VIRGINIA WOOLF ICON

WOMEN IN CULTURE AND SOCIETY   *A Series Edited by Catharine R. Stimpson*

VIRGINIA WOOLF ICON

Brenda R. Silver

The
University of
Chicago Press
Chicago &
London

BRENDA R. SILVER is professor of English at Dartmouth College. She is the author of *Virginia Woolf's Reading Notebooks* (1983) and coeditor of *Rape and Representation* (1991).

The University of Chicago Press, Chicago 60637
The University of Chicago Press, Ltd., London
© 1999 by The University of Chicago
All rights reserved. Published 1999
Printed in the United States of America
08 07 06 05 04 03 02 01 00 99   1 2 3 4 5

ISBN: 0-226-75745-5 (cloth)
ISBN: 0-226-75746-3 (paper)

Parts of this book originally appeared in the following places: "What's Woolf Got to Do with It? Or, the Perils of Popularity," *Modern Fiction Studies* 38/1 (spring 1992): 21–60; reprinted with permission of *Modern Fiction Studies*. "Mis-fits: The Monstrous Union of Virginia Woolf and Marilyn Monroe," *Discourse* 16/1 (fall 1993): 71–108. "Tom & Viv & Vita & Virginia & Ottoline & Edith . . . ," *Woolf Studies Annual* 2 (1996): 160–74. "Whose Room of Orlando's Own? The Politics of Adaptation," in *The Margins of the Text,* ed. D. C. Greetham (Ann Arbor: University of Michigan Press, 1997), 57–82; © University of Michigan 1997, reprinted with permission. "Retro-Anger and Baby-Boomer Nostalgia: A Polemical Talk," in *Virginia Woolf and Her Influences: Selected Papers from the Seventh Annual Conference on Virginia Woolf,* ed. Laura Davis and Jeanette McVicker (New York: Pace University Press, 1998), 221–33.

Library of Congress Cataloging-in-Publication Data

Silver, Brenda R., 1942–
   Virginia Woolf icon / Brenda R. Silver.
      p.   cm.—(Women in culture and society)
   Includes bibliographical references and index.
   ISBN 0-226-75745-5 (alk. paper).—ISBN 0-226-75746-3 (pbk. : alk. paper)
   1. Woolf, Virginia, 1882–1941—Appreciation.   2. Woolf, Virginia, 1882–1941—Criticism and interpretation—History.   3. Women in popular culture—Great Britain—History—20th century.   4. Women in popular culture—United States—History—20th century.   5. Public opinion—Great Britain—History—20th century.   6. Public opinion—United States—History—20th century.   7. Feminism and literature—Public opinion. 8. Women and literature—Public opinion.   9. Women novelists—Public opinion. 10. Fear—Public opinion.   11. Fear in literature.   I. Title.   II. Series.
PR6045.072Z87633   1999
823'.912—dc21   99-36175
                                                                                              CIP

⊚ The paper used in this publication meets the minimum requirements of the American National Standard for Information Sciences—Permanence of Paper for Printed Library Materials, ANSI Z39.48-1992.

FOR PAUL

CONTENTS

ILLUSTRATIONS

Virginia Woolf was born in 1882. She became a writer. She died in 1941. These are the barest of factual bones. Since her death, she has become more and more famous. The interest in Woolf has transmuted the bones of fact into the complex body of her achievements and their meanings. In turn, this complexity has stimulated even greater interest and fame. More picture postcards of Woolf are sold in the National Portrait Gallery in London than of anybody else. A Woolf poster has hung prominently on the set of the television show *Murphy Brown*. In brief, she is a phenomenon—icon, celebrity, star. No god, no omnipotent master of the universe has made this happen. Her cultural legatees have. What we have done to this greatly creative writer is an important story, not only about her but about us and the relationships that we have bred and breed. Brenda R. Silver, the scholar and critic, tells this story brilliantly. Indeed, I cannot imagine it better told.

Woolf had become a public figure before her death. In 1937, her novel *The Years* was a best-seller in the United States and she appeared on the cover of *Time* magazine. Silver locates the beginning of Woolf's stardom at this moment; this is true particularly in the United States, which has been far more receptive to Woolf than a Great Britain that often still casts her as a representative of an old cultural order. Silver analyzes this discrepancy incisively. In the hierarchy of reputation, stardom trumps fame. *Time*'s covers are, of course, pictures, usually photographs. Photographs of Woolf rivet and command one's gaze. The grand-niece of Victorian photographer Julia Margaret Cameron, Woolf was a sophisticated student of the genre. An exceptional reader of the photographs of Woolf and her family, Silver is acutely aware that they illustrate two linked truths about fame. First, every icon is an image. An icon is visual. A portrait in words will not do. Next, photography provides images that can be broadly circulated and constantly recirculated. This both accelerates and reaffirms the process of iconization and celebrity making. Modern celebrity is unthinkable without the presence of the camera.

In the 1960s, Silver argues, Woolf became a major icon, in part because of Edward Albee's play *Who's Afraid of Virginia Woolf?* and in part because of a renewed interest in the Bloomsbury Group, of which she was a prominent representative. In the 1970s this evolution continued with the rise of the women's movement and its strong cultural and educational interests, the publication of a biography by Woolf's nephew Quentin Bell, new critical frameworks such as poststructuralism and discourse theory, and, not to be dismissed, the appearance of the popular Historical Products Inc. T-shirt with an imprint of Woolf's face. Yet while icons can inspire both iconoclasts and idolaters, the public has not divided neatly over whether to adore her or loathe her. As Silver shows persuasively and stylishly, Woolf's own complexity—as a public figure and as a writer—helps to shield her against this cultural vulgarity. Part of her complexity arises from her residency at the borders between long-established dualisms, for example, those of mind and body, powerful and female, the voice of high culture and of popular culture. Doing so, Woolf emblemizes not one side or the other but the possibility of dwelling on both or all sides and, as a result, the possibility of disrupting familiar categories and boundaries.

Not surprisingly, the proliferating responses to Woolf have been frag-mented and competing, especially during periods of struggle over gender and sexuality, and, linked to these struggles, over cultural authority and legitimacy. Silver usefully applies the concept of "versioning," by which new versions of a text or image keep it in constant flux. This multiplicity of texts and the responses to them have defeated any effort to impose a single, unitary, dominant interpretation—for example, Quentin Bell's belief that his was the "insider's" truth, and thus the truth, about his aunt. Despite the welter and chaos of Woolfs, Silver finds a consistent and perhaps surprising pattern: the association of Woolf with fear. She can become a modern Medusa or Sphinx. After Albee's play, she is guilty by association with childlessness and homosexuality. As Silver tells us, she hopes to examine places where "Virginia Woolf becomes symptomatic of embedded layers of cultural anxiety, in an effort to formulate as precisely as I can the issues—and the stakes" (p. 5).

Each of the three major sections of *Virginia Woolf Icon* takes on a different place. Part 1, "Negative Encounters," is about the intellectual media, especially the *New York Review of Books,* and the academic curriculum, especially the founding father of the core curriculum, the literary humanities course at Columbia College in New York City. For the most part, the Woolf they admire is the writer who explores private, interior, feminine spaces. In a double move, they strip Woolf of her politics, including her feminism, and dismiss as angry harridans the feminist critics who vigorously and rigorously study the totality of Woolf's career. One element in the post-1960s culture wars, this rejection found its risibly crude extreme in Rush Limbaugh's characterization of feminist critics, including Silver herself, as "feminazis." Part 2, "Starring Virginia Woolf," traces the rise of Woolf from her appearance on the 1937 *Time* cover to household-name status—a face on a T-shirt that proclaims a group identity, a name deployed by graffiti artists, a figure used by the fashion industry, a presence in the 1987 Hanif Kureishi film *Sammy and Rosie Get Laid,* for some a most un-Woolfian piece of diction. I am no newcomer slouching toward the Bethlehem of Woolf studies. I have read nearly all of Woolf and much of the biographical and critical literature about her; made my pilgrimages to the historic sites of Bloomsbury; written about Woolf, her work and circles. Silver's mapping of the extent of her presence in United States and British culture since her death still astonishes me.

Part 3, "Doubled Movements," begins with a dazzling analysis of stage and screen adaptations of Woolf's texts. Unsurprisingly, given the age of spectacle and image in which we live, many people "see" Woolf before they read her. Sharp contrasts to each other, these adaptations claim Woolf for almost every position, versioning her as both the voice of universal truths and of an edgy, sexually fluid, "postfeminist" or "queer" moment. Despite these differences, the adaptations together illustrate the nature of performance and performative acts. Part 3 ends with a disturbing, provocative history of the conjunctions of Woolf and Marilyn Monroe, perhaps beginning as far back as Albee's play and most graphically realized in the six-foot photomontage, constructed by café owners in North Carolina, that placed Woolf's head on Marilyn Monroe's body. Oh, the amazing artifacts of American popular culture. The figure is monstrous and frightening because, as a hybrid, it displaces familiar categories, because it evokes both sex and intellect, beauty and death. It might, however, also open up new spaces, reveal gaps and fissures, in which culture might renew itself. It might prove to have the power of the Cyborg, so influentially crafted by Donna Haraway. Certainly, as Silver proves, Woolf has engaged the imagination of those who imagine the future, our writers of speculative fiction. For the "boundary-defying monster allows us to see and think and speak and act differently, to become, like Virginia Woolf icon and star, a multiple, intertextual proliferation of always partial images, acts, and words" (p. 272).

Virginia Woolf Icon ends with a series of brief meditations on various allusions to, evocations of, and summonings up of Woolf, including an editorial about the dangers of political correctness; an academic symposium; a film version of a Woolf novel; a big biography; a television comedy about generations of contemporary women, among them two bawdy publicists; and, finally, a poster sold by a branch of the Italian Communist Party. This "Afterword," an artful collage, weaves together Silver's great themes. They go beyond Woolf, immense though she is. For Silver is exploring, deeply and lucidly, how late twentieth-century culture, pluralistic and self-divided and democratic and full of ordinary people, constructs its *extraordinary* people, its icons, stars, celebrities, monsters, heroes and heroines. In a more limited sphere, how does it construct its extraordinary writers and artists, its canonical figures? In addition, she asks how, given such pluralism and self-divisions, it stages its debates about value and meaning. Framing her inquiries are a number of suggestive ideas about culture. From Stuart Hall she has learned that popular culture is a "double movement of containment and resistance" (p. 13). Deft and far-ranging, Silver also explores the tension between theories in which meanings, like identities, tend to be "authentic" and postmodern theories in which meanings, like identities, are "continually refashioned" (p. 197). Throughout *Virginia Woolf Icon* Silver seeks to situate this struggle in the material realm. "Like others committed to a postmodern multiplicity of meanings," she writes, "I, too, would insist on the necessity of exploring the historical and social contexts of each and every manifestation of Virginia Woolf, of charting the patterns" (p. 201).

Woolf is reported to have once said, "This celebrity business is quite chronic." Her skepticism is palpable. For "chronic" means that something is always with us and that this something smacks of illness, an ache, a pain. *Virginia Woolf Icon* permits us to share this skepticism about a celebrity culture when it goes to seed. It also helps us to grasp patterns, to understand how culture operates and reseeds itself with new meanings. Doing so, *Virginia Woolf Icon* is a model of inquiry and of cultural studies. Though the Virginia Woolf whom Silver studies is the Virginia Woolf whom others have made, she permits us to remember that Virginia Woolf was a woman who was born in 1882, who died in 1941, and who, between these years, so acted that reading and writing was never the same. For all this, Silver's readers should be many, and in her debt.

Catharine R. Stimpson

For years now, much to my friends' amusement and annoyance, I've been in the habit of saying that Virginia Woolf is everywhere. She is, and the fact that I can state this so categorically owes a great deal to the individuals, most known but some unknown, who when they heard I was writing about the construction of Virginia Woolf as cultural icon began sending me visual or verbal proofs of her numerous appearances. (One friend, having stared for weeks during his Long Island Railroad commute at the larger-than-life Virginia Woolf featured in a Bass Ale ad, finally eased it off the wall of the train to give to me.) But toward the end of the project, when I spent a month at an international research institute among scholars and artists of different ages and from diverse disciplines, I was reminded that others do not automatically share my perceptions of this phenomenon. One resident, a young composer, wanted to know why I even considered her appearances notable. After all, he stated, if advertisers or whoever want a woman writer, of course they're going to use Virginia Woolf. Another, a sociologist, had a different concern. Virginia Woolf may be everywhere, he said, but how did I know that people on the LIRR other than my friend recognized her face or even her name in the Bass Ale ad?

Coming from different perspectives, both questions raise issues central to the multifaceted narrative of Virginia Woolf's iconicity I am recounting here. Growing up at a time when Virginia Woolf had already achieved canonical status, the young composer was unaware of the contested history that brought her into public prominence, transforming her in some circles into a female Shakespeare readily available when one needs a well-known literary figure, a celebrity, to illustrate a point. The answer to the sociologist's question about how I know that people recognize her is, I don't know; moreover, I often find myself mystified as to who a writer or designer thinks will "get" an unidentified reference or picture and, if they do, what they will make of it. What I do know is that visual and verbal representations of Virginia Woolf continue to appear and to change, presenting such mobile, contradictory images of her as to make her role in the stories we tell about our culture a more than academic question.

Indeed, her academic reputation, the well-known story of her elevation to canonical superstar, is only one part of the phenomenon that has made Virginia Woolf so pervasive a concept and image; on its own it cannot explain either her extraordinary iconicity or the powerful, often iconoclastic, reactions it generates as it cuts across the boundaries between nations, genders, and cultural classes. Yes, her now assured stature as "major author" and literary figure within an increasingly global scholarly community has played a role in this process; in addition to the International Virginia Woolf Society, independent societies exist in France, Japan, and Great Britain, and an online Virginia Woolf e-mail list attracts participants worldwide. But her unusual ability as icon to transgress the borders supposedly separating the academy from the intellectual sphere and the world of popular/mass culture, where she has also achieved star billing, has proved far more significant in making her such a highly contested figure. Not only does each realm claim her for itself, but within each realm her advocates and her critics alike insist that they alone know the "real" or "authentic" Virginia Woolf, however different these Virginia Woolfs may be, adding to the profusion of images; moreover, they state, if she were alive today she would assuredly direct her famous scorn at whomever or whatever the claimant disapproves of and scathingly demolish it. (In a less antagonistic mode her claimant might say, "She would have appreciated the irony. . . .") Reading these statements, one gets the feeling the writers think she *has* returned from the dead to speak in their persona and voice: would-be Virginia Woolf impersonators.

But when we look more carefully at this seemingly random proliferation of images, patterns begin to emerge, the most dramatic of which is the persistent association of Virginia Woolf with fear. A further look unexpectedly reveals a considerable number of intersections between the academic and the popular. In both locations the "versioning" of Virginia Woolf—the production of multiple versions of her texts or her image—however contentious the debates this versioning elicits, has become a recognized and recognizable practice. In the academic realm, for example, "authorial intention" and the "author" have for the most part, however grudgingly, given way to or come to coexist with "postmodern" texts and readings, while in the popular realm, continual enactments and reenactments of Virginia Woolf as name, image, spectacle, fashion, or performance have become the norm. Only in what I have come to call the self-styled "intellectual" media, for the most part located in the world of New York journalism, has Virginia Woolf remained more or less fixed.

Virginia Woolf, then, may be everywhere, but her meanings remain undecided. The battles to name or unname them, to freeze them or put them in motion, are ineluctably tied to specific, competing institutions and ideologies within our culture and society. These battles constitute the subject of this book.

ACKNOWLEDGMENTS

However clichéd it may be to write "without whom," in the case of *Virginia Woolf Icon* it's the appropriate gesture, for without the many individuals who provided sightings of Virginia Woolf, often sending along a clipping or a tape, or who shared with me their recollections of events I chart, this book would not have happened. I also wish to acknowledge—and thank—those who willingly shared their expertise with me; those who read and reread either parts or the whole, offering invaluable suggestions; my dedicated and creative research assistants; my sisters and brothers-in-law, who were always there; and those who participated at every stage of the book as friends, colleagues, and interlocutors: Michael Amberger, Michele Angers, Joanne Trautmann Banks, Michèle Barrett, Matthew Benedetto, George Bornstein, Julia Briggs, Rachel Brownstein, Michael Cadden, Julie Carlson, Gianna Celli, Mary Childers, S. N. Clarke, Michael Cohen, Richard Corum, Jonathan Crewe, Melba Cuddy-Keane, Nathan Currier, Mary Desjardins, Madelyn Detloff, Jonathan Eburne, Martin Favor, Helene Foley, Jon Gilbert Fox, Louise Fradenburg, Carla Freccero, Christine Froula, Blynn Garnett, Sally Greene, Leslie Hankins, Carolyn Heilbrun, Lynn Higgins, Marianne Hirsch, Amy Hollywood, John Horgan, Lois Keates Horgan, Mark Hussey, Alexis Jetter, Keala Jewell, Ellen Carol Jones, Wolf Kittler, Robert Koelzer, Gisela Kommerell, Hermione Lee, Melissa Llewelyn-Davies, Nicola Luckhurst, Kay Menand, Nancy Miller, Tania Modleski, Peter Nardi, Annelise Orleck, Constance Penley, Sandy Petrey, Laurence Rickels, Matthew Rowlinson, Peter Saccio, Rolf (Sander) Schlichter, Alix Kates Shulman, Anna Snaith, Abigail Solomon-Godeau, Margaret Spicer, Susan Squier, Carol Starrels, Michael

Starrels, John Sutherland, Peter Swaab, Sasha Torres, Gerard Touroul, Nancy Vickers, Pierre-Eric Villeneuve, Barbara Will, Mark Williams, J. J. Wilson, Melissa Zeiger, and, in memoriam, Elizabeth Richardson.

Others were equally generous: Peter Samuelson, who gave me access to his archives and permission to quote from the script for *Tom & Viv;* Robert Archer-Carr, Alan Bennett, and Stephen Frears, who allowed me to quote from letters responding to my own; and Cora Kaplan, Peter Stallybrass, and Ann Rosalind Jones, who permitted me to quote from their unpublished manuscripts.

I am enormously grateful to Dartmouth College for providing me with both research funds and research time. The English department at the University of California, Santa Barbara, did much to facilitate my research there. A grant from the National Endowment for the Humanities made the completion of this project a reality. A residency at the Rockefeller Foundation's Bellagio Study and Conference Center provided the ideal place for writing and an interdisciplinary group of scholars whose questions and suggestions made all the difference to the work's final shape.

Those at the University of Chicago Press could not have been more helpful: Alan Thomas, Randy Petilos, Leslie Keros, and, from the beginning, Catharine Stimpson. Rachel Bowlby's and Christine Froula's discerning readings for the Press have, I hope, been reflected throughout.

Finally, a special thank-you to Alice Gambrell, whose insights permeate the book. Paul Tobias's unfailing sense of proportion made it all possible; I dedicate this book to him.

THE VERSIONING OF VIRGINIA WOOLF

"This celebrity business is quite chronic," Virginia Woolf once remarked. . . .

—Richard Schickel, *Intimate Strangers: The Culture of Celebrity*

In February 1994 the *New York Times Magazine* ran an extract from Lani Guinier's book about her nonconfirmation as head of the United States Justice Department's Civil Rights Division during Bill Clinton's first term as president. A call from a friend alerted me to the article; in the picture on the cover, she said, Guinier looks just like Virginia Woolf. My friend was right: the face, in profile, bears an uncanny resemblance to Woolf's profile in one of the lesser-known Man Ray photographs taken of the writer in 1934, a portrait that emphasizes the strength and the stark beauty of her features (figs. 1, 2). Given this cover and the controversy surrounding Guinier's views and persona, I was not surprised to find that the piece was called "Who's Afraid of Lani Guinier?"

The controversy over Guinier, at that time a professor at the University of Pennsylvania Law School, hinged to a great extent on her writings about political representation: how to ensure that all groups within a community have a voice in the decisions that determine their lives. One of her goals was to find alternatives to the controversial practice of redistricting as a means of achieving "minority" representation; but the options she considered, such as cumulative voting and legislative supermajority requirements, both examples of proportionate interest representation already in use across the nation, proved more controversial still.[1] Her nomination set off a one-sided firestorm of criticism, which included the accusation that she wanted to

FIGURE 1. Cover, *New York Times Magazine*, February 27, 1994.

FIGURE 2. Virginia Woolf. Photograph by Man Ray. Copyright © 1999 Man Ray Trust/Artists Rights Society, NY/ADAGP, Paris.

destroy the basic tenets of American democracy, a charge she never got to respond to before her nomination was withdrawn.

Several factors played a role in the furor incited by the woman and her ideas, illustrating the fractured nature of American identities and politics. For one thing, race counted: Guinier, of mixed race, is identified as African American; one critic noted that she wanted blacks to have a veto in legislation affecting them. The label "Quota Queen," which was coined to discredit her views, also bears a distinct racial marking, linked as it is both to the "Welfare Queen" already used to portray African American women and to fears of affirmative action taking educational opportunities and jobs away from whites. Class counted as well, cultural class: Guinier's professional status at one of the country's most prestigious law schools made her an academic, a specialist, ensconced in her ivory tower and hence out of touch, according to this argument, with the realities of public life. (Even Bill Clinton, her longtime friend, claimed that had he read her published articles more carefully, he would not have nominated her.) But gender also counted, as the evocation of Virginia Woolf, mediated by the title of Edward Albee's play, makes clear. Here was a formidable intellectual woman speaking out in public about ways to restructure our system of political representation, and that proved scary indeed. No wonder government officials and journalists alike spent almost as much time talking about her appearance, in particular her "strange hair," as about her ideas: one look at Medusa Guinier and you might turn to stone.[2] Linked as the Guinier affair was to the aftermath of a series of events centered on powerful women—the Anita Hill–Clarence Thomas hearings and Hillary Rodham Clinton's perceived ascension to political power, for example—it accurately anticipated the large role played by self-declared "angry white men" in the 1994 congressional elections who were fighting, they claimed, to restore their illegitimately lost power.

At first glance it might seem that Virginia Woolf's role in this drama of public, political life is nothing more than a cliché, a verbal tic made possible by the "well-knownness" of Albee's title, which has taken on a life independent of the writer and her works in our cultural consciousness.[3] Not so. Virginia Woolf's appearance as Lani Guinier's mirror image graphically highlights the phenomenon at the heart of this study: the extensive visual and verbal representations of Virginia Woolf that have circulated in Anglo-American culture for the past thirty-five years, giving her a visibility and an immediacy, a celebrity, rare for a living writer and even rarer for one from the past. Occurring across the cultural terrain, whether in academic discourses, the intellectual media, or mass/popular culture, the proliferation of Virginia Woolfs has transformed the writer into a powerful and powerfully contested cultural icon, whose name, face, and authority are persistently claimed or disclaimed in debates about art, politics, sexuality, gender, class, the "canon," fashion, feminism, race, and anger. The debates themselves have varied, and they have generated often radically conflicting versions of "Virginia Woolf," who must be understood in this context as an image or representation, under erasure, between quotation marks. (Throughout this study the term *Virginia Woolf* will refer to this polysemous image; when the "real" or historical woman/writer enters the story she does so as Woolf.) But however various the representations, one motif keeps recurring, that which links Virginia Woolf to fear: the fears she is said to have experienced in her own life, often read through her suicide, but even more important, the fears she evokes in others. For that reason I have come to take Albee's question "Who's afraid of Virginia Woolf?" very seriously indeed. By looking more closely at the *who* and exploring the contexts in which she is presented as or perceived to be frightening, we can begin to understand how Virginia Woolf has become the site of conflicts about cultural boundaries and legitimacy that continue to rage today.

Virginia Woolf Icon takes Virginia Woolf's multiple and diverse cultural appearances as its starting point. Using a series of case studies, it explores the conflicting constructions of Virginia Woolf as cultural icon and the issues they raise, including the fears provoked by the proliferation of her meanings. The majority of the cases are located in the United States and in the context of its social/cultural structures, making this at one level a study of Virginia Woolf American icon; but they also cross the Atlantic, either evoking a text that originated in Great Britain or drawing British writers into the fray. The result is to foreground the local conditions that have made the history of her reception and her iconic status so different in the two cultures, even as it underlines the reiterative similarity of the responses. Equally important, the cases crisscross the realms of "high culture" associated, variously, with the academy and/or intellectuals and the realm of mass-produced and/or popular culture; these transgressions lead me to ask in what ways Virginia Woolf's mobility—her ability to cross the boundaries between categories that so many people, particularly those who defend high culture, would dearly like to keep in place— undermines or undoes both the categories and the distinctions claimed for them. This tension underlies the first series of cases, which occur in the determinedly nonacademic realm claimed by the "public intellectual" writing in the "intellectual" press. From there, my narrative moves into the intersecting worlds of "Art" and popular culture, where Virginia Woolf often plays a starring role in plays and films and television and fashion; these appearances project her, through the reviews, back into the realm of the journalistic media, both mainstream and intellectual, where so many cultural battles are fought.[4] Both her appearances and their reception in the more popular media soon reveal the same fractures and anxieties found in the realm of high culture: anxieties about gender and sexuality, anxieties about social class and cultural class. Even more surprising, I will argue, they reveal a pattern of parallels and crossovers between the academic sphere and the popular sphere that helped transform Virginia Woolf into a multifaceted iconic figure, a pattern and a result that differ from her seemingly fixed positions within the self-styled "intellectual" media.

Situated within this framework, each case focuses on a particular text or set of texts and its reception by one or more specific audiences within a particular time and/or place. In each, I am interested in how Virginia Woolf's image generates custody battles over who gets to define her meaning—over whose representation counts as "truth"—that inscribe clearly demarcated historical moments and ideological positions. Taken together they begin to suggest the links between Virginia Woolf icon and the impact of the second wave of the women's movement on shifting attitudes toward gender, sexuality, and cultural class.

My choice of cases and the necessarily limited representations of Virginia Woolf icon present here are no less situated than the examples I explore. Having been there, done that—having participated, that is, as a North American, East Coast feminist with strong ties to Great Britain, in the project of constructing new versions of Virginia Woolf's texts and meanings, and then studied their evolution and reception—I am keenly aware of the heated conflicts such moves have generated among those of all persuasions who consider themselves the powers that be. This includes the ire and/or condescension of those who insist on a Virginia Woolf made only in their image, an "authentic," legitimate Virginia Woolf to whom, they assert, they have a direct line. While I am not immune to the kinds of identification that led me to experience surprise when I first heard Virginia Woolf's voice and realized it didn't sound like mine or to feel that a Virginia Woolf dressed in the Gap T-shirt I myself wear seemed just right—and while I am not above feelings of intense annoyance at renderings that undercut or recuperate those representations of Virginia Woolf associated with feminisms and/or a postmodern penchant for border-crossings and multiple shapes—my distrust of those who would fix her into any single position, either to praise or to blame her, remains my strongest motivation. We cannot stop the proliferation of Virginia Woolfs or the claims to "truth" or authenticity that accompany each refashioning of her image; nor would I want to, however much I might disagree with or be scared by the effect produced by any particular representation. Instead, I have focused on those places where Virginia Woolf becomes symptomatic of embedded layers of cultural anxiety, in an effort to formulate as precisely as I can the issues—and the stakes.

To the extent that the representations of and reactions to Virginia Woolf that I am tracking have been so consistently associated with fear, the question of who fears her and why becomes an inextricable aspect of the struggles over authority, legitimacy, and authenticity that concern me here. This question is inseparable from the double movement of iconization and iconoclasm—the claim that Virginia Woolf, or a particular Virginia Woolf, is a false idol—that I chart throughout. During the writing of this book, as I have watched the public battles in the United States over multiculturalism and "political correctness," including the simultaneous backlash against and appropriation of feminism, civil rights, gay and lesbian rights, and an activist commitment to social change, I have come to see a formulation of these struggles as increasingly important. As the Lani Guinier case illustrates, representation—who controls it, who enacts it—

matters. In the cultural and political climate at the end of the twentieth century, understanding the complex construction of Virginia Woolf as cultural icon, whether exploring its performative role in the naming and policing of norms that continue to fix women into particular cultural and social positions, or positing its subversive potential, becomes a strategy for imagining a different future.

1. Icons and Iconicity: Why Virginia Woolf?

In this last decade of the twentieth century, studies of icons and iconicity have become hot commodities in both the academic and the popular marketplace. The enormous presence of the media in our lives, along with our postmodern awareness of the role of spectacle and sound bites, photo ops, spin control, and advertising in the construction of "leaders" and concepts, has led a large number of writers to turn to the processes by which cultural icons are produced, disseminated, and read by various self-defined or demographically defined audiences. Books and articles about stars, fame, celebrity, and fandom, written by sociologists and political scientists as well as film and television critics, literary critics, cultural critics, and journalists, have been appearing regularly and receiving more than academic attention. Wayne Koestenbaum's *Jackie under My Skin: Interpreting an Icon,* published shortly after Jacqueline Kennedy Onassis's death, was widely read, reviewed, and talked about; Ramona Curry's *Too Much of a Good Thing: Mae West as Cultural Icon* was one of several works that earned the actress a retrospective profile in the *New Yorker;* Paige Baty's postmodern rendering of a mass-mediated *American Monroe: The Making of a Body Politic* elicited a review in the *New York Times.*[5] Meanwhile, a conference called "Icons of Popular Culture: Elvis and Marilyn," organized in conjunction with an art exhibition called *Elvis + Marilyn = 2 × Immortal* and hosted by George Washington University in April 1994, brought together curators of art museums, art historians, artists, photographers, anthropologists, sociologists, musicologists, and literary critics; similarly eclectic international conferences devoted entirely to Elvis, including scholars, fans, and Elvis impersonators, were held at the University of Mississippi in 1995 and 1996.

Also in 1995, *Bartlett's Familiar Quotations* produced a CD-ROM "Expanded Multimedia Edition," which included visual images, bits from speeches, and musical extracts. Explaining this addition in a newspaper article headed "Notable Quotables: Why Images Become Icons," Thomas Hine points to the iconicity of nonverbal expressions such as image, sound, and gesture that are "regularly used, reused, parodied and appropriated" today; his examples include the opening of Beethoven's Fifth Symphony, Rodin's sculpture "The Thinker," Edvard Munch's painting "The Scream," and Botticelli's "Venus," as well as Marilyn Monroe with her skirt flying. So great is this phenomenon, Hine argues, that " 'high' Western culture is not dead. Quite the contrary. We're swimming in it." "Even people," Hine continues, "can be turned into quotations if they acquire strong associations": Albert Einstein ("pure braininess"), Che Guevara with beret ("romantic revolutionary"), Winston Churchill and Richard Nixon making the V-for-victory sign ("men trying to win").[6] Holly Brubach might well have had this statement in mind when, introducing a 1996 *New York Times Magazine* special issue, "Heroine Worship: Inventing an Identity in the Age of Female Icons," she defined an icon as "a human sound bite, an individual reduced to a name, a face and an idea."[7]

Every time we open a magazine or turn on the TV one ramification of this transformation appears: the power of icons to sell. The culturally attuned Calvin of the cartoon *Calvin and Hobbes* got it just right; holding a square frame before his face he says to Hobbes, "Now that I'm on television, I'm different from everybody else! I'm famous! Important! Since everyone knows me, everything I do now is newsworthy. I'm a cultural icon." "Watch," he continues, "I'll use my prestige to endorse a product!"

Writing in the "Heroine Worship" issue of the *New York Times Magazine*, William Safire reminds us of the origins of *icon* in the Greek *eikon*, "to resemble," and describes its earliest meaning as "the material representation, or image, of a saint or angel in the Eastern Orthodox Church," a meaning that "evolved into 'revered symbol.' " Today, he notes, the "vogue word" has at least three different meanings, the simplest of which is " 'a graphic representation of an idea' "; his example is computer icons. The second meaning makes *icon* a " 'symbol,' a sign that represents, or a token that stands for something else," with an emphasis on likeness; it still has, he adds, an element of reverence about it similar to that accorded to the earliest icons and inherent in the power of visual images. The third meaning he offers is " 'idol.' By this," he adds, "most of us mean 'living idol, superstar,' and its subset, 'media celebrity, the famous famed for being famous.' "[8]

Finally, we need to throw Russell Baker, the longtime humorist and commentator on American life, into the mix: his campaign against the ubiquity of the word *icon* itself. In the first of two 1997 articles on the subject, he writes, "This lovely word with its odor of incense and hint of Byzantine religious mystery is now reduced to a pretentious way for depraved language butchers to speak of computer cartoons and of entertainers and athletes once dismissed as 'heroes' or 'stars.' "[9]

All of this might seem a far cry from Virginia Woolf, whom her detractors in the 1930s labeled the "High Priestess of Bloomsbury" and identified with a literary and cultural elite and elitism: hardly the stuff, one would have thought, contemporary cultural icons are made of. Nevertheless, Virginia Woolf, along with Dale Evans, Helen Keller, Greta Garbo, Mae West, Catherine Deneuve, and Naomi Campbell, was on Brubach's 1996 list of female icons ("Virginia Woolf has her own T-shirt"), and she received an extended write-up later in the issue, indicating the extent to which she has been "taken up by the media and made famous, packaged as [a commodity] and marketed to a public eager for novelty and easily bored."[10] And Baker himself, in a subsequent column lamenting his lack of success in banning the word, evinces as one example the cover of the *New York Times Book Review,* of all places, which declared Virginia Woolf "an icon and a beacon for most of a century."[11]

Virginia Woolf may not have been an icon "for most of a century," but starting in the 1960s the public appearances, recognition, and market value of Virginia Woolf's name and face have steadily increased. Wherever one looks, it often seems, whether in academic journals, newspapers and magazines, television and film, or billboards, Virginia Woolf is there, endorsing by her presence and status whatever product—whether intellectual or material—is being offered for our attention; Virginia Woolf, it is clear, sells, and not just to one audience. In 1979 a *New Yorker* cartoon depicted the "Virginia Woolf Bookshop," with sections devoted to "novels," "journals," "husband," etc., an indication of the large number of autobiographical and biographical books by and about her that made her attractive to nonscholarly readers; and in 1991 the *New York Times Magazine* put her at the top of "What's In" in the Modern Language Association, reflecting her popularity among academics. Both are noteworthy, if not particularly surprising for a writer. But for years now, Virginia Woolf's face has also sold more postcards at London's National Portrait Gallery than that of any other figure; and she has been used to market wares ranging from the *New York Review of Books,* to fashion clothing, to the Communist Party of Rome, to Bass Ale. Even more striking are the breadth and diversity of places where her name and face appear without any explanatory identification, as if it is assumed readers and viewers will recognize her and understand her role as cultural marker: *Los Angeles Times* editorials; George Will columns; discussions of Ruth Bader Ginsburg's legal philosophy; ACTUP anticensorship marches; Michael Innes mysteries; the science fiction novel *I Vampire;* the television shows *Sesame Street, Beverly Hills 90210,* and *Absolutely Fabulous;* the rock groups "Virginia Wolf" and "Virginia and the Wolves"; a mutoscope (a mechanical device used in the early twentieth century for creating and viewing moving images) featuring an image of her face and the legend "TO BE HAPPY See What Every Married Woman Must Not Avoid" (laundry); a photomontage that combined her head with the body of Marilyn Monroe; and Hanif Kureishi's 1987 film *Sammy and Rosie Get Laid.*

To some extent we have *Who's Afraid of Virginia Woolf?* to thank for this visibility; during the 1960s, Albee's play, especially the film version starring Richard Burton and Elizabeth Taylor, transformed Virginia Woolf into a household name. Even if you hadn't seen the film, which garnered fourteen Academy Award nominations and extensive media buzz, you were more than likely to have heard of it. Virginia Woolf, we could say, became a "celebrity," "known for [her] well-knownness"[12] to a broad spectrum of people who might never have read a word of her writing or even realized that a real woman named Virginia Woolf had lived. From this moment on, and the point cannot be overstated, Virginia Woolf acquired an iconicity that exists independently of her academic standing or literary reputation, of her perceived value as a writer and the perceived value of her works.[13]

But Albee's play was not the only force at work. By the end of the 1960s, Michael Holroyd's biography of Lytton Strachey had helped inaugurate a tidal wave of interest in the Bloomsbury Group, as much for its sexual relations—its homosexuality and bisexuality, with their concomitant fears and pleasures—as for its contributions to intellectual life;[14] and by the early 1970s, the emerging women's movement had made Woolf's words— "a room of one's own," for instance—into public slogans and her face, emblazoned on T-shirts, into a public sight. By the middle of the decade, feminist literary critics in the academy had begun to make their mark; at conferences (1974) and later in journals (1977), drawing upon the publication and interpretation of previously unpublished writings, they declared and presented to their skeptical colleagues "Another Version of Virginia Woolf," one that foregrounded her political, social, and feminist concerns and led, they argued, to "another and perhaps more comprehensive version of Virginia Woolf's works."[15]

Keenly aware of the politics of representation and cultural authority, American feminists in the 1970s, both outside and inside the academy, subversively laid claim to Virginia Woolf's image and her writings in order to articulate a new social and cultural text. In many ways, they were wildly successful, making Virginia Woolf and her association with feminist agendas a cultural force. But as so often happens, success transformed subversiveness into respectability, producing both her elevation to canonical status and the iconoclastic desire to overthrow it. As Virginia Woolf's value increased, so too did the struggles over who would define her cultural standing and meaning, struggles intensified by the intervention of those who wanted to reclaim her for more traditional sites of cultural power. By 1982, the year of her centenary, her iconicity in the United States had already generated this reaction, evoking denunciations of a Virginia Woolf "cult" apparent in both academia and popular culture and provoking journalists to call for her return to her more appropriate—i.e., intellectual—sphere. The *New York Review of Books,* long considered the most eminent of intellectual journals, set one example; responding to her new stature, it elevated Virginia Woolf into an icon of Western civilization on a par with Shakespeare, the other figure simultaneously featured during the 1980s in its "special offer to . . . readers" for David Levine T-shirts, even as it persistently ignored the popular interventions and the majority of (feminist) critical studies that had recently made her an important cultural figure or found a "respectable"—that is, nonfeminist—critic to review the feminist works negatively. Their own political and cultural agenda, we could say, their claim to speak for "legitimate" culture, manifested itself graphically every time the advertisement appeared.

By the early 1990s, the situation was decidedly mixed. At the *New York Review of Books,* Shakespeare had disappeared from the ads and Virginia Woolf reigned alone; and at the MLA, as we've seen, Virginia Woolf was definitely "in." In Britain, meanwhile, where Virginia Woolf's reputation has always faced a conjunction of local restrictions deeply embedded in systems of social/cultural class, her elevation to iconic status, even among feminists, had been decidedly slower; her centenary, for example, passed almost unnoticed. But by 1991, when she appeared as a protagonist/target in the television series *J'Accuse,* wherein cultural icons were brought to trial and found wanting, the situation had clearly changed. To Tom Paulin, who wrote and narrated the program, Virginia Woolf's extraordinary popularity was both inexplicable and dangerous; rather than legitimizing Virginia Woolf, his goal was to dethrone her. During this same period Eileen Atkins's highly praised declamation on TV and stage of *A Room of One's Own,* the book that had done more than anything to make Virginia Woolf a powerful cultural force, became a vehicle for discrediting "contemporary feminists" on both sides of the Atlantic.

What is it about Virginia Woolf that elicits such widely divergent responses, these struggles over whose image and meaning will prevail, over her legitimacy and cultural capital? What "strong associations" can explain the phenomenon? Why is it so easy to separate images of the woman from the writer in these struggles, and why is it that her being a woman may ultimately be the most significant factor in her conflicting iconic representations, including their inscription of fear?

My study begins with the premise that Virginia Woolf's elevation to transgressive cultural icon and the contradictory, often vehement, responses provoked by it reside in her location on the borders between high culture and popular culture, art and politics, masculinity and femininity, head and body, intellect and sexuality, heterosexuality and homosexuality, word and picture, beauty and horror, to name just a few. This borderline existence reflects the multiple, contradictory sites she occupies in our cultural discourses: British intellectual aristocrat, high modernist, canonical author, writer of best-sellers, Bloomsbury liberal, Labour Party socialist, feminist, sapphist, acknowledged beauty, suicide, and woman. Situated on the borders, Virginia Woolf continually threatens to undo them and the categories or norms they name and contain; in this sense she becomes aligned with the monsters whom culture and cultural critics have always placed on the boundaries of what is acceptable, policing them by their very presence. "A construct and a projection," Jeffrey Cohen writes, "the monster exists only to be read: the *monstrum* is etymologically 'that which reveals,' 'that which warns,' a glyph that seeks a hierophant. Like a letter on a page, the monster signifies something other than itself: it is always a displacement . . . ,"[16] but one that marks both the place of social/cultural disruption and the space for change. "It is by no accident," Slavoj Žižek notes, "that 'monsters' appear at every break which announces a new epoch," threatening to "[dissolve] all traditional . . . symbolic links and [marking] the entire social edifice with an irreducible structural imbalance."[17] One of his examples is Virginia Woolf.

As the case studies I examine make clear, the boundary disruptions and social struggles marked by Virginia Woolf's contested appearances can be located in historical periods characterized by major shifts in the status of women in society, whether the 1920s or the period from the end of the 1960s on, periods when a substantial number of women began to enter the public arenas associated with higher education and the professions.[18] I would call the fear provoked by these shifts a fear of feminization, except that the term in its current usage is too strongly biased in the direction of sentimentality and the feminine, whether in terms of the private sphere, or religion, or literature and art (including the contemporary study of literature and the humanities in general), to make my point. What I am talking about is more accurately described as a fear of feminism, although feminism need not be present in an overt form; this was the case, for example, in the early and mid-1960s, when, taking advantage of the expansion of higher education following Sputnik, women began to go to college and to graduate school and then into the professions, including academic ones, in ever-increasing numbers, and not just in the humanities.[19]

Gender, then, with its crucial role in social relations and social power, takes center stage in the struggles to define Virginia Woolf and her meaning, although it never stands alone. In this sense my avowedly feminist approach aligns itself with Margaret Ferguson's and Jennifer Wicke's definition of feminism as "materialist feminism, feminist theory and practice—however divergent—premised on material conditions, on the social construction of gender, and on an understanding of the gender hierarchy as relational and multiple and never in itself simply exhaustive."[20]

As I have already indicated, the category that intersects most powerfully with gender in the contradictory and fiercely contested renderings of Virginia Woolf is that of cultural class, often tied, particularly when the example is British, to social class, but not always and not necessarily.[21] For one thing, any discussion of Virginia Woolf's role as complex marker of cultural class cannot escape the contradictions inherent in her "highbrow" status, a status she cheerfully claimed for herself, and her established position today as a "high modernist" within what is generally considered "high culture." Having said that, however, we find ourselves immediately drawn back into gender, an effect of the many arguments by cultural critics that have aligned high culture with the masculine, and low or popular or mass culture with the feminine. Andreas Huyssen, to take just one pertinent example, argues with great clarity that modernism, the modernism of "the Flaubert–Thomas Mann–Eliot axis" as well as of "modernists such as Marinetti, Jünger, Benn, Wyndham Lewis, Céline, et al.," is not only characterized by "a powerful masculine mystique" but defines itself in opposition to a mass culture persistently gendered "as feminine and inferior."[22] Writing of this distinction in his introduction to *Joyce and Popular Culture,* R. B. Kershner notes that "this idea has proved so influential that contemporary critics sometimes take it as an assumed point of departure."[23] What neither Huyssen nor Kershner nor others seem to wonder about or question is where Virginia Woolf, who aligned herself with both "highness" and the modern, would fit. I would say she doesn't, unless, perhaps, we grant her honorary masculine status. As we shall see, this is what happens when she gets subsumed into the supposedly gender-free, androgynous, disinterested world associated not only with high art but with "intellectuals" and the "public sphere." How much, I find myself asking at moments like these, is the threat posed by Virginia Woolf to these categories and arguments a question of cultural class, and how much is it a question of gender?

The answer will vary, depending on the particular context in which the question arises, including its location on the cultural terrain. Because of this multiplicity, I have found myself crossing between and among critical frameworks in articulating both my questions and my answers, drawing upon different ones at different times as I've followed Virginia Woolf icon on her transgressive journeys. Only by adopting a similar mobility can we begin to map the multifaceted phenomenon signified by Virginia Woolf's iconization and its effects.

2. *Frameworks: Border Crossings*

When feminist critics in the 1970s announced the introduction of "Another Version of Virginia Woolf" and turned to Woolf's texts to illustrate their claim, they were evoking a concept central to this study: versioning. A concept with ties to both the academic world and the popular, versioning suggests both the process and the effects integral to Virginia Woolf's construction as contested cultural icon across the cultural terrain. Often presented as a democratic practice in which all the participants are potentially equal, versioning in actuality has proved more limited. In this sense versioning becomes aligned with theories of cultural conflict and cultural change that posit what Stuart Hall calls a "double movement of containment and resistance," perhaps as good a phrase as any to summarize Virginia Woolf's iconicity and its impact.[24]

In literary studies, versioning describes and usually advocates the practice of publishing all the different "versions" of an individual work, including prepublication texts (holographs, typescripts, etc.). The immediate effect, Donald Reiman writes, is to provide "enough different *primary* textual documents and states of major texts" for readers to explore their "distinct ideologies, aesthetic perspectives, or rhetorical strategies";[25] but the larger impact of the practice is to challenge the authority of any one version of the work and, by implication, both the author's intention and the editor's authoritative final word. Seen in this light, versioning signifies a rebellion among textual scholars against the eclectic edition of a single "authorized" text and posits the coming-of-age of the unstable, unfixed, postmodern work whose meanings are derived by readings of the differences among the multiple versions. As David Greetham explains the implications of this practice, "instead of postulating a single, consistent, authorially sponsored text as the purpose of the editorial enterprise, [the new textual scholars] suggest multiform, fragmentary, even contradictory, texts as the aim of editing, sometimes to be constructed *ad hoc* by the reader." The shift from " 'intention' (an authorial prerogative) to 'affect' (a reader's)" must be understood as part of the larger shift in critical theory from "reliance on an author's imputed meaning to the free play of meaning associated with post-structuralism," creating a situation in which "it seems that all we have are competing texts and competing readers." The term Greetham uses to describe the practice of producing texts and meanings— of versioning—at the end of the century is *democratic pluralism.*[26]

In the popular realm, versioning arises in conjunction with "black linguistic and musical practices that accent variance, variability—what reggae musicians call 'versioning.' "[27] Here, too, the appeal to the democratic is strong. In his book on Caribbean music, for example, Dick Hebdige writes that " 'versioning' is at the heart not only of reggae but of *all* Afro-American and Caribbean musics: jazz, blues, rap, r&b, reggae, calypso, soca, salsa, Afro-Cuban and so on." For Hebdige, the British cultural critic long associated with the study of oppositional subcultures, versioning is distinctly subversive, and its subversiveness lies in part in the continual shifts and changes in a text that privileges—as, he argues, African, Afro-American, and Caribbean music all do—the "collective voice" over the "individual voice," helping make reggae a "rebel music." Comparing versioning to a quotation in a book, he describes both as "an invocation of someone else's voice to help you say what you want to say. . . . And every time the other voice is borrowed in this way, it is turned away slightly from what it was the original author or singer or musician thought they were saying, singing, playing." The benefits of this practice, he concludes, reside in the lack of fixity, the continual flux: "That's the beauty of quotation. The original version takes on a new life and a new meaning in a fresh context. . . . And that's the beauty, too, of versioning. It's a democratic principle because it implies that no one has the final say. Everybody has a chance to make a contribution. And no one's version is treated as Holy Writ."[28]

While the two usages of the term and their contexts differ, I am struck by the similarity of the utopian vision, voiced in both cases as a potentially subversive practice whose end is multiplicity, fluidity, and change. The realities, however, even if we leave aside the question of which versions of a text get published and used—and the even larger question of copyright law, at least in the United States—often seem more sobering, raising as they do questions of social and cultural hierarchies and power. The power relations operative in the act of versioning motivate poet and critic Nathaniel Mackey's less optimistic view of its possibilities when placed in a North American cultural landscape. In Mackey's formulation, versioning in black art and culture operates in tension with a dominant white culture that can, at any point, appropriate an emergent cultural form for its own ends. On the one hand, versioning can be read as "resistant othering," an act by which those who are subjected by the forces of "power, exclusion, and privilege" to a "social othering" that fixes and marginalizes them can claim their own agency: "The black speaker, writer, or musician whose practice privileges variation subjects the fixed equations which underwrite that denial [of agency to them] (including the idea of fixity itself) to an alternative." On the other hand, this power of agency is always under threat of erasure, as evidenced in the example of "swing": the white musical form, articulated as a noun, that, he argues, was borrowed from blacks who used the verb to indicate a way of responding to a particular form of black music. "As in Georg Lukács's notion of phantom objectivity," Mackey writes, "the 'noun,' white commodification, obscures or 'disappears' the 'verb' it rips off, black agency, black authority, black invention." The result is not only aesthetic impoverishment, but "on the political level, a containment of black mobility, a containment of the economic and social advances that might accrue to black artistic innovation."[29]

Here Mackey's argument, read as a corrective to rather than a canceling of a versioning that is understood to be subversive only, intersects with Stuart Hall's useful definition of popular culture in terms of "the play in cultural relations," a realm in which "what matters is *not* the intrinsic or historically fixed objects of culture, but . . . the class struggle in and over culture" itself. For Hall, popular culture is best defined as a process or site of contention inscribing the structural and institutional "relations which define [it] in a continuing tension (relationship, influence and antagonism) to the dominant culture," including that which constitutes "high" or "elite" culture. This definition "treats the domain of cultural forms and activities as a constantly changing field," one in which

> the meaning of a cultural form and its place or position in the cultural field is *not* inscribed inside its form. Nor is its position fixed once and forever. This year's radical symbol or slogan will be neutralised into next year's fashion; the year after, it will be the object of a profound cultural nostalgia. . . . The meaning of a cultural symbol is given in part by the social field into which it is incorporated, the practices with which it articulates and is made to resonate.

Elsewhere in his essay, Hall describes this process and the class struggle it demarcates in the phrase I have already evoked: a "double movement of containment and resistance."[30]

If we substitute *icon* for *cultural form* in Hall's formulation, we can begin to understand the processes at work in the versioning of Virginia Woolf across the cultural terrain: the often subversive versions of Virginia Woolf that have emerged and the struggles to reclaim or contain them. Those engaged in the latter gesture often enact Michel Foucault's rendering of the "author function": "a certain functional principle by which, in our culture, one limits, excludes, and chooses; in short, by which one impedes the free circulation, the free manipulation, the free composition, decomposition, and recomposition of" cultural texts by evoking the author; "the author is therefore the ideological figure by which one marks the manner in which we fear the proliferation of meaning."[31] When scholars or, for that matter, journalists or filmmakers or reviewers claim to speak with and for an "authentic" or authorized Virginia Woolf who has one meaning only—theirs—we are in the realm of the author function.

While this gesture occurs across the cultural terrain, it may be strongest in the realm of the "intellectual" media, where the process of exclusion, including the exclusion of the academic and the popular as illegitimate usurpers of Virginia Woolf's image and meaning, is basic to both its self-construction and its construction of Virginia Woolf. The element of ownership also comes into play here, metaphorically if not literally, though the issues often seem the same. As Jane Gaines has illustrated, when it comes to the laws governing the use of another person's name, face, words, images, and sounds, the question of ownership intersects with what counts as legitimate culture and what doesn't. Using as an example the California Civil Code known as the "Celebrities Rights" act (1985), she highlights its distinction between cultural forms that have " 'cultural or informative functions' " (books, plays, and magazines, for example, or works that are "single and original"), and are hence " 'accorded a social value that transcends commercial enterprise,' " and those that don't ("posters, coffee cups, lunch pails, magazine ads, T-shirts, playing cards, ashtrays, statuettes, postcards, mementos"); this distinction attempts to contain the celebrity's image by denying its use to those subcultural groups that have traditionally used more "popular" forms to articulate alternative or subversive cultural meanings.[32] But as Gaines also notes, regardless of who "owns" the image or its status as private property, "meaning" will always escape or be defined anew. Building on the ironic coincidence that the case precipitating the "Celebrities Rights" act was brought by the heirs of Bela Lugosi over the rights to his image as Count Dracula, Gaines makes a case for the subversive/disruptive return of the undead.

With Lugosi I come to another critical framework central to my argument: recent studies of stars. While most pertinent in that part of the book exploring Virginia Woolf's appearances in popular culture (part 2), its concepts can be applied to the history of Virginia Woolf's iconicity in general. Identifying Virginia Woolf as a "star" has a number of attractions, not the least of which is Richard Dyer's characterization of the star as a "star image" situated at the intersections of semiology and sociology.

To see Virginia Woolf as a star, then, is to approach her as an image that is simultaneously textual (realized in a media text), social fact, and ideological (grounded in and expressive of the contradictory sets of "ideas and representations in which people collectively make sense of the world and the society in which they live"). The concept Dyer uses to explore the complexity of the star image and its necessarily ideological existence, "structured polysemy," captures both the multiple, contradictory representations of Virginia Woolf and their necessary limitations: limitations of available texts and of ideological/institutional constructs at any particular cultural moment. In Dyer's words, structured polysemy suggests "the finite multiplicity of meanings and affects they embody and the attempt so to structure them that some meanings and affects are foregrounded and others are masked or displaced."[33]

Dyer's analysis focuses on Hollywood film, but the concepts, he notes, are applicable to "stars" in other realms as well. When he uses the term *structured polysemy*, for example, the *structured* contains within it the possibility of the "various elements of signification" reinforcing each other, legitimating, as in John Wayne's case, "a certain way of being a man in American society," or in the case of "intellectual" representations of Virginia Woolf, a certain way of being a high cultural figure. But it also contains the possibility of oppositions or contradictions, which can become so extreme, as in the case of Marilyn Monroe or of Virginia Woolf in her more popular forms, that "they threaten to fragment the image altogether." For Dyer, star images are inseparable from the contradictions at the heart of our social and psychic lives, and these contradictions are both "managed" and "subverted" in the production and consumption of the star image itself, the two processes often occurring simultaneously. The meaning of the star image, then, is never divorced from a production/consumption dialectic in which consumers are potentially as significant as producers, a concept that resonates in a wide array of studies of cultural articulations of stars, including those posited by queer theorists.[34]

Dyer's insistence on the textuality of the star image proves equally generative: his argument is that the "structure" at work in the star image, however contradictory, is provided by the interplay of the various and numerous media texts that constitute the image, including the interplay of the "vehicle" developed to feature or foreground a star and the responses to it by critics and commentators. The star image is always intertextual and always changing. Elsewhere Dyer expands the components of the star image to include "what people say or write about him or her, as critics or commentators, the way the image is used in other contexts such as advertisements, novels, pop songs, and finally the way the star can become part of the coinage of everyday speech."[35] Because of this complex intertextuality, Dyer notes, any reading of a star's "meaning" has to take into account the particular historical moment and the specific group that is responding.

It also has to consider the star image's "complex configuration of visual, verbal, and aural signs,"[36] and I want to foreground *visual*. There is no question in my mind that the visual aspects of Virginia Woolf icon are crucial to her visibility and her resonance. Virginia Woolf, we know, is an extraordinary-looking woman, and we know this because of the many extraordinary photographs of her that have circulated in our culture. This is particularly true of the photograph of the young Virginia Stephen, in profile, taken by G. C. Beresford when she was twenty (fig. 3), which provides the image most often reproduced on T-shirts, mugs, posters, etc.; but several of the portraits by the Lenare studio (figs. 4, 5), by Man Ray (figs. 2, 6, 7), and by Gisèle Freund (figs. 8, 9, 10, 11) have also contributed substantially to the construction of her star image and made her transformation into *icon* particularly feasible. But being on the side of the visual has its price in our culture, linked as image, spectacle, and often the grotesque are to women and/or the feminine, contained by the power of the word but—and here we return to the concept of fear—always containing within it the threat of subversion, of rebellion, as well.[37]

Star theory, then, provides inroads into the complex intertextuality of Virginia Woolf icon, but it has another attraction as well: its role as antidote to those theories that frame studies of cultural figures deemed worthy of respect in terms of heroes and the heroic, a frame that almost by definition excludes women. Here it is worth recalling Russell Baker's lament that the word *icon* is being reduced by "depraved language butchers" to a label for those "once dismissed as 'heroes' or 'stars.'" Baker's formulation elides the long-standing distinction made by cultural commentators *between* the hero and the star, a distinction that, like Baker's, implies a descent. Daniel Boorstin provides a classic example; his chapter in *The Image, or What Happened to the American Dream* on the "human pseudo-event" is called "From Hero to Celebrity," and the movement is all downhill.[38] More recently, the untimely death of Princess Diana in 1997 and the outpouring of emotion that followed generated articles with headings such as "Once We Had Real Heroes; Now There Are Only Stars. . . ."[39] Both are manifestations of a powerful cultural myth about the twentieth century that is predicated on a fall: the fall of the hero into the star.

As my reading at the start of this project soon made clear, any attempt to understand Virginia Woolf's cultural status through models grounded solely in the heroic was doomed to fail. The difficulty is that throughout

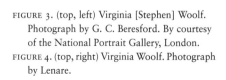

FIGURE 3. (top, left) Virginia [Stephen] Woolf. Photograph by G. C. Beresford. By courtesy of the National Portrait Gallery, London.

FIGURE 4. (top, right) Virginia Woolf. Photograph by Lenare.

FIGURE 5. (bottom, left) Virginia Woolf. Photograph by Lenare.

FIGURE 6. (bottom, right) Virginia Woolf. Photograph by Man Ray. Copyright © 1999 Man Ray Trust/Artists Rights Society, NY/ ADAGP, Paris.

FIGURE 7. (above)
Virginia Woolf. Photograph by
Man Ray. Copyright © 1999
Man Ray Trust/Artists Rights
Society, NY/ADAGP, Paris.

FIGURE 8. (left)
Virginia Woolf. Photograph by
Gisèle Freund. Copyright ©
Gisèle Freund, Photo
Researchers.

FIGURE 9.
(left) Virginia Woolf.
Photograph by Gisèle
Freund. Copyright © Gisèle
Freund, Photo Researchers.

FIGURE 10.
(below, left) Virginia Woolf.
Photograph by Gisèle Freund.
Copyright © Gisèle Freund,
Photo Researchers.

FIGURE 11.
(below, right) Virginia Woolf.
Photograph by Gisèle Freund.
Copyright © Gisèle Freund,
Photo Researchers.

most of Western culture and much of this century the concept of the hero, like the concept of high culture, has been located squarely in men and/or the masculine. As Gloria Steinem noted in a 1997 *Life* magazine devoted to "celebrating our heroes," "When I was growing up, there were really no female heroes except Wonderwoman."[40] Instead, there were female stars, the one category in studies of public figures where you could count on finding women. Boorstin, for example, includes Joan of Arc in his list of traditional heroes, and he talks on occasion of the unsung "men and women" who might provide heroic models, but the only women who enter the story after Joan of Arc are movie stars: Mary Pickford, Mae West, Elizabeth Taylor. Eight years later (1970), a collection of essays titled *Representative Men: Cult Heroes of Our Time* puts no women into the chapters titled "Politics," "Social Commentary," "Race," "Literature," "The Arts," or "Science"; the two women who do appear are located in "Films," where Elizabeth Taylor enters the scene, and "Popular Culture," where an essay on Jacqueline Onassis, the last in the collection, presents her as "The Existential Heroine"—not hero. Richard Schickel goes even further in his 1986 book on the culture of celebrity when he calls his chapter on film stars in the 1950s, with its focus on Marlon Brando and Marilyn Monroe, "Super Hero, Super Victim." And no women appear in the introduction to the 1978 *Icons of America,* suggesting that when the hero is the model, women can't be icons either.[41]

Given this history, when John Rodden argues in the introduction to his study, subtitled "The Making and Claiming of 'St. George' Orwell" (a literary figure who, like Virginia Woolf, crosses cultural class lines), that "the typically unscholarly question of heroes and hero worship hovers at the border of any study of the making of a literary figure," he sets up barriers for applying his model to women, however literary they may be. These barriers are reinforced by the title of the introduction, "Appraising Famous Men: Mediating Biography and Society," and by his location of the discourse of the hero and the heroic in the nineteenth-century interest in "great men." For Rodden, "the sense of passionate identification expressed toward Orwell by some observers and the variety of inspirational images in which they have cast him sometimes make him appear almost like Joseph Campbell's 'hero with a thousand faces,'" incarnated as "Rebel, Common Man, Prophet, and Saint." But most of all, Orwell emerges as the "intellectual hero" for a multitude of Anglo-American men on both the Left and the Right who claimed him as their own, and *men* is the operative word: not one woman appears in Rodden's extensive introductory list.[42]

This gendered beginning is not improved by Rodden's location of Orwell's appeal as intellectual hero in his "virile image," his "capacity to make intellectual life seem manly, not effeminate"; nor does his statement, apropos of the often negative feminist responses to Orwell, that these responses reflect "the urge for a heroism that transcends gender modeling, the longing for intellectual heroes who are heroines too" alter the situation. Not only does the concept "intellectual heroine" read like an oxymoron, but Rodden's configuration fails to consider that *hero* and *heroine* have not had symmetrical meanings and/or equal value in our cultural narratives. Joanna Russ, to take just one wittily trenchant example of an extended discourse, vividly illustrates this point in her 1972 essay "What Can a Heroine Do?" where, presenting scenarios that reverse the gender of the protagonists in eight well-known narratives, including *Moby Dick,* "The Bear," and *The Day of the Locust,* she argues that in their perverse form they are unthinkable. Heroines, she adds, unlike heroes, have been severely restricted in Western literature and culture, being reduced, for the most part, to being the protagonist in a love story, and more recently to going mad; "woman as Intellectual is not one of our success myths."[43] Toril Moi certainly discovered this when writing *Simone de Beauvoir: The Making of an Intellectual Woman;* not only, she illustrates, is Beauvoir not considered an intellectual in France, but the level of animosity apparent in her reception led Moi to speculate that its source is less Beauvoir's writings than her illegitimate claim to participate as an intellectual in the public sphere.[44]

While not ignoring the hero and the heroic as important elements in the constructions of the star and her/his cultural roles, Dyer presents them in terms of the distinctly gendered and decidedly ideological issues they raise; moreover, they are only one factor in a richly nuanced network of approaches to the production, dissemination, and reception of the far more inclusive and mobile star image. For Dyer, the (gendered) heroic aspects of a star are never divorced from the overall image or construct, emerging as an effect rather than the origin of the discourses of the hero, including those that, like Rodden's, posit different heroic types.[45] In this way, Dyer reveals the performative aspects of the discourses of the hero in works such as Rodden's: their role in the production of cultural norms, values, and meanings that are the effect, in Judith Butler's terms, of processes of reiteration, sedimentation, citation, and exclusion;[46] he also suggests ways in which they are subverted. Arguing that every star image (and I would include Virginia Woolf) is necessarily finite, constrained by the available texts and ideological/institutional norms at any moment, he also argues it can be altered by practices that dislocate and/or shift the meaning of old texts, opening the space for revision. "Audiences cannot make media images [or, I would add, texts of any sort] mean anything they want to," Dyer writes, "but they can select from the complexity of the image the meanings and feelings, the variations, inflections and contradictions, that work for them," a response that "is often tantamount to sabotage of what the media industries thought they were doing." This process, he adds, becomes doubly important for those "groups—the working class, women, blacks, gays—who have been excluded from the culture's systems of representations in all but marginal or demeaning forms."[47] It can be read, once again, as a form of versioning.

If the unacknowledged gender bias that aligns the (male) literary figure with the (male) hero and never asks what would happen to the model if the literary figure were a woman limits its applicability to Virginia Woolf, it does prove useful in understanding some of the issues raised by her positions within the intellectual media—once she was admitted, that is, during the 1980s. Here, another of Rodden's assumptions points to the difference between Orwell's trajectory and hers: his claim that in the making of Orwell's reputation, as in that of literary figures in general, the originating source of recognition and elevation occurs in the intellectual or avant-garde sphere, in the "non-specialist 'intellectual' quarterlies or 'advanced' magazines, rather than in the specialist academic journals."[48] Not so Virginia Woolf in her posthumous rise to fame and iconicity, whose appearances in the intellectual press were few and far between—as well as being strictly controlled by her husband—from the time of her death until her emergence as a "major author" and feminist icon in the 1970s, neither of which would have occurred without the agency of the women's movement. As Susan Koppelman Cornillon wrote in the introduction to one of the first feminist anthologies (1972), "People—both women and men—are beginning to see literature in new perspectives which have been opened up by the Women's Liberation Movement."[49]

Rather than making Virginia Woolf icon, then, the intellectual press, once they decided she had cultural value, felt compelled to remake her. One anticipatory sign of the coming reclamation, as I've noted, appears in the negative renderings of the American celebrations, celebrants, and formats (academic conferences; T-shirts and calendars) at the time of her centenary. As Helen Dudar wrote in a *Saturday Review* article called "The Virginia Woolf Cult," Virginia Woolf "has become the Marilyn Monroe of American academia, genius transformed into icon and industry through the special circumstances of her life and work."[50]

The implication of the contrast between *genius,* on the one side, and *cult, icon,* and *industry* on the other—that Virginia Woolf had fallen and needed rescuing from her academic and popular incarnations—places her squarely within Boorstin's narration of our fall into an image and celebrity culture. In addition to asserting the fall of the hero, Boorstin offers a number of motifs pertinent to the contradictory threats and promises of Virginia Woolf icon: the role of the star as prototypical celebrity and the way in which stardom becomes the rule in all aspects of society (political, artistic, intellectual, and personal); the assumption that the changes being charted are inseparable from changes in technology, specifically the technologies for reproducing and disseminating words and, even more important, visual images; and the distinctions made, especially by American commentators, between American and European cultural models that oppose the democratic principles of the former to the vestiges of a more aristocratic, *rentier* system in Europe. For Boorstin, the "aristocratic survivals" in British culture have "retarded" not only the impact of what he terms the Graphic Revolution, the "ability to make, preserve, transmit, and disseminate precise images[,] images of print, of men and landscapes and events, of the voices of men and mobs," but also the shift from hero to celebrity, allowing great men and serious books to endure. Explicit in this longing is a contradiction that underlies much of the debate in the United States at least since World War II about the perceived debasement of culture: a simultaneous distrust of and desire for hierarchical European models of distinction and value that plays itself out in representations of and reactions to the figure of Virginia Woolf.[51]

The question of how Virginia Woolf fits into the intellectual realm, of course, is a question of gender as well as cultural class, with significant implications for the academic/intellectual split that I am positing. Here yet another framework comes into play: the myth of the fall of the disinterested intellectual, the *Luftmensch* ("airman"), as New York intellectuals often call him, into the professional, including the academic, that is assumed by its narrators to have been completed by 1960. At the heart of this myth is the idea of transcendence: of a flight or escape from the grounded, particular, private, weighted, bodily existence so often located in women and/or the feminine; in the American version, cultural class and cultural power are inseparable from gender.[52] Under the rubric of this myth, writers in the so-called "intellectual" journals, who might well be academics but who do not identify as such, have increasingly claimed the mantle not only of intellectual but of preserver of a high culture threatened by both the academy and popular/mass culture, which are often described as interchangeable; the most effective way to define oneself as an intellectual seems to be to distance oneself from and attack academics. Yet as Bruce Robbins and others have illustrated, we can chart a clear historical connection between the dissemination of this myth in the 1980s and 1990s and the perceived impact of feminism and ethnic studies in the academy:

> The argument that intellectuals in the independent, public sense no longer exist has also been an argument . . . by which the arguer, who remembers the greatness of intellectuals past, shows in so doing that he himself (it almost always is a he) retains a true intellectual's public voice and truly, legitimately speaks for the public. . . . At the same time, he claims priority over the specialized professionals, feminist academics, and so on, who, he is implying, have usurped its place.[53]

When the "intellectual" critique of the academic profession turns to a critique of its philosophical relativism, its secular refusal of a transcendent truth or a final authority,[54] it intersects with the critique of a postmodernism characterized by its undecidability, its undoing of borders and categories, its emphasis on the circulation of meanings, all of which come into play in the academic and popular versioning of Virginia Woolf. Although the conflict between a (postmodern) proliferation of meanings and the claim to a fixed, authoritative truth about an authentic Virginia Woolf occurs in all three spheres, it has been substantially undercut in both the academy and popular culture by methodologies and ideologies that spill over from one sphere to the other. When Rachel Bowlby wrote in 1988 of an " 'exemplary' " Virginia Woolf who had not only come to stand in for women writers and/or feminist criticism but who "doesn't easily stay put"—one whose texts and whose life, "like the Bible," lend themselves to multiple readings—she was also making an argument for the "French-inspired theoretical criticism" associated with the deconstruction of fixed positions or identities that by the 1990s had "naturalised" itself in the academic world.[55] Her turn in her subsequent writings on Virginia Woolf to the "varied relationships between literature and modern culture," mass/popular culture included, foregrounds the turn during the 1990s toward cultural studies that has increasingly brought the academic and the "constantly changing field" of the popular into conjunction.[56] Only in that self-styled "intellectual" sphere where writers define themselves as intellectuals by labeling versions of Virginia Woolf that differ from their own "academic," or "feminist," or the lowbrow product of a mindless mass/popular culture, has Virginia Woolf remained frozen into fixed (if contradictory) positions.

But the turn toward cultural studies so lamented by these "intellectuals" does not necessarily correlate with an uncritical or unqualified acceptance of an unending circulation of meanings, whether in the field as a whole or in my own study. As we know from the work of those associated with the Birmingham School in Britain, represented here by Hall, Dyer, and Gaines, the cultural is never distinct from the material, even or particularly when writing about public figures, icons, stars. Gaines's definition of the star underlines this point: "At once ego ideal for the spectator-subject, ideological rectifier of cultural contradictions, industrial product, and economic strategy in the studio's bid for monopoly domination of the market."[57] These multiple roles have led to debates about whether the star rectifies ideological and cultural contradictions or exposes them; in the case of Virginia Woolf, I would argue, it exposes them. The intertextual star image imbricated in the name and face "Virginia Woolf" highlights the dispersal of any fixed meaning, moving her into the realm Dudar so laments, the realm of "cult," "icon," and "product" that lies more on the side of stardom, fashion, play, spectacle, and the role of the audience as consumer/producer of images and meanings—the side of poststructuralism and/or postmodernism—than on the side of nostalgic renderings of the hero or the intellectual. Or, rather than opposing the star and the hero, we might argue that Virginia Woolf illustrates the star *as* hero in a productive sense: a site of identification and/or rejection, interpellation and resistance; the space where we enact our responses to the demands made upon us by society.

The doubleness or multiplicity implicit in the production of and responses to Virginia Woolf icon I am suggesting here has ramifications throughout my study and leads to a multiplicity in my relationships to the materials I present. It underlies my insistence on the circulation of meanings, on versioning, even as I insist on the local circumstances of their production and effects and add my own interpretations; in this sense the battles between versions I chart become symptomatic of larger cultural debates. It also underlies the doubleness of my rendering of Virginia Woolf icon as border-defining and border-defying monster, leading to a dual trajectory: on the one hand, the recurrence of the motif and its association with fear; on the other, the ways in which this fear has been and can be rearticulated and reinscripted for new possibilities and pleasures. These oscillations, grounded in the complexity of particular texts and moments, inform my resistance to the more starkly poststructural vision of the "mass-mediated rememberings and representations" that Paige Baty, writing of Marilyn Monroe, posits, representations that exist independently of the processes by which individuals or groups interpret a figure for their own ends. For Baty, mass-mediated culture, conceived as a matrix, undoes even the dialectics of dominant and subordinate, center and margins; "the center is central by being everywhere and nowhere all at once," while the mass-mediated rememberings through their circulation "constitute cultural expressions of common relationships to knowledge, power, and identity. They do not capture a preexisting reality so much as they generate and express, though their construction of the world, the character of the real at a given moment."[58]

However seductive Baty's vision of "common relationships to knowledge, power, and identity" may be, it fails to take into account the only too real question of who has access to the various media that constitute this matrix and how these "rememberings" translate into the norms and institutions and laws that make some representations and some identities more important—and more rewardable—than others. As Mackey reminds us, versioning is not always the "democratic principle" Hebdige extolled; nor does it always signify a "democratic pluralism," Greetham's formulation. Occurring within specific social and cultural contexts, it inscribes substantive struggles for subjectivity and power. Concerned about the "irresolvability of the contents of stardom" and the "political flaw in the poststructuralist challenge to 'the real' as a category to which we can appeal," Gaines does "not want to lose sight of the reality of material conditions";[59] nor do I. For Gaines, this means concentrating on the star as labor and examining the material implications of battles involving the legal ownership and hence the commercial exploitation of the star's images. For me, with the initial example of Lani Guinier clearly in mind—the only too real struggles for representation her views and her person generated in a government and in media that were more than willing to play on their constituents' fears—it means stepping back from the endless proliferation of virtual Virginia Woolfs to ask what role they have performed during specific historical moments, in specific national and cultural configurations, in defining and policing cultural hierarchies. Or to return to Hall's formulation, it means tracking the "double movement of containment and resistance" at work in Virginia Woolf's reformulations as "genius," "icon," "industry," cult figure, or star, and the double movement of elevation and iconoclasm that arose in response to them.

3. Preview

Virginia Woolf Icon is divided into three parts, each one with a structure and logic expressive of its origins and ends. Part 1, "Negative Encounters: The 'Intellectual' Media," takes as its assumed starting point Virginia Woolf's steady rise during the 1970s and 1980s to academic canonization and the central role played by the women's movement and feminist criticism in this process; one result was to make Woolf studies synonymous with feminist criticism itself. The response within the academic establishment, particularly in the United States, which couldn't fail to see the handwriting on the departmental walls, was a two-pronged counterattack: on the one hand, an attempt to reclaim Woolf for a theoretically "universal" but in fact male civilization and/or literary tradition defined in its own theoretically impersonal, objective image; on the other hand, the assertion of a "universal" standard of criticism that authorizes its discourse but is inaccessible to Woolf's feminist critics, characterized in this rendering by their anger and presented as barbarians at the gates.[60] The intensity and implications of this battle over Virginia Woolf became clear to me in the late 1980s when I set out to trace the reception history of *Three Guineas,* the 1938 feminist/pacifist tract that has probably generated more controversy than anything else she has written. Raising the question of how women can find a voice to speak in the public sphere, Woolf's text evokes reactions that illustrate powerfully the difficulties of going public that still confront women, including a deeply embedded cultural fear of female anger.[61]

Conceived as an afterword to my analysis of the role of anger in representations of Virginia Woolf and her critics, "Negative Encounters" soon turned into a polemic on what I have come to describe as the self-styled "intellectual" media: the would-be successors to the New York intellectuals, the late, lamented *Luftmenschen,* and the journals in which they appear. I have called this section "Negative Encounters" to register one of the strongest refrains in these writers' claim to speak the truth about Virginia Woolf: that they speak *not* as academics—in other words, that they are *not* elite or specialized or jargon-ridden, *not* deconstructive or poststructuralist—and even more emphatically that they speak *not* as academic feminists. Most of the writers who define themselves against the negative Other "academic feminism" make no effort to define the term; nor do they seem to recognize how plural both the theory and the practice have always been. Instead, they invoke a singular, monolithic "academic feminism" as if it were a mantra, in the apparently secure belief that having said "not me," they have achieved the authority and legitimacy to speak in and for the "public" sphere. Another part of this negative legitimacy resides in their *not* being seduced by popular culture or the dislocation of the boundaries between the cultural spheres.

"Negative Encounters" begins on the margins of the academy, with those who write about it and Virginia Woolf for a supposedly disinterested media and public. The first section uses Virginia Woolf's symptomatic appearances in two intersecting stories connected with Columbia University,

Carolyn Heilbrun's early retirement and David Denby's *Great Books,* to suggest the processes by which this self-enclosed segment of the intellectual sphere produces and normalizes its discourses, freezing them into truths. The second section goes to the heart of the matter, the *New York Review of Books,* still considered by many commentators the leading intellectual journal in the United States, tracing the journal's iconization of Virginia Woolf as "one of us," not the false idol erected by "feminists," and the cultural contradictions exposed in the process. The final section anticipates Virginia Woolf's shift from the academic and "intellectual" into the popular by foregrounding her destabilization of categories when it comes to battles of the brows.

Part 2, "Starring Virginia Woolf," explores specific instances in Virginia Woolf's career as "star" of theater, cinema, television, and fashion, not to mention poster-girl and product endorser.[62] These instances, chosen for their inscription of the particular cultural thematics I am charting in this study, including that of fear, are presented as a series of "takes." Here, the duality or multiplicity that arises so often in conjunction with Virginia Woolf icon comes to the fore; for if these takes evoke the definition of the term, *"Cinematogr.* A continuous section of film photographed at one time; an instance of such filming. Also preceding a number to distinguish individual sections of film" (*OED*), the numbered sequence also signifies another of the term's meanings: the repetition of a single scene shot over and over again. The feeling of déjà vu implicit in this latter usage becomes stronger and stronger as the narrative unfolds, suggesting that however distinct the individual sections are, they can in many ways be read as multiple takes of the same scene or scenes; proliferation and reiteration continually intersect. The early takes (2–5) present the media texts that contributed to the construction of her star image; in Dyer's terms, these can be read as manifestations of promotion, publicity, texts, and commentaries or criticism.[63] The sequence here is for the most part chronological, starting with her appearance on the cover of *Time* magazine in 1937 and running to 1972–73, when Quentin Bell's biography of his aunt was published and Historical Products Inc. produced the first Virginia Woolf T-shirt.

The subsequent takes interrogate different facets of Virginia Woolf's proliferating appearances, her iconicity, once she had become an acknowledged star. Take 6 focuses on the extraordinary power of Virginia Woolf as visual icon, signified by the large number of reproductions of her face and the strong responses it evokes in viewers. Take 7 looks at the history of British attitudes toward Virginia Woolf that intersect in two of her more fascinating star appearances, both of them visual: Alan Bennett's television play *Me, I'm Afraid of Virginia Woolf* and Hanif Kureishi's *Sammy and Rosie Get Laid.* Take 8, which foregrounds the film *Tom*

& Viv, uses Virginia Woolf's cameo appearances as the starting point for ruminations on the status of the "Artist," capital *A,* in cultural productions of the 1990s, and the role of gender in the high/low divide. And Take 9 takes up Virginia Woolf's role as fashion icon, generating a discussion of the refrain "Virginia Woolf, like fashion, like postmodernism . . ." and its implications for contemporary cultural battles. The open-endedness of the refrain may provide a last word on the takes, but it is by no means the end of a story characterized by an ongoing interplay of proliferation and reiteration.

Part 3, "Doubled Movements," foregrounds this complex interplay by focusing on two examples of Virginia Woolf icon's role in the exposure and rectification of ideological and cultural contradictions; these in turn are inseparable from the "double movement of resistance and containment" so central to my argument. The first essay, "The Politics of Adaptation; or, The Authentic Virginia Woolf," revisits the question of proliferation and fashion raised in Take 9. Taking as my examples the nearly simultaneous adaptations of two of Woolf's most popular works, *A Room of One's Own* and *Orlando* (the latter of which has experienced at least five incarnations since the early 1980s), I concentrate on two interconnected issues: the continuing invocation of an "authentic" Virginia Woolf, and the way authenticity was translated into descriptions of and prescriptions for gender and sexuality during the "postfeminist" or queer moment of the early 1990s. All three spheres participated in the production and reception, the performances, of these texts: Woolf scholars, the "intellectual" media, and mass-circulation journalists/reviewers all jumped into the discursive fray, powerfully enacting the fractures and fractiousness of the cultural scene. The second essay, "The Monstrous Union of Virginia Woolf and Marilyn Monroe," returns to the recurring motif of fear. It begins with the photomontage that combined the head of Virginia Woolf with the body of Marilyn Monroe, called in recognition of its place of origin the "Chapel Hill hybrid," and uses it to explore the manifestations of the monstrous feminine that are so prevalent in Virginia Woolf's intertextual star image.[64] Here Medusa and the Sphinx, who make uncanny appearances as Virginia Woolf's shadowy alter egos throughout the narrative, become actors in their own right, and reiteration itself gets into the act, generating a multiplicity that both empowers and subverts its normalizing functions.

In the Afterword, "Virginia Woolf Episodes," the episodic appearances of Virginia Woolf in television shows serve as a pretext for speculations on Virginia Woolf's mobility as we move toward the end of the century, with an emphasis on shifting generational perceptions. I see this moment as an episode in an ongoing series rather than a "conclusion"; there are no final credits.

NEGATIVE ENCOUNTERS *one*

The "Intellectual" Media

B renda," my sister said over the telephone in June 1994, "did you know that Rush Limbaugh had named you by name on his radio show?" I didn't, but soon learned the details from others: Limbaugh's rant was about angry "feminazis" in elite institutions, and included an anecdote about my once being so angry that I almost burned a building down. It took me a while to realize he was citing my story about leaving an artichoke on the stove while writing a footnote in my essay "The Authority of Anger"; it took even longer to remember that I had told this story during my comments on the panel called "Anger, Strategies, and the Future" at the October 1992 conference honoring Carolyn Heilbrun. The conference was called "Out of the Academy and into the World with Carolyn Heilbrun"; the occasion was Heilbrun's very public retirement from Columbia University, a retirement taken early as a "protest against the denial of tenure to a woman colleague in the English and Comparative Literature Department," a sign of the ongoing resistance of the "old boy network" to feminist scholarship.[1] Although one of Limbaugh's sources was Christina Hoff Sommers's conservative-inspired and -funded *Who Stole Feminism?* his staff must have gone directly to the videotape of the conference to find that particular tale. Despite several attempts by scholars to obtain a transcript of the show, none has succeeded.[2]

What fascinates me about this sequence is the transmutation of this panel in the right-wing telling of it. In Sommers's version, the speakers were a group of "aggrieved," "chronically offended" feminists from some of the country's most prestigious institutions who, despite our "fine and expensive educations" and our tenure, were complaining yet again about being victims of patriarchy; she gives no further details.[3] Granted, the academics on the panel taught at Dartmouth, MIT, Harvard, or Rutgers, and Gloria Steinem, the other panelist . . . well, at that moment she was very much involved in the upcoming presidential election; and granted, the moderator, Jane Marcus, introduced me as "having been angry at Dartmouth since 1972." But to my recollection, and the tape bears this out, only one of us even mentioned patriarchy, and that was in a quotation from Heilbrun. Basing my remarks on my experience teaching at UCLA during the Los Angeles uprisings the previous spring, I talked about the presence of racial tensions in the classroom and strategies for channeling student anger; others talked about conservative attacks on multiculturalism and lawsuits filed against feminist scholars, about the necessities and dangers of the new information technologies and the importance of understanding global capitalism, about organizing and education occurring outside the university, and about the imminent election. We were talking issues, strategies, politics, pedagogy, hopes, fears, history, the future, the relationship of the academy to the world. We were talking about the need to speak out, to translate anger into public words and public acts, to enter the political realm. Who, I find myself asking, is really "aggrieved" in this scenario and why?

The "[familiar] irony of angry counsel against anger" accruing to this story, in Daniel Cottom's phrase, has a long history in Western aesthetic and cultural criticism. Virginia Woolf's presence in the title and body of Cottom's "The War of Tradition: Virginia Woolf and the Temper of Criticism"[4] provides a jumping-off point for my concerns here: an eccentric, elliptical look at the role played by "Virginia Woolf" (decidedly in quotation marks) in cultural wars waged in the United States over the past thirty-five years, including those waged over the canon, the curriculum, the role of feminism in the academy, and, most of all, whose voice carries cultural authority or legitimacy when these wars are fought in the public sphere: when anger, like Heilbrun, moves out of the academy and becomes a "media spectacle."[5] The media I am concerned with here take a specific form: the New York–based journals associated with a self-styled "intellectual" media, those "'influential' periodicals read by a general audience" such as the *New Republic, Commentary, Partisan Review,* the *Nation,* the *New Yorker,* the *New York Times Book Review,* and the *New York Review of Books.*[6] During this period, these journals have increasingly defined themselves by what they are not: *not* academic, *not* pandering to mass or popular culture, *not* feminist, and most decidedly *not* academic feminist.

Virginia Woolf's symptomatic appearances within these "battles of the brows," whether they occur at Columbia University, over the *New York Review of Books,* or in conjunction with the slippery terrain of middlebrow culture, reveal not only competing definitions of what constitutes cultural capital and for whom, but startlingly contradictory impulses. There are, it appears, elites and elites within the American intellectual scene, and what constitutes their desirability or authority depends not only on who has the power within particular contexts to draw the boundaries between categories and designate what goes where—that is, on cultural class—but also on gender and its ideological configurations. Constructed as a "special interest" group and weighed down by what is presented as a monolithic ideology, feminists find themselves continually excluded from the realm of detachment, transcendence, and universality asserted by and for "intellectuals" and the public sphere: the "high" culture, and/or the understanding of "greatness" they claim as their own. Where, I am left asking, can feminists speak in an "intellectual" sphere so deeply class- and gender-encoded? Or, equally significant given the attention accorded Sommers's book, what counts as "feminism" and who gets to define it in these "intellectual" media?[7]

In exploring these issues, my itinerary is as serendipitous as Virginia Woolf's appearances in the debates. If there is a gravitational pull, it is toward Columbia University and by extension New York, where so many of the battles over Virginia Woolf's iconic status and its relationship to "high" culture have been fought. This decidedly East Coast bias reflects the belief among many participants that New York and its journals remain the primary site of intellectual life in the United States, a fixation that mirrors itself in the fixed if contradictory representations of Virginia Woolf found there.

Prelude. Anger and Storytelling: Whose Story Counts?

In his explication of "The War of Tradition," Daniel Cottom provides a history of that strand of Western cultural criticism that defines anger as a distorting "anamorphosis," a perversion, and outlaws it in the name of " 'sweetness and light,' " harmony, reflection, and most of all reason; this definition, he argues, is as familiar as the self-righteous anger associated with its defense: the "irony of angry counsel against anger" so endemic to the critical tradition as to become a commonplace, a "mere figure of speech" that "as such is dismissable from the terrific patriarchal thrust of tradition" (145, 147–48). This tradition is "patriarchal," he adds, for reasons equally familiar: because anger has long been marked as feminine (in Cicero's formulation, " 'sharp exclamation injures the voice and likewise jars the hearer, for it has about it something ignoble, suited rather to feminine outcry than to manly dignity in speaking' " [146]), and because of the historical exclusion from the public sphere and public speech of those considered "especially prone to intemperance": "children, women, servants and inferior sorts of freemen" (149–50).

The critics who challenge this tradition, Cottom argues, do so by show- ing that "the familiar irony," rather than being "exceptional, marginal, and dismissable," was "constitutive" of the outlawing of certain kinds of speech (149) and, equally important, that this process was implicated in so- cial struggle: "When these [oppositional] critics addressed anger, they lost track of the very term . . . because it was bound to turn into other issues . . .

in which the name of anger was no longer able to bear the complexity of the historical differences through which human destinies have been defined" (159). "Like Milton before him," Cottom adds, naming some of his examples, "and Woolf, [Audre] Lorde, [June] Jordan, and [David] Wojnarowicz after him, Blake argued that anger could be identified only in the context of differing desires, conflicting wills, and words expunging one another—in short, in the contested dimensions of politics through which our cultures take shape and our histories are written and rewritten. . . . [Blake] knew that whatever else we may be and whatever else we do, we are fighting words" (157).

As Cottom's list makes clear, those whom he privileges with a recognition of the politics of anger in the early 1990s, his time of writing, include feminists of all colors, racial and ethnic minorities, antiwar activists, and gays and lesbians. This is not surprising given his premise that "currently the anger of those who claim not to be political in their criticism and art, the anger that defines this claim for them, has arisen in response to public movements of protest, resistance, and rebellion," movements that insist that "neither art nor criticism has ever dwelt in a room of its own" and that the "imaginary tradition [of a disinterested art or criticism] has functioned as [a means] of censorship for the very people who claim to represent the principles of free inquiry" (162). What distinguishes Cottom's perspective on the topic is his concern that the term *anger* alone cannot move us beyond either "the familiar irony" of the status quo *or* the opposition's equally limited presentation of anger as "a matter of truth-telling, self-revelation, and the overthrow of censorship" (153): that anger alone cannot project us into the realm where it is recognized as "a question of rhetoric and politics" (152). Even as Cottom insists that anger is "undeniable," then, he also calls for a recognition of the potentially "divisive political implications, identifications, and possibilities historically bound up in the name of anger" (159) when it lacks a clear political grounding or articulation.

Cottom's history of the exclusion of women and/or feminists, among others, from the public sphere on the grounds of anger or special interests sets the stage for the stories of exclusion and inclusion that follow, as well as establishing their imbrication in a *two-sided* contest of vested interests. It also anticipates Ellen Rooney's more recent reading of discourses that exclude or distance feminist anger, one that focuses on feminisms within the academy but is applicable to the public sphere as well. Rooney's concern is the danger that an unselfconscious association of feminism with anger may obscure and hence leave unchanged the more complex social and cultural forces at work when it comes to political power and political change, a danger she confronts through an analysis of the apostrophic address "*you* would have been so angry" as constitutive of the feminist subject.[8] While this address, she argues, will win you, the feminist addressee, " 'a place in other people's stories' " it can also, she notes, "serve the peculiarly contrary purpose of *displacing* feminist intent away from the speaking subject who narrates" (2). When told by unsympathetic men or women such as Rush Limbaugh, she adds, who "tells stories about feminists, thematizing feminism" that "he plainly hopes . . . feminists (and especially 'feminazis') will hear," these stories underscore "the sometimes curiously intimate relation between feminist and 'anti-feminist' narratives" (23) that can be as self-perpetuating and as self-defeating as the confessional responses to Cottom's "familiar irony." But even when the address and the story are narrated by men and women sympathetic to feminism, the figure of the (female) feminist addressee allows a split to occur by which "you," the feminist subject, not only absorbs the speaker's anger but enacts his story, leaving him curiously distanced and uninvolved.

If, in this scenario, "*you* would have been so angry" assumes the narrative form "I tell *my* story as the story of *your* feminism," other forms and rhetorical strategies, Rooney argues, are available. One of these is "I tell *my* story as the story of *my* feminism," a form that makes a "direct claim upon feminist anger" and that still informs the ongoing project of "many contemporary U.S. feminisms . . . despite the differences and even the mutual incompatibilities among them" (10, 11, 12). This story remains, Rooney notes, a powerful and productive tool for altering what constitutes power and knowledge across academic disciplines. Another strategy is "I tell *your* story as the story of *my* feminism," an act of disjunction that when practiced by critics such as Nina Auerbach and Gayatri Spivak allows one to tell another's story, acknowledge another's anger, "without evading or disavowing political responsibility, and without claiming identity or an 'authentic' voice, but only a critical position and an 'impure' [Auerbach's term] feminist anger" (18). This process of "de-identification," she continues, "potentially unhinges anger from feminist discourse," revealing how often and how thoroughly the knee-jerk identification of feminism with anger has served to obscure the radical nature of feminist insights and their revisionary power, a comment easily borne out by the representation of "feminism" in the media. "Perhaps," she writes, "the apostrophe to anger is . . . a veil over the inescapable recognition that feminism lies in an instantaneous rereading of events, a rereading that is only belatedly attributed to the feminist or feminism and only then tagged with her dead-give-away anger. In this evasion or veiling of feminist insight, we may begin to read the process by which feminism becomes ideology" (19).

But the rhetorical strategy that haunts me most is Rooney's final example: "I tell *your* story as the story of *your* feminism," a formulation that reduces feminism and feminist narratives to something happening over there (perhaps in "Women's Studies"): something that can be observed and reported but has no authority or performative bite, a "postfeminist" phenomenon in which the feminist subject and object both disappear (21–22). It is this strategy, I believe, that in concert with "the process by which feminism becomes ideology" increasingly permeates that sector of the public sphere dominated by self-styled intellectuals for whom feminist critique is definitely "over there" in the academy or in journals such as the *Women's Review of Books* and *Ms.* or in "special interest" groups, and hence has no place in a public conversation committed to the idea of a common, rational, disinterested discourse.[9] Given the power of this narrative strategy, Rooney's conclusion that "the politics of storytelling can never be allowed to take care of themselves" (22) becomes a crucial warning.

Section 1. The Columbia Stories

The narrative act of "disappearing" feminism—of relegating it to the academy except when it can be evoked as spectacle or the spectacular eruption of an illegitimate and dismissible anger—is graphically illustrated by the Heilbrun conference and its media coverage. As noted above, Heilbrun was neither quiet nor shy about stating her reasons for her early retirement, much to the individual and institutional anger of her colleagues for whom such matters as promotion and tenure are resolutely private. Nor was the conference honoring her a private affair; held at the CUNY Graduate Center, it drew so many scholars and nonscholars from New York and elsewhere that the organizers had to set up peripheral sites where the attendees could watch a video relay of the panels. But despite the public nature of this event—and despite Heilbrun's wide public visibility as both the mystery writer Amanda Cross and the author of two best-selling crossover books on androgyny and writing women's lives[10]—as *event* the Heilbrun story failed to capture the public's attention, receiving little coverage in the intellectual journals or mass-media magazines such as *Time* or *Newsweek*. In other words, it failed to become an actor in what Dana Polan has described as the transformation of intellectual debate, often located initially in the academy, into media spectacle. Only the *New York Times* covered the various moments in the unfolding story in any sustained way, a fact that can be attributed as much

NEGATIVE ENCOUNTERS   41

to its New York connections—Columbia and CUNY—as to its perceived cultural import.[11]

In contrast, the academic story that dominated the media at the time can be summarized by the term *culture wars.* Feminist anger in the academy, it seems, becomes newsworthy only when it translates into actions that threaten the critical traditions and the "canon" so dear to the hearts of the cultural conservatives—and many of the "liberals"—who control these journals. In this way, the culture wars become an illustration of the process that allows us to gauge the success of feminist anger and action, among other forces, through the angry reassertions of power they generate. Unfortunately, the backlash had ramifications that extended far beyond the realm of abstract theory so often associated with the academy or the more concrete realm of the classroom, migrating into the distinctly public realm of politics, elections, the media, and the law, where it intersected with perceived threats from "special interest groups," affirmative action, and immigration; the results include the "angry white men" phenomenon of the 1994 elections, which led to legislative restrictions on immigrants, and the ongoing dismantling of affirmative action, to name just two obvious examples. As we now know only too well, the battles over what gets taught to whom in colleges and universities proved to be lightning rods anticipating exclusionary legislative measures.[12]

Given Cottom's argument that anger is always historically specific, it is not surprising that in the context of the emerging culture wars Cottom himself turns not to *Three Guineas,* usually considered Woolf's angriest work, but to *A Room of One's Own,* Woolf's acidly etched map of the social and cultural factors that are necessarily inseparable from any consideration of the Western canon and its history. What is surprising is that unlike many commentators, Cottom reads *A Room of One's Own,* often portrayed as the reasonable, ironic alternative to the angry *Three Guineas,* as an exemplum of an anger as deeply committed to historical necessity, public rhetoric, and strategies for action as *Three Guineas* itself.

David Denby would be very angry at Cottom; he would admit as much. Denby, at that time a film critic for *New York* magazine, returned to his alma mater, Columbia University, in 1991–92 (the year Heilbrun resigned) to retake the two required courses in Western literature and culture, Contemporary Civilization and Literature Humanities ("Lit Hum"), the heart of the college's eighty-year-old core curriculum; his record of the experience, *Great Books,* was published in 1996. Denby, as he never tires of repeating, is deeply committed to the belief that "great books" and their classroom study are and should be kept separate from what is happening "out there" in the political realm. He is also deeply committed to the belief that Virginia Woolf would have unhesitatingly agreed with him. Bringing *A Room of One's Own,* which he read in Lit Hum, to his aid, he foregrounds Woolf's discovery, made possible by the legacy that gave her £500 and a room of her own, of the ability to "think of things in themselves," which is exactly what he argues the study of literature should be. Moreover, he loves Woolf for what he calls her privileging in her fiction and her essays of "the private theater of the emotions," located in the private and domestic (*To the Lighthouse* is his example), an attribute, he adds, that has traditionally been devalued by male literary critics and our culture as a whole.[13]

Denby's words of praise, of course, lock Woolf squarely into the private, feminine world of emotion, sensibility, and aesthetics that so much feminist criticism has tried to undo, but that is not all Denby wishes to accomplish. Although he admits the role of feminist critics in establishing Woolf's "greatness" and her current place in the canon, his grudging acknowledgment is followed by an angry attack on the supposed perversions of academic feminism that is worth citing in full:

> It was a famous victory [Woolf's ascension to "the eternal canon"], and in gratitude to the feminist critics, who were mainly responsible, I have tried to ignore the women in the universities who were using and misusing Woolf, claiming the most private of artists as a public possession, reading her entire work as an attack on the patriarchal family, or in terms of the childhood sexual abuse she was subjected to at the hands of her half-brother George Duckworth, and so on. I struggled to forget the mad American victim-consciousness and the separatist fantasies that have been directed onto Woolf in a manner alien to her nature as a writer and to her life as a social being. Though she disliked the word itself, Virginia Woolf was most assuredly a feminist. But to reduce her immense, varied output to a variety of current-day feminist agendas, and to marshal her iridescent metaphors as dull-edged weapons in the struggles for turf within the university, is to engage in exploitation, expropriation, and slander. If Woolf were now brought into contact with some of her academic champions, there would follow an explosion of scorn without parallel in English literature. Anyone who reads her carefully could prove as much.[14]

Strong words, particularly from someone who elsewhere in his book not only argues that there is never a single or fixed interpretation of a text—that readings will always change—but who illustrates through his own changed reactions to reading Woolf and his differences from the younger students how much context matters in responses to a work. The level of vitriol achieved in this passage is equaled only by Denby's attacks elsewhere in his book against those "academic leftists" who question the value of a core curriculum grounded in Western culture and art, and can be traced to some of the same sources.

Just look at his choice of *expropriation,* for example. The word derives from *expropriate,* defined in the *OED* as "dispossess (from estate, etc.); take away (property)," with its linguistic insistence on ownership, legal or otherwise. In this way it differs from the more linguistically neutral *appropriate:* "take possession of; take to oneself; devote to special purposes." *Expropriation,* then, signals that Virginia Woolf belonged to someone else whose "estate" was deprived of *his* (almost certainly) property by "academic feminists" (generic; no distinctions made). And this someone has, moreover, no agenda *except,* one might reasonably conclude, the restoration of Virginia Woolf to her rightful owners. Having regained their property, they, like Denby, can condemn the improper readings and the illegitimate or unauthorized uses made of Woolf by (generic) academic feminists who want to wrench her out of the "private" realm and make her a "public possession." But if a writer and her works are not a "public possession," what are they?

Cultural capital, John Guillory (for one) would answer, particularly when they are included in required courses on Western culture such as the Lit Hum course Denby took (twice) at Columbia, whose function is "to install a *class* habitus in the subjects of its pedagogy" defined by "a relation of *ownership.* It is not the ideas expressed in the great works that account for their status in arguments such as [Denby's], but the fact that these works are appropriated as the cultural capital of a dominant faction" in the society.[15] If, then, we ask, as Virginia Woolf did in *A Room of One's Own,* why people like Denby are so angry, we can conclude, as she did, that to understand it one has to do some digging, for "it was anger that had gone underground and mixed itself with all kinds of other emotions,"[16] including the fear of no longer being in a position to see oneself as superior by naming the Other inferior; the fear of loss of ownership and property; the fear of loss of power. Ironically, Denby got it just right when he associated "feminists" with "struggles for turf within the university," as Woolf herself did in *Room;* what he seems to have missed here is that it takes at least two factions to have a contest, and every one of them transforms Virginia Woolf into fighting words in very public battles over legitimacy.

If David Denby's undiscriminating diatribe against feminist criticism in the name of a more objectively derived Virginia Woolf sounds depressingly familiar, Columbia's recurrence as its site is equally predictable. For one thing, it is no accident that Denby's criticism of the feminist misuse of Woolf directly echoes Columbia professor Michael Rosenthal's defense of *Three Guineas* and its author as a "civilized" antidote to angry feminist critics; Rosenthal is acknowledged by Denby for his "general support." There is no mention of Heilbrun, despite the fact, as all the stories reporting on her retirement noted, that she was "one of the professors who helped" make Virginia Woolf "front and center" in the field.[17] In contrast, Heilbrun used the publicity surrounding her retirement to emphasize the lack of support given by Columbia's senior men to junior women who were feminists, and her frustration at not being able to change the situation.

Equally important, at the time of Heilbrun's public articulation of her anger, Columbia was emerging from an internal struggle over the nature of its core courses, including the question of whether Lit Hum should include women writers and, if so, which ones. Despite Denby's passionate desire to divorce the course from what is happening "out there" in the politicized public realm, "out there," in the form of Columbia's admission of women in 1983, precipitated the debates that led, ultimately, to Woolf's appearance in the course in 1990. If Columbia College had been a "male preserve," so had the core, and "partially as a nod to women undergraduates," Timothy Cross notes, "Jane Austen first made it on to the syllabus in 1985; Sappho and Virginia Woolf joined later." But the transition was not easy, as Cross, an in-house historian of the core curriculum, tells the story: ". . . the inclusion of women authors (and women's issues) added a new element of rancor to curricular decisions. Professor John Rosenberg remembers that the quarrel within the Lit Hum staff over [*La Princesse de Clèves*] 'was more bitterly divisive than any in my long memory of the course.' In the 1980s, curricular decisions were *again* becoming politicized. . . . Ideological concerns were *once again* undermining the validity of the entire educational enterprise" (my emphasis). Gender, it seems here, leads inevitably to anger, "politicizing" debates "again" (the reference being to the 1960s, when the core curriculum came close to being abolished) that at all other times had presumably been purely "educational," concerned, as Cross argues the course as a whole is, not with "indoctrination" but with "the notion of sensibility and *humanitas.*"[18] No wonder Heilbrun's assertion during a 1986 speech at Columbia that "the life of the mind is organized to reflect the politics of the mind, particularly the politics of a wholly male-centered culture and university" self-defined as "universal," could be conceived as heresy. As one of the articles on her retirement noted, "In academia, those are fighting words."[19]

Nancy Miller, who had taught Lit Hum for three years before the inclusion of women writers, drew a different lesson from the intrusion of gender into the debates. Writing in 1986, she worries more about the larger issues raised by the decision to add Austen because of the admission of women: the dangers inherent in the identification of women writers with women readers; the dangers of an overly simplified "reflection" relationship between literature and reality or experience; the dangers of adding a single woman writer to a "canon" without questioning the very concept of the "canon" or a core curriculum, particularly at an institution like Columbia, where "the names of the masterpiece writers are inscribed on the library's facade," are literally "carved in stone." At the same time, she notes, not to make the argument about women writers and women readers—the argument about representation, we could say—"authorizes the fiction of a certain hegemony." What is needed, she continues—once the particularity of the dominant culture becomes as apparent as the particularity of "minority" cultures (i.e., once "European white elite men, generally heterosexual, typically empowered" are also understood to be a "special interest")—is study of the way the dominant record is institutionally "rationalized and canonized."[20]

But the story doesn't end there. A footnote to the passage about the library in Miller's essay refers the reader to the October 1989 *New York Times* photograph of Columbia's Butler Library, "upon which one can read the names Plato, Aristotle, Demosthenes, Cicero, etc., graced by a one hundred and forty-foot-long banner 'bearing the names of great female authors': Pizan, Sor Juana, Brontë, Dickinson, Woolf, etc." The other names on the banner were Sappho and Marie de France.[21] When the creator of this banner, Laura Hotchkiss Brown, unfurled it during Columbia's graduation ceremony the previous May, she was arrested; later Columbia agreed to display it for a week, in conjunction with an exhibition and lecture series on women writers. By 1989, one might have assumed, both the action and the list would be fairly unexceptionable, but not so, at least in certain media circles. Miller quotes the comment in *New Criterion*'s "Notes and Comments" about this "radical initiative": "The names that adorned Brown's banner are interesting, of course, as an example of what happens when the study of literature becomes radically ideologized. For what is striking about the majority of these names is that they are minor, if not indeed, marginal, figures."[22] In 1992, this same banner hung over the stage at the conference honoring Heilbrun's retirement from Columbia; and in 1993 the *New York Times* photograph of the library and banner reappeared on the cover of Guillory's study *Cultural Capital,* cropped so as to place "WOOLF" between the author's name and the title, where, owing to the shading, it takes center stage.

Why does this matter? Where does the serendipitous appearance of *Woolf* lead us? In Guillory's book, contrary to what one might expect from the cover, her presence does not lead to arguments for the "representation" of women and minority writers in core courses, or for challenges to the canon, or for the development of alternative canons within women's studies and African American studies, for example—all of which, he believes, become immaterial when weighed against the larger issue of how the universities, as part of the School system, work to produce and reproduce a cultural capital that operates in terms of class, rather than race or gender; from this perspective, changing the content of what is taught to include women and minority writers will make no difference. Moreover, he notes, the system relies on admitting members of otherwise disadvantaged groups into its mysteries, thereby encouraging participation in the reproduction of the system rather than altering or dismantling it, an argument vividly illustrated by Denby's insistence that, within certain limits (i.e., that they are European), it doesn't matter what "representative" texts of Western culture are included in Columbia's core; what matters is the process of reading them that shapes the students' sense of themselves as the sharers of a particularly valuable form of cultural capital. Woolf or Dostoevsky, no matter; the sense of entitlement in reading great books is all.

How does this story end? It doesn't, but it branches out into a number of intersecting scenarios that suggest the stakes. The first occurs in the academy, where the Columbia story suggests that Woolf's elevation to the canon does not guarantee that English departments or universities will be more open to feminist issues; Virginia Woolf can not only be recuperated for a "tradition" that leaves cultural class very much in place, whether it has to do with the tenuring of feminist scholars or with arguments about what constitutes the "life of the mind," but can also be used against those, such as "academic feminists," who challenge the institution and its critical traditions.[23] But without insisting on Virginia Woolf, we run even more risk of reinforcing the positions of those, like Denby, who claim ownership of an "objectivity," "universality," and "truth" that render women writers and feminism "special interests" when they don't ignore them completely. One striking example of this blind spot occurs in Sven Birkerts's defense of the printed word and reading in *The Gutenberg Elegies,* where the first chapter opens with the statement, "It was Virginia Woolf who started me thinking about thinking again. . . . The magnet that pulled [my thoughts] into a shape was Woolf's classic essay, *A Room of One's Own.* Not the *what* of it, but the *how.* Reading the prose, I confronted a paradox that pulled me upright in my chair. Woolf's ideas are, in fact, few and fairly obvious—at least from our historical vantage. Yet the *thinking,* the presence of animate thought on the page, is striking."[24] But in his subsequent chapters on the reading he did as a child, a student, and a young man, all of it intricately linked to movement, adventure, and most of all his desire to be a writer, one finds a different paradox: that not one work he mentions was written by a woman, and none would have given a woman reading it the sense that she too, like Birkerts, could become a thinker or a writer—exactly the problem Woolf was addressing in *Room*. So much for the obviousness of her ideas.

Ironically, a similar process of "disappearing" women in the name of universality is reproduced in Guillory's own work, where, despite the promise of the cover that "Dickinson" and "Woolf" will figure in the text, they are both conspicuously absent, as is any reference to Miller's seemingly similar concerns. Instead, one is tempted to say, in this book the white boys for the most part talk only to and about other white boys, except when they criticize those who emphasize "representation" in the curriculum or those, like Barbara Herrnstein Smith, who want to question how "value" is defined and determined. At the end, when Guillory adduces Pierre Bourdieu's insistence that " 'We must . . . work to *universalize in reality the conditions of access* to what the present offers us that is most universal,' " one is left wondering *who* will be deciding what these "universals" might be.[25]

The second scenario moves out of the academy into the world of the self-styled intellectual media, where Denby's book received an enormous amount of mostly laudatory attention. One of the few exceptions, written by one of the few academics to review it, Helen Vendler, illustrates in great detail the book's lack of historical, philosophical, and literary understanding,[26] but no matter: Denby couldn't care less what she thinks. His audience from the beginning was composed of those self-identified, determinedly nonacademic "writers" or journalists like Denby himself whose access to the media still does so much to shape public perceptions of what happens inside the academic world, even though academics have begun to talk back.[27] The widely held negative view of what those "special interests" in the university, including feminists, are doing to our great traditions and to our youngsters illustrates the importance of tracking how Denby's arguments played in the press. Ironically, despite Denby's stated desire to move the study of literature away from the ideological and into the universal, his reviewers, even when they emphasized and praised his skill and enthusiasm as a reader, recognized that "the underlying premise of 'Great Books' is frankly political" and that his bias in the book is conservative.[28] But this did not hurt him in his chosen sphere; instead, his access to and defense of the "great books," coupled with his attacks on "leftist academics," including "academic feminists," provided him with an elevation of audience and authority. Excerpts from *Great Books* were published in the distinctly more upscale *New Yorker,* where, leaving *New York* behind, he has since become a regular film critic, and he is apt to appear in the journal that many writers still believe confers the greatest cultural prestige, the *New York Review of Books.*

There is, however, one place where Denby proved vulnerable to critique: his legitimation of Virginia Woolf's elevation to the canon. The specificity of the opposition generated by Virginia Woolf's inclusion but not Jane Austen's or Sappho's underscores that it *does* matter who or what is included or represented in a particular cultural category; it also underscores the importance of who gets to choose. Denby implicitly acknowledges this in his overdetermined attempt to distance Virginia Woolf from the political realm in general and "academic feminism" in particular, associating her instead with the aesthetic, the universal, the transcendent; but the iconography that links Virginia Woolf to anxieties about gender, cultural class, "sensibility," feminism, anger, and/or "special interests" proved too strong for him. The recurring refrain in the reviews, regardless of the politics of the reviewer, laments not only Woolf's inclusion but the necessary exclusion of a more worthy male writer. "One hopes," Joyce Carol Oates writes in the *New York Times Book Review,* "that it wasn't cynicism that provoked the 'Lit Hum' committee, under pressure from feminists, to drop 'Crime and Punishment' for 'To the Lighthouse' "; she also laments that a more "appropriate" modernist text such as *Portrait of the Artist* or *Women in Love* was *not* chosen because it was written by a man. And another reviewer, Roger Kimball, who's made a career of bashing "tenured radicals," comments in the *New Criterion* that by 1991 the Columbia courses, which in the past had "consisted entirely of acknowledged masterpieces," "had been corrected to include Jane Austen and politically corrected to include Virginia Woolf. . . ."[29]

At this point, the story branches yet again, suggesting diverse yet intersecting answers to the question of why Virginia Woolf should generate such strong reactions in reviewers. The simplest arises from her clear association with feminism, especially in the academy, which Denby acknowledges and protests. But another would point toward two divergent representations of Virginia Woolf: (1) as the private, aesthetic, "feminine" writer presented by Denby; and, conversely, (2) as public intellectual. The latter status is linked in part to her extensive critical writings and in part to the polemical works such as *A Room of One's Own* and *Three Guineas* that proclaim women's right to speak in the public sphere. Here, we need to return to the myth of the fall of the intellectual into the academic that I discussed

NEGATIVE ENCOUNTERS   49

in my introduction—a myth, as Bruce Robbins has illustrated so well, whose perceived origins correspond in time with the entrance of women and minorities into the universities, and which effectively excludes them from having a public voice. To pose "academic" and "public" as opposites, Robbins argues, is to highlight how centrist or "elitist" the "public" was presumed to be: "Blacks, Chicanos, Native Americans, even women— those groups whose new representation in American universities, curricula, conferences, book lists, and so on has drawn so much fire in the antisixties backlash—were not, [it] appears, 'the public.' " "The so-called missing generation" of intellectuals, he adds, would be "largely composed of fe-male, working-class, black, Hispanic, and other groups who simply *were not represented* in the white, male, largely upper- middle-class intelligentsia of the past."[30]

In raising the question of who or what constitutes the "public," we are plunged into an ongoing debate about definitions of the "public sphere," a term, it is often noted, that is etymologically related to the Latin *pu-bic,* from *pubes:* adult man.[31] Here Jürgen Habermas's description of the ideal or classic or bourgeois public sphere, which came into being in the eighteenth century, remains the norm against which other definitions assert themselves. Conceived as a "body of 'private persons' assembled to discuss matters of 'public concern' or 'common interest' "—and the idea of talk has always been crucial to it—the public sphere was meant to foster a discussion among peers, open and accessible to all, by banning "merely private interests."[32] But critics have long recognized, and here I am citing W. J. T. Mitchell, that while "the fictional ideal of the classical public sphere is that it includes everyone[,] the fact is that it can be constituted only by the rigorous exclusion of certain groups—slaves, children, foreigners, those without property, and (most conspicuously) women."[33] Writing of its American incarnation, Janice Radway confirms that "women, blacks, Indians, the unpropertied, criminals, and various other subjects marked at once by their illiteracy and by their bodies, by 'the humiliating positivity of the particular,' were denied access to the public arena."[34]

When writers lament the fall of the intellectual into the academic, they are reproducing this disembodied/embodied, universal/particular, man/woman dichotomy, especially when the intellectual is troped as a *Luft-mensch.* This is especially true in that the "intellectuals" evoked in these laments are almost always those known as the New York Intellectuals, "that tight-knit group of literary men that coalesced around *Partisan Review* in the 1930s and 1940s,"[35] who for many of their would-be suc-cessors are the "last intellectuals." Although there were women associated with the group, they tended to be undervalued in their time and have all but disappeared in the numerous books written about the group.[36] The one exception, the one woman accorded full "intellectual" status—and there was only one at a time—was the "Dark Lady": "that mysterious and fearsome woman who could tantalize an entire generation of (male) intellectuals by virtue of her superior wit, style, wisdom, command, and combativeness."[37] The first to hold the position was Mary McCarthy; she was followed by Susan Sontag. Despite Sontag's rejection of the concept as misogynist, it has a strong afterlife; Norman Mailer for one echoed it when defending the virtual exclusion of women speakers at the 1986 PEN Congress in New York: "There are not that many women, like Susan Sontag, who are intellectuals first, poets and novelists second."[38]

Another aspect of the Dark Lady brings us back to Virginia Woolf, fear: a fear that encompasses both the intellectual woman *and* the "feminine" woman, creating a double bind for female writers and intellectuals caught between being too bitchy or too feminine. The bitchiness surfaces in descriptions of the Dark Lady's aggressiveness, her bloodletting. As Harvey Teres notes, sharp criticism and polemical skills characterized the group as a whole, but where the men were usually "identified with the more balanced, circumspect aspects" of their writing, "the women were often identified with the aggressive aspects" of theirs.[39] But being too feminine, as Virginia Woolf was perceived to be by the New York intellectuals, also had its dangers. Scorned, Denby tells us, by men such as Lionel Trilling, who despite his academic role was one of the premier members of the tribe, for the aesthetic, feminine nature of her writing, Virginia Woolf became a marker of what one would *not* want to be if one were a woman within that group.

Nevertheless, these women could not ignore Virginia Woolf, in part because they were often assigned those topics considered less crucial to the public discourse of politics: theater reviews or reviews of fiction and poetry. As a result, when Woolf's works were reviewed in journals such as *Partisan Review* or the *New Republic* or the *Nation,* the reviewer was often a woman who to some extent was forced to define herself against what was perceived as Woolf's "femininity." The references I have found to Woolf in books written about the group usually place her squarely in the realm of the private, the aesthetic, the distinctly nonpolitical, often associated with "women's writing." Sidney Hook, for example, in an attempt to denigrate the portrait of male intellectuals drawn by Tess Schlesinger in her novel *The Unpossessed,* wrote, "She never understood a word about the political discussions that raged around her. . . . Tess could talk about Virginia Woolf, Jane Austen, some of the characters in Dostoyevski—not Ivan Karamazov—but the political isms" were the men's concerns; "she was a political innocent until the day of her death."[40] Mary McCarthy makes the point from the other side when she populates the category "Woman Writer"—those "interested in décor," "drapery," and "sensibility"—with Virginia Woolf, Katherine Mansfield, Elizabeth Bowen, and Eudora Welty, and rejects it in favor of the "sense" found in Jane Austen and George Eliot.[41] When Joyce Carol Oates lambastes the choice of *To the Lighthouse* for Lit Hum on the grounds that novels such as *Portrait of the Artist as a Young Man* or *Ulysses* or *Women in Love* or *The Sound and the Fury* would be "much more appropriate to represent modernism," she is echoing earlier women intellectuals' ambivalent attitude toward women writers and Virginia Woolf.[42]

The no-win designation of women writers and intellectuals as either too bitchy or too feminine that fed into their exclusion from serious public discourse helps explain why the 1960s post-Sputnik entrance of women into areas previously preserved for men, the academy and hence potentially the "public sphere," provoked such great anxiety. This anxiety often took the form of fear of feminization: a feminization associated paradoxically but not surprisingly with both traditional "femininity" and the second wave of feminism that began to make itself felt in the early 1960s (feminist-ization). One example will have to suffice: Leslie Fiedler's 1965 essay "The New Mutants," an articulation of the nostalgia and sense of betrayal afflicting the aspiring New York male intellectual. In Fiedler's telling the new mutants or "new barbarians," especially those populating the universities, his primary site of concern, are not only anti-reason and anti-humanist, but post-human, post-modern, post-white, post-heroic, post-Jewish, and most of all post-masculine and post-male. This latter refrain occurs repeatedly in Fiedler's essay, whether he is talking about the turn from "*polis* to *thiasos,* from forms of social organization traditionally thought of as male to the sort of passionate community attributed by the ancients to females out of control"; or "the effort of young men in England and the United States to assimilate into themselves . . . that otherness, that sum total of rejected psychic elements which the middle-class heirs of the Renaissance have identified with 'woman' "; or the conversion of the literary hero into "the non- or antimale"; or the whole discussion of the fascination with the "polymorphous perverse," the "revolt against masculinity," that surfaces everywhere in culture, from "camp" to nonviolent or passive resistance to the passivity of the drug cult ("what could be more womanly . . . than permitting the penetration of the body by a foreign object which not only stirs delight but even [possibly] creates new life?").[43] In making his argument, the literary work Fiedler evokes to illustrate the perils of feminization is Edward Albee's *Who's Afraid of Virginia Woolf?*

Rather than being "out of control," women who arrived at the universities in the 1960s found themselves in an inherently contradictory position. Given Russell Jacoby's argument that "by the end of the 1950s, American intellectuals decamped from the cities to the campuses," thereby creating the negative split between intellectual and academic, women were already entering a debased world of professional behavior and commitments and discourse and journals that, Jacoby asserts, made true intellectual independence, as well the ability of the intellectual to speak as a *public* intellectual, difficult if not impossible. "Academic" and "public" were perceived to be antithetical. Moreover, Jacoby continues, whatever success "radical, feminist, Marxist, or neo-Marxist scholarship" may have had in assailing or even changing academic disciplines, it had no *public* import: "it is largely technical, unreadable and—except by specialists—unread." Rather than New Left and feminist intellectuals invading the university, they were in turn invaded by "the academic idiom, concepts, and concerns."[44]

Damned if you do, damned if you don't: feminists within the academy are either too political (Denby) or not political enough (Jacoby), a double bind that Robbins argues Virginia Woolf anticipated in *Three Guineas'* vision of the woman in the 1930s poised on the bridge between the private house and the public, professional world: "Behind us lies the patriarchal system; the private house, with its nullity, its immorality, its hypocrisy, its servility. Before us lies the public world, the professional system, with its possessiveness, its jealousy, its pugnacity, its greed."[45] Woolf, as he notes, urges women to go forward as long as they keep in mind the price they will pay by being an insider/outsider in the system they want to change. But neither women's ambivalence about entering the public sphere posited by Woolf nor the contradictions confronting contemporary feminist intellectuals within the academy are likely to be aired in or given credence by an "intellectual" media that uses Virginia Woolf, as Denby does, to categorically dismiss "academic feminism" or, as Denby's detractors are wont to do, to categorically dismiss Virginia Woolf herself.

Gender, then, particularly when linked to feminization or feminism, plays a central role in the strong responses to Virginia Woolf among Denby's "intellectual" reviewers, but it does not tell the whole story; cultural class enters the narrative as well. British, born into the intellectual aristocracy, Virginia Woolf represents *par excellence* the *rentier* class identified with European cultural systems that simultaneously tempts and antagonizes American "intellectuals" who want to claim a high cultural position distinct not only from the academy but from "middlebrow" and/or popular culture as well. To understand the role Virginia Woolf plays in the intersecting anxieties of gender and cultural class within this "intellectual" sphere, we need to turn to its most "eminent" site, the *New York Review of Books.*

Section 2. *The* New York Review of Books

When the *New York Review of Books* set out in 1963 to produce a more trenchant analysis of contemporary culture than was currently available, it also produced the conditions that made it as significant a player in establishing Virginia Woolf's contested iconicity as women's 1960s entrance into the universities or Albee's 1962 play. Firmly established in the public, intellectual sphere, albeit with an academic following, a 1960s progeny of the New York intellectuals and the world they inhabited, the *NYRB* epitomizes the pervasive discourse that, like Denby's, demonizes academic feminism even as it legitimates Virginia Woolf. The British critic Frank Kermode's review of *Great Books,* with its obligatory trashing of American academics in general and academic feminists in particular and its unremitting praise for the pleasures of reading displayed by Denby, provides a good introduction to the journal's cultural stance, in many ways similar to that of other self-styled "intellectual" journals.[46] But unlike in other "intellectual" journals, you will not find any carping about Virginia Woolf as a "great" or high cultural figure here. After all, this is the journal that for years featured Virginia Woolf as its come-on: subscribe today and you will get a T-shirt or tote bag with David Levine's drawing of Virginia Woolf on it. So strong is this identification that one writer on the journal's thirtieth anniversary commented, "Mention *The Review*'s name among the nonacademic literate, and you may hear someone groan, 'Oh, no, not Virginia Woolf again!' "[47]

The headline for this article—"Q: Who's Not Afraid of Virginia Woolf?"—gets it just right, for in iconizing Virginia Woolf, or more accurately a particular image of her, the journal took a position that put it at the center of America's long-standing anxieties about "culture," including its relationship to Britain. Ironically, *NYRB*'s Virginia Woolf icon, British to the core and proudly embodying the high end of that nation's class-inflected cultural heritage, enjoys a fixed, seemingly impregnable stature in its pages that was long denied her in her own country and that maintains itself by ignoring her mobility almost everywhere else: the rough-and-tumble world of academics, the constantly shifting field of popular culture, and the prevalence of alternative sites within the public sphere. But this fixity may prove the icon's undoing, simultaneously locking her into the position of perpetual target within the increasingly narrow range of self-styled intellectual discourse that characterizes the *NYRB* and its New York detractors. Ultimately, Virginia Woolf's ability to cross borders and undo categorical distinctions fractures this discourse, revealing its internal contradictions and transforming it into an increasingly predictable sideshow.

From its beginnings, the *New York Review of Books* has been considered the preeminent intellectual journal in North America, although in the beginning it was read as much if not more for its political and social analysis, which was notably left of center, as it was for its literary or cultural reviews.[48] In fact, what commentators about the *NYRB* have described from the start is a split between its political and cultural stances: its political stance leaning from liberal to radical before returning to the center; its cultural stance distinctly conservative. For the avowedly conservative Joseph Epstein, writing in the rival journal *Commentary* about the *NYRB* in 1993, this split not only characterizes the journal but provides whatever redeeming virtues it has as the "representative intellectual journal of our age, with the important qualification that it has not been a great age and the *New York Review of Books* has done more than its share to diminish it."[49]

Epstein's characterization of the journal includes much that is agreed upon by almost everyone who has written about it, regardless of the writer's ideological position. On the political side, this includes its support for the New Left in the early 1960s, its staunchly anti–Vietnam War and pro–civil rights stance even when the movements turned violent, and its refusal to condemn communism; this latter gesture distinguished it from journals such as *Commentary* and *Partisan Review*, which moved increasingly to the right during this period. While there is disagreement about how far to the center it moved once the 1960s were over, for the New York neoconservatives whom it left behind it was never center enough. Its post-sixties politics, Stephen Fender noted in 1986, which takes "a line mildly Keynesian in economics, pro-Israeli but Anti-Zionist, sceptical of Reagan's Latin-American policy," consistently evoked their ire and fueled their overriding argument: that it is anti-American.[50]

On the cultural side Epstein finds less to quarrel with, as his list of what the *NYRB* is and is not, what it has and has not done, makes clear. Resolutely committed to "highbrow journalism," it did not jump "on every passing cultural bandwagon"; it

> steered clear of post-structuralism, deconstruction, and other zany English-department dalliances, . . . Derrida, Foucault, and the rest of the French gang; . . . [it] never mistook rock and roll for art, nor pro-

claimed the music of the Beatles to be the cultural equivalent of T. S. Eliot's *Four Quartets*. It has lost its head neither over movie directors nor over contemporary visual artists. The detritus of publicity culture has not attracted it. Quite properly, *NYR* prizes all those dear dead white males whose works comprise the chief treasures of Western civilization. Far from being trendy, in its approach to culture the journal has if anything tended to be conservative, even a little staid. [42–43][51]

Perhaps most important for my point, Epstein also notes that "while feminist in its general stance, it has also shied away from the madder kinds of academic feminism that see a phallo under every centrism"; and, although advocating tolerance and allowing Gore Vidal to contribute "homosexual gossip," it has neither supported nor criticized "the gay/lesbian-liberation movement," with its call for the normalization of homosexuality (43).

Unsurprisingly, the one (dead, white) literary figure besides Eliot named in Epstein's 1993 essay is Virginia Woolf, who appears as a parenthetical interruption to a list of examples of the *NYRB*'s revolutionary politics: "Stokely [*sic*] Carmichael (right on the heels of Sir Stuart Hampshire writing about Virginia Woolf) informing his readers that black neighborhoods in American cities were essentially colonies" (41). That her presence here is not surprising speaks directly to the canonical status that by 1993 she enjoyed outside the academy as well as within, a status given a substantive boost in the "intellectual" world by her role as celebrity endorser of the *NYRB,* a position she initially shared with Shakespeare. Starting on 21 July 1983, the *NYRB* began to run ads offering readers T-shirts picturing either Shakespeare or Woolf; "Here's your chance to sport your literary preferences," the copy repeatedly promised, and both images were prominently displayed (fig. 12).[52] But from March 29, 1990, on, which is roughly the same time she entered Columbia's Lit Hum course, Shakespeare disappeared; Virginia Woolf stood alone.[53]

For my purposes the best way to approach both Virginia Woolf's controversial elevation and Epstein's Virginia Woolf/Stokeley Carmichael riff is through the cultural contradictions she so vividly brings to light; Tom Wolfe's 1970 indictment of the *NYRB* as "the chief theoretical organ of Radical Chic" provides a good starting point. Evoking the infamous diagram of how to make a Molotov cocktail that once appeared on its cover and the journal's axiomatic belief that Huey Newton, Eldridge Cleaver, and the Black Panthers were "the legitimate vanguard of the black struggle for liberation" as his initial grounds for the attribution, Wolfe continues:

FIGURE 12. Advertisement, *New York Review of Books*.

In fact, the journal was sometimes referred to goodnaturedly as *The Parlour Panther,* with the *-our* spelling of *Parlour* being an allusion to its concurrent motif of anglophilia. The *Review*'s embracing of such contradictory attitudes—the nitty-gritty of the ghetto warriors and the preciosity of traditional English Leavis & Loomis intellectualism—was really no contradiction at all of course. It was merely the essential double-track mentality of Radical Chic—*nostalgie de la boue* and high protocol—in its literary form.[54]

The emphasis on the English is crucial to Virginia Woolf's status at the *NYRB,* for from the beginning the cosmopolitanism of the *NYRB*'s contributors and perspective, in particular its ties to England, has been one of its defining characteristics. Not only were many of its regular reviewers of literature, art, history, and philosophy British, but the journal, Epstein repeatedly notes, was distinctly Anglophilic. (Others make this point by noting that Karl Miller, formerly literary editor of the *Spectator* and the *New Statesman* before becoming editor of *NYRB*'s British protégé, the *London Review of Books,* once said that "*The Review* had borrowed so much from him that it 'was the best English magazine he had ever edited.'")[55] This association has been consistent over the years. Russell Jacoby's "unscientific check of ten random issues from early 1985," for example, found that over half of the 116 major reviews were "by British writers and professors; of these, 20 were from Oxford and Cambridge."[56]

At this point we find ourselves face to face with the contradictions inherent in the conservative critique of the *NYRB,* for at the same time that Epstein praises its "highbrow journalism" and its allegiance to the canon, he is bothered by the cultural elitism signified by the English connection: "If culture can be said to have a class hierarchy, *NYR* was clearly upper-class in its intellectual pretensions" (40); "its English writers have been preponderantly Oxbridge," many of them lords, and "its American academics chiefly from Ivy League schools" (42). Ultimately, however, what irks Epstein most about the journal's cultural elitism is its use as a "cover for the review's politics" (40); the result, and for Epstein the journal's major and most dangerous innovation, is to make "an unrealistic and damaging politics . . . indistinguishable from high culture" (43). Apparently, it is not just academics who are guilty of injecting politics into culture, according to the neoconservatives; intellectuals can sin as well.

Expatriate Fender provides a different perspective. In his reading, the righteous horror voiced by the journal's American detractors for its fusion of politics and culture is particularly American. To the British reading public, with its long tradition of quarterlies such as the *Edinburgh Review,* the

Quarterly Review, and the *Westminster Review,* which were "ostensibly book reviews" even while "frankly political journals, actually established to further the aims of political parties," this fusion represented the best kind of journalism.[57]

Taken together, its Oxbridge and titled reviewers, its unproblematic relationship to a hierarchical European culture, and its adherence to a more British model of journalism all contribute to *NYRB*'s perceived un-Americanness, a position confirmed by Virginia Woolf's position as its poster girl. For if there was one thing readers knew about Virginia Woolf, it was her link to the "status group" that Noel Annan (Lord Annan, Epstein points out), one of the *NYRB*'s most frequent English contributors, describes as an "aristocracy of intellect," held together by family as well as intellectual ties and passed on to one's children.[58] In this sense, the iconic status granted Virginia Woolf by *NYRB* becomes as potentially antithetical to an American culture that had mixed feelings about the European *rentier* class as the rest of the journal's politics is perceived to be.

Epstein's critique also foregrounds another version of cultural elitism associated with the journal that in his eyes makes it dangerous: that associated with Ivy League schools and hence with the professionalization of culture so lamented by "intellectuals," a connection that is perceived by its detractors to have become even more prevalent in *NYRB*'s later years. To the extent the universities are the enemy, Virginia Woolf's canonization, which crosses the borders between the academy and the *NYRB,* becomes distinctly suspect. Recall that it was the "nonacademic literate" who had grown weary of the *NYRB*'s Virginia Woolf by 1993; in telling the story, Nicolas Von Hoffman also notes that "the neoconservative social critic Midge Decter dismisses [the journal] today for its 'Anglophiliac snobbery. . . . It's become like the academy. . . . Dishonest, chaotic and full of posture.' "[59]

But not, one should observe, feminist, a telling omission, and one anticipated by Epstein's careful distinction between *NYRB*'s feminism and that found in the academy. After displaying some interest in the early scholarly publications on Woolf that were self-identified as feminist, the journal soon abandoned them, ignoring the critical studies, so many of which were feminist, that made Woolf a major author, a potential "great." In this sense, contrary to Epstein's analysis, the cultural as well as the social/political started more to the left and moved increasingly to the center. When it did notice an academic feminist text, as was the case with Louise DeSalvo's controversial study of child abuse in Woolf's life and writings, Quentin Bell, Woolf's nephew and biographer, who for years had been waging a public battle against a "lupine" criticism characterized as academic and feminist, was asked to review it.[60] This choice precluded a broader discussion not only of the intellectual and cultural issues raised by DeSalvo's approach, but also of what it means to make the family the authority in defining a public figure's meaning. Here one feels that the metaphor so often applied to the New York Intellectuals—the Family—is still very much at work.

Having turned away from academic, critical studies, the journal's coverage of Virginia Woolf from the end of the 1970s on has consisted entirely of Woolf's letters, diaries, memoirs, and the occasional book of essays, or of biographies, memoirs, or reminiscences about the writer and/or Bloomsbury. For the most part the articles were written by Englishmen and Englishwomen, most of them appearing over and over: Stuart Hampshire, Noel Annan, Stephen Spender, Frank Kermode, V. S. Pritchett, Karl Miller, John Bayley, and Rosemary Dinnage. The exceptions are Elizabeth Hardwick, one of the founding members of the *NYRB* and the only New York–identified intellectual to write about Virginia Woolf in its pages; Phyllis Grosskurth, a historian of British social and cultural life, who did two Bloomsbury reviews; and more recently, Janet Malcolm. The result of this conjunction of Brits, biography, and Bloomsbury was to focus attention on Woolf's private life and social milieu rather than her fiction or her literary criticism or her polemical works or the phenomenal role she played in the contemporary feminist and peace movements from the late 1960s on. The other versions of Virginia Woolf and her writings constructed as a result of shifts in critical and theoretical perspectives, feminist and otherwise—versions that crossed over between the academic and popular realms and became markers of powerful cultural battles—are rendered invisible. The effect is that of a time warp or vacuum, where, just as Denby would have it, nothing from the outside intrudes. Virginia Woolf has become, as it were, fixed like an exotic insect in amber.

In order to illustrate this process, I want to go back to the beginning and track the freezing of *NYRB*'s Virginia Woolf icon. The earliest article, Stuart Hampshire's 1966 review of *Virginia Woolf and Her Works* by the Frenchman Jean Guiguet (alluded to by Epstein), introduces one of the few critical works on Woolf to be reviewed in the journal. While occasioning a critique of academic criticism in general and the "now dreaded affectation and apparatus of so much Anglo-Saxon criticism" in particular, it also admits that Guiguet's more philosophical, French approach, while it "tries too hard to be exhaustive and definitive in an academic way," is at least "immensely informative and his perceptions are often unexpected and convincing." But what interests me even more about Hampshire's review is its insistence that the time had come to think again about her achievement, away from the local prejudices which, at least in England, have absurdly concealed some of the true qualities of her genius. Some of the dominant academic critics in England have for many years parroted phrases about the Bloomsbury Group, and smothered her work with nervous polemics. Her elaborate play with language in her lighter works, and as a critic and journalist, seems to have aroused a sense of social grievance among critics, because her tone and style were taken to be a return to a genteel tradition of *belles lettres* which should have been discredited. A remoteness, a bookishness, a conscious poise and cultivation of literary manner in the widely read *The Common Reader* established a public character which obscured, at least for a time, her deeper purposes as novelist.[61]

Here Hampshire lays the groundwork for *NYRB* to become a revisionary force.

To the extent that this revision occurred, however, it did so with little to no reconsideration of Woolf's novels; instead, the journal turned increasingly to Virginia Woolf in her Bloomsbury context. One explanation lies in the 1968 publication of Michael Holroyd's *Lytton Strachey,* which precipitated the widespread writing about and interest in the Bloomsbury Group; from this point on, books about Bloomsbury proliferated, and the *NRYB* seemed to review them all. As a result, articles on Virginia Woolf during the 1970s always present her as part of the group. But true to form, Virginia Woolf refused to stay put; her mobility and the excitement generated in the broader culture by her rise to stardom occasionally broke through before being constrained once and for all.

The first eruption occurs in Elizabeth Hardwick's ostensible review of Quentin Bell's biography of Woolf and a collection of Strachey's essays in February 1973; virtually ignoring both works, Hardwick talks instead about what really interests her: Bloomsbury's "gay liberation, its serious high camp," the American interest in androgyny, and Woolf's novels. In the process, she ranges from Woolf's class-inflected, distinctly nasty presentation of figures like Miss Kilman in *Mrs. Dalloway,* who, despite their desires, will never attain the cultural class they desire; to E. M. Forster's treatment of the same subject in *Howards End;* to Woolf's narrowness when compared with Henry James or George Eliot; to the harmful aspects of her "femininity" and its relation to her "feminism"; to the privileging of "androgyny" in the academy and its problems; and, finally, at the end, to the "great mind" at work in her fiction.[62] The result is a strangely ambivalent rendering of Virginia Woolf: a discomfort with both the worship of cultural class that often seemed to surround "intellectual" discussions of Virginia Woolf and Bloomsbury and the too-easy dismissal of her; and a simultaneous fascination with and distrust of the revisionary representations of her surfacing at the time, whether they came from more Bloomsbury-friendly Brits or from American feminists.

Ultimately what most characterizes Hardwick's review is its uniqueness in the *NYRB:* a direct confrontation of the larger issues of gender and cultural class that were then being generated by academic and public representations of Virginia Woolf written by a reviewer who is not only both female and American, but openly conflicted.[63] The seemingly disconnected quality of the essay bears this conflict out; it is almost impossible to give a summary of her argument. Once again we encounter the powerful double binds confronting women intellectuals in the New York scene: given the need to walk a fine line between "feminine" and aggressive/bitchy/feminist that manifests itself in Hardwick's resistances, it becomes impossible to take a stand. Writing elsewhere, Hardwick agrees with Mary McCarthy that the concept of "woman writer" was not particularly useful: "Woman writer? A bit of a crunch trying to get those two words together. . . . I guess I would say no special difficulty, just the usual difficulty of the arts." But she also recognizes the role of gender in attacks on Susan Sontag: "I think her being a woman, a learned one, a *femme savante,* had something to do with it. As an intellectual with very special gifts and attitudes, it was somehow felt that this made her a proper object for ridicule of a coarse kind. I believe the tone was different because she was seen as a very smart, intellectually ambitious woman."[64]

If, as Teres argues, contemporary feminists underestimate the feminism of the generation of intellectual women represented by Hardwick, the *NYRB* must bear some of the blame, for consistently refusing to open its pages to a genuine public debate (theoretically the preserve of the "public sphere") about the issues confronting a newly emerging generation of women struggling to define their public role. To some extent, this failure reflects one of the recurring critiques of the journal, that it has not reached out to younger reviewers in general; but in the case of Virginia Woolf, the exclusion/absence was exacerbated by the anti-academic-feminist bias. What was lost was the opportunity to bring before the public the full range of representations of the emerging Virginia Woolf. Rather than contributing to the enrichment of intellectual life, the *NYRB*'s separation of "academic" and "intellectual" considerably diminished it.

There is one exception to this pattern, but only one: Noel Annan's April 1978 omnibus review of a number of works by and about Woolf, which marks the *NYRB*'s single foray into a more inclusive representation of the increasingly multifaceted—and feminist—Virginia Woolf. By the end of 1978, when Frank Kermode announced her canonization and the welcome resurgence of male voices in the discussion ("Roger Poole, sympathetic to feminism, nevertheless makes some sturdy qualifications here, and one is glad of them, for a bass voice strengthens the chorus"), he announced as well the disappearance of the rich array of academic and/or popular Virginia Woolfs, including the feminist versions, from the journal's pages.[65]

Annan's article stands out in a number of ways, providing both a glimpse of what might have been and a blueprint for what happened. The glimpse occurs in Annan's openness to the new scholarship and its feminist underpinnings, rare not only in the NYRB but in the "intellectual" media as a whole. The grounds are the two scholarly works among the eight under review: The Pargiters, a transcription of an early manuscript version of what later became Woolf's novel The Years; and the Bulletin of the New York Library: Virginia Woolf Issue that included a number of essays about The Pargiters, The Years, and Three Guineas. What's important here is not only the NYRB's momentary acknowledgment of the academic scholarship so crucial to the versioning of Virginia Woolf, but Annan's enthusiastic rendering of it. In direct contradiction to Denby's assertion, for example, that Virginia Woolf would have scorned the "academic feminists" who claimed her, Annan believes that the New York Public Library Bulletin would have "given Virginia Woolf satirical pleasure. To have nine articles by women devoted to The Years and Three Guineas might have convinced her that there were signs of a new age dawning and that offensive male superiority had received a check."[66] For Annan, apparently, a love of literature and "culture" does not necessitate the rejection of a feminist politics, for Virginia Woolf or for her like-minded critics and readers. To understand how unusual his stance is we can compare it to Rosemary Dinnage's far narrower conception of what is appropriate to Virginia Woolf. Claiming her for the category "serious writer" in 1984, she ridicules young women's fascination with Virginia Woolf (her iconization) and declares The Years a book "dogged from the start by a feminist propagandist aim which soon became irrelevant"; it "would now, I suppose, be considered the least successful of her books."[67] Woolf scholars clearly don't count in this assessment.

Annan's article, then, stands out for its unusual acceptance of feminist criticism, but it also stands out for its establishment of Virginia Woolf as an emblem of the British system of cultural class so central to NYRB's representations of Virginia Woolf and to its detractors' ire. Unlike Hardwick, the New York intellectual, who has little patience with the private pond filled with "thoroughbred fish" called Bloomsbury, Annan doesn't think that we've had too much of the group, or that Bloomsbury, including Virginia Woolf, represents a dangerously class-inflected culture. Instead, he praises the resurgence of both the individuals and the group from the status of "artifact" assigned to them by the "skillful tactics of the Leavises," a tactic seemingly as effective in the States as in Britain. Annan had addressed the American attitude as early as his 1968 review of Holroyd's *Lytton Strachey,* where he both praises and questions American conceptions of "culture":

> The long serious debate on culture as a mode of criticism, carried out in the Fifties and early Sixties by New York intellectuals, has thrown some doubt on the self-confident assurance, once regarded as a state of grace, with which certain styles of life were condemned and dismissed. Neither Strachey's life nor works will stand up, of course, to such strenuous examination, if only for the reason that neither his feelings nor his intellect was strenuous or self-critical enough. But some do not understand that what they detest in him is his homosexuality and what they call corrupt is the camp world and its jokes. Others are offended by his sense of humor and would be indignant if they were told the truth—namely that they themselves are devoid of humor and, not understanding it, are frightened by it.[68]

By 1978, Annan's claims had become political as well as cultural; the members of Bloomsbury, he writes, "were the first example of the modern English intelligentsia," not so much for their sexual license or their homosexuality, which "in the European capitals" of the time "was more openly acknowledged," but for breaking "with the style of upper-class life and [setting] a new fashion in living": "the cheap, unfashionable town house or flat . . . ; the contempt for moneymaking and the status which money brings, and the spending of it on the arts and travel; refusal to wear respectable clothes; . . . rejection of 'the glittering prizes' . . . ; adherence to certain causes dear to the hearts of progressives . . . ; and finally support for equality for women, anti-imperialism, pacifism, and in general suspicion of the Establishment and of those who wield power however petty. . . . In the Thirties," Annan concludes, the new left-wing intelligentsia seemed to make a break with Bloomsbury, but in retrospect those "middle-class revolutionaries look more and more like those whom they spoke of as old fashioned."[69]

In Annan's rendering, Bloomsbury appears closer to the young middle-class intellectuals of the 1960s than to the older New York intellectuals who, despite their immigrant and outsider status and their left-wing credentials, had by 1978 become increasingly conservative and establishment and wanted no truck with the 1960s turn toward "equality for women, anti-imperialism, pacifism, and in general suspicion of the Establishment and of those who wield power however petty." No wonder Epstein worries about Lord Annan's frequent appearances in the journal, and conservatives in general have reacted against the *NYRB*'s identification with Virginia Woolf and Bloomsbury. Gertrude Himmelfarb, for example, has made a habit of routinely naming Bloomsbury as one of the prime culprits in the destruction of those Victorian morals and morality she would like America to return to; her book *Marriage and Morals among the Victorians* begins with the devastation wrought by Strachey's *Eminent Victorians*.[70] As Jonathan Arac has pointed out, not even J. M. Keynes is immune from the Bloomsbury taint; he may, in fact, embody it. In this sense the "mildly Keynesian" line Fender attributed to the journal involves more than economics, denoting as well "the sexual permissiveness that does not set the reproduction of the human race as its highest goal."[71]

Virginia Woolf and Bloomsbury, then, as represented in the *NYRB*, become emblematic of the doubleness many American intellectuals bring to European high culture, whatever their political perspectives: an admiration for the value of high culture and of "dead white males" (a category that often includes Virginia Woolf by default) mixed with a deep suspicion of a European-style culture grounded in history, class, tradition, and the mutual engagement of the political and the cultural.[72] From this perspective Virginia Woolf is also implicated in another charge brought against the *NYRB*: that it eschewed the encouragement or even the judgment of new writers and new literary ideas in favor of contextualizing them. Kurt Vonnegut, for example, attributed the journal's 1970 retrospective damning of his six published works to its preference for those who respond " 'to art history so far,' " those who "present their credentials that they are in fact educated—in effect, have a European education, a European outlook; and names of great authors, great works of art, will be dropped" in this sort of work. In contrast, Vonnegut associates himself with those artists who " '[respond] to life,' " who do not "present [their] credentials. There's no evidence in my work that I am sufficiently well educated to write a book."[73] To the extent that Virginia Woolf represents a "European outlook" where "credentials" are all-important, she becomes anathema to a more democratic, free-ranging American literature and cultural ethic.

Given these contradictions, what's a red-blooded American "intellectual" to do? What stand can he or she take on the "culture" associated with the Virginia Woolf–Bloomsbury–Anglophilia axis represented by the *NYRB*? This is especially problematic if you are a conservative horrified by what you perceive as the turn away from a European-based high culture and the "disinterested" intellectuals who upheld it, which began, such conservatives argue, in the politicized 1960s and continues with the politicization of culture under the banner of feminism and multiculturalism. In these circumstances, terrible as it might be, you might even need to reclaim Virginia Woolf and European standards, might have to declare her and her cultural class something worth preserving, even in democratic America. Cultural elites who define a national agenda may not be so bad after all, as long as they are not the "cultural elites" associated with the marxist-feminist-multiculturalist academy.

To take just one example of the ironies of this situation, I want to introduce Diana Trilling, who will return as a featured player in part 2. Trilling was as closely linked to the New York Intellectuals as any woman and became one of the *NYRB*'s most outspoken critics. In 1948, she wrote an extremely snide review of a posthumous collection of Woolf's essays for the *New York Times Book Review;* the review was called "Virginia Woolf's Special Realm" and damned Woolf's elitist class presumptions. But in 1962, responding to Albee's *Who's Afraid of Virginia Woolf?* as a consummate threat to cultural class distinctions, she found herself (almost) defending Virginia Woolf. Trilling subsequently reprinted both essays in a collection she called *Claremont Essays,* a reference to the street on the Upper West Side of New York near Columbia where she and her husband, Lionel Trilling, along with other New York intellectuals, lived. We know this because her introduction calls attention to the role this geographical and social/cultural space played in her own intellectual beliefs and practices, her clear sense of place.[74] While Trilling does not mention the connection between "Claremont" or even "New York" (intellectuals) and "Bloomsbury"—and would have rejected it with horror—others have not been so silent; a 1986 review of yet another history of the New York Intellectuals ("the *Partisan Review* crowd") bears the headline "America's Bloomsbury."[75]

Where does the history traced through the *NYRB* leave Virginia Woolf in the New York intellectual sphere? Locked, I would say, into a struggle over an increasingly limited concept of "culture," frozen in place in a debate between the journal and its critics that is short-circuited before it begins by the narrowness of its focus and the unending reappearance of the same reviewers voicing the same ideas. Meanwhile, the real intellectual excitement has been occurring elsewhere, in all those places, whether academic, popular, or intellectual, scorned by both camps within the self-styled New York "intellectual" media. When it comes to the intellectual, to stick to my topic here, one could go to any number of other journals than those named by Jacoby as "intellectual" journals and find a rich public debate

about a wide range of intellectual and cultural issues, including Virginia
Woolf. As historians and other scholars have argued and illustrated, even in
the eighteenth century there existed multiple, contestatory, counter or alternative public spheres to those identified as *the* public sphere by Habermas,
and this is still true today.[76] A 1993 *Chronicle of Higher Education* article
on the increasing role of academics as public intellectuals, for example,
notes that one of the questions asked by these intellectuals is, "Just what is
the public anyway? For answers, they look to postmodern theory, the black
church, [and] television talk shows" as well as the work of Habermas.[77]
And more recently, a forum in *PMLA* presented a wide range of answers
to the questions "What defines an intellectual?" and where she or he is
to be found, including one by J. Hillis Miller that argues, "No one . . .
expects to find in the *New York Review of Books* or the *New Yorker*
essays of the caliber of Benjamin's or Arendt's, nor do such periodicals
represent the views of more than a small segment of the educated class.
From an outsider's perspective they often seem as much anti-intellectual as
intellectual. No large, highly educated public with common interests and
goals exists in the United States."[78]

Even closer to my topic, one could go to either the *London Review of
Books* or the *Women's Review of Books,* modeled after the London rather
than the New York journal,[79] and find versions of Virginia Woolf and the
debates surrounding her that remain absent in the *NYRB.* In the *WRB,*
for example, which began publication in 1983, one will find a broad range
of books about Virginia Woolf's life and writings reviewed by academics
and nonacademics alike. Feminist scholarship in many although not all its
variations (anything that might be deemed poststructuralist, e.g., seems to
be omitted) finds a voice here, as well the disagreements that exist within
it; the letter columns have been a rich source of discussion and debate. No
one reading the *WRB* could talk about a monolithic, canonized Virginia
Woolf or a monolithic "academic feminism"; nor could one doubt the
contributions of academic *feminisms* to public debate.

In the *LRB,* one would find an ever-widening divergence from its
predecessor. Although Karl Miller declared his journal's independence and
differences in the first issue (October 25, 1979), the journal featured many
of the same reviewers when it came to Virginia Woolf and Bloomsbury:
John Bayley, for example, or Frank Kermode. But it has also consistently
reviewed scholarly studies, feminist and otherwise, as well as Woolf's
diaries and letters, and has called upon academic feminists such as Gillian
Beer to write about them. More recently, as the paper changed editorship,
the nature of the essays on Virginia Woolf has also changed, moving away
from reviews of individual books to more general assessments of Virginia

Woolf's relationship to a culture wider than Bloomsbury. In 1985, for example, Michael Holroyd wrote a thoughtful essay on Virginia Woolf and Beatrice Webb that ends by arguing the need of the principles represented by both women (both sexual and economic reform, both poetry and a "contented people") in surviving and countering Thatcherite Britain. In 1995, Peter Wollen, (feminist) filmmaker, cultural critic, and academic, used the publication of James King's biography of Woolf to reexamine Raymond Williams's depiction of the role of the Bloomsbury "fraction" in the class-inflected cultural history of Britain, arguing that it was Virginia Woolf, not any of the others, including Keynes, who made the most subversive and effective contribution to cultural change. Finally, Jacqueline Rose, feminist psychoanalytic writer, literary critic, and academic, brought her concerns for the darkness of the human mind and human nature to her review of Hermione Lee's 1996 biography of Woolf, providing an insightful exploration of current attitudes toward Freud, reason, and madness.[80]

What has the *NYRB* been doing? For the most part, more of the same, although in 1993 Virginia Woolf lost her status as its primary come-on; the ads featuring her on her own disappeared. Her fall might or might not reflect the many disparaging comments linking the *NYRB* to Virginia Woolf, Bloomsbury, and academia when it celebrated its thirtieth anniversary that year; it does suggest the journal's perception, at least at the business level, that its representation of Virginia Woolf no longer sold.[81] But the editorial department seems not to have gotten the message, blissfully ignoring the signs of the times. Rosemary Dinnage's 1997 review of Hermione Lee's biography, for example, with its "I am a serious intellectual" stance, presents a distinct contrast to the wider-ranging reviews by Jacqueline Rose in the *LRB* and by Carolyn Heilbrun in *WRB*.[82] Echoing her advice to readers in 1984 that they "forget the T-shirts, the ballyhoo, the copies of That Picture of the angelic Virginia Stephen pinned up by a multitude of seventeen-year-olds next to Millais's *Ophelia* and the worn teddy bear," Dinnage's 1997 article begins by asking, rhetorically, what Virginia Woolf would have made not only of the biographical outpourings about her, but of the "doctoral dissertations, the pro- and anti-Bloomsbury arguments, the iconization of herself as feminist queen, the tourists at Charlestown farmhouse, the T-shirts, the innumerable student bedrooms with their wistful early photograph tacked to the wall."[83] No extraneous, regrettable factors such as new approaches by scholars to Woolf's work or a serious look at Virginia Woolf's extraordinary popularity must be allowed to sully the *NYRB*'s pages.

At this point we need to move on before, like Virginia Woolf "intellectual" icon, we fall into the black hole of the *NYRB* and cannot climb out. Our next stop is the world of "middlebrow" culture, where Virginia Woolf has experienced a far more varied and generative iconicity.

Section 3. How the Greats Are Fallen

If you do a computer search for "great books" in data bases such as Books in Print or an online university library catalog, you will more than likely retrieve not only David Denby's defense of the Columbia core curriculum but the multivolume *Great Books of the Western World*. Published originally in 1952 by Encyclopaedia Britannica and the University of Chicago under the editorship of Robert Maynard Hutchins and Mortimer Adler, it was reissued in an expanded version in 1990 with Adler as the editor-in-chief. The revised edition includes women for the first time: Jane Austen, George Eliot, Willa Cather, and Virginia Woolf. Despite its association with the University of Chicago and indirectly with the Columbia core, *Great Books of the Western World* (hereafter *GBWW*) was from its beginnings a commercial enterprise, which set out to sell "culture" to the "2% cream on top of our society . . . the eggheads," but soon turned to "the mass market—the butcher, the baker, the candlestick maker."[84]

The crossover of both Virginia Woolf and the concept of "greatness"— from a university curriculum ostensibly dedicated to the disinterested development of the humane individual (Cross's "oasis of order"), to public intellectuals (eggheads), to the commercial promise that "great books," or more specifically the two-volume Syntopicon of "Great Ideas" developed by Adler, will improve your cultural and perhaps social standing— highlights the inherent contradictions in the concept of "greatness," contradictions that are inseparable from intersections of authority and cultural capital. From this perspective the selling of Virginia Woolf as a cultural commodity in a "mass market" indicates a trickle-down theory of cultural growth and improvement, with the value of a particular commodity determined by those on high. The irony of this theory is that long before *GBWW* included Virginia Woolf in its catalog of greats, she was already a highly salable commodity in the "middlebrow" or mass culture targeted by *GBWW*, a mobility that illustrates once again her ability to highlight and fracture the intersecting categories of gender and cultural class.

My entrée here is Katha Pollitt, one of the few progressive or feminist women to have a regular voice in the self-styled "intellectual" media.[85] My source is her clear-sighted discussion of the battles over the canon, "Why We Read: Canon to the Right of Me . . . ," which begins with her surprised discovery that, with one exception, she "agreed with all sides in the debate at once"; the exception, true to her tribe, negates those academic "ultraradicals, who attack the 'privileging' of 'texts,' as they insist on calling books, and think one might as well spend one's college years deconstructing 'Leave It to Beaver.'" Her agreement ranges from the conservative position that there are books, even those written by dead white Western men, that are "more essential to an understanding of our culture" than others, and that she wishes her students had read or would read; to the liberal position that, once we understand the grounds of exclusion and recognize the way the canon has always changed, "why can't we dip into the sea of stories and fish out Edith Wharton or Virginia Woolf?"; to the radical position that we need to scrap the whole concept of "canon" or "greatness," grounded on the exclusion of the "others—women, blacks, Latinos, Asians, the working class, whoever," and recognize that ours is a "multifaceted and conflict-ridden society." She dismissed this last position, she notes, until she recalled how important it was to her as a child to find poems by women in the *Oxford Book of English Verse* when they were so markedly absent in other anthologies.[86] Representation counts.

Pollitt also recognizes the power inherent in who gets to decide and how the categories are drawn. Turning to the "recent fuss over the latest edition of the Great Books series published by Encyclopedia Britannica, headed by that old snake-oil salesman Mortimer Adler," she uses it to illustrate that "if we leave the broadening of the canon up to the conservatives," it will never include "different kinds of greatness" or produce a shared culture that "reflects the true range of human experience." The most glaring example of the project's biases resides in its total exclusion of nonwhite writers from the list; but the inclusion of the four women, described in the media as a "token victory for feminists," also underscores the arbitrary yet self-legitimating nature of such lists:

> That's nice, I suppose, but really! Jane Austen has been a certified Great Writer for a hundred years! Lionel Trilling said so! There's something truly absurd about the conservatives earnestly sitting in judgment on the illustrious dead, as though up in Writers' Heaven Jane and George and Willa and Virginia were breathlessly waiting to hear if they'd finally made it into the club, while Henry Fielding, newly dropped from the list, howls in outer darkness and the Brontës, presumably, stamp their feet in frustration and hope for better luck in twenty years, when *Jane Eyre* and *Wuthering Heights* will suddenly turn out to have qualities of greatness never before detected in their pages. It's like Poets' Corner at Manhattan's Cathedral of St. John the Divine, where mortal men—and a woman or two—of letters actually

vote on which immortals to honor with a plaque, a process no doubt complete with electoral campaigns, compromise candidates and all the rest of the underside of the literary life. "No, I'm sorry, I just can't vote for Whitman. I'm a Washington Irving man myself."[87]

Pollitt's vision of Adler handing out "greatness" as if it were a prize stands in stark contradiction to John Guillory's insistence in *Cultural Capital* that "the literary curriculum is precisely not the site of mass cultural production and consumption" of what he calls "a politics *of the image*," a politics that belongs in "the same political domain" as the critique of minority images in the national media, of stereotyping, and of exclusions; nevertheless, he continues, "the critique of the canon has proceeded as though it were, as though canon formation were like the Academy Awards."[88] This distinction, however elevating it might be to the academic curriculum, just won't do, especially when you take a closer look at the long history of intercourse between "the literary curriculum" and the "sites of mass cultural production and consumption" at work in the "great books" philosophy. This is true even when we factor in class, Guillory's concern, and the social struggles at work at any particular moment of canon formation. It is no accident that Mortimer Adler, the leading figure behind *GBWW,* not only started the Western Civilization course at the University of Chicago but had been a student and protégé of John Erskine, the man responsible for instituting what became the Lit Hum portion of the Columbia core. Erskine's own list had previously been sold by the American Library Association as *Classics of the Western World* (1927, 1934, 1935), illustrating the inherent market value of the concept from its beginnings. As Joan Shelley Rubin argues in her detailed study of the "great books" ideology in *The Making of Middlebrow Culture,* both these commercial enterprises contributed to one of the "great books'" overriding aspects: the "temptation to regard culture as a commodity."[89]

Virginia Woolf's appearance in *GBWW* plunges her into the realm that Denby, in explaining why Columbia never called its core courses "great books," characterizes by its "taint of consumerism and middlebrowism," a taint that is "never too far from lists of classics" (his choice of the term for his title says something about his desired market).[90] This was not a new position for Virginia Woolf, whose relationship to middlebrow culture illustrates once again her unstable position on the borders that are meant to police both cultural and gender categories. On the one hand, she wrote one of the earliest critiques of the middlebrow, proudly claiming for herself the status of highbrow and promising to "take [her] pen and stab" dead anyone who hinted otherwise;[91] on the other hand, she used that pen to write for some of the leading middlebrow journals in the United States, and had a distinct following among those organizations associated with middlebrow culture, including the Book-of-the-Month Club. That these organizations are also linked in our cultural topographies to the feminine, as middlebrow culture in general is, reinforces the multiple forcelines within the cultural field thrown into relief by the figure of Virginia Woolf and illustrates why, despite her claims, we so often find her associated not with high but with middlebrow or even popular culture.

When Russell Lynes cited Woolf's "Middlebrow" in his 1949 *Harper's Magazine* essay "Highbrow, Lowbrow, Middlebrow," calling her "the first, I believe, to define the species,"[92] it helped establish the terms of subsequent discussions of the topic in the States, including those that argue for the separation of cultural classes. Woolf's essay is unequivocal about the middlebrow's negative capacity to destroy cultural classes and categories: to undercut the clear-cut but mutually beneficial distinctions between high-brow and lowbrow, including those between mind and body. Describing the highbrow as "the man or woman of thoroughbred intelligence who rides his mind at a gallop across country in pursuit of an idea," and the lowbrow as "a man or a woman of thoroughbred vitality who rides his body in pursuit of a living at a gallop across life," the middlebrow emerges as "the man, or woman, of middlebred intelligence who ambles and saun-ters now on this side of the hedge, now on that, in pursuit of no single object, neither art itself nor life itself, but both mixed indistinguishably, and rather nastily, with money, fame, power or prestige." In addition, one of the middlebrow's main characteristics is consumption: of objects, of culture. The middlebrow buys "bound volumes of the classics" that he or she keeps "behind plate glass"; and "first editions of dead writers—always the worst; pictures . . . by dead painters; . . . but never anything new . . . for to buy living art requires living taste."[93] So much for *GBWW*.

If Woolf saw distinctions between highbrow and lowbrow, she also had a vision of the lowbrow's ability to understand literature without the middlebrow's intervention. Dwight MacDonald, the American cultural critic who coined the term *midcult*, would, one might think, agree, his own writings on middlebrow culture making him in many ways Virginia Woolf's discursive heir. In his rendering, midcult, defined as exhibiting the same emphasis on homogenization and popularity as "masscult" but covered with a "cultural figleaf," pretends "to respect the standards of High Culture while in fact it waters them down and vulgarizes them." Taking *GBWW*, which he calls "a hundred pounds of Great Books," as a prime example, MacDonald associates the project with Julian Benda's "*le trahison des clercs*": in his translation, "the treason of the *academics*," not the *intellectuals*, the usual phrase. But here he differs from Woolf, for one of the most powerful aspects of this betrayal, MacDonald argues, is the *clercs'* complicity with the belief that the perceived "problem of vulgarization" so prevalent in American culture by 1960, the threat of a homogenized mass culture, could be solved by "[integrating] the masses into high culture," a solution that MacDonald unequivocally rejects. No crossing of the high/low boundary for him. Instead, he argues forcefully, what is needed is a hard and fast distinction, an "attempt to define two cultures, one for the masses and the other for the classes," where the "classes" are carefully defined as a cultural elite and not "a social or economic upper-class."[94]

Again, given Woolf's defense of the highbrow and the shared attitude toward the middlebrow (if not the lowbrow), one might think Virginia Woolf would be a prime candidate for citation and emulation by those in the States who, like MacDonald, have in the second half of the twentieth century increasingly identified high culture with a hierarchical system such as that which existed in England and with the modernist avant-garde, both of which are descriptive of Virginia Woolf.[95] But no; after her appearance in Lynes's essay (which, despite the quotations from Woolf's essay, includes almost no women in its examples of highbrow writers, artists, and intellectuals) she disappears from the American "intellectual" and academic debates about the battles of the brows until feminist historians such as Rubin and Janice Radway began writing about middlebrow culture in the 1990s. Clearly Virginia Woolf's cultural class—her status as highbrow, aristocrat, elite, and/or avant-garde—cannot overcome her gender, and in American versions of the story the intellectual or highbrow or hallowed modernist artist is always already male.[96]

But as we know, what we cannot see is often the most powerful force at work, and Virginia Woolf's uncanny ability to cross borders and reveal their arbitrary nature enacts the power of gender to intersect and fracture cultural class, distinctly queering the picture. What propels Virginia Woolf back and forth across the borders that police the high/middle/low categories are the intersections between her cultural class and the rhetoric that associates middlebrow culture with the feminine: with an embodiment that, as in the case of the "intellectual," prevented women from participating in the realm of disinterested rationality associated with debate within the public sphere. As Radway illustrates in her study of the negative reactions to one of the prime sites of middlebrow culture, the Book-of-the-Month Club, more was at stake than the presumption that most of its readers were women. Instead, the fear of standardization, of homogenization, so often cited in these arguments, needs to be read as a fear of the masses, who exemplify a "lack of differentiation associated with the feminine and the effeminate"; "middlebrow agencies . . . were feminized as smothering authorities who threatened the differentiation and individuation of those who were dependent upon them."[97]

More specifically they threatened the rational, autonomous, disinterested, individual reader, who, in these arguments, as in the others I've been tracking in this chapter, is perceived to be masculine if not male. Middlebrow culture, that is, represented as feminine, threatened the construction of the rational bourgeois subject and a public sphere constructed to exclude "special interests" in favor, Radway notes, of "abstract subjects defined by their universality, their generality, and their responsiveness to the inherent qualities of true literature and rational argument." These abstract subjects stood in opposition to "standardized and feminized consumer-subjects" characterized as "masses of bodies redundantly materialized through the display of products by Maybelline, Helena Rubinstein, Frigidaire, Lux, Aunt Jemima, and, of course, the Book-of-the-Month Club." The fear of the feminization and commodification of culture underlying the fear of the middlebrow so prevalent in the 1920s, Radway argues, can be read as a response to the increasing admission of middle-class women "to the public world of work through the portals of a much-expanded public education system," which put them "for the first time in a position to compete with middle-class men for status, financial rewards, and authority."[98] Haven't we heard this before?

The illusion of detachment, transcendence, and weightlessness associated with the abstract subject and the "intellectual" reader also permeates the construction of the "ideology of greatness," where it is achieved, Marjorie Garber argues, by the "evacuation" of the specificity of the persons or circumstances concealed behind the curtain of objectivity—exactly the process at work in rationalizations for *GBWW*.[99] In the case of *GBWW*, this meant the supposed exclusion of any intervention by specialists or experts on the grounds that the great works were great exactly because they spoke directly to readers across time and place and culture. As the editors put it in 1952, " 'great books contain their own aids to reading; that is one reason why they are great. Since we hold that these works are intelligible to the ordinary man, we see no reason to interpose ourselves or anybody else between the author and the reader.' " In this way, they continue, they avoid the " 'reduction of the citizen to an object of propaganda, private and public.' "[100]

As Katha Pollitt might say, excuse me! (What about the Syntopicon?) This rationalization becomes even more suspect when we factor in subsequent justifications for the project that transform the "great books" into best-sellers. Arguing in 1988 that he (or his board) doesn't choose the books, they choose themselves, Adler makes this equation explicit:

> . . . of all the book lists ever made, the list of the great books results from the most democratic or popular method of selection. . . . We did not choose them. The great books were chosen by the largest reading audience of all times, as well as by a consensus of expert opinion.
>
> A best-seller is a best-seller, not by authoritarian judgment, but by popular consent. So the fact that certain books have interested a vast multitude of men through the centuries is one of the signs that they are great books. It is not the only sign, but it is that mark of a great book which shows it to be not the choice of a special elite, but the choice of mankind generally.[101]

How the greats have fallen! Aligned with best-sellers, with "popular consent," they become part of rather than an alternative to the perceived degradation of American culture that the best-seller is often believed to exemplify. In Daniel Boorstin's telling, the philological shift that turned *The Bookman*'s 1885 lists of "Best-Selling Books" into "Best-Sellers," implying that "the book somehow sold itself," created a tautology in which "a best seller [or a great] was a book which somehow sold well simply because it was selling well"; it becomes part of the star system that increasingly dominated American culture and American life, including literary culture.[102] While Boorstin would undoubtedly deny the crossover between "great books" and "best-sellers," just as Guillory denies any association between the canon and the Academy Awards, the rhetoric (universal value; popular consent) brought to the defense of inclusion/exclusion lifts the curtain of objectivity to reveal the special interests (white, male, European) at work in the desire to maintain cultural hierarchies and their vested authority.[103]

Where does Virginia Woolf fit into this scenario? Everywhere, it seems, crossing the boundaries, dislocating the categories, illustrating how culturally specific and arbitrary they are. In the same collection of essays where Adler sets out his theory of greats as best-sellers, we learn that Virginia Woolf did not originally make it onto his A-list of greats from the first half of the twentieth century (1900 to 1945); instead, she appears as an "also-ran," as the author of *Mrs. Dalloway*, not *To the Lighthouse*, the work featured in the 1990 edition.[104] But Virginia Woolf, ironically and revealingly, may well be the only writer Adler includes on either list who had literally achieved best-seller status, "popular consent" about her novel *The Years* having projected her onto the best-seller lists in the United States in 1937 and as a result onto the cover of *Time* magazine. Nor was this her first brush with "popular consent." In 1933, *Flush,* her fictional biography of Elizabeth Barrett Browning's spaniel, was selected as an alternate in the Book-of-the-Month Club;[105] and earlier still she had established a place for herself in a venue that signified to many of those lamenting the blurring of cultural distinctions the worst of the popularization associated with middlebrow culture: the *New York Herald Tribune Books* section. Created in 1924 by its editor, Stuart Sherman, a former academic, to provide a middle road in literary journalism between the "higher journalism" of the highbrow weeklies and monthlies, where criticism and judgment were the norm, and the daily newspapers' reporting of books and authors as trade, gossip, or "news," it undertook to combine "aspirations of 'criticism' with an awareness of 'news value,' " an undoing of boundaries that horrified die-hard highbrows.[106] Virginia Woolf proved eminently suitable for Sherman's agenda, combining high visibility with cultural class; appearing as the star of one of Sherman's front-page columns designed to champion "modern" writers, no matter how difficult, to a distrustful audience of "common readers," she is presented in terms of her inheritance of a "robust and sinewy" (male) literary tradition, her sympathy for and appeal to the common reader, and her modernism.[107] Woolf reciprocated; one month later, she began publishing articles and essays in *Tribune Books,* graduating to front-page "visiting critic" after Sherman died.[108]

Given the reiterated discourse that consistently codes middlebrow and mass as grounded, embodied, commodified, and feminine while insisting on a supposedly transcendent, disembodied, intellectual value or "great-ness" that just happens to exclude women, it is not surprising that the *New York Herald Tribune Books* section, the Book-of-the-Month Club, and *Time* had less trouble negotiating Virginia Woolf's transgressive mix of cultural class (both high and popular) and gender than the self-defined defenders of class distinctions and the arbiters of the "greats," even when the "greats" are defined as "best-sellers." The need felt by Denby and by the *New York Review of Books* to recuperate her for their own brand of supposedly disinterested cultural value, to grant her cultural capital, illus-trates the potential her refusal to stay in place poses to the entire structure. When Rosemary Dinnage dismisses *The Years* in the *NYRB* as Woolf's least successful novel, more than its "feminist propagandist" background is at work; the novel's ability to cross cultural boundaries by becoming a best-seller and the author's celebrity/star appearance on the cover of *Time* come into play as well.[109] But Virginia Woolf has proved too powerful an image to remain in any one location. The men who still control so many of the organs of the "intellectual" sphere may think they have contained her, fixed her into positions that make her safe or dismissible, but like all boundary-dwelling, border-disrupting figures, Virginia Woolf continually escapes, returning in both old and new guises. To understand the full extent of her protean image and its powerful, frightening disruptiveness, we need to turn to the realm of popular culture, where Virginia Woolf icon has become a multifaceted star.

STARRING VIRGINIA WOOLF

PRODUCTION NOTES

On April 12, 1937, shortly before *The Years* made its way to the best-seller list in the United States, Virginia Woolf made her way to the cover of *Time* magazine. Man Ray provided the photograph (fig. 6); the caption reads, "Virginia Woolf. 'It is fatal to be man or woman pure and simple.'" By that time in its history *Time*'s cover article had become a significant measure of a person's cultural status or prestige, so much so that when the magazine put Al Capone, just released from prison, on its cover, it received a number of letters from readers outraged that "*Time* had inferentially honored the man." As the editorial response explained, "If it is considered an honor to be pictured on *Time*'s cover, *Time* is glad that is so. But in selecting national figures for its cover, *Time* does not presume to be 'honoring' those figures. If they are outstanding nationally or internationally, that is solely and definitely to their own and to society's credit and not by virtue of anything *Time* has done for them."[1] Disclaimers notwithstanding, such an appearance carried with it the connotations of celebrity, of stardom, bestowed as much as earned; the figure was assured his or her fifteen minutes of fame.

Virginia Woolf's projection into the public consciousness and its aftermath, the rise of her novel to the top of the best-seller list, carry within them the fleetingness that even then was associated with fame; it also evokes that aspect of "culture" so lamented by those cultural commentators who see the advent of the "best-seller" as a degrading commodification of literature and its authors, transforming them from transcendent heroes into flash-in-the-pan celebrities or stars. Aware of these pressures, the anonymous writer set out to distinguish Woolf from the previous year's best-selling woman novelist and her novel in terms that emphasize Woolf's long-term value:

> Last year Margaret Mitchell of Atlanta, Ga. wrote her first novel, *Gone With The Wind.* Last week Virginia Woolf of London, England published her seventh, *The Years.* Margaret Mitchell's book has sold more copies (1,300,000) than all Virginia Woolf's put together. But literary brokers who take a long view of the market are stocking up with Woolfs, unloading Mitchell's. . . . Their opinion is that Margaret Mitchell was a grand wildcat stock but Virginia Woolf a sound investment.[2]

Ironically, though, both the reasons offered for this prediction and the writer's inducements to his middlebrow audience not to ignore Woolf introduce exactly the quality he hoped to counter: fear. Responding to those "jealous juniors" who "derisively style her 'The Queen of Bloomsbury' " and dismiss her works, and insisting that she is "not just a highbrow writer but perhaps a great one," whose audience is "the Intelligent Common Reader" and who "writes about the common gist of things," the writer nevertheless sketches a portrait of Virginia Woolf as potentially very scary indeed. For one thing, "Nervous readers will find *The Years* not nearly such heavy going as their knowledge or hearsay of Virginia Woolf might lead them to expect"; the novel is "straight," not experimental. In addition, although she comes from a "thoroughbred" English literary background, where she knew and read everyone significant, her own criticism is tolerant and appreciative, like "Sam Johnson's." She might have "done her bit for woman's cause," setting forth "the now-classic requisite of modern women who want independence: '£500 a year and a room of one's own,' " but she still believes that what the writer needs is an androgynous mind and that "it is fatal to be a man or woman pure and simple; one must be woman-manly or man-womanly" when one writes. Finally, when young, she may have been "in appearance a pure pre-Raphaelite, [but] she was actually more like an emancipated Bryn Mawr girl," participating in a hoax on the English navy; now, at fifty-five, she may be "tall, gaunt, haunted-looking," "the picture of a sensitive, cloistered literary woman," but instead of being an "invalid's retreat" (like Proust's) or a "chamber of nightmares" (like Joyce's), her workroom is "a room with a view."

The uncanny evocation of fear in this article, located variously in Virginia Woolf's experimental fiction, cultural class, role as public intellectual, feminism, sexuality, and photographic images, sets the stage for her appearances in the cultural productions that dominate this section:

plays (performed in the theater and on TV), films, television arts program-
ming, photographs, posters, fashion magazines, biographies, newspaper
and magazine articles, and T-shirts. At times she appears as a name,
a verbal evocation; more often she appears as a visual image, usually
represented through her head or her face. In some she plays a starring
role; in others she shares the billing or makes a cameo appearance. But
each appearance becomes an integral part of the ongoing construction of
her intertextual star image, an image whose multifaceted, contradictory
makeup inscribes a complex pattern of reiterations and a shifting array of
meanings. In the process, Virginia Woolf becomes a significant participant
in the "double movement of containment and resistance" that characterizes
popular culture.[3]

Presented as a series of takes—some of them quite short, more like
snapshots; some of them generating more extended treatment—Virginia
Woolf's appearances trace two intersecting narratives associated with the
term *take:* "A continuous section of film photographed at one time; an
instance of such filming. Also preceding a number to distinguish individual
sections of film" (*OED*); and the repetition of a single scene shot over and
over again, each one a slight variation on the others, often called a retake.
One narrative tracks the versioning of Virginia Woolf: the proliferation of
texts and responses that produce an increasingly multifaceted, postmodern
Virginia Woolf who changes with the text, the medium, the discourse, the
historical/cultural moment. (Here, *take* accrues another of its meanings:
"an opinion or assessment; an approach; treatment: *a new take on an
old idea*" [*Random House Webster's College Dictionary, 1996 ed.*].) This
Virginia Woolf remains endlessly open, like fashion, to reformulation
and refiguring, however retro the "new" style may be. As this narrative
progresses, it begins to evoke the refrain "Virginia Woolf, like fashion,
like postmodernism . . ." and with it the dangers of an unending, free
circulation of signifiers and meanings unattached to the "material" or
the "real." The often conflicting representations make Richard Dyer's
proposition—that the contradictions within a star image might become
so great that it could shatter altogether—a distinct possibility.[4]

A second narrative tracks the repetitions, the reiterations, enacted in and
through Virginia Woolf's star appearances, highlighting those that have
so powerfully tied her image and its meanings to fear. These repetitions,
including those that link her to the mythic figures of Medusa and the
Sphinx, suggest a contemporary incarnation of fears that would seem
to go much deeper, reaching down to forces embedded in our cultural
psyche. While susceptible to and evocative of psychoanalytic readings, my
emphasis here is more on the performative role played by these reiterations,

these sedimentations, in normalizing and policing our understanding of gender and sexuality both on their own and in their intersections with social and cultural class. What, I found myself asking, does the figure of Virginia Woolf, continually poised at the crossroads of beauty and terror, tell us about the role of female icons in the transgression and/or recuperation of cultural spaces and authority?

The intersecting narratives draw upon texts that range across the categories associated with popular or mass-produced culture, including those, like Albee's play or *Sammy and Rosie Get Laid* or *Tom & Viv,* that come at the "high" or "arty" end of the scale, from what can be called elite popular culture,[5] and those, like T-shirts, with a more populist orientation. But even here, the categories get blurred. *Sammy and Rosie,* for example, deliberately, parodically, mixes genres and registers, juxtaposing *The Waste Land* with Motown; and the *New York Review of Books,* as we've seen, puts Virginia Woolf's image on T-shirts and tote bags advertising its wares. Both narratives also rely heavily on reviews that appeared in mainstream media (newspapers, magazines) and the journals associated with the "intellectual" media. While criticism and commentaries are often described as "expressing" an already existent view about a star, Dyer puts them on the side of construction: of "[contributing] to the shaping of 'public opinion' about a star," although "the relationship of what the media call 'public opinion' to the opinion of the public must always remain problematic." The reception, then, which is often at odds with the views of the producers of the text, constitutes an essential aspect of the star's polysemy, providing glimpses into the social facts and ideological forcelines at issue at any particular historical/cultural moment.[6]

The transformation of Albee's theatrical version of *Who's Afraid of Virginia Woolf?* into a commercially and critically successful film provides one example of the kinds of cultural crosscurrents at work. Elizabeth Taylor, who starred with Richard Burton, appeared on the cover of both *Look* and *Life; Vogue* had a review by Arthur Schlesinger, Jr.; the film received fourteen nominations for Academy Awards and won five; and *Mad* magazine published a parody called "Who in Heck Is Virginia Woolfe?" One result, as I've noted, was to make "Virginia Woolf" a household name even among people who had no idea there was an actual woman behind the name or what she was known for. Among others, however, particularly those in the media, the play provoked discussions about the (dangerous) presence of homosexuality in both the New York theater scene and culture in general, establishing motifs that reappear intertextually in later works. This is true whether, as in Alan Bennett's *Me, I'm Afraid of Virginia Woolf,* the text explicitly cites Albee's play, or whether, as in Frears and Kureishi's *Sammy and Rosie Get Laid,* the citations operate more as a cultural unconscious.

Another way to address the impact of Albee's text is to say that through it Virginia Woolf entered fully into the "play in cultural relations" that for Stuart Hall defines the realm of the popular itself: a process or site of contention, where class struggle is the norm, positions are never fixed, and "this year's radical symbol or slogan will be neutralised into next year's fashion; the year after, it will be the object of a profound cultural nostalgia." Within this realm, a cultural symbol or icon is never divorced from the "social field into which it is incorporated, the practices with which it articulates and is made to resonate."[7]

Projected as cultural symbol into the ongoing struggle over forms and meanings and power relations, Virginia Woolf soon became a highly visible player in a broad range of battles that had as great (if not greater) a cultural impact as those occurring in the academic realm. While to some extent linked to her status in the academy and the intellectual press, Virginia Woolf's popularity, the articulation of and responses to her popular meanings, has its own rhythms and valences, not the least of which is its provision of a far more extensive field for subcultural interventions that disrupt the claims of dominant or "legitimate" culture. In other words, like the academic realm—though with a broader reach—the realm of the popular allowed for, generated, and reacted against versions of Virginia Woolf that were distinctly associated with a feminist and/or gay/lesbian and/or queer agenda.

For one example of the complexity of the social field at any particular moment, we could look at Virginia Woolf's appearance in the 1993 Bass Ale ad that featured a huge reproduction of the Beresford profile (fig. 3) with the legend "When Are Words Not Enough?" above it and the legend "Bass Helps You Get to the Bottom of It All" below. Part of a campaign that also used such figures as Mark Twain, H. G. Wells, Rudyard Kipling, Franz Kafka, and Albert Camus, Virginia Woolf, the only woman, earned the campaign a write-up in *Vogue*. There, a snippet in the "People Are Talking About" feature begins by calling the campaign "one of the more curious variations on the time-honored celebrity endorsement theme"; it then describes Virginia Woolf as "the long-suffering author of *A Room of One's Own, The Waves, Mrs. Dalloway, Orlando,* and a lot of very sad letters" and as "Vita Sackville-West's lover—which is to say Leonard Woolf's something-less-than-faithful wife"—before commenting that for her, "words were not enough" when she "put down her pen" and drowned herself. This doubled appearance of Virginia Woolf becomes even more polysemic and intertextual when read through her two other appearances in the same issue of *Vogue:* a huge spread on Sally Potter's film version of *Orlando,* and a short comment about the film in an article about the new lesbian visibility in the mainstream media that states, "While the book was an homage to Woolf's married lesbian lover, Vita Sackville-West, you wouldn't know that from watching the movie."[8] Which one is the "real" Virginia Woolf? Or, more to the point, what cultural, social, and political ends are articulated and served by the disparate uses of her name and face?

The other useful aspect of this particular example is to highlight the central role of visual images in the "complex configuration of visual, verbal, and aural signs" characteristic of Virginia Woolf's star image.[9] Finding her face on Barnes and Noble shopping bags or Quality Paperback Book Club mugs or Largely Literary T-shirts may not be surprising; nor, perhaps, given the nature of advertising, is her appearance in the Bass Ale ad, which had a limited circulation in cities such as New York, San Francisco, Chicago, and Philadelphia. But Virginia Woolf's face appears in a wide range of cultural productions that feature her picture without identification or words— *Sammy and Rosie* and the television sitcom *Ab Fab,* for example—giving her visual image a life of its own.

The strong visual component of Virginia Woolf's iconicity stands in direct opposition to the construction of the literary figure and his reputation proposed by John Rodden in his study *The Politics of Literary Reputation.* Rodden uses many of the same terms applied to stars in his study of what constitutes literary reputation—image, face, portrait, star—but in his formulations they remain metaphoric, rooted in words, not visual images. Locating the etymology of *reputation* or *repute* in the process of "re-thinking" ("L. *re-putare,* to think again"), he defines it as a "public 'image' [that] signifies the Other's perception of the subject as an embodiment or type of [a] stated quality, e.g., 'the image of' integrity." "To talk about reputations is therefore to talk about images," but these images are " 'a picture made out of words.' " Although he frames his narrative as "a tour of a portrait gallery" and argues that without a "*face* . . . the clear image of the literary (and sometimes private) personality," a writer will neither move beyond literary circles and into the mass media nor cross the "inter-generational divide," the discourse of image, face, and portrait Rodden employs never escapes from the domain of the word, from verbal portraits of the man.[10]

Man may be the key word here, introducing gender into Virginia Woolf's popular appearances; perceived as part of the star's structured polysemy, Rodden's abstract, metaphoric "face" not only becomes visceral, visual, but marks a field where a number of ideological and cultural contradictions in Western culture get played out. One of these involves the long-standing binary opposition between verbal and visual—between word and visual image—that from the start has had distinctly gendered implications, including that of domination and subordination. In his study of iconology and aesthetic theory in Western culture, W. J. T. Mitchell places gender, along with race, nationality, and social relations, at the heart of any attempt to answer the question, "What is at stake in marking off or erasing the differences between images and words? What are the systems of power and canons of value—that is, the ideologies—that inform the answers to these questions and make them matters of polemical dispute rather than purely theoretical interest?"[11]

Conceived as "a struggle for territory, a contest of rival ideologies," the gulf between word and image signifies the larger struggle between culture and nature. While the terms of the argument often shift, aligning word and image alternately with both sides of the nature/culture divide, what emerges most clearly from Mitchell's historically located studies is the dynamic that constructs

> the image as the site of a special power that must either be contained or exploited; . . . [Edmund] Burke and [G. E.] Lessing treat the image as the sign of the racial, social, and sexual other, an object of both fear and contempt. The contempt springs from the assurance that images are powerless, mute, inferior kinds of signs; the fear stems from the recognition that these signs, and the "others" who believe in them, may be in the process of *taking* power, appropriating a voice.

Not surprisingly, the threat of eruption or subversion located in the image, and by extension with spectacle, is almost always aligned with the feminine and/or women, who for this reason must be contained and constrained by law and custom lest they become or produce hybrids, monsters, "freaks of nature"—or revolution.[12] As we shall see, Virginia Woolf incarnate.

But if Virginia Woolf often appears as a face, that face is nevertheless connected to a head and the head to a body, both of which prove equally threatening. As head, Virginia Woolf becomes emblematic of the mind or intellect, the intellectual (a "talking head"), and hence a threat to the social and political division of genders that have excluded women from the public realm. But by virtue of her being a woman, her face and head can never be divorced from her body, the body that by weighing her down should ground her in the realm of the reproductive, the material, not the intellectual or transcendent. *Should:* the body, we know, particularly a woman's body, is never that simple or safe. Located on the side of the visual, for example, of spectacle or performance, including that associated with cross-dressing and refashioning—of women "making a spectacle of themselves"—it threatens the overthrow of hierarchy and order, including that of gender itself. Nor can woman's body be divorced from the sexual, with its lures and threats, including the lure and threat of death. And if, as is the case with so many representations of Virginia Woolf, the body becomes so frail and fragile as to become ghostly, this too is frightening, carrying within it the taint of death. So does the nonreproductive body, whether the failure to reproduce is chosen or not. Finally, when the body of Virginia Woolf disappears into the body of Marilyn Monroe, as it does in the Chapel Hill hybrid explored in part 3, the threat posed by the woman's body becomes apocalyptic, signifying an explosion of boundaries that opens up spaces for new inscriptions.

When Slavoj Žižek uses Virginia Woolf's face to mark "the boundary that separates beauty from disgust" that he associates with the sublime, or Hanif Kureishi presents Virginia Woolf as a visual image inseparable from horror and contrasts it to the life-giving poetry of T. S. Eliot, we can begin to see the complex role Virginia Woolf plays in what are distinctly ideological battles.[13] Her position on the borderline of so many of the divides outlined by Mitchell in his study, whether that between mind and body, eloquence and silence, or beautiful bodies and monsters, becomes a measure of her ability to transgress borders and undo categories that our culture has fought so hard to keep distinct. When manifested in the popular realm, this transgressiveness threatens to undo the binary between high and popular culture itself.

Each take that follows evokes specific historical and cultural moments, often associated with a specific date; the sequence, particularly in the early takes, is more or less chronological, charting the appearances that marked her emergence as star and anticipating subsequent manifestations. The overlap and overlay that soon become apparent suggest the powerful cultural undercurrents imbricated in Virginia Woolf's ever-evolving star image.

TIME: VIRGINIA WOOLF JOINS THE

"ALL-STAR LITERARY VAUDEVILLE"

When the founders of *Time* set out to create an innovative news magazine in 1922, they defined their function as serving "the modern necessity of keeping people informed" and doing so in a way that appealed not only to the college-educated but "to every man and woman in America who has the slightest interest in the world and its affairs." The way to achieve this, they decided, was to keep the articles short and to the point; to develop a style that was telegraphic and did not demand that people think too hard; and most of all, to get the information "off its pages into the minds of its readers."[1] This last injunction they met in part by translating events and ideas into a human figure: by locating them in an emblematic man or woman. The epitome of this strategy was the cover portrait and story: "The notion was that by investigating the intersection of personality and achievement in the life of a single individual, the magazine could offer its readers an approachable emblem of any matter," whether political, social, or literary, "that might otherwise prove to be disagreeably abstract." Writing of this "masterstroke" in 1986, Richard Schickel, himself a film critic at *Time,* had no trouble pinpointing the origins of this "emblematic journalism": "reporting about show people."[2]

Given this origin, it makes perfect sense that one of Virginia Woolf's earliest star appearances occurred in the United States, home of Hollywood, and that the vehicle was *Time.* By 1937 Hollywood had not only established itself as the premier producer of films, but had a well-established system for producing stars. This system, as disgruntled critics of twentieth-century cultural life never stop repeating, insinuated itself into every area of our life, producing those "human pseudo-events," celebrities, known for their well-knownness, their image, which was in turn based more on their "personality" than on their innate character or their deeds. Hollywood, then, becomes the central player in the American cultural narrative of the fall of the hero into the star.

The transposition of the star system from movies to literature was also well established and strongly lamented by 1937. Edmund Wilson's 1926 essay "The All-Star Literary Vaudeville," whose title I have made my own, hints at its beginnings, critiquing not just the thinness of most contemporary American literature but the literary reviewers who fail to pass honest judgment on it. Instead, they provide a "publicity service" that makes it "scarcely possible nowadays to tell the reviews from the advertising: both tend to convey the impression that masterpieces are being manufactured as regularly and as durably as new models of motor-cars." Pointing specifically to Stuart Sherman, editor of the influential *New York Herald Tribune Books* section, "the central desk of authority," he paints a picture of "each of the performers in the all-star circus [stepping] up to receive his diploma."[3]

Although Wilson does not make this point, one aspect of this transformation of the writer into the performer can be linked to an increased emphasis on an author's personality by reviewers such as Sherman, who, borrowing heavily from advertising prose, created verbal portraits of writers;[4] in Dyer's schema, we might see these portraits as part of the "promotion" of the star, instituted to create a particular image. Another aspect resides in the increased use of photographs of authors not only in reviews but in advertisements for books, which provides the star with "publicity."[5] The writer's face, then, especially if attached to a best-seller, might appear in ads for weeks on end, long after the review and perhaps the book had faded into a distant memory or been forgotten.

The particularly American status of the "best-seller" also comes into play here, with its connotations of a media-produced and -generated star system that transformed a literary work into a celebrity in its own right. Britain has never shared the American enthusiasm for best-seller lists; books, it is believed, do not compete with each other. Although the British journal *The Bookseller* ran a monthly article called "Books in Demand" during the late 1920s and early 1930s, based on publishers' statements of what they had sold, the publishers' resistance to going public with their figures soon ended the column.[6]

The term *vaudeville* in Wilson's title suggests yet another approach to the seemingly changed status of literature and authors in the United

States by the early twentieth century: that they, along with reviewing, had been "barnumized," absorbed by the spectacularization of advertising universally associated with P. T. Barnum and described as a process that employed newspapers (both "news" stories and ads), books, posters, and performances to create a "tautological threshold" where advertising led to more advertising, which led to more advertising. The phenomenal spectacularization of Oscar Wilde during the 1880s, so extensive and so effective that even a sunflower could evoke the man, provides one vivid example, epitomized by images depicting Wilde sauntering down the street with Jumbo, the elephant made famous by Barnum, who wears Wilde's trademark sunflower on his chest.[7]

There are, of course, other ways to look at this transformation of the author into star and its cultural meanings that are less negative, less apocalyptic, than the American jeremiads about loss and decay, and show more historical continuity. In her study of the long-standing intersection of literature and advertising, Jennifer Wicke points out that ever since Gutenberg, literature has had advertising as its shadow partner, and that this advertising has used visual images of the writer, along with "prefatory remarks, . . . paeans to cultural classics," etc., to create "cults of authorship": "The advertising exordiums at the front of printed material were focal in allowing books to be seen as intellectual property also, with authors as celebrity figures (and here we can think of Erasmus, Paracelsus, Galileo), so these two aspects of early advertisement converged in the formation of 'authorship' as a new property category." By the nineteenth century, authors, along with other famous people, had become a staple of advertising in general, their names and faces appearing on trade cards and posters and packaging without any necessary connection to the product being sold. One nineteenth-century cigar band, for example, reads "Shakespeare Gorki Macbeth Maud Muller Sancho Panza Harriet Beecher Stowe."[8] Authors also sold in their own right, evidenced by the numerous photographic *cartes de visite* of writers for sale individually or as part of albums.

Leo Braudy's history of fame, *The Frenzy of Renown,* offers a further challenge to the myth of a twentieth-century fall into a celebrity or image culture. Writing explicitly of Boorstin's depiction of the deleterious effects of media culture, Braudy questions "his assumption that, say, heroism and its expression can ever really be fully separated": "Whatever political or social or psychological factors influence the desire to be famous, they are enhanced by and feed upon the available means of reproducing the image." For Braudy, moreover, the increased dissemination of a famous person's image brought about by changes in technology was not necessarily a bad thing, resulting, from the eighteenth century on, in the "democratization of fame": "Beyond any previous period, the eighteenth century marks a diffusion of the image of the famous into places, social as well as geographical, it had never gone before." "To dismiss the circus of contemporary notoriety with pat versions of . . . Boorstin's phrase, 'a celebrity is someone who is famous for being famous,'" he warns, "too easily allows us to ignore the importance of even celebrity in shaping the values of our society, not always for the worse."[9] From here we need take only a short step to reach Dyer's argument that stars are always implicated in ideological contradictions at both the individual and the group level, and that consumers are just as crucial as producers in determining the star's social and cultural meanings.

To the extent, then, that Virginia Woolf's appearance on *Time*'s cover signifies her arrival as star in the United States, it establishes a persona that becomes the basis of her future roles and sets the stage for the battles fought over her meaning.[10] If, as some critics have argued, the star image, like Foucault's author function, serves to set limits on a text's meaning by making the star a limit or boundary, this early construct becomes even more significant.[11] One way to approach it is through Schickel's formulation of the star's emblematic nature—"shaggy Einstein was the symbol of intellectuality; fierce-featured Toscanini was the artistic temperament personified; Hemingway was the artist as adventurer; Gertrude Stein the artist as incomprehensible"[12]—which translates into the question, What is Virginia Woolf emblematic of?

Before turning more directly to this question, I want to reiterate a point made earlier: that the *Time* cover and the advertising blitz that accompanied it, both featuring the Man Ray photograph, were a distinctly American phenomenon, linked in part to *The Years*' best-seller status but also endemic to American book advertising in general. American publishers, that is, spent more money for more elaborate ads, including those bearing the author's picture, than was the norm in Britain. This practice ensured that Virginia Woolf's star image in the United States was shaped from the beginning by her visual image.[13] In contrast, Hogarth Press, the press owned and run by Woolf and her husband, Leonard, which published her writings in Britain, did not use authors' pictures in advertisements for its books; in fact, it hardly ever veered from the most understated announcements. Leonard expressed the general view of British publishers between the wars when he wrote in 1927, "My own belief is that books are, in general, not a commodity which, like patent medicines, cigarettes, or mustard, the consumer buys or can be induced to buy by the skill of the advertiser alone."[14] While Leonard did make some concessions, including the skillful use of a wolf's-head logo designed by E. McKnight

Kauffer, an American painter and designer, he never used authors' pictures in his ads. But Harcourt Brace and Company, Woolf's American publisher, made full use of all the available techniques and resources, a practice that often bemused Woolf, even as she appreciated the results.[15]

A brief survey of the ads in the *New York Herald Tribune Books* makes the point. On Sunday, April 11, 1937, the same day Isabel Paterson's front-page rave review of *The Years* appeared, Harcourt used the top half of its full-page ad to announce the book. The large-font heading reads, "Virginia Woolf," and the Man Ray photograph (fig. 6) is center stage; the ad also announces "Second large printing before publication."[16] Woolf's *Time* appearance occurred almost simultaneously (April 12, 1937), and the following week Harcourt's two-column ad includes the blurb, " 'She is certainly the foremost woman author of her day.'—TIME MAGAZINE," along with a blurb from the *New York Times* (April 18, 1937). By April 25, the ad includes a blurb from Dorothy Canfield, *Book-of-the-Month Club News,* and we learn that the novel is in its fourth printing. Two weeks later a half-page ad on the back cover of *Books* announces *The Years* as "The best selling novel in the United States. First on the 'What America Is Reading' chart in *N.Y. Herald Tribune Books*" (May 9, 1937); and two weeks after that, another back-page ad, this time devoted entirely to Woolf's novel and featuring the photograph, tells us the book had been the best-selling novel in America for four weeks (May 30, 1937).[17] Ads foregrounding the best-selling status of the novel and, for the most part, the Man Ray photograph, continued to appear for the next four months.[18]

By the time this run of publicity ended, Virginia Woolf's face would have been as familiar to readers of *Books* as her name or her novel; given the extraordinary foregrounding of her face—and the extraordinary aspect of the face itself—it might be argued that the photograph was intended to catch the reader's eye and direct it to the more prosaic details. No such publicity would have been necessary in Britain, even if it had been the norm, where, given the centralization and stratification of the cultural scene, neither Virginia Woolf's name nor her face (not to mention her parentage, her Bloomsbury address, or her literary and social associates) would have needed any introduction or explanation by 1937.[19] Moreover, during the 1920s, while still a rising star, she had made appearances in Britain that extended her visibility beyond literary and intellectual circles. In 1924 she was featured in British *Vogue*'s "Hall of Fame" accompanied by a photograph by Beck and Macgregor, fashionable studio photographers who specialized in the intelligentsia (fig. 13), an appearance that Jane Garrity argues established a split between Virginia Woolf writer and Virginia Woolf beautiful woman and fashionable icon.[20] The nomination reads, "Because she is a publisher with a prose style; because she is a daughter of the late Sir Leslie Stephen and a sister of Vanessa Bell; because she is the author of 'The Voyage Out,' 'Night and Day,' and 'Jacob's Room'; because in the opinion of some of the best judges she is the most brilliant novelist of the younger generation; because she also writes admirable criticism; because with her husband she runs The Hogarth Press." Five years later a more "popular" Virginia Woolf, again accompanied by the Beck and Macgregor portrait, appeared in *Vanity Fair*'s "We Nominate for the Hall of Fame." Here she is nominated "Because she is the first woman in English letters; because despite the fact that her style is advanced and her subject matter recondite, she has become a popular novelist; because her hobby is printing and typography; because she has exerted a tremendous influence on her fellow writers; and finally because *Orlando* has made her a favourite with the public as well as with the intelligentsia."[21]

Despite these positive portraits, competing texts that focused less on her pursuits and her popularity than on her more ethereal, ascetic attributes were also making their way into public view, introducing the motif of fear into Virginia Woolf's evolving star image. To take just one significant example: the drawings and description of Virginia Woolf in the British photographer Cecil Beaton's 1930 *Book of Beauty*. The drawings are based on the Beck and Macgregor photograph already familiar from *Vogue* and *Vanity Fair*, where Woolf wears a Victorian dress, complete with leg-of-mutton sleeves, that had belonged to her mother. Beaton was forced to reproduce another photographer's image because Woolf had consistently refused to sit for him, making her, he wrote, the only person besides Queen Mary "reluctant to do his bidding."[22] Not that this stopped Beaton, the photographer of "beautiful people" and later Hollywood stars; he simply appropriated her image, leading her to write a series of angry letters to the *New Statesman* in protest that might have added to the aura of elitism so central to her British persona.[23] Forced to rely on already available images, Beaton chose one that might well have been in the *Time* writer's mind seven years later when he described the young Virginia Woolf as "Pre-Raphaelite," a designation that carries with it traces of the beautiful Julia Prinsep Jackson Duckworth Stephen, Woolf's mother, whose face appeared both in numerous photographs taken by her aunt Julia Margaret Cameron and in paintings by Burne-Jones.[24] Beaton's drawing also exaggerated the fragility of the woman encased in the dress. Given this representation, Virginia Woolf's visual presence in Beaton's book brings both beauty and death in its wake.

The verbal portrait leaves us in no doubt about Virginia Woolf's other-worldly quality and its association with fear. "Mrs. Virginia Woolf is one

FIGURE 13.
Virginia Woolf.
Photograph by Beck
and Macgregor.

of the most gravely distinguished-looking women I have ever seen," the
entry begins, and *gravely* is the operative word:

> In her we do not find the conventional pink cheeks and liquid eyes
> and childish lips. Although she would look like a terrified ghost in
> an assembly of the accepted raving beauties, she would make each
> one separately appear vulgar and tawdry in comparison with her.
> She has all the chaste and sombre beauty of village schoolmistresses,
> housekeepers, and nuns, and one cannot imagine her being powdered
> and painted: the mere knowledge that *maquillage* exists is disturbing
> in connection with her, for when one sees her so sensitively nervous
> and with the poignant beauty of the lady in the faded photograph
> in the oval frame, the lady who is one's grandmother as a girl, one
> realises that a face can be a reverent and sacred thing. Her fine skin
> is parchment-coloured, she has timid startled eyes, set deep, a sharp

bird-like nose and firm pursed lips. Her lank hair and aristocratic wrists are of a supreme delicacy, and one imagines her spending eternities of dreamy leisure sewing and gazing out of the window. She wears cameo brooches and cotton gloves, and hatpins, and exudes an atmosphere of musk and old lace and the rustle and scratch of stiff ivy-coloured taffeta, but her old-fashioned dowdinesses are but a conscious and literary game of pretence, for she is alertly contemporary, even a little ahead of her time. Many of her confrères see her as Juno, awe-inspiring and gaunt, but she herself is frightened, a bundle of tentative gestures, and quick nervous glances, as frail and crisp as a dead leaf; and like a sea-anemone she curls up at contact with the outer world.[25]

Even if we take into account Beaton's predilection for representing women as *memento mori*,[26] this description of Virginia Woolf as uncanny, a fearful and fear-evoking figure of beauty-as-death, death-in-beauty, is both overdetermined and prescient: not only of her suicide in 1941 but of subsequent renderings of her emblematic nature.

By the time of her appearance on *Time*'s cover, then, the images of Virginia Woolf circulating in the British media, linked as they were to the class-inflected designation "The Queen of Bloomsbury" current in (some) intellectual circles and the descriptions of her uncanny otherworldliness, provided ample reason for *Time*'s writer to want to humanize and democratize her, to bring her into the American fold. This democratization anticipates the widely divergent attitudes in Britain and the States toward Virginia Woolf later in the century, whether in terms of her iconization by the women's movement in the 1960s and 1970s or in terms of her versioning by feminist scholars and critics; both of these phenomena depended in part on an ability to see the woman and her writings outside the contexts and prevailing images that govern her British persona, including those linked to her social/cultural class. *Time* does not hide her class position; it makes it very clear, although it scrupulously avoids the presumably taboo term *class* itself, evoking instead the concept of the "thorough-bred": "The best steeplechasers are bred in Ireland. From England come literary thoroughbreds."[27] In Woolf's case, this involves a pedigree that includes William Makepeace Thackeray, Darwins, Maitlands, Symondses, and Stracheys, who are all "related to her," in addition to her father, who "kept open house for the great literary men of his day." But despite this pedigree and her own association with many of the leading writers of the day, *Time* insists, "her books are addressed not to a literary clique but to the Intelligent Common Reader. And the address is written in such a fine and flowing hand that even when it is illegible the hopeful addressee can find some profitable pleasure in puzzling over it. Even her obscurer books have something about them that attracts popular attention, for more than most stylists, she writes about the common gist of things."

The popular and the common cross over into the representation of "The Woman" as well as of her writing, presenting the feminist as the advocate of the androgynous mind and transforming the young Virginia Stephen into an "emancipated Bryn Mawr girl" who, if not the girl next door, is at least a version of her, fun-loving, bright, independent.[28] Significantly, the images refuted in the discussion of "The Woman" are predominantly visual, whether those that gave the young girl her Pre-Raphaelite appearance or more recent ones: "Careless of her clothes, her face, her greying hair, at 55 she is the picture of a sensitive, cloistered, literary woman." This latter image is supported by the information that she "lives quietly," "rarely makes a public appearance," and "has no children." It seems unlikely that the physical description here is motivated by the Man Ray photograph of a sharply delineated Virginia Woolf on *Time*'s cover, and the only other photograph that appears in the article shows a cross-dressed ("emancipated") Virginia Stephen and her disguised collaborators at the time of the Dreadnaught Hoax (1910). Instead, it depends on a general and generalized image of Virginia Woolf powerful enough to impel the writer's insistence that despite all appearances, "the world of her own" she has created, unlike that of Joyce or Proust, is a "room with a view."

The comparison of Virginia Woolf's workroom to Joyce's at the end of the article provides one more angle on the construction of her early persona, one that emanates from Joyce's own appearance on the cover of *Time* when *Finnegans Wake* was published two years later. Schickel describes Joyce in his last decade as well known for his "unknowableness," and the *Time* piece as "a kind of reward for being so widely unread, so famously unreadable."[29] The article both supports and counters this view. Beginning with the statement "All children are afraid of the night," and identifying Joyce as chronicler of the dreams we associate with it, the writer declares, "*Finnegans Wake* is a difficult book—too difficult for most people to read. In fact, it cannot be 'read' in the ordinary sense. It is perhaps the most consciously obscure work that a man of acknowledged genius has produced." Nevertheless, more than two pages are devoted to explicating the "Story" and "Method," with quotations from "Critic Edmund Wilson" brought in to help. The writer then turns to "The Author," tracing his somewhat nomadic existence and his career, and to "Nono" [sic], "grandfather," the name used by his grandson: to the artist's appearance, his near-Miltonic blindness, and his role as family man and friend.[30] In addition to the cover image, a photograph by Gisèle Freund of Joyce reading what looks like a manuscript through a magnifying glass, three pictures accompany the story: one of Joyce and Eugene Jolas, one of Nora Joyce, and one of Joyce with his father (a painted portrait above his head), his son, and his grandson.

Juxtaposing this article to the one on Woolf two years earlier, I am struck by the seriousness of the piece on Joyce, which employs little of the *Time*-ese that often made a portrait indistinguishable from a caricature or parody. We are left with the sense that Joyce, however little he is read, has indelibly changed literature and the way we think of the English language. Moreover, the man and his family do not need reconstruction for an American audience; Joyce fits easily into the traditional categories. In contrast, for all the emphasis on Virginia Woolf's status as a "great writer" and her value as a long-term literary "investment," the article leaves us with a portrait of the reclusive woman, seemingly without family or friends, alone in her workshop. If, then, we return to the question posed at the beginning and ask what Virginia Woolf is emblematic of, the answer is paradoxical: everything frightening the article tries to convince us she is not. She may be the "foremost woman author" of the day, but if so the emblematic "woman author" is simultaneously sensitive, aesthetic, and asexual; aristocratic, feminist, and intellectual. In a word, potentially very scary indeed.

A WRITER'S DIARY AND THE

"REAL" VIRGINIA WOOLF

In the years following Virginia Woolf's death in 1941, the images re-pressed in the *Time* essay became the prevailing intellectual and popular view. Highbrow, mandarin, elite; sensitive and fragile: any way you looked at it, her name and her face evoked images of "sensibility," class privilege, experimental prose, distinction.[1] Although Woolf's novels were taught in college courses, at least in the United States, *The Years,* the book that led to her star turn in America, fell into an abyss of critical and pedagogic silence; even her feminism, like feminism in general, faded from popular view.

The first notable event in Virginia Woolf's reemergence as public persona—the publication of *A Writer's Diary,* edited by her husband, Leonard Woolf, originally in Britain (1953) and then in the United States (1954)—illustrates the inability of any one person or group or factor to control a star's image and meaning. Leonard's clearly stated editorial choice to present Virginia as a writer, period, introduces into my narrative the family's desire both to disseminate and to contain Virginia Woolf's image; it also introduces the uncontainable power of competing market and social forces, for the Virginia Woolf who emerges from this vehicle is already well on her way to shifting her status from writer to personality to star. *A Writer's Diary,* then, marks a significant moment in the complex interplay of text and audience at work in the construction of Virginia Woolf's star image.

Histories of the Hogarth Press make clear that Leonard, who controlled his wife's literary estate, carefully planned the posthumous publication of her works to stretch them out over time; in the years immediately after her death these included her final novel, *Between the Acts,* and collections of her essays. In this sense, Leonard could be said to have both promoted and marketed Virginia Woolf, keeping her in the eye of at least that public that reads serious literature or its reviews in the literary and intellectual journals. Virginia Woolf became merchandise, an illustration of the star as commodity, property.[2]

But stars and their images, as Jane Gaines reminds us, however much they may be property and hence subject to legal ownership, are also signs and carry within them social uses that escape legal consignment; this is true even after the star's death and even—or especially—when the ownership is deemed to belong to the family. For Gaines, the struggle of families of deceased celebrities to "own" the rights to their image has as much to do with "the desire to secure meaning" as it does with "an attempt to secure real property": "While legislators in the state of California were concerned about a particular point of law—the extension of post mortem property rights to the dead—the families of deceased celebrities borrowed these legal mechanisms in an attempt to rearticulate the image of an ancestor." This is particularly so, she adds, when the images in question can be considered "offensive," as is often the case with representations of the celebrity's sexuality.[3]

From this perspective Leonard Woolf's selections from his wife's extensive and diverse entries for *A Writer's Diary* can be seen as an attempt to limit Virginia Woolf's public persona to that of writer or literary figure. And for the most part he succeeded; the reviews, which appeared in the usual literary and intellectual journals on both sides of the Atlantic, generally concentrated on what the diary tells us about her as a writer and include some assessment, based on the reviewer's location in the national and/or international literary/cultural scene, and hence his or her biases, of Woolf's current status. But inevitably, because this was after all a diary, the reviewers also put a great deal of effort into constructing a portrait of the private woman revealed in or by the writing, which then became the subject of either defense or critique. Not surprisingly, as theorists of the star phenomenon have long argued, these portraits can also be read as a process of identification or rejection. The question then becomes, what attributes provoke the reviewers' reactions and projections?

While much of the answer is to be expected—her family and class background, her association with Bloomsbury, and her attitude toward contemporary writers such as Joyce, all of which lead to accusations of or refutations against elitism, snobbery, etc.—other aspects of the reception anticipate future shifts in the articulation of her image. For one thing, even when the reviews express more or less serious reservations about her work and her character, most of them suggest she had not escaped, as W. H. Auden argues she has in his review, the fate of becoming "a sacred cow of whom everyone speaks in tones of hushed and bored reverence"; in fact, the more dismissive reviews take this stance as their starting point.[4] For another, contrary to what one might have expected from her *Time* appearance, the more negative portraits came not from Britain, but from America, particularly those, all written by men, that appeared in those self-defined "intellectual" journals—the *New Republic;* the *Nation;* the *Saturday Review*—that had clearly decided by the 1950s that Virginia Woolf and Bloomsbury were anathema to whatever literary and cultural standards they stood for.[5] Most of the positive portraits in the American journals came from men or women who were themselves writers—Elizabeth Bowen in the *New York Times Book Review;* Rumer Godden in the *New York Herald Tribune Books;* Auden in the *New Yorker.*[6] Significantly, all three are British; Bowen and Auden knew Woolf personally.

Women reviewers (all of them writing in American journals, although the anonymous review in London's *Times Literary Supplement* may well have been written by a woman)[7] on the whole created a more sympathetic and rounded portrait, one that acknowledged the otherwise conspicuously missing concept of gender; this absence indicates the quiescence of feminist consciousness or activity at the time. Bowen, for example, talks about Woolf's dislike of being considered a woman writer or being called " 'one of our leading female novelists,' " even as she describes where Woolf "shows herself most a woman"; Auden, always the exception, noted in his assessment of why Woolf responded so strongly to criticism of her, "the fact that she was a woman was a further aggravation. She belonged to a generation in which a woman had still to fight to be taken seriously as a writer." A more unexpected—and prescient—note is sounded by Anne Fremantle, writing in the Catholic *Commonweal,* who, citing Ashley Montagu's suggestion that "women have not excelled in the creative arts because their creativity was total, physical and spiritual no less than intellectual and imaginative," comments that, like "almost all the greatest women writers," Woolf was childless.[8]

As always visual images play a role, although, as was still usual, they appear only in the American reviews. Joseph Wood Krutch's dismissive piece in the *Saturday Review,* for example, is accompanied by the 1939 Gisèle Freund photograph that shows Woolf looking down, her head leaning against her hand (fig. 10); the caption reads "Virginia Woolf— 'morbidly affected.' " It is unclear whether the quotation comes from the *Diary;* it does not appear in Krutch's review. Another photograph by Freund, this one the full-figure profile where Woolf holds an open manuscript with one hand and a cigarette holder in the other (fig. 9), appears in Bowen's far more positive review, captioned with a remark from the *Diary* that is repeated in the article as a sign of Virginia Woolf's strength: "Virginia Woolf: 'Praise and fame must be faced.'" In these examples, the visual image mirrors the verbal rendering: picture and text become one. What strikes me in reading them is how much the combined visual-verbal construct also mirrors the reviewer, a reflection that is unself-conscious and unexamined within the reviews.

A slightly different but just as telling illustration of the power of her visual image, this time one of the 1929 Lenare portraits (fig. 4), occurs in Mark Schorer's ambiguous and ultimately negative review in the *New Republic,* headed "A Writer's Mirror": "Fear. This is what a stranger, who knew her face only from the many august and sometimes admonitory photographs, would least have expected to find in her. But fear, by which one means uncertainty about her own worth, was apparently among her first qualities."[9] Schorer's reading, provoked by Woolf's statement that she feared the "taunt Charm & emptiness," provides no context; he doesn't tell us that Woolf made this statement about her deep political passion in writing *Three Guineas* and her desire that the book be taken seriously: a realistic response, given attitudes toward feminism and pacifism at the time it was published. But what interests me even more is the doubling of the fear located in Virginia Woolf: the fear she is perceived to experience and the fear her "august" image elicits in others. Whose fear, one begins to wonder, are we really talking about? Is Virginia Woolf a mirror that reflects back the viewer him- or herself?

Finally, the aspect of Virginia Woolf that proved most significant to her later articulations reveals itself, like gender, by its absence: the fascination exerted by her private life, including her personal relationships. True to the process at work in the construction of the star system during the early part of the century, what the public desired, even the literary public represented by these reviewers, was information about the private woman: what she did, at home and elsewhere, when she was not writing. Like readers and spectators from at least the eighteenth century on, the reviewers want to find the "real person" behind the persona projected by the public text; they were behaving like fans.[10] For Richard deCordova, the transformation of the "picture personality," who was indistinguishable from the films in which she or he appeared, into the "star" occurred only when the "private lives" of the individuals became public and were "constituted as a site of knowledge and truth."[11]

Despite Leonard's decision to exclude almost everything that did not pertain to Virginia's "intentions, objects, and methods as a writer," then, the publication of *A Writer's Diary* generated almost as much interest in knowing more about her personal life as it did about her work. In particular, the reviewers wanted to know what Virginia had said about her friends and acquaintances that was so damning Leonard chose not to publish any of it, "to protect the feelings or reputations of the living."[12] Ironically, one of the people hinting at the richness of the excluded materials was Benedict Nicolson, who knew what he was talking about. For Ben was the son of Vita Sackville-West and Harold Nicolson and the brother of Nigel Nicolson, the man who, twenty years later, reflecting a different world, projected both his parents and Virginia Woolf into the popular imagination and a great deal of scandalous outcry when he published *Portrait of a Marriage:* a detailed presentation of his parents' homosexual relationships, including that between Vita and Virginia.[13]

But by the time this happened, Virginia Woolf had left behind the self-enclosed arena of literary reviews and reviewers and entered the wide-open field of the popular. However illuminating an example of Virginia Woolf's potential star power *A Writer's Diary* and its reception may be, the audience was still self-selected and limited.[14] The vehicle responsible for propelling Virginia Woolf once and for all into the popular realm and a different level of stardom did not appear until nine years later: Edward Albee's *Who's Afraid of Virginia Woolf?* And what a vehicle it was. Virginia Woolf entered the 1960s and its cultural frays with her hair flying.

WHO'S AFRAID OF VIRGINIA WOOLF?

VIRGINIA WOOLF BECOMES

A HOUSEHOLD NAME

A review of Quentin Bell's biography of Virginia Woolf in 1972 begins with the anecdote of a woman nudging an editor carrying the book and asking, "Was there a real person called Virginia Woolf? I saw the play but not the movie"; another recounts an exchange in which Gordon Haight used the name "Virginia Woolf" to recall to the wife of a retired British major what Bloomsbury was. "Her face lighted up at once. 'Oh, yes, she was the one in that dirty movie!' "[1] These women are not alone; in 1997 a professor in Australia noted that many of her older women students, if they knew Virginia Woolf, knew her in conjunction with Albee's work, not her own.[2] Given this history, it would be hard to overstate the importance of *Who's Afraid of Virginia Woolf?* in constructing and securing Virginia Woolf's name recognition and the persona attached to it. Produced on stage in New York in 1962 and then in London in 1964 before becoming the film starring Richard Burton and Elizabeth Taylor in 1966, Albee's play did more than make his title and "Virginia Woolf" household words, "part of the coinage of everyday speech." Both the texts and their reception highlight the contradictions and tensions inhering in Virginia Woolf's star image and illustrate "how meanings and the affects they embody" are either "foregrounded" or "masked or displaced" in the elaboration of what are clearly ideological disputes.[3] In addressing these topics I will concentrate on the ramifications of the title, taking its question, its riddle, with its emphasis on fear, very seriously indeed. For whatever else people may have taken away from the play or film, and however they interpreted the term "Virginia Woolf," her name became synonymous with the power to elicit fear and wreak psychological death or destruction.

Even before the play opened the title provoked talk and controversy; writing in the *New York Times* column "News of the Rialto," Lewis Funke claimed to have received "letters of protest [about the title] to this department's mailbag": "How, indeed, did Mr. Albee dare poke fun at the late English novelist, who, to many on both sides of the Atlantic, was one of the greats of this century?"[4] I am reminded here of Woolf's description of certain of Jane Austen's admirers, who, she wrote, would "resent any slight upon her genius as if it were an insult offered to the chastity of their Aunts";[5] Virginia Woolf, it seems, despite Auden's 1954 protest, had herself become a "sacred cow." Funke's sarcasm thus signals a significant aspect of Woolf's iconicity at the time the play appeared, a form of protectionism that needs to be distinguished from her iconization by feminists during the 1970s; an example of this attitude occurs in a review of the film that begins, "No one would be particularly surprised if that fine and sensitive English novelist Virginia Woolf were turning over in her grave at every mention of the most talked-about movie these days," not because of the title (she liked a joke) or the treatment of illusion and reality, "but because of the foul language and profanity."[6] Albee himself showed a certain amount of compunction about the title: he wrote to Leonard Woolf for permission to use Woolf's name, apparently worried, in Malcolm Muggeridge's telling of the story, that "in view of Virginia's tragic end, it might be distasteful to her relict."[7]

Virginia Woolf's presence in the title would not have incited this particular protective response if the play had been other than it was: an acid depiction of the destructive and self-destructive words and actions of two academic couples at a small New England college. Both couples are childless. The older couple (George, a historian, and Martha, the college president's daughter) and the newly arrived younger couple (Nick, a biologist, and Honey) enact a night of "fun and games," the title of the first act, punctuated by heavy drinking and characterized by the viciously funny undermining of the others' pretenses and defenses. The titles of the following acts, "Walpurgisnacht" and "The Exorcism," give some sense of this interaction from hell, which ends only after George's exorcism of the fantasy son he and Martha had created and maintained between them.

But the angst created by the play's title and content had deeper roots than protecting an individual writer; looked at more closely, the reception reveals a tangled web of social, cultural, and sexual anxieties. At the most

obvious level, perhaps, Virginia Woolf's cultural class or literary persona
appears to be the issue: her long-standing association with high culture,
the British intellectual aristocracy, and a femininity that is both ascetic
and aesthetic. We are on familiar ground here: that place where the battle-
of-the-brows, particularly as manifested in the United States, finds itself
so ambivalent about Virginia Woolf, only now it is not just middlebrow
culture but its links to mass culture that become the perceived threat. The
British reviews were generally more explicit about the play's contribution
to these battles than the American (one said it had "a lowbrows-will-
be-persecuted title");[8] they were also more ironic. It was the New York
intellectual Diana Trilling who undertook to critique *Virginia Woolf,* as
the play immediately became known, for its cultural pretensions.

At first glance a reading of Virginia Woolf from the perspective of
cultural class would appear self-evident; as noted above, the image of her
that dominated the intellectual world in the States was the upper-middle-
class, snobbish, intellectual aristocrat with impeccable literary and social
credentials, definitely a lady and definitely a highbrow. At this level the
title becomes an academic or intellectual joke, made possible by the happy
conjunction of her name with the animal in the fairytale and the Disney
song.[9] Here again Lewis Funke provides an insight into the way the title
was initially read. Three weeks after his sarcasm about the angry letters
he'd received, he passed on to his *Times* readers the information that in
the mid-thirties Professor John Hawley Roberts of Williams College used
to give an extracurricular lecture on Woolf with the title "Who's Afraid of
Virginia Woolf?" a title that rather than being "a sneer at a writer" was
meant to encourage readers who might at first glance find her too difficult.[10]
In contrast the "sneer" perceived in Albee's use of the phrase and in his
play would be equivalent to thumbing one's nose at a figure associated
with (European) standards of taste and authority, of order, civilization,
manners—an act of defiance. This reading is supported by Janet Flanner's
report on the Paris production in the *New Yorker,* where she records that
the French saw the "American academic couple . . . as true and informative
natives of our land and . . . the complete opposites of any professional
couple imaginably connected with the Sorbonne."[11]

Trilling's essay, published originally in *Esquire* as "Who's Afraid of the
Culture Elite?" with the epigraph "You are, Reader: that's why it's so
reassuring to see intellectuals at each other's throats," and in a slightly
different version in her *Claremont Essays* as "The Riddle of Albee's *Who's
Afraid of Virginia Woolf?*" accepts the association of Virginia Woolf
with high culture but reads the title less as an act of defiance than as
an act of appropriation: a dangerous blurring of distinctions between

the cultural classes.[12] For Trilling the riddle is why this play, which she intensely disliked and which she describes as a "canvas of hopelessness and desperation," whose message, like that found in so many areas of contemporary culture, is that "life is nothing, and we must have the courage to face our emptiness without fear," should be so extraordinarily popular among "the American theatregoing public, . . . decent respectable middle-class people" (211, 214, 211). Her answer is that its popularity has less to do with its explicit message than with its concealed purpose and appeal: its seduction of its audience by granting them a sense of privilege, of being "in," in "an exclusive club," a cultural club or "closed circuit" (a phrase she borrows from Mary McCarthy) located within the play in an academic, intellectual community where "virtue . . . is defined by taste" (218–19, 217, 221). In this light, the intellectual joke inscribed in the title is directed to the audience, which receives a "gift of cultural status" (221) by having shared in what Trilling identifies as the play's very specific class humor: "the humor of the present-day intellectual class"; it participates in "a conspicuous consumption of literacy" ("Culture Elite," 82). People go to the play, as they read advertisements, to learn "the signals by which we advance in prestige and leave the indiscriminate democratic masses behind us" (224).

Although Trilling deplores the elitism promoted by the culture club, she is *not* making an argument for a democratic middlebrow or mass culture, which she calls variously a "fabrication" or a "monolithic culture," dictated by the "officers of the cultural club" (226). While she is willing to admit that her own cultural location in a university community made the wit (if not the academics uttering it) familiar to her—even more, that it "made me feel cozy and privileged . . . to have this advantage over other members of the audience" ("Culture Elite," 74)—she rejects the idea of cultural diffusion. Mass art's borrowing from high art, she concludes, its narrowing of the divide between the two, might be perceived as a victory for democracy, but for her it represents something different and dangerous: an attitude of conformity, linked to the "complacency of the radical intellectual" in the postwar period, that needs to be exposed and fought (226–27).[13] "The cultural radical has become a Broadway success— and this alone should be enough to alert us to the need to reassess his premises" (227).

What Trilling feared, then, was not Virginia Woolf as aristocratic arbiter of taste but the homogenization of culture, associated in part with a democratization of education and changes in the media that characterized American cultural life in the early 1960s, and the particular ideological stance inscribed by this process. The new cultural establishment and the new academicism, she laments, have appropriated what *appears* to be "our most radical impulse in the theatre," a phenomenon that extends far beyond cosmopolitan New York: "Tomorrow it will be everyone in the United States who will have the requisite sophistication for Mr. Albee's play, having been prepared for it, if not by their novels, then by their television programs, and if not by their television programs, then by their mass-circulation magazines" (225–26). Significantly, Trilling's source for the latter is the editor of a "slick women's magazine," who told her that in order to succeed "every smooth-paper magazine . . . had to make a decision, whether to try to strengthen its mass appeal or raid *Partisan Review*," and that only those who chose to go with the intellectuals increased their circulation ("Culture Elite," 88).[14] Again the message is clear: what we see in this process is not an elevation but a dangerous leveling of art and culture.

At this point the contradictory status accorded Virginia Woolf in the high-low discourse constructed by American intellectuals in the postwar period becomes significant. Fourteen years earlier, reviewing the reissue of the *Common Reader*s and a posthumous collection of Woolf's essays, Trilling had dismissed the writer as a culturally insignificant icon, arguing that she represented a form of elitism that, while pleasant enough to share for a moment or two, was not only gender- and class-specific but divorced from the material realities of the broader social community.[15] Now, however, as Trilling turned away from a community perceived to be more and more influenced by the cultural manipulation exemplified by Albee's play, she is forced to recognize Virginia Woolf as a sign whose cultural significance was greater than she, Trilling, had been willing to admit: to see her as an emblem of the true cultural elite under attack by Albee and the "mass *non*-thinking" (227) he and his play represent:

> *Who's Afraid of Virginia Woolf?* Mr. Albee calls his play, and even this title, which really has no perceptible relation to the story Mr. Albee is telling, suddenly reveals its purpose. Who indeed need be afraid of the lady-writer of Bloomsbury, that quintessential literary aristocrat whose cultural fortress could once be thought so impregnable to the assaults of a vulgar democracy? Certainly not Mr. Albee, or George and Martha, or Nick and Honey. And certainly not a public let in on Mr. Albee's cultural secret—that distinction, whether of birth or achievement, is merely a joke, that the values which once supported our society no longer prevail, and that modern man is on his desperate, ugly, and meaningless own. ("Culture Elite," 83)

But however powerfully Virginia Woolf, both the persona and the play, may function as a synecdoche for class distinctions in the intellectual realm Trilling claimed as her own—however much Trilling fears Virginia Woolf's appropriation by a mass culture meant to lull us into a false complacency—the focus and fears of the mainstream media took a different direction, one that proved immensely significant for subsequent articulations of Virginia Woolf in the popular realm. Here Virginia Woolf signifies less cultural class than an ambiguous and, to many, a monstrous sexuality. Before turning to this other response, however, I want to note that Trilling's ambivalence about Virginia Woolf's cultural status already anticipates the eruption of gender and sexuality into the discourse, pointing once again to the strong tradition that identifies high culture, high art, including the modernism that for many exemplified high art's last beleaguered moment, as masculine and mass culture as feminine.[16] The figure of Virginia Woolf inscribes the fault lines revealed in this tradition when an actual woman, not "Woman" or "the feminine," is involved, and the play, in terms of both its title and its reception, makes them visible. The title, that is, leads in two different directions. One puts Virginia Woolf and the fear she evokes on the side of high culture, a high culture that is either cheekily defied or dangerously appropriated, depending on your point of view. The other associates the fear elicited by Virginia Woolf with fear of the feminine or feminized masses, including those who read popular culture ("slick women's magazines"), and hence with fear of consumption (or of being consumed), of excess, of the potential destruction or feminization of the cultural (not to mention the political) powers that be. This projection ties Virginia Woolf to the fear of dominant women and of gender blurring that characterizes the popular reception of the play and the film.

Again the title provides an entrée. Albee himself explained publicly only that he had seen the phrase written on a blackboard in a bar in Greenwich Village;[17] what he didn't say was that it was a gay bar. The latter is crucial to one increasingly explicit subtext in the discourse surrounding *Virginia Woolf*: that associated with (male) homosexuality and its complex intersections with both homophobia and misogyny.

One of the first expressions of this subtext occurs in a letter to the drama editor of the *New York Times* on December 2, 1962, about six weeks after the play's opening:

> I was at a party the other night where a gentleman gleefully clapped his hands and said: "Isn't it marvelous? All the married couples seeing 'Who's Afraid of Virginia Woolf?' will go home and act in the same way and pretty soon men and women will be living like homosexual

pairs." And there, it suddenly struck me, is the key to the play: it is not about men and women; it is about male homosexuals. The author has extrapolated the vicious, waspish, gratuitous destructiveness of people living in special circumstances to all people. His gifts have allowed him to get away with it, but the play is deeply flawed at its heart and, I think, invalidated. I don't suppose this can be discussed in print, but what a pity, as you once wrote, that the homosexual influence is so pervasive—and distorting—in our theater.[18]

By the spring of 1963 the discussion had gone more or less public both in the *New York Times* and in theater journals. Howard Taubman's "Modern Primer: Helpful Hints to Tell Appearances vs. Truth," published in the *Times* in April 1963, provides "helpful hints on how to scan the intimations and symbols of homosexuality in our theater," most of which pointed directly to Albee's conspicuously unnamed play. "If only," he ends, "we could recover our lost innocence and could believe that people on the stage are what they are supposed to be!"[19] Unlike Taubman, Richard Schechner, in an editorial "Comment" in the *Tulane Drama Review,* names names, explicitly using *Virginia Woolf* to make essentially the same point. His list of everything wrong with contemporary American theater states "I'm tired of morbidity and sexual perversity which are there only to titillate an impotent and homosexual theatre and audience," before concluding that "the lie of [Albee's] work is the lie of our theatre and the lie of America. The lie of decadence must be fought . . . for it is a lie in current usage these days, and one which is likely to have an infective and corrosive influence on our theatre."[20]

The links among Albee's play, the "special circumstances" of homosexuals, and the corrosive influence of homosexuality in the theater increased during the next few years, revealing the depths of homophobia in the culture. By the time the film was reviewed, this response had filtered down to the popular press. *Newsweek*'s reviewer was explicit about both the homosexuality and what it represented: "[Albee] has not really written about men and women, with a potential for love and sex, however withered the potential may be. He has written about saber-toothed humans who cannot reproduce, and who need to draw buckets of blood before they can feel compassion for each other."[21]

What do these reviewers fear? Albee, writing years after the fact, perceives the reading of the couples as gay as a heterosexual defense mechanism: "because it would let them off the hook; they don't have to think that the play is about themselves." Vito Russo, in his study of homosexuality in the movies, likewise argues that this particular reading of the play is a "straight fantasy," though to different ends: "How else could this unmarried playwright know so much about *their* lives?"[22] But more is at stake than homophobia in these responses to Albee's study of impotence and sterility, personal and cultural; misogyny is as well, leading me to ask once again, what do these reviewers fear? Is it the feminizing effect of male homosexuality? Or the threat of strong women like Martha, the female protagonist, whose role as castrating bitch is commented on by almost every reviewer of the play if not the film, where Martha's power is generally believed to be eclipsed by George's? (One critic, for example, in his search for the "source of the savage events that follow," asks, "Is it some acquired sexual frigidity which causes her to seek gratification in a constant emasculative assault on her husband?")[23] Most tantalizing, what's Virginia Woolf got to do with it?

From our perspective today one obvious place to start answering these questions is Bloomsbury; situating ourselves there, we can see Albee's play and its reception anticipating the appearance of Michael Holroyd's biography of Lytton Strachey in 1968 and the subsequent flood of memoirs and biographies that made the homosexuality and bisexuality of its members public knowledge. Although the initial performance of the play in New York preceded the emergence of the Bloomsbury phenomenon, as well as of an openly gay culture and press after Stonewall (1969), enough underground knowledge existed in the gay community and in the theater community to link the name Virginia Woolf to a homosexual subplot and, hence, to alarm its attuned but antipathetic straight reviewers. By 1966, when the film appeared, the cultural terrain had shifted, making the threat of the perceived homosexual subtext more worrying and hence more susceptible to popular condemnation. One aspect of the shift suggests the emergence of camp into public consciousness and discourse, associated in part with Susan Sontag's influential "Notes on 'Camp'" in 1964.[24] The camp element had been implicit in the play from the beginning, located in Martha's imitation in the opening scene of the line made famous by Bette Davis, a camp idol, "What a dump!"[25] This line, Marjorie Garber reminds us, was "a staple of female impersonators," a history, one commentator implies, that led Bette Davis, who was Albee's first choice for the role of Martha in the film, to refuse "to play it, and rightfully so! because it is really a part for a drag queen."[26] When Liz Taylor did her rendition, the scene took on an added layer of campiness, and imitations of Liz imitating Bette became a staple of the gay party scene.

But Bloomsbury, and to some extent camp, however obvious as referents today and however much a part of the gay underground they may have been at the time, remain afterthoughts; the initial attacks on the play's closeted homosexuality evoke less Bloomsbury and/or camp than the anxieties surrounding the (insidious) inroads made by homosexuality and, I would argue, feminism in the culture at large during the 1960s. Philip Roth's hostile 1965 *NYRB* review of Albee's *Tiny Alice,* "The Play That Dare Not Speak Its Name," for example, may criticize both plays for not being openly homosexual, but it describes their subject as "emasculation . . . male weakness, female strength, and the limits of human knowledge."[27]

At this point in my argument the implication that *Virginia Woolf* is a closet play, a genre in which homosexuality, often defined as a condition that cannot enter language directly and has therefore concealed itself within a dominant discourse, forces us to look more closely at the specific signs read by the critics as revealing the secret: to explore the moment when all the signs come together to reveal the couples to be not "men and women, with a potential for love and sex," as *Newsweek* put it, but "saber-toothed humans who cannot reproduce." In this context the childlessness of the two couples, taken by most reviewers to signify the sterility of contemporary life in general, takes on a more ominous cultural meaning, one in which the two childless women become the focus. And this in turn introduces the powerful intertwining of homophobia and misogyny in the play, its reception, and the culture at large. Several things are at stake here. First, to the extent that the play was perceived as a masquerade for male homosexual relations, the misogyny directed toward Martha raises the vexed issue of male homosexual misogyny. For Sky Gilbert, whose critique of the play resides in his desire for an openly gay theater, closet plays in general and Albee's in particular are characterized in part by their misogynous representation of women, often located in a fear of women's physicality and sexuality. The "constant references by George to Martha's promiscuity and her bulk," Gilbert argues, not only make her horrifying, but evoke the taboos still prohibiting women's expression of their sexual desires. But as Gilbert also notes, if *Virginia Woolf* were really about gay men, this representation would be homophobic, not misogynistic, linked less to a fear of women than to fear of the gay lifestyle itself: an aspect of homophobia that Gilbert, like other postliberation gay critics, believes is endemic to closet plays.[28] Given the complexity of the strands here, we would do well to heed Alexander Doty's warning that while "men have misogyny in common, . . . gay men's misogyny . . . needs to be discussed with more attention to its specific psychological and cultural foundations and patterns."[29]

But other forces, other cultural patterns, are at work as well when it comes to the intersecting fears evoked by the play. One resides in Leslie Fiedler's derisive characterization of the increasing feminization of culture

in the early 1960s, exemplified by what he calls the "new mutants,"
including its "polymorphous perversity":

> If in *Who's Afraid of Virginia Woolf?* Albee can portray the relation-
> ship of two homosexuals (one in drag) as the model of contemporary
> marriage, this must be because contemporary marriage has in fact
> turned into something much like that parody. And it is true that
> what survives of bourgeois marriage and the bourgeois family is a
> target which the new barbarians join the old homosexuals in reviling,
> seeking to replace Mom, Pop and the kids with a neo-Whitmanian
> gaggle of giggling *camerados*.[30]

Martha, moreover, frightens for more reasons than her role as "giggling
camerado" or her manifestation as drag queen; she also frightens by her
(masculine) strength. Cynthia Grenier, one of the few women to review
the play, saw the Paris production and had no trouble detecting that "the
'Virginia Woolf' [the characters] are afraid of, of course—there is no way
around this, a hundred details in the play point to it—is the specter of the
dominant female."[31]

Finally, we need to factor in a central facet of *Virginia Woolf*'s representation of both Martha and Honey, the younger, more traditionally
"feminine" woman in the play: their shared childlessness. For in 1962
one of the areas where fear of women was beginning to manifest itself
was that of reproduction: a fear linked to the development of the Pill
and the specter of women taking control not just of their sexuality but of
procreation as well.

Some facts are pertinent here. The first contraceptive pill, Enovid,
was approved by the FDA in May 1960. As David Halberstam tells the
subsequent story, "By the end of 1961 some 408,000 American women
were taking the Pill, by the end of 1962 the figure was 1,187,000, and by
the end of 1963 it was 2.3 million and still rising. Of it, Clare Boothe Luce
said, 'Modern woman is at last free as a man is free, to dispose of her own
body, to earn her living, to pursue the improvement of her mind, to try
a successful career.' " Gloria Steinem seemed to bear this out in her 1962
Esquire article "The Moral Disarmament of Betty Coed," which talked
explicitly about college girls' wanting to take the Pill and their feeling that
they did not have "to choose between a career and marriage." For Fiedler
the usurpation of birth control by female "new mutants" during the 1960s
exemplified one of the most virulent forms of the feminization/feminist-
ization of the culture; whereas "the invention of the condom had at least
left the decision to inhibit fatherhood in the power of males, its replacement

by the 'loop' and the 'pill' has placed paternity at the mercy of the whims of women."[32]

In the destabilization that characterized the decade, then, women became powerful—and frightening—by refusing to become mothers, the role enacted within *Virginia Woolf* by the younger Honey. George, the older man, the historian, understands the implications. Having badgered Honey into confessing she is scared of getting pregnant, he asks her, "How do you do it? Hunh? How do you make your secret little murders stud-boy doesn't know about, hunh? Pills? PILLS?" (177). Coupled with the earlier statement that she threw up regularly, this question accuses Honey not of using birth control (though *the* Pill shadows the statement), but of what Robert Brustein, reviewing the play, calls "surreptitious abortions."[33]

Again, some perspective is needed; as one document on abortion during the 1950s and 1960s makes clear, a woman could get "drugstore abortifacients" from "her 'friendly' druggist" at the time, "which, all expensive, endanger her life to varying degrees and almost never work." Among these were "suppository tablets of potassium permanganate, a caustic tissue-destroying agent that damages the vagina walls and can cause massive hemorrhaging, ulcers, and infection"; "quinine pills and Humphrey's Eleven pills," which are useless; and "castor oil and other strong purgatives," which similarly have no effect.[34] When the pills failed you could, if you had money and contacts, arrange an illegal abortion, and women did; whether any woman would go through this process month after month, as the play suggests Honey does, is another question. Nevertheless, George and/or Albee as well as the (male) critics not only seem to believe in the effectiveness of these pills but to fear them. To this end Honey becomes an exemplar of all those things that Brustein, whose article is headed "Albee and the Medusa-Head," argues Albee and we fear in contemporary life but cannot yet face directly: "For if Albee can confront the Medusa-head without the aid of parlor tricks or mirrors, he may yet turn us all to stone."[35]

Brustein's metaphor makes explicit the overt and covert links in our culture between childlessness and a deadly monstrosity, including their imbrication in the intertwined discourses of homophobia and misogyny. In this way the play and its reception establish a motif that recurs obsessively in popular representations of Virginia Woolf to this day. For one thing, the *Newsweek* film reviewer was not alone in characterizing homosexuals by their lack of reproduction; the inability—or refusal—to reproduce becomes a marker of homosexuality and of Albee's play even for those more sympathetic to homosexuality itself. But true to societal bias, when this refusal *is* presented sympathetically, the nonreproductive figure becomes George, not Honey or Martha, and he emerges as a "hero."

This is the message of Donald Kaplan's 1965 "Homosexuality and American Theatre: A Psychoanalytic Comment," a response to the "increasing alarm" generated by *Virginia Woolf*. Kaplan explains the play's success by its implicit endorsement of the idea that genital sexuality and procreation—especially the ability of *men* to perform in this way—can be successfully resisted without loss of power or sexuality, however perverse (in the psychoanalytic sense) this sexuality might be: "Albee's answer . . . is that genitality is after all an unnecessary burden—the audience sighs with relief—and that one can prevail through the tactics of pregenital perversity, precisely as George prevails. The sexuality of the parental bedroom (Nick and Martha offstage) is no match for the multifarious derivatives of George's oral aggression, anality, voyeurism, masochism, and procreative reluctance." Later, quoting Herbert Marcuse, Kaplan notes: " 'Psychoanalytic theory sees in the practices that exclude or prevent procreation an opposition against continuing the chain of reproduction and thereby of paternal domination.' The homosexual, then, is a rebel. . . ."[36]

And in this paradigm a man; female homosexuality is not part of Kaplan's equation. Instead, women who do not reproduce, whether by choice (rebelliously) or because, like Martha, they do not conceive, are far less reassuring; in fact, they become monstrous. Blaming her husband for the lack of a child, Martha turns against him, transforming her thwarted desire into acts of psychological destruction. I would maintain that this dynamic dominates *Virginia Woolf* despite the fact that it is George who "kills" their fantasy child, an act that can be read as a triumph over his monstrous wife. But the mostly male critics didn't see it that way, arguing almost to a man that the fantasy child and its "murder" were unbelievable; in the process they show a stunning blindness to the realities of the pressures on childless women—whether in the 1950s when the "feminine mystique" predominated, or in the 1960s in a society increasingly worried about gender blurring and women's sexual and reproductive freedom, or, for that matter, in the first part of the century when Virginia Woolf embodied the childless woman. No wonder Martha wants to maintain the fiction of her womanhood.[37]

One final take on Martha's unnaturalness occurs in a scene written into the film script by Ernest Lehman and later removed. Working against Martha's verbal denials within the play ("I'm loud, and I'm vulgar, and I wear the pants in this house because somebody's got to, but I am *not* a monster. I am *not*" [157]), Lehman represented Martha "seated at her dressing table" using "an eyebrow pencil to apply a mustache and connect her eyebrows; she becomes at once a man and a monster (the Cyclops that George calls her), two dominating but finally oppressive roles."[38]

At this point I want to step back from both Trilling's horror at the play's undoing of class distinctions and the strong responses to its queering of the heterosexual family to look more closely at two of the mythic figures projected to signify the fear evoked by Virginia Woolf: Medusa and the Sphinx. Both are distinctly female; both are traditionally perceived as destructive. Brustein introduces Medusa into the discourse surrounding the play, linking her directly to Virginia Woolf: everything we fear but cannot yet face directly; the Sphinx enters through Albee's title, with its status as a riddle that we need to answer in order to survive. But survive what? Here, we need to turn to the Sphinx's appearances in the long-standing discourse that equates the masses with the "mob" or "crowd" and genders them all feminine. As Andreas Huyssen describes this discourse at the end of the nineteenth century, a time when culture, as in the 1960s, was facing not only feminization but feminism, a fear of the mob and of revolution was inseparable from "a fear of woman, a fear of nature out of control, a fear of the unconscious, of sexuality, of the loss of identity and stable ego boundaries in the mass." For Gustave Le Bon, writing during this turbulent period, the danger of the crowd was best understood through the figure of the Sphinx. "Crowds," he wrote, "are somewhat like the sphinx of ancient fable: it is necessary to arrive at a solution of the problems offered by their psychology or to resign ourselves to being devoured by them."[39] Albee's title may be only one of a number of riddles within the play, but it has the first and the last word; tauntingly introduced by Martha at the beginning, George, in his victory over her, appropriates it for the penultimate line. As a result, that which we must understand or risk being devoured by is Virginia Woolf.[40]

The conjunction of images that links Medusa, Sphinx, and Virginia Woolf radiates outward in a number of critical directions. One, which points to the anxieties of the early 1960s that I have been tracing, suggests the powerful role gender played both in discourses about the family and in the discourses surrounding high and mass culture during the period, an intersection we can again link to the entrance of women into areas where their presence was previously limited. To illustrate this, we need only ask, why not *Who's Afraid of Thomas Wolfe?* The pun would still work (though the Disney song wouldn't), the hint of high culture and its defiance would still be there, but we would lose the fear of the feminization/feminist-ization of culture that Fiedler makes so clear. Mass or popular culture may well use a figure from high culture to legitimize itself and seduce its audience, as Trilling argued Albee's play did, but when that figure is a woman, especially a strong woman, she brings with her the threat of annihilation as well. Men can never be that scary.

Medusa, however, is. Here the conjunction of Medusa, Sphinx, and Virginia Woolf moves us in less localized directions. One, rooted in Freud's equation of Medusa with castration, points to the associations made between Medusa's head and male hysteria; another to studies of Medusa and the evil eye; and still a third to readings of the Medusa story as a ritual sacrifice for the sake of the community.[41] But any approach to Medusa and the Sphinx must confront the dominant affect at work, fear and perhaps envy: a fear of powerful female figures that, among other things, locates the violence perpetrated against women in the women themselves. (Medusa, you may recall, is in some versions of the story a beautiful woman who was punished by Athena for having either attracted the attentions of Poseidon or been raped by him.) From this perspective, women too have much to fear in this construction of Virginia Woolf; they have certainly understood the stakes. Patricia Joplin, for example, exploring the intersection of violence and the repression of women's voices, writes that "Behind the victim's head that turns men to stone may lie the victim stoned to death by men." And Teresa de Lauretis prefaces an analysis of the silencing of women's desire in narrative and culture with the rhetorical question, "What became of the Sphinx after the encounter with Oedipus on his way to Thebes? Or, how did Medusa feel seeing herself in Perseus' mirror just before being slain?"[42]

De Lauretis's response to her revisionary riddle foregrounds yet another aspect of the conjunction of Medusa, Sphinx, and Virginia Woolf at work in the construction of Virginia Woolf's popular persona. Although the answers are known—at least to the question about the Sphinx, who committed suicide (an end not inconsequential to the fear evoked by Virginia Woolf, as at least one reviewer of Albee's play noted at the time)[43]—de Lauretis argues that we don't know them offhand because "Medusa and the Sphinx, like the other ancient monsters, have survived inscribed in hero narratives, in someone else's story, not their own."[44] For the most part, that is, although there are exceptions, women have not been represented in our culture as either heroes or creators of culture.

This leads to my final question about Albee's play: does its foregrounding of Virginia Woolf make her, and with her Medusa and the Sphinx, a potentially heroic figure? If not, what would it take to effect this transformation? Can she cross the gender divide and become the kind of heroic figure that both legends and heroic reputations are based on in our culture? Or, does her appearance in Albee's play make her a star: an image open to reconfiguration by a variety of subcultures for ends that challenge the legitimacy of the prevailing boundaries and alter the cultural terrain? Both,

I would say, depending on where you look, as the following takes illustrate, where the attempts of Woolf's family and the "intellectual" media to contain the image, to keep it from becoming heroic, while capitalizing on its star quality, increasingly vie with a proliferation of uncontainable Virginia Woolfs. For once Albee had made Virginia Woolf a part of the popular, once she had become a household term whose naturalized, descriptive meaning was inseparable from fear, she became subject to articulations and rearticulations that not only track the ups and downs of feminism, but indicate the power of popular representations to shape cultural meanings.

QUENTIN BELL'S BIOGRAPHY

AND HISTORICAL PRODUCTS INC.:

FAMILY PORTRAITS

The publication of *A Writer's Diary,* Frances Spalding observes, "did much to stir interest in Virginia Woolf as a person and before long Leonard Woolf had three distinguished biographers—the Countess of Huntingdon, Leon Edel and Joanna Richardson—all wanting to write her biography. He chose his nephew, Quentin Bell, and the first authorised biography of Virginia Woolf appeared in 1972."[1] In Hermione Lee's telling of the story, the choice of Bell was part of Leonard's " 'husbanding' " of her public appearances, entailing the decision "that the first biography should be written by a member of the family."[2] By the time Bell's two-volume work was published, however, Leonard was dead and Virginia was well on her way to becoming a figure or sign far beyond the control of the family. The near-simultaneous appearances of *Virginia Woolf: A Biography* and the original Historical Products Inc.'s T-shirt featuring Virginia Woolf's face mark a key moment in the increasingly diverse and divisive articulations of Virginia Woolf icon. For the image and circulation of Virginia Woolf generated by the T-shirt phenomenon created an alternative discourse to that evoked by the Bell biography; from then on, Virginia Woolf would become a primary site for the waging of a large number of cultural battles, not least among them those about feminism and its challenges to established authorities.

The years 1972 and 1973 set the stage for these confrontations. In the United States, where the women's movement had begun to make its mark, the 1972 presidential election that pitted Richard Nixon against George McGovern gave us not only Watergate but Shirley Chisholm, the first African American woman to run for president. Coeducation and affirmative action were going strong. Dartmouth College, the last of the previously all-male Ivies, admitted women in September 1972; Congress passed Title IX of the Education Amendments, a law aimed at prohibiting sex discrimination in federally assisted educational institutions, and sent the Equal Rights Amendment to the states to be ratified. Then, in February 1973, the Supreme Court decision in *Roe v. Wade* ensured a woman's legal right to abortion. Meanwhile, women's studies was becoming a reality, not just in the creation of academic programs but in the intensive un-earthing of ignored and forgotten women writers and artists and thinkers at all levels of culture. In 1972 the academic journal *Feminist Studies* began publishing; by 1973 approximately 5,000 women's studies courses were being offered in the United States.[3] On the streets, *Ms.* magazine published its first issue in July 1972; Jill Johnston, outspoken author of *Lesbian Nation,* was writing a regular column in the *Village Voice; Our Bodies, Ourselves,* originally published in 1970 by a small Boston press, went commercial; Alix Kates Shulman published *Memoirs of an Ex–Prom Queen;* and in March *Time* published a special issue, "The New Woman, 1972."[4] Style also plays a role in this story, becoming increasingly androgynous; in 1973, for example, Levi-Strauss won two achievement awards for the creation of jeans and for changing the lifestyle of both sexes in the States.[5]

The years 1972 and 1973 also play a central role in stories of the changes in artistic and perceptual frameworks associated with postmodernism and poststructuralism, which also posed challenges to established authorities. David Simpson, for example, points to the 1973 publication of Hay-don White's *Metahistory,* "a study roughly coincident with the incursion of French poststructuralist theories into the anglophone academy," as a crucial marker of the moment. White's revisionary theorization of what constitutes history, with its emphasis on the " 'linguistic protocol' " used by the historiographer " 'to fashion a "story" out of the "chronicle" of events contained in the historical record,' " destabilized the writing of history and, we could add, the writing of biography; history and biography reemerged as storytelling or narrative rather than documentary or factual "truth."[6] By 1972–73, that is, the theoretical and critical frameworks asso-ciated with poststructuralism, postmodernism, and discourse theory that would increasingly destabilize traditional claims for narrative as well as cultural authority were gaining strength, including those that emphasized the crucial role of language, discourse, and performativity in constructing knowledge, power, and truth.

Virginia Woolf was in the thick of the action, both feminist and postmodernist, as responses to the Bell biography illustrate. In charting these responses and their inscription of the deeply ideological cultural battles being fought at the time, I want to concentrate on four interrelated points. Each one provides insights into the diverse roles a post-Albee Virginia Woolf began to play during this pivotal moment and the emerging contradictions within her increasingly intertextual and multifaceted star image.

The first focuses on diversity itself, in particular the diversity of the cultural sites where by this time Virginia Woolf regularly appeared. Robert Gish's overview of the American scene in his review succinctly makes the point:

> The increasing interest in Virginia Woolf is accounted for in large part by the latest surge in the feminist movement which finds in her an old friend. Try to order *A Room of One's Own* for class use and read the publisher's reply: "Unavailable at this time." Read the Autumn 1972 issue of *Modern Fiction Studies,* a special Virginia Woolf issue, and note the feminist stance of many of the articles. Read *The Politics of Literature* (Pantheon Books, 1972), which ends on the question, "Who's Afraid of A Room of One's Own?" Appropriately, the first issue of *The Virginia Woolf Quarterly* is recently out. And self-confident co-eds may be heard referring to the Virginia Woolf they read about in *Ms.* magazine. The Virginia Woolf bibliography swells *in the library and the drug store.* [My emphasis.][7]

The overlap between library and drugstore is central to Virginia Woolf's increasing visibility and popular personae, for unlike the reception of *A Writer's Diary,* reviews of the Bell biography extended beyond the literary and intellectual press; both *Time* and *Newsweek,* for example, having reviewed the work, included it in their list of the year's best books.

My second point concerns the reasons offered by reviewers for Virginia Woolf's surging popularity: the rise of feminism; the interest in Bloomsbury; and the widespread notoriety achieved by Albee's play, especially in its movie version. Almost no one attributes it to her novels or her stature as a writer, modernist or otherwise. When her literary reputation is mentioned, it is often to complain (especially if the reviewer is American) that enough is enough: we don't need any more criticism of her admittedly experimental but ultimately not very significant novels, which have been talked to death by academics as it is.[8]

To a certain extent the authority for this exclusion resides in what is my third point: Quentin Bell's decision *not* to make the work a literary biography: *not* to explore her writings; reviewers predisposed to discount the novels responded by arguing that given their critical overexposure, this was a good thing.[9] Instead, Bell, who noted that his "purpose" in writing was *"purely historical,"* chose to concentrate on providing "a clear and *truthful* account of the character and personal development of my subject,"[10] and this, we know, is what the public had long been waiting for. Writing in the *New Yorker,* William Maxwell is blunt: "what one wants to know about and has always wanted to know about, is Sir Leslie Stephen's high-strung, overimaginative youngest daughter." What did they find? Again, Gish's review nicely sums it up: "Insanity, incest, homosexuality, lesbianism, promiscuity, frigidity, hate, envy, snobbery, love, friendship, artistic genius."[11] Who could ask for anything more?

A few reviewers did, but before turning to them I want to note some of the ramifications of the reception I have already mentioned, including an irony neither Bell nor his enthusiastic reviewers could have anticipated: the ways in which his revelations, rather than fixing Virginia Woolf's image and meanings, opened the door to the fragmentations, contradictions, and competing versions of Virginia Woolf that followed. The result was to produce numerous Virginia Woolfs that Quentin Bell subsequently spent a great deal of time trying, unsuccessfully, to repudiate or erase—an impossible task. Once the details of her life became part of her star image, once they were available for consumption, the process of rearticulating them took on a life of its own.[12] This process accelerated in the years after the biography as her letters and diaries appeared, but even in the initial reviews the fractures, expressing clearly demarcated ideological positions, were beginning to show.

These fractures extended even to those aspects of Virginia Woolf's image considered central to her popularity: her role as feminist icon and her reigning position in Bloomsbury. Not surprisingly, the most immediately visible fracture occurs in the reaction against the articulation of a political, feminist Virginia Woolf by an increasingly powerful women's movement. Also not surprisingly, this reaction, condescending and dismissive, appears most often in the self-styled "intellectual" press in the United States; in Britain, where feminism had not made as many inroads and where class and cultural class more than gender were still at the top of the agenda, no threat was perceived and hence no counterattack deemed necessary. The sharpest and most specific critique comes from William Pritchard, who warns his *Hudson Review* readers against those who would make her "the feminist heroine who preceded Sylvia Plath—artists, though married, who eventually cracked under it all"—and deems "particularly offensive" Jill Johnston's attempt in the *Village Voice* "to add Virginia Woolf to her ever-burgeoning list of tragic lesbians."[13]

When women, particularly those who acknowledge Virginia Woolf's feminism, enter into the debate they bring a different set of concerns, one that reflects divisions about what constitutes an appropriate feminist theory and practice. The unwitting dialogue between Cynthia Ozick, often named as a possible successor to Susan Sontag for the position of Dark Lady among New York intellectuals and committed to most of their positions, writing in *Commentary,* and Barbara Hardy, one of the first British academic feminist critics, writing in the *Spectator,* provides one clear example. Their disagreement can be read in terms of broader disagreements between a feminism that emphasizes sameness or equality and a feminism that emphasizes difference, a debate in which both—or more accurately all—sides claim Virginia Woolf as their authority, locating their feminist politics in her own. But first they had to establish that Virginia Woolf was "political," a process necessitated by Leonard Woolf's categorical assertion that "Virginia was the least political animal that has lived since Aristotle invented the definition," an assertion that Bell, most reviewers, and many subsequent writers on Virginia Woolf uncritically accept as the last word on the subject.[14]

Ozick agrees with Bell that Virginia Woolf "was not political—or, perhaps, just political enough, as when Chekhov notes that 'writers should engage themselves in politics only enough to protect themselves from politics,' " but she strongly disagrees with Bell's portrait of Virginia Woolf, offering as "antidotes" "the autonomous authority of the fiction, the more public authority of the essays," and that which is "implicit in the whole of the work and in the drive behind the work": "Virginia Woolf's feminism." But this feminism, she argues, "was what can now be called 'classical' feminism," which is "inimical to certain developing strands of 'liberation' ":

Where feminism repudiates the conceit of the "gentler sex," libera- tion has come to reaffirm it. Where feminism asserts a claim on the larger world, liberation shifts to separatism. Where feminism scoffs at the plaint of "sisters under the skin," and maintains individuality of condition and temperament, liberation reinstates sisterhood and sameness. Where feminism shuns self-preoccupation, liberation ex- periments with self-examination, both psychic and medical. Classical feminism as represented by Virginia Woolf meant one thing only: access to the great world of thinking, being, and doing.

As a result, she argues, "the latter-day choice of Virginia Woolf, on the style of Sylvia Plath, as a current women's movement avatar is inapposite and mistaken."[15]

Both Ozick's claiming of Virginia Woolf for a rational feminism aimed at a "unitary culture" defined in terms of the traditional concept of the (male) public sphere and her use of this claim to disparage other versions of contemporary feminism stand in opposition to Hardy's rendering of Virginia Woolf, one that would gain increasing support within the academic community and in popular representations. In Hardy's telling, Virginia Woolf

> struck Quentin Bell as unable to see world events in economic terms, but her radical feminism was a good deal less flimsy than one would infer from reading these pages and not knowing *Three Guineas*. She didn't just tell the Girton girls to emulate masculine comfort, but also asked the urgent question which has to be asked by anyone arguing for sexual, racial, or political equality—are the exclusive privileges worth having? Her contempt for the professional masculine world is a fine one, with real political implications.[16]

But despite the clarity of the competing claims for feminism found here, in most of the reviews feminism is notable for its absence, eclipsed by the seemingly endless discussions of Bloomsbury that reviewers bemoan but can't seem to get enough of. Significantly, the fascination with Bloomsbury comes from its perceived status as precursor to the radical subcultures of the 1960s and early 1970s, a representation of the group and its social/cultural import elaborated more fully and far more subtly by British reviewers than American. Located within the class system they are describing, the British recognize gradations of behavior and attitudes invisible to most mainstream American intellectuals, who often cannot see beyond the privilege and snobbery.[17] The *Times Literary Supplement,* for example, asserts that "it becomes clear that many of the protagonists [of the 'Bloomsbury' world] who experimented with personal relations were claiming freedom from rules and conventions in the name of good sense, honesty, candour and generosity, very much as some young people today assert their freedom on principle." Even those, like Malcolm Muggeridge, who were less inclined to honor either group's motives acknowledge the significance of the overlap: "Nevertheless, interest in the Bloomsburyites would seem to me to be justified . . . because of the great influence they have had on the generations that came after them. So many of their attitudes and ways have become the contemporary fashion, especially among the young. . . . A social historian may well decide that this was, in fact, the birth of the permissive society as we know it today, and that the Bloomsburyites were its true founders; the first dropouts deluxe."[18]

Ultimately, however, the image that emerges most powerfully from the reviews is neither Virginia Woolf feminist nor Virginia Woolf freedom fighter, which brings me to my fourth point: the authority almost universally granted Quentin Bell on the grounds of his family relationship to Woolf. Almost without exception—and the exceptions were all women—no one questioned what it meant that her biographer was her nephew, presumably with a vested interest in the family portrait of Virginia, a portrait premised on the assumption that yes, she was a precocious "genius" (and the deployment of the word *genius* both in the biography and the reviews serves to empty it of any substantial meaning)[19] and extremely good company, but that she was also difficult, delicate, frigid, apolitical, and often out of touch with reality. Families, it should go without saying, have a way of labeling or assigning places to their members that often bears little relationship to the individual's social relations and image in the rest of the world. But again almost without exception, instead of questioning Bell's position vis-à-vis his subject and/or the storytelling nature of biography itself, the vast majority of reviewers credited his inherited insider's view as revealing "the truth" (his own term), granting him an authority that grew even stronger when he began to review subsequent works on Woolf. This "truth" helped create the image of Virginia Woolf as twentieth-century madwoman with a bedroom of her own—witty and malicious, yes, and productive, but again, all of the above: delicate, ethereal, asexual, apolitical, etc.—that survived well into the 1990s and still surfaces today.

Not everyone accepted the official image, however, and the grounds for their objections register both specific countercurrents and a broader postmodern/poststructuralist questioning of whose story counts as "the truth." These reviewers recognize how Bell's linguistic reiterations produce the "reality" he claims merely to document, producing in the process norms that erase alternative perspectives or possibilities. Jill Johnston's *Village Voice* review, "The virgins of the stacks," so offensive to Pritchard, takes issue with one of the major ideas presented in the biography and accepted overwhelmingly by the reviewers: the portrait of Virginia Woolf as sexually unresponsive either to men or, despite her clear emotional attachments, to women. In a passage cited extensively in the reviews—"she was . . . terrified back into a posture of frozen and defensive panic"—Bell suggests that the origins of this frigidity lay in her sexual molestation by her Duckworth half-brothers, chronicled by Woolf herself. For Johnston, this depiction of what one reviewer called her "thoroughly muddled" sexuality depicts instead a "male freudian view" that assumes heterosexuality as the norm: "The implication that virginia would have grown up to enjoy a proper heterosexuality had she not been subjected to the trauma of an incestuous invasion of her privacy at a tender age is a projection based on the notion that only heterosexuality is normal and natural and that its failure must therefore be due to a serious psychological setback: it's a way of considering women only in relation to the males of their family and not to the women. . . ."[20] Ellen Hawkes Rogat's review, "The Virgin in the Bell Biography," published in the academic journal *Twentieth Century Literature,* agrees, but situates the biography's view of sexuality in its unquestioning acceptance of the most conventional clichés about what it is to be masculine, feminine, or (shudder) a spinster. The result, she argues, bolstered by the family bias, was to resurrect the "phantom" that "has haunted Woolf for years": "the pale figure of a neurotic virgin cloistered from experience."[21]

Cynthia Ozick's attack on the family portrait, in some ways the strongest and most explicit, shares some of Johnston's and Rogat's assumptions, but her premise and her concerns differ, arising from her rejection of one of the most powerful themes to emerge from the book's reception: the construction of Leonard, not Virginia, as the hero of the story. Commenting tartly in 1995 on "the revisionist works 'purporting to demonstrate that both Leonard and Quentin had completely misrepresented [Virginia]' " in presenting " '*their* preferred image—and one in which Leonard himself figured as hero,' " Anne Olivier Bell rewrites history, ignoring the fact that it was the laudatory reviews of her husband's biography that initially declared Leonard the hero, loudly, clearly, unequivocally: "Leonard, who watched over and protected her . . . comes out as the hero of this biography" (Stephen Spender); the couple's "curious happiness . . . makes Leonard Woolf the hero of the second volume" (Stanley Weintraub); "in his devotion, equanimity, and indifference to the criticism of those who, not knowing the truth, were vexed with him for acting as his wife's dragon, he becomes the hero of this book" (Noel Annan).[22] Setting out to counter this all-too-readily accepted image of "a madwoman and her nurse," Cynthia Ozick lays the blame squarely on "that particular intimacy of perspective— of experience, really—which characterizes not family information, but family bias": "The Virginia Woolf that comes off these pages is a kind of emanation of a point of view, long settled, by now, into family feeling. . . . The Stephens are bold, the Pattles are fair, the Fishers are self-righteous. And Virginia is mad."[23]

While her critique of this image has as much to do with her feelings about Leonard (his attitude toward his Jewishness and his reasons for marrying and then nursing Virginia) as with the biography, Ozick succinctly characterizes just what gives Bell's version of his aunt its authority: "He knows, he does not doubt. It is the note of self-recognition; of confidence; of inheritance. Everything is in his grip."[24] A quarter of a century later this note of authority and the family portrait it paints continue to seduce readers, even when they acknowledge that there are other versions of the story. Janet Malcolm, for example, rhapsodizing over "the novel of Bloomsbury" she finds so compelling and the biographies and letters that created it, writes,

> What makes Quentin's biography such a remarkable work . . . is the force of his personality and the authority of his voice. He is perhaps more a butler than a chambermaid. . . . He has been with the family for a great number of years, and he is fiercely, profoundly loyal to it. . . . More important, he knows its members very well . . . and he has chosen sides, has discriminated and judged. In making his judgments and discriminations, he has picked up certain habits of mind from the family—habits of mind for which the family is famous—together with a certain tone.

Thus, even when another member of the family, his half-sister Angelica Garnett, challenges his authority and his view, he will, Malcolm argues, because of this tone, win: "The struggle between the obedient, legitimate son of Bloomsbury and its disobliging, illegitimate daughter is an uneven one, and Quentin will prevail."[25]

To return, then, to the question posed at the end of Take 4: can Virginia Woolf achieve the status of hero? Can she become the active agent, the heroic figure, in the story of her life? Not, it appears, while the story remains within the family orbit: remains a portrait painted by a family that, at all costs, wants to prevent its Virginia Woolf from escaping, from deconstructing the narratives and norms so dear to its and much of its culture's construction of itself. And they have been enormously successful, both in the self-styled "intellectual" media and in some areas of popular representation. When I originally wrote about the biography's role in authorizing the view of Virginia Woolf as frail, politically naive "genius" in 1992, I had no trouble finding examples of its ongoing currency and power: Edward Gorey's cartoon, drawn for the cover of the revised edition of *From Beowulf to Virginia Woolf* in 1984, which pictures an elongated, frail Virginia Woolf in the arms of a strong, muscular Beowulf (fig. 14); Alistair Cooke's introduction to the 1990 Masterpiece Theatre presentation of *A Room of One's Own,* performed by Eileen Atkins. In

Cooke's representation, "Mrs. Woolf," the "saint of the Bloomsbury set," was characterized at the time of the original talks at Cambridge by her "tremulous voice" and her total lack of financial reality. And while most reviewers of Atkins's rendition, ignoring Cooke, praised her embodiment of Woolf's intellectual strength and humor, critics such as John Simon could not resist adding that "Miss Atkins, sturdier by far, could have blown Mrs. Woolf with one breath from Bloomsbury to Billingsgate."[26]

The question is, what cultural need has been satisfied by the persistence of the image of the etiolated, fragile, apolitical Virginia Woolf, often in the face of clearly contradictory evidence and counter-representations? As Nell Irvin Painter argues about Sojourner Truth, there are times when the "symbol . . . is stronger and more essential in our culture than the complicated historic person" revealed by scholars, so much so that no amount of historical evidence or argument will "talk [individuals] out of the convictions [they] need to get through life"[27]—or maintain their credentials. Even the publication of Hermione Lee's 1996 biography, which carefully documents those contexts (whether events or relationships) and those persons that have generated the persistent myths, revealing them as a family portrait, could not overcome this need.[28] While reviewers for the most part enthusiastically applaud her revisionary portrait, a few, all of them British, strongly disagree, and their disagreement takes the form of reauthorizing Bell's version for the same old reasons. Bell's supporters, that is, reiterate the authority of Quentin's legitimate son's version in a self-conscious counterattack against academic and popular versions presumed to be feminist: the illegitimate daughters' versions. John Bayley covers the bases in his emblematic review:

> [Woolf] was not heartless, but she was malicious: and like many melancholics she was deeply frivolous, the last person, one would have thought, to have become a Woman's Lib ikon. Yet she has become one, and this enormous and, it must be said, rather indigestible book is one more tribute laid on the altar. Her own nephew, Quentin Bell, did the job of a critical biography better, and with more innate understanding. But the industry about her she would have so heartily despised goes grinding on.[29]

"A Woman's Lib ikon": Bayley's dismissive (not to mention anachronistic) phrase is more historically insightful than I'm sure he knows, pointing directly to the event that exemplifies the unauthorized, wildly popular portrait of Virginia Woolf in the States that would so forcefully counter the Bell biography: the 1973 founding by a group of women of a company called

Drawing by Edward Gorey

FIGURE 14. Beowulf and Virginia Woolf. Drawing by Edward Gorey. Copyright © 1984 by Edward Gorey. Reprinted by permission of Donandio and Ashworth, Inc.

Historical Products Inc. This company undertook to bring history alive by making its actors, including its women actors, literally visible, in this case on T-shirts, and Virginia Woolf's image was one of the first printed and sold. Soon, it seemed, her face was everywhere in the women's movement as it then constituted itself, signifying a sense of political excitement, activism, and camaraderie, and generating images that carried an equally powerful symbolic charge. Virginia Woolf had escaped the family portrait and taken to the streets.

VIRGINIA WOOLF'S FACE

No single object presented to our senses . . . engrosses so large a share of our thoughts, emotions, and associations as that small portion of flesh and blood a hand may cover, which constitutes the human face.

—Lady Eastlake, "Physiognomy," *Quarterly Review,* 1851

When Virginia Woolf's face began to appear on T-shirts and then postcards and posters, it signified the most distinctive and perhaps the most powerful aspect of her iconicity. Visual images of Virginia Woolf have from the beginning played a central role in the production of her star image, evoking responses that transform her features into a mirror of the viewer's own. This mirror is as much cultural as individual; perceived on one level as a template for reading her private character and her social meanings, Virginia Woolf's face, through its very repetition, has acquired the aura of myth. The strong visual component I am insisting on here affirms the origins of *icon* as "likeness, image, portrait, semblance, similitude, simile" (*OED*), inscribing in the dislocations and the doublings implicit in the term an uncanny familiarity and fear.

The reviews of Hermione Lee's 1996 biography of Virginia Woolf capture one aspect of this doubleness, presenting her iconicity in terms of both its role in the process of self-definition—why "generations of young women have sought to identify with [her]"—and its cultural meanings: modernist icon, feminist icon.[1] To this extent Virginia Woolf foregrounds one of the central contentions of star theory: the crucial role of identification in the star's ideological nature and hence of the construction of his or her meanings, whether identification is defined as social/cultural, "cinepsychoanalytic"/subjective, or a combination of both.[2] Rosemary Coombe, for example, describes the star ("the celebrity image") as "a cultural lode of multiple meanings, mined for its symbolic resonances, and, simultaneously, a floating signifier, invested with libidinal energies, social longings, and political aspirations."[3]

The multiplicity bears reemphasizing; during the period between the appearance of the first T-shirt in 1973 and Lee's biography, when Virginia Woolf's status as icon and the strong iconoclastic response it generates became so well established as to be commonplaces, her meanings proliferated and diverged. For some she has been and always will be a "matron saint," an inspiration; that goes without saying.[4] But for others she poses more threat than promise, and it is here, in the realm of the frightening, the uncanny, that the symbolic resonances articulated in and through Virginia Woolf's star image begin to acquire their reiterative power, become a guide to cultural obsessions that seem compulsively to repeat themselves in the very act of staking out specific historical moments and cultural claims. Nowhere, perhaps, do these obsessions enact themselves more vividly than in the fascination exerted by Virginia Woolf's face. Possessing from the beginning a public aspect rooted in her family background and her own ambitions, Virginia Woolf's face—whether printed in newspapers, magazines, or albums of beautiful women, worn on T-shirts, hung on the walls of bedrooms and studies, or carried during political rallies—transcends the individual woman to become an image-sign, sending disconcertingly mixed messages into the cultural realm.

While the process of identification and symbolic transcendence has proved especially important for subcultural groups, whether adolescents, women, or gay ghetto culture, all of whom "share a peculiarly intense degree of role/identity conflict and pressure, and an (albeit partial) exclusion from the dominant articulacy of, respectively, adult, male, heterosexual"— and, Dyer would add, white—culture, it is not limited to them.[5] Nor do these groups' subversive articulations go unchallenged by the status quo. Virginia Woolf's face on T-shirts and posters, two of the most widely circulated forms of popular culture, might signify acts of individual assertion or political speech, might claim Virginia Woolf for social activism and social change, but once she was established in that role, the inevitable processes of reaction, reabsorption, appropriation, and commodification came into play, as they did for feminism and activism themselves. In tracking this "double movement of containment and resistance," one thing becomes particularly clear: Virginia Woolf's face has proved remarkably resistant to the freeze-frame.

In order to illustrate this point, I want to turn to the photographic portraits that have played so extraordinary a role in Virginia Woolf's star image. Today the most reproduced and recognizable is a portrait of Virginia Stephen taken by G. C. Beresford in 1902 when she was twenty (fig. 3).[6] Here we see the young Virginia, in almost full profile, looking into the distance. This is the photograph that appears on the front cover of the Bell biography and in many of the reviews; it hangs in the National Portrait Gallery in London and is reproduced on many of their products, as well as providing the model for the images of Virginia Woolf seen on most T-shirts, posters, and mugs. Hermione Lee, doing her own reading of the face, speculates that the constant reproduction of this portrait has done as much as anything to perpetuate her ethereal, refined, vulnerable image: "The sensual, down-curved lips, the large sad gazing eyes, the dark lashes and strong eyebrows, the lovely straight nose and delicate curve of the chin, the long elegant neck, the high cheekbones, the soft, loosely-coiled bun, the pretty ear-lobe, and the aetherial lacy dress were to be crucial items in the making and maintaining of the Virgin Virginia legend."[7]

Viewed from another angle, however, this portrait conveys a different message, carrying within it a less ethereal, more self-conscious Virginia Woolf, who well understood the power of visual images, including their sociality; in this sense even this seemingly private image has a distinctly public resonance. For one thing, the photograph has a family history, both in terms of the pictures of Virginia and her father, Leslie Stephen, taken by Beresford later that year, and in terms of its reinscription of her mother's image. For Virginia Stephen bore a distinct resemblance to her mother, Julia Prinsep Jackson Duckworth Stephen, whose beauty, known to the public from her appearances in Julia Margaret Cameron's photographs and in Burne-Jones's paintings, was legendary. Julia bequeathed her beauty to her three daughters—Stella Duckworth, from her first marriage, and Vanessa and Virginia, her daughters with Leslie Stephen—a beauty often conveyed through photographs of mother and daughters that depict the family profile and neck (figs. 15, 16).[8] Woolf herself contributed to the public recognition of her mother's beauty in her descriptions of Mrs. Ramsay in *To the Lighthouse* and in the Hogarth Press publication of a collection of Julia Margaret Cameron's photographs, where Woolf provided an introduction about her great-aunt.[9]

Photographs, then, as both art/representation and cultural document, are an integral part of Woolf's inheritance, one she used effectively in her two interrogations of biography, *Flush* and *Orlando,* and in her political manifesto *Three Guineas.* Equally important, as Woolf became a public figure in her own right, she allowed herself, however grudgingly, to be

FIGURE 15.
Julia Duckworth Stephen.
Photograph by Julia
Margaret Cameron.

FIGURE 16. Vanessa Stephen, Stella Duckworth, Virginia Stephen. Photograph by H. and R. Stiles.

photographed by some of the most famous studios and artists of her time for exhibition in highly public places.[10]

The next series of photographs to consider, the studio portraits of Virginia Woolf taken in the mid-1920s, reflects the growing visibility of her public persona at the time, occasioned in part by her increasing fame as a novelist and in part by her verbal and visual appearances in *Vogue London*.[11] One, used in the *Saturday Review of Literature* in 1924, shows Woolf wearing a lace shawl; the studio is unidentified. Not so the next set of photos, which provides well-defined cultural markers: the two portraits (one full-face and almost full-length; one three-quarter-view face) of Virginia Woolf in her mother's dress (fig. 13). Taken by Beck and Macgregor, regular contributors to *Vogue*, in conjunction with the essays she wrote for the journal between 1924 and 1926, they denote her association, as Cecil Beaton comments, with the " 'intelligentsia,' a word that came into much use at that time" and was often signified by the "strongly Bohemian atmosphere" of Beck and Macgregor's portraits.[12] A subsequent Beck and Macgregor portrait (1925), which appeared in *Vogue*'s Late May 1925 issue, uses another of their trademark poses, placing Woolf, seated on a stool, before a screen depicting tropical birds and flowers.

Although all of these images have appeared regularly in later editions of Woolf's works (letters, diaries, etc.) as well as in books about her, with the exception of the Beck and Macgregor portrait used in her *Vogue London* and *Vanity Fair* Hall of Fame appearances and appropriated by Beaton for his *Book of Beauty*, they did not have much media exposure at the time. But the final (unidentified) studio photograph from this period (c. 1927) did, and in many ways this is the most glamorous of them all; wearing a fur-collared coat, Woolf jauntily leans her chin in her hand and looks more or less directly at the viewer (fig. 17). Appearing in a number of Harcourt Brace ads and articles about Woolf and/or her works in the States during the late 1920s and 1930s, this image created a version of Virginia Woolf that was far less ethereal and "bohemian" than those appearing in the British press.

At the end of the decade Woolf sat for the first of the three sets of portraits that, after the Beresford, have played the greatest role in constructing her public image: those taken by the Lenare studio, known for its society portraits, and those taken by the photographers Man Ray and Gisèle Freund. Two of the Lenare portraits (figs. 4, 5), taken in 1929, are among the most widely reproduced of her images: at first officially, in advertisements for and reviews of her books, and later less officially, in popular appropriations. Wearing a dark dress with a V neck and simple

FIGURE 17.
Virginia Woolf.
Photographer
unknown.

jewelry, Woolf appears either full-face or almost full-face, looking just past the camera; one portrait pictures her down to her waist, where her hand lies on a magazine resting on her lap, but this photograph is usually cropped below the pin at the bottom of the V (Richardson, 295), emphasizing her face rather than her whole figure. The photographs conform to what one writer describes as the Lenare style: "uncluttered by ornamental setting, trimmed of nature's irrelevancies of wrinkle, pouching and sag, his sitters squarely dominate the frame. They are seen against a peach-fuzzed light into which they themselves will often half melt—not for nothing was Lenare's long-time motto, '*Artistry in Diffusion.*' . . ." This style, the writer continues, suggests that of early British portraiture referred to by David Piper in *The English Face* as " 'The Polite Mask of the Augustan Age.' "[13]

Then, in 1934, possibly at the request of *Harper's Bazaar*, Woolf was photographed by Man Ray;[14] each of the five portraits I have seen is taken from a very different angle, and each is extraordinary in its own way. Again, Woolf is dressed simply: long jacket, print blouse, earrings. The best known is the photograph that appeared on the cover of *Time* in 1937 (fig. 6); a second shows Woolf sitting with her arms crossed over the back of a chair, staring at the camera (fig. 7); and a third, to me the most extraordinary, is a half-length profile against a dark background, head tilted slightly back, the light falling on her hair and face (fig. 2). Two other portraits, not listed in Richardson, are both three-quarter-length profiles of Woolf sitting sideways on a chair.[15]

Situated at the center of the avant-garde art scene in Paris and a sought-after portraitist, Man Ray was in the habit of writing about his famous subjects as well as photographing them; in one place he commented, "Virginia Woolf, whose ascetic face was framed in a severe arrangement of her hair—I had to put some lipstick on her mouth, to which she objected at first, but I explained that it was for technical reasons and would not show in the picture. When she left, she forgot to remove the rouge."[16] Richardson, like others, objects to the addition of the lipstick, arguing that it contributes to "the incongruous lushness of the image" (Richardson, 300). Elsewhere, Man Ray tells us that "in making the portraits of the personalities" he photographed, "the photographer was interested only in the faces of his models, and did not take into account their situation or their fame, or the greater or smaller sympathy that they inspired in him personally." After the fact, however, he did, ranking his sitters according to their sympathy for his work; having "recourse to a little game once popular with the Surrealists[,] he granted the mark 20 when he was in full sympathy with the personality and when his interest in the photograph was unreserved. On this basis he gave a mark from 0 to 20 to each image." Virginia Woolf, presented through the photograph where she looks most directly at the camera (fig. 7), received a 3.[17]

This was not the response of Gisèle Freund, the expatriate German photographer living in France during the 1930s, who, like Man Ray, photographed many of the most eminent literary and intellectual figures of the day; both her visual portraits of Woolf, taken in Woolf's home in June 1939 when Woolf was fifty-eight, and her verbal portraits tell a different story. Unlike Man Ray, Freund appears to have found Virginia Woolf a sympathetic and compelling figure, describing her as "frail and luminous, . . . the very embodiment of her prose," which is in turn presented as "giving permanence not to the external facts of existence but to elusive and complex thoughts, made up of ever-changing and multicolored images and memories"; both looks and prose are described as a reflection of her "purely cerebral life."[18] In two of the pictures, Woolf is sitting on a sofa in a dark jacket, skirt, and plaid blouse, a cigarette in hand. In a second set, the blouse has changed (eyelet embroidery), but the cigarette in its holder is very much in view. In one of these, she is tilted forward, holding the cigarette in front of her and smiling (fig. 8); in the other, which is better known, she is pictured side-on down to the waist in front of panels painted by Vanessa Bell and Duncan Grant (fig. 9). One hand holds the cigarette, while the other rests on a manuscript in her lap; more manuscripts are piled on the table next to her. The third set of portraits, which presents her more close up, is more somber. Here she wears a dark dress broken only by a stiff white frill at the neck; in one she rests her head on her hand while looking down (fig. 10); in a second, she looks off to the side and down (fig. 11); a third pictures her almost full-face.

In Freund's telling, years after the fact, the sitting, brought about by the Argentinian writer and editor Victoria Ocampo, had an auspicious—and domestic—beginning. Taken by Ocampo to tea at the Woolfs, Freund showed her some color transparencies, which she was experimenting with at the time; Woolf "was very much interested, especially in the psychological significance disclosed by each picture," and she responded by recounting her family relationship to Julia Margaret Cameron and showing Freund the Hogarth edition of her work. Then, after some hesitation, she agreed to a future sitting; at that time "Virginia Woolf submitted to all my demands. She showed me her dresses, and the two of us chose the colors. She asked me to photograph her husband as well, and at the end they posed together, the little dog at their feet." When she returned to London later that summer while Woolf was in Sussex, Freund showed the pictures, as yet unseen by Woolf (who never did see them), to others, provoking an extremely angry letter from Woolf to Ocampo, followed belatedly by an apology.[19] Woolf's version of the story differs, indicating that she felt betrayed by Ocampo into agreeing to the sitting and even more betrayed by the exhibition of photographs of her that she had never seen. For however much Woolf might have recognized photography as an art or the role of photographs in the advancement of her professional career, she was never happy about having them professionally taken or about their public appearances.

Her uneasiness about her public persona had some justification; when Beaton appropriated her photographic image for his ghostly description in *The Book of Beauty*, he anticipated what became a major aspect of her construction as icon: the verbal portraits of Virginia Woolf that read her character in and through her photographs. Virginia Woolf is not alone in being characterized by her visual image; the long-standing intersections among physiognomy, phrenology, anthropometrics, and portraiture in the West attest to the strength of the belief that "the body, and especially the face and head, [bear] the outward *signs* of inner character."[20] This belief remains a powerful impetus in the twentieth century, even among individuals who consider physiognomy itself an outdated and discredited "science," as those who feel compelled to read Virginia Woolf through her face never tire of telling us. Photography, the visual medium most associated with Virginia

Woolf's face, also plays a role here, having been characterized from its beginnings by its perceived ability to convey the essence of an individual, his or her innermost nature and qualities, an attribute inseparable from its presumed "realism": its seemingly direct portrayal of the individual; its authenticity or veracity. "The earliest portrait photographs," Graham Clarke writes, "most notably the daguerreotype, insisted on their realism; they were literally mirror-images of those photographed"; a hundred years later, despite the changed technology, many photographers still argue, as Edward Weston has done, that the photograph provides "a vivid representation of a living person," conveying "that quality of authenticity that makes [the observer] accept the photograph as a truthful picture, a genuine likeness." When well done, the photograph shows not "how this person looks, but . . . what he is."[21]

Others have taken another tack, equally important in the readings of Virginia Woolf's face, arguing that photographic portraiture, like portraiture in general, depicts not the individual, but the type: that it is inseparable from the codes, both aesthetic and social, that govern its production and reception. "Portraits," Richard Brilliant writes, "reflect social realities. Their imagery combines the conventions of behaviour and appearance appropriate to the members of a society at a particular time, as defined by categories of age, gender, race, physical beauty, occupation, social and civic status, and class," demanding close attention to the "subtle interaction between social and artistic conventions." The photographic portrait, Clarke adds, "consistently offers the promise of the individual through a system of representation which at once hides and distorts the subject before the lens. Thus the portrait's meaning exists within wider codes of meaning: of space, of posture, of dress, of marks, of social distinction." When we add to this sociality theories of the role of the mask—the argument that "the emergence of the subject revealed in the portrait must take into account the fact that self-effacement behind the mask is consistent with the social nature of men and women, of all who (re)present themselves in public," we are led to the area where readings of photographs—interpretations of the mask and what lies behind it—tell us as much about the reader/viewer as about the photographic subject. As Brilliant notes, the viewer is always complicitous "in answering the question posed by the portraitist, 'Who is "the You" that I am looking at and how may I know it?' "; "knowledge of others is also knowledge of oneself."[22]

Looking at a portrait, then, is looking in a mirror, however much we think we are viewing a mirror image of the other. Roland Barthes makes this point in his description of what he calls the *punctum,* the "wound" or "punctuation," "sting, speck, cut, little hole—and also a cast of the dice" that "pricks" him in a photograph, dislocating the *studium,* the photograph's relation to a shared "ethical and political culture." "To give examples of *punctum,*" he writes, which speak perhaps to him alone, "is, in a certain fashion, to *give myself up.*"[23]

When viewers turn to photographs to discover the authentic Virginia Woolf and/or her social meanings, then, they reveal themselves in the process. What makes this exchange, common enough in representations of a public figure, so significant in Virginia Woolf's case is the intensity of the reactions, reactions so powerful and so self-revealing (Barthes's *punctum*) as to suggest a form of psychic investment that cannot be totally explained by more social factors (Barthes's *studium*). At one level there seems to be little in the images to distinguish them from those of women such as Edith Wharton or Willa Cather, also featured in *Vogue*'s or *Vanity Fair*'s Hall of Fame "for outstanding achievement," who "exhibit a direct gaze and business-like stance." Woolf does, perhaps, look more often past the camera into the distance, a gaze that in nineteenth-century celebrity photography conveyed "an air of weighty seriousness," of farsightedness,[24] but might strike some viewers as anachronistic or too detached in a more free-for-all, engaged environment. Equally striking, no one photograph stands out as especially provoking, although the Man Ray portrait domesticated in *Time* seems to have that effect on some viewers. And while the choice of visual image will affect the verbal portrait based on it, there is no consistent pattern; the same image can produce radically divergent readings.

What does distinguish Virginia Woolf's face from that of Edith Wharton or Willa Cather is its appearance in anthologies of beautiful women, projecting Virginia Woolf out of the cerebral intellectual world and into that occupied by women more traditionally associated with beauty, fashion, spectacle: society women, actresses, royalty. Once again Virginia Woolf proves transgressive, crossing boundaries, creating category crises, provoking anxiety. Cecil Beaton's verbal rendering of Virginia Woolf as an icon of ghostly or deathly beauty haunting his *Book of Beauty* provides one prototype for subsequent responses (see Take 2). In his introduction to the 1930 collection, which, like all such collections, can be read as having an anthropological or typological function, Beaton writes that "modern beauty," that which he is presenting, needs to be "backed up by intelligence" to "signify." In Virginia Woolf's case, intelligence crosses into "intelligentsia," where, with two exceptions, Edith Sitwell and Anita Loos, she finds herself alone. Beaton's description of Edith Sitwell, accompanied by a photograph that shows her lying as if in a coffin, includes some of the same tropes applied to Virginia Woolf, but the elements of threat and fear are missing. Edith Sitwell might be gaunt, characterized by a spectral thinness, and she might possess "the mad moon-struck ethereality of a ghost," but her uncanniness, unlike Virginia Woolf's, is vitiated by Beaton's declaration that "she is too gay and human to be frightening."[25]

For the sake of contrast to Beaton's reading of Virginia Woolf's face, listen to Victoria Ocampo's, based on the same Beck and Macgregor photographs that inspired Beaton's drawings:

> Try to imagine a mask that even without life, without intelligence would be beautiful. Then imagine this mask so impregnated with life and intelligence that it would seem to have been modelled by them. Imagine all this, and you will still have only a faint idea of the charm of Virginia Woolf's face, a charm that is the result of the most felicitous encounter of matter and soul in the face of a woman.[26]

Intelligence is also present in my next example, Virginia Woolf's appearance in L. Fritz Gruber's 1965 *Beauty: Variations on the Theme* WOMAN *by Masters of the Camera—Past and Present,* where she is identified as an "authoress," but life and charm are not; instead the emphasis is once again on death. The image, the Man Ray profile, is cropped and blown up so that her head and face, sharply delineated against the dark background, fills the entire page (fig. 18); it is the most powerful image of Virginia Woolf I know. The verbal portrait once again presents Virginia Woolf in terms of her uncanny otherworldliness:

> The ethereal, almost Gothic profile bears witness to the genius of this outstanding woman. The open face suits the deep-set, expressive eyes, and the finely arched nose is balanced by the strong chin. Only the unusually full lips strike an odd note in the harmony of her features. The photographer admits to having tinted the delicate pink of her mouth with a little lipstick, fearing that the pallor of her lips would tend to make her face seem more remote than ever from mankind. Who can say whether or not this was justified? The *Encyclopedia Britannica* makes the following comments about Virginia Woolf: "*The merit of her books lies partly in her understanding of those about whom she wrote, partly in the facility with which she used words. These gifts placed her among the best literary critics of her time.*"
>
> Here, too, foreshadowed in her haunted face is Virginia Woolf's eventual suicide by drowning.[27]

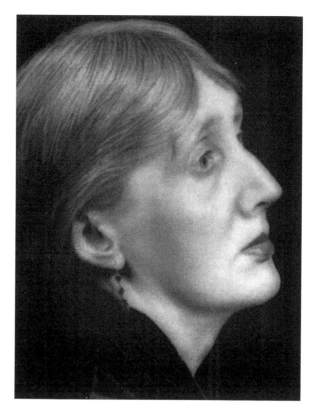

FIGURE 18.
Virginia Woolf.
Photograph by Man
Ray. Copyright ©
1999 Man Ray
Trust/Artists Rights
Society, NY/ADAGP,
Paris.

The choice of photograph and the context create a very different portrait of Virginia Woolf in Diana Trilling's snide review of two collections of Woolf's essays in 1948, where gender and class rather than intelligence and beauty are the ostensible issue; Man Ray's widely reproduced portrait of Virginia Woolf with arm raised (fig. 6) accompanies the piece, bearing the caption "Virginia Woolf: 'An Extreme Sensibility . . . A Pride More Imposing Than Suffragettes with Banners' ":

> Probably anyone acquainted with the name of Virginia Woolf is familiar with the remarkable photograph of her which appears on this page—the long, tense face at once so suffering and so impervious, the large, too-precisely socketed eyes and the full, too-precisely outlined mouth rimmed with humor but also with conscious vanity, the aristocratic nose and the surely troublesome hair dressed in such

defiance of whatever fashion. Unmistakably it is the portrait of an extreme feminine sensibility, of a spirit so finely drawn that we can scarcely bear to follow its tracings. But just as unmistakably it is the portrait of a pride of mind a thousand times more imposing than an army of suffragettes with banners! Here without question, we decide merely on appearances, is someone who conforms to the rules of neither the feminine nor the feministic game, someone we must recognize as a special instance of her sex.[28]

Trilling's response beautifully illustrates the process that naturalizes the photographic message as purely denotative: as inherent in the image and not in the cultural codes of the producer and/or consumer; Trilling, we are meant to believe, contributes nothing to the process. It also suggests the lingering belief that the face captured in a photograph reveals, however unintentionally, the person rather than the mask, in this case the "portrait of an extreme feminine sensibility" inscribed in the facial features. At the same time, Trilling not only recognizes but names the mask constructed for public consumption: "conscious vanity," "defiance of whatever fashion," "pride of mind." In Trilling's view, as the rest of the article makes clear, Virginia Woolf's face, with its mixed signs, becomes a marker of the writer's ability to get the response she demands from her public, whether from critics or from common readers, who treat Virginia Woolf as a "special instance, both of her sex and her profession"; but she, Trilling, who can decode the message for its social meanings, refuses the gambit. In this sense Trilling would agree with Barthes's argument that "the great portrait photographers are great mythologists" because "Photography cannot signify (aim at a generality) except by assuming a mask. It is this word which Calvino correctly uses to designate what makes a face into the product of a society and its history." When Barthes adds that only those with a trained critical faculty have the "capacity to perceive the political or moral meaning of a face,"[29] Trilling might well say, "indeed."

Given the negativity of her response to the "political or moral meaning" of Virginia Woolf's face, Trilling's compulsion fourteen years later to side with Virginia Woolf against Albee in the name of high culture must have been galling indeed.[30] To understand why, we need to look more closely at two details of Trilling's anatomy of Virginia Woolf. The first, her reference to the "aristocratic nose," foregrounds a physiognomic feature still recognized in England as a class and to some extent a "racial" marker: a sign of Virginia Woolf's upper-middle-class status and origins, which, if not Norman, the mark of the true aristocrat, were at least not Celtic. In her study of the intersections of physiognomy, anthropology, art, and class in nineteenth-century England Mary Cowling writes, "By its very nature obtrusive, and given to a marked variety, the nose developed especially strong class connotations and was the foremost feature by which the status of any one individual was usually determined." The belief, Cowling continues, that "there is something 'dominant' in the form and expression of the Roman and aquiline noses" extended beyond the physical to the social, illustrated, as one writer in 1842 put it, by the fact that " 'such noses frequently belong to persons of superior intellect and high moral sentiment, and are often found indicative of great strength of mind and decision of character.' "[31]

More than half a century later, Bloomsbury concurred. Lytton Strachey, for example, detected "the sign of power in the dominating curve of [Florence Nightingale's] thin nose"; and Woolf herself tells the story of how, caught without money to pay for a purchase, she "remembered [her] grandfathers nose and gave [herself] such airs they let me go off with three pound ten worth."[32] Hermione Lee comments that "certainly that Stephen nose—and the ability to look down it—was visible through the generations," adding that many people saw her father in Woolf's face as a whole. Nor has time diminished the significance of her nose in representations of Virginia Woolf's class status; Alan Bennett's parodic portrait of Virginia Woolf in his first play, *Forty Years On* (first performed in 1968), relies on an understanding of its prominence, in all senses of the word, including the phallic, for the parody to work: "And then there was Virginia herself elegant and quizzical, those great nostrils quivering and the sunlight playing over her long pale face. She never used cosmetics, except to powder her nose. But then she had her father's nose."[33]

The multiple codings governing cultural meanings of the nose suggest that Trilling's reference to the "aristocratic nose" carries with it a critique of the European *rentier* class so powerful among those American intellectuals, many of them of immigrant, working-class, and/or Jewish background, who were carving out professional and social spaces for themselves in the pre- and postwar period; more than Virginia Woolf's genetic heritage is at stake. The other of Trilling's markers I want to highlight, "the surely troublesome hair dressed in such defiance of fashion," is less a matter of physiognomy or genes than self-representation, but proves equally freighted. In talking about her hair, Trilling strikes a recurring note, for over the years descriptions of Virginia Woolf's untidy hair and clothes, often read as a sign of her bohemian disregard for conventions or, more ominously, as a sign of her mental disorder, have become a trope in themselves.[34] But in this case Trilling's reading stands in direct contrast to Man Ray's when he noted the "severe arrangement of her hair," indicating how much we find what we want or expect in photographs of others. Equally telling, Trilling's emphasis on defiance in her portrait links Virginia Woolf's unruly hair to an act of transgression, which *could* signal a liberating break from the constraining mores that kept women's hair and by extension women themselves in place; but Trilling reads this defiance otherwise: as a sign of the class privilege that allows those inside the system to reject its codes, something Trilling, by her own accounts, would have found difficult if not impossible to do herself. In at least two essays she details her meticulous preparations for formal social occasions outside her usual range of experiences: one at the home of the then president of Columbia University, Nicholas Murray Butler, in 1938, who shortly after appointed her husband, Lionel, to the faculty of the English department, making him the first Jew to achieve that status; the other at the Kennedy White House in 1962. On the first occasion she called both the fashion department of *Vogue* and the fashion adviser at Bonwit Teller, an upscale department store, to ensure that she would be dressed correctly.[35] No wonder Trilling found Virginia Woolf's seemingly cavalier attitude toward her appearance a sign of pride, class privilege, and confidence at odds with her own struggles for self- and social definition.

When we turn from Virginia Woolf's appearances in anthologies of beauty and in reviews (and one should recall here the captions attached to her photographic images in reviews of *A Writer's Diary* [Take 3]) to the mass replication of her face on T-shirts and posters, we move out of the realm of the physiognomic or socially coded portrait and into the realm of the image-sign, which Richard Brilliant links to the symbolic and mythic. Repetition is the key to this "consolidated portrait image": an image so familiar through repetition or redundancy that no label or caption is necessary. Brilliant's examples are political figures such as Lenin or Mao and "celebrities," especially film stars; Warhol's *Marilyn Diptych,* with its fifty identical images, provides the model. In it, Marilyn "retains her identity in the public consciousness despite the fact that her image has been reduced to her smiling face with its crown of blond hair." Repetition, he adds, can also transform "highly individualist, descriptive images" into "depersonalized" signs, "because they come to possess some other, and greater, symbolic value."[36] Both processes can be traced in the transformation of Virginia Woolf's face into iconic sign, although I would qualify the term "depersonalized"; Virginia Woolf may have become an image-sign, but she carried a very personal resonance for many of her wearers and viewers.

By the time of the Bell biography and the first T-shirt in 1972–73, the repeated appearances of the major photographs of Virginia Woolf had provided the necessary conditions for this transformation; Virginia Woolf's face was readily available for the articulation of widely divergent renderings of the figure's meaning, used for widely divergent political ends. Under the circumstances, the photograph chosen in any particular discursive situation becomes an ideological statement. David Levine, for example, caricaturist for the *New York Review of Books,* chose the Beresford profile of the young Virginia as the model for the drawing accompanying Elizabeth Hardwick's ambivalent review of the Bell biography, but altered it by exaggerating the length of the face and even more the famous family neck, the sharpness of the nose, the thrust of the chin, the shaded eyes. "Attenuated," one might say about the woman portrayed, perhaps "dreamy," and certainly "beautiful," but not "young" and not "fragile"; "aristocratic" seems to go without saying. Frightening? I think not; too self-enclosed to be a direct threat. It is this caricature, rather than any of the others that Levine did of Virginia Woolf over the years, that subsequently appeared in the *NYRB*'s ads and on its T-shirts: Virginia Woolf icon for the intellectual class.

In contrast, in or around 1972–73, the publicists for Everywoman's Center at UMass, Amherst, chose a full-face Lenare photograph, where Woolf looks more directly at her viewers, as the model for a poster sold to raise funds for textbooks for poor women attending college (fig. 19); the poster also includes a defiant passage from *Three Guineas:*

> And let the daughters of uneducated women dance round the new house, the poor house, the house that stands in the narrow street where omnibuses pass and the street hawkers cry their wares, and let them sing, "We have done with war! We have done with tyranny!" And their mothers will laugh from their graves, "It was for this that we suffered obloquy and contempt! Light up the windows of the new house, daughters! Let them blaze!"

At the time the Virginia Woolf poster appeared, the center was engaged in an active battle with the university to recognize that poor women, often older, many of them on welfare, had different financial and living needs than more traditional students; the Poor Women's Task Force, which ran this program, writes, "Major questions for us have been, and continue to be: is higher education an obsolete idea or a revolutionary force? Is it practical for poor women? Is higher education for poor women political pornography?"[37] Given this context, Everywoman's Virginia Woolf icon, like Woolf's *Three Guineas,* challenges more than Bell's image of the unpolitical esthete (or Levine's otherworldly profile); assuming a frontal

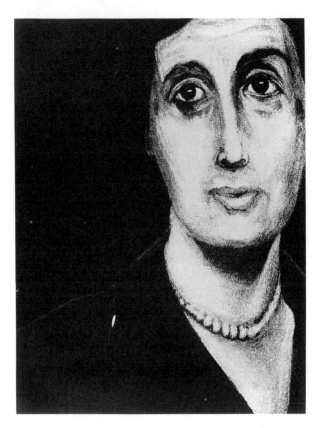

FIGURE 19.
Poster, Every-
woman's Center,
University of
Massachusetts at
Amherst.

position that "functions like the 'I-You' relation," Virginia Woolf not
only insists on the viewer's presence, drawing her or him into the discursive moment, but demands a dialogue.[38] Virginia Woolf becomes "fighting words."

Like the Levine caricature, the Historical Products Inc. T-shirt also
featured the Beresford profile but kept its youth and softness intact; here,
though, the context and the medium—the specificity of the cultural cur-
rents at work in 1973 and the rich semiotics of the T-shirt as a cultural
form—considerably altered its meaning. Numerous readings of the T-
shirt have been put forward over the years, including those that locate
its significance, like that of clothing in general, in revealing "a person's
drives and propensities, internal state and external status"; but the T-shirt
also functions more specifically as political statement, a form of subcultural
assertion often described as getting something off your chest by putting it
on your chest.[39]

This is especially true of the 1973 Virginia Woolf T-shirt, which coincided with a distinct shift in the nature and significance of the T-shirt itself. As historians of the genre note, during the 1960s message T-shirts had not yet become the norm: "For much of the 1960s, coats and ties were so *de rigueur*" for men, and wearing men's clothes and the increasing appeal of androgyny were still so new for women, that " 'the gesture of wearing a T-shirt at all was sufficiently rebellious . . . no message was needed.' "[40] In this form, J. D. Reed adds, "the T-shirt became the uniform of radical youth, male or female," so much so that by the end of the decade Tom Wolfe had claimed it for radical chic. But when the technological process of plastisol-ink heat transfer made it possible in 1970 to produce full-color images and slogans, T-shirts with messages, many of them political, quickly took over as an expression of rebellion.[41] One fashion writer, asked in 1996 to name which works produced in the late twentieth century would still be talked about a hundred years later, named the logo T-shirt and associated it with freedom of expression: "The logo T-shirt represents what fashion historians fear most: the liberalization of fashion. No effort need be made to decode the messages here, because the wearers are willing to (literally in some cases) wear their identities on their sleeves."[42]

Significantly, the political messages that did appear on T-shirts in the late 1960s tended to promote women's liberation or the NAACP, or declare resistance to the Vietnam War. For Edith Mayo, former curator in the political history section of the Smithsonian, feminist T-shirts carried on the strong tradition of the political button within the women's movement from the nineteenth century on, which often featured images of leaders such as Susan B. Anthony, Elizabeth Cady Stanton, and Lucy Stone. The visibility of the early leaders, she adds, gave them the status of icon, a tradition continued in the second wave by feminists who, wary of "charismatic personalities" and leaders, may have put words, not faces, on their buttons, but proudly displayed their historical icons, including Susan B. Anthony and Virginia Woolf, on T-shirts, a more spectacular mode of assertion. Women of all ages and from all walks of life wore these T-shirts, illustrating the continuing importance of popular forms such as T-shirts and buttons for those, like women, who "generally cannot afford access to electronic media dissemination of their [political] message."[43]

The power of these forms to shape a figure's image and meaning is enormous: witness Alix Kates Shulman's history of the Emma Goldman T-shirt. Created for and sold at a 1973 Central Park celebration of the end of the Vietnam War as a way to raise money for the anarchist cause, the original run (about two gross) displayed the photographic image "of a stalwart hatless Emma in pince-nez" and the legend, "If I can't dance

I don't want to be in your revolution." Goldman herself never said or wrote these words, which instead offer a "succinct abridgement" of a story told by Goldman in her 1931 autobiography. "But history (and fashion) exploded so quickly in those hungrily feminist days," Shulman writes, "that the slogan on the original shirt-run was soon dispersed and copied and broadcast nation-wide and abroad, underground and above," with the legend changing along the way, until it "soared up into the realms of myth."[44]

By 1973 Virginia Woolf needed no legend to sanction her iconic, mythic status or her role as a source of self- and group identity, although one can easily imagine the phrase "a room of one's own" serving this function; her image alone offered those who bought and/or wore her T-shirt the opportunity for personal self-declaration and what Reed calls "instant familiarity among strangers—an index for passers-by to what you thought, liked or wanted to be associated with."[45] The result was to create a strong sense of community among the wearers: we are here, we are legion, and we will prevail. Another way to approach the promise of individual and communal identification articulated by the T-shirt is through Laurence Rickels's association of adolescent and group psychology with replication: the desire to be "different like the friends they like to be like."[46] In this way, however much the T-shirt enacts the impulse to distinguish or declare one's self by the choice of the image, it ultimately becomes the sign of a group identity that is forged in part by rejection of the coupling ultimately expected of them: an act of replication rather than reproduction. We are back in the world feared both by critics of Albee's play and by Leslie Fiedler: a refusal, whether homosexual or heterosexual, to reproduce the previous generation. By (metaphoric) extension, the replication of the Virginia Woolf T-shirt becomes an act of subversion of the generational demand to become like one's parents, both a psychic tool and a subcultural statement.

Analogously, the wearing of Virginia Woolf's image on one's chest, like Perseus's or Athena's or the Greek warriors' apotropaic wearing of Medusa's head on their aegis or shield, becomes an act of both self-protection and defiance: a claiming of Virginia Woolf's powers, including her feminist agency, for oneself. Rather than retreating from the association of Virginia Woolf with fear of the powerful and potentially monstrous female, the T-shirt declares, "you'd better believe it."

Here, perhaps, is where the T-shirt presents its strongest challenge to Quentin Bell's fragile, apolitical, neurasthenic Virginia Woolf: its role as image and spectacle, with their historical links to the (feminine) masses and hence to the revolutionary overthrow of the self-proclaimed legitimacy or rule of the (masculine, patriarchal) order claimed by Bell's words. Edmund Burke would have understood the gesture, having represented the overthrow of the established family and state during the French Revolution, exemplified by the overthrow of the monarchy, as an unnatural spectacle, the work of " 'furies of hell, in the abused shape of the vilest of women' ": an "unnatural, feminine violence, a reversal of the natural order of strength and weakness; perhaps even worse, the 'abused shape' of a transvestite mob." "For Burke," W. J. T. Mitchell writes, "the threatening 'speculative' and 'spectacular' images (feminine, barbaric, and French) must be met with counterimages which certify the beauty and sublimity of the native, natural order of things, and which 'reflect' the new, threatening images as monstrous, grotesque freaks of nature."[47]

Women in the early seventies, rejecting the fear taught them by their mothers and society as whole of "making a spectacle" of themselves, were having none of it; they were out to overthrow the old regime, and Virginia Woolf served as an avatar, a woman whose revolutionary politics, as feminist critics were beginning to argue, were never distinct from her life or her art. If their acts made them monstrous, so much the better, given the etymological origins of *monster* in *monstrum:* "something marvelous, originally a divine portent or warning" (*OED*), which Mary Russo extends to freaks, and links, via the demonstrations of the 1960s, to identity politics:

> Although the tradition of the freak as monster—literally the de-*monstrater* of the marvelous power of the divine—has a long history in European culture, the demonstrations of the sixties in the United States were characterized by a new articulation of heterogeneous social groups, and by a mixing of external and internal demands for dramatic visibility. Being a freak was, and remains, an individual choice for some and an oppressive assignment for others. . . .[48]

Making a spectacle of themselves, the wearers of the T-shirt were anticipating Hélène Cixous's 1976 call in "The Laugh of the Medusa" for women to write themselves "into the text—as into the world and into history—by [their] own movement," to follow that desire to "sing, to write, to dare to speak" that had made women in the past accuse themselves of being monsters. Having confronted their fears, Cixous writes, they will see that Medusa is "not deadly. She's beautiful," and, like the Virginia Woolf on the UMass poster, "she's laughing," scary, and strong.[49]

There is still one more way to gloss the performative role of the original T-shirt, one that reads it as a speech act whose function is to initiate processes or procedures. Here, the T-shirt wearer parallels the feminist critic described by Tania Modleski, "who, participating in a community whose values she both shares and 'helps to form,' is in the process of challenging 'accepted conventional procedures' and forging new ones."[50] One way to understand this synergy is through the concept of the gift; for the giving or receiving of the T-shirt, a common practice at the time, functioned to bring about and maintain "human, personal, relationships between individuals and groups."[51] Conceived as a form of symbolic exchange, the circulation of the T-shirt and its status as gift served to counter the conventional image of Virginia Woolf constructed by the Bell biography. For whereas the Bell biography pushed the writings and the writer into the realm of a "high culture" where the genius/artist was divorced from politics and the public realm, the exchange of T-shirts by women in the 1970s undid the boundaries between high culture and popular culture, private and public, elite and mass. The result was to rewrite Virginia Woolf's relationship to the public realm, transforming her into a sign or token of an activist community.

Ten years later, 1982, when Virginia Woolf celebrated her centenary, the prevalence of the T-shirt and the rearticulation it signified became a central point of contention in the debates over who would define her meaning; the spectacular nature of the image had all the markings of a rebellion, and it looked to many as if the barbarians had won. The result, as we've seen earlier, was a regrouping of the powers that be; the process of creating counterimages that would "certify the beauty and sublimity of the native, natural order of things, and . . . 'reflect' the new, threatening images as monstrous, grotesque freaks of nature" had begun,[52] and it too had a visual component. In Britain, which saw itself as the "native, natural order" when it came to Virginia Woolf, the barbarian Other was the United States, where virtually all of the celebrations, both academic and mainstream, occurred.[53] For those within the States claiming to represent the "natural order of things," the Other became those feminists and popularizers whose responses to her were not only misguided but signs of a cult. The subtitle of Helen Dudar's derogatory essay, "The Virginia Woolf Cult," says it all: "On the 100th anniversary of her birth, she has become both a feminist icon and a flourishing industry, complete with T-shirts and calendars. Through it all, much of her writing endures brilliantly."[54] Dudar's target is as much academic critics, for the most part feminist, as T-shirts, but she spreads her net wide; it is left to Carolyn Heilbrun, introduced into the article as an example of the excesses of the cult mentality, to point out the linguistic demeaning of women writers and women readers implicit in the term *cult*— a term, she notes, that was not applied to those celebrating James Joyce's centenary that same year. In Dudar's telling, " 'If you admire Auden, that's good taste,' Professor Heilbrun notes sardonically. 'If you admire Sylvia Plath, it's a cult. Women are always in a defensive position. One has to be awfully careful to call something a cult.' " Four years later, Heilbrun spoke in her own voice: "When Woolf began to be studied, and written about, and to have her letters and other writings published, the result was a howl of laughter that echoed from *New Yorker* cartoons to newspaper articles discussing the 'cult' of Virginia Woolf. . . . It is the usual no-win situation: either a woman author isn't studied, or studying her is reduced to an act of misplaced religious fanaticism."[55]

When Peter Watson transmitted Dudar's article to a British public, he too pointed to the T-shirt as the prime example of her unwarranted, excessive popularity: "First there are the tee-shirts. Virginia Woolf tee-shirts have always outsold Jane Austen and even Emily Dickinson tee-shirts, but this year there is no contest." For Watson, this was just one more example of the poverty of American culture;[56] others in both Britain and the States, recognizing Virginia Woolf icon's selling power and its indication of a shifting cultural terrain, appropriated it for their own ends. The *New York Review of Books* ad featuring Virginia Woolf and Shakespeare, introduced in 1983, makes the visual and cultural point, as well as illustrating, in Paul Fussell's words, that "intellectuals" as well as "proles" experience the need to "[fuse themselves] with some successful commercial commodity—whether it be a pop star or a brand of pop—and [become] for the moment, somebody"; T-shirts "stamped with the logo of *The New York Review of Books*, . . . or printed with portraits of Mozart and Haydn and Beethoven . . . assure the world, 'I am civilized.' "[57]

Soon even the family recognized the potential of Virginia Woolf's un-bridled popularity. In 1991 the Charleston Trust, in conjunction with its money-raising campaign to restore Charleston, the home and studio of Vanessa Bell, Duncan Grant, and their family that Janet Malcolm calls "Bloomsbury's shrine," issued its own calendar, which reproduces many of the most popular photographs. If you can't stop the proliferation of Virginia Woolf icon, you can at least benefit from it.[58] While some of the Charleston Trust's constituency, many of them American, may be the same people who bought the original T-shirt in 1973, the context and the significance have changed dramatically, for here they are supporting rather than challenging the authority of the family. Nevertheless, the calendar's existence speaks to the widespread effect of the original T-shirt wearers in the production of Virginia Woolf icon.

Ironically, Charleston Trust's capitalizing on Virginia Woolf's iconic status stands in opposition to—and could be said to fuel—one of the predominant strands in the *British* construction of Virginia Woolf's image, whether in the academy or popular culture: that which reads Virginia Woolf icon not as subversive articulation of subcultural desires and power but as emblem of the reigning cultural system, the old order, that must itself be overthrown. This is certainly the case in another manifestation of Virginia Woolf icon in 1991, Tom Paulin's *J'Accuse* program on Britain's Channel Four, where visual images steal the show.[59] Faced with Virginia Woolf's "enormous and extraordinary" popularity, Paulin finds himself hard put to explain it, but he is absolutely certain of two things. First, he is clear that this popularity would evaporate if people actually read her works, including her letters and diaries, and realized not only how badly written the fiction is but how Victorian—how racist, imperialist, anti-Semitic, and snobbish—she and her characters are; this reading would leave her with little to offer the innumerable British women for whom she is a "feminist icon." More to my point, Paulin is equally certain that "part of the explanation lies . . . in the fragile beauty of her more flattering portraits, coupled with the enticing air of tragedy that surrounds her." At the moment Paulin utters these words, the Beresford profile of Virginia Stephen fills the screen.

In fact, visual images of Virginia Woolf vie for attention with Paulin's words and those of the other witnesses for the prosecution (Marxist critics Terry Eagleton and John Lucas; novelists Angela Carter and A. S. Byatt) throughout the program. Early on Paulin declares that although he has "never been able to understand [the] slavish and uncritical adulation" of Virginia Woolf, who in his view is "one of the most over-rated literary figures of the 20th century," "wherever you go these days Virginia Woolf is all around you." The point is illustrated by shots of a bookstore checkout counter flanked by a poster-sized reproduction of a Lenare portrait, where a young woman purchases a large quantity of Woolf's books; we also see close-ups of the portraits of Woolf on the covers and frontispieces.[60] Virginia Woolf's face continues to be "all around" for the rest of the program, providing, one assumes, visual proof of the accusations. For the most part the Beresford profile plays this role, often taking up at least half the screen; it is particularly visible during the scenes when the actress playing Virginia Woolf sardonically reads Woolf's written words, words that are meant to illustrate Paulin's critiques. Other photographs replace the Beresford to support specific points. Each image begins as a long shot of a framed picture and ends, almost inevitably, as a close-up; as the words become more damning, Woolf's face grows larger. The effect is mesmerizing—and subversive, for despite the forcefulness of the denunciations and Paulin's pain-stricken voice, the images prevail. Dissolving the framework and undermining the words, Virginia Woolf's face cannot be contained by the surrounding discourse.

But when we turn to other, more sophisticated British texts that juxtapose word and image in their explorations of Virginia Woolf's iconic significance—Alan Bennett's 1978 TV play *Me, I'm Afraid of Virginia Woolf* and Hanif Kureishi's 1987 film *Sammy and Rosie Get Laid*— the meanings become more complex. Here, the gender and class anxieties presented so naively in *J'Accuse* cross and recross, producing an almost unreadable network. Both texts are located in a specific time and place, and both explore specific class contexts and issues, but when read through the figure of Virginia Woolf icon, they reveal as well the increasingly mythic nature of the image-sign, including its incarnation of the monstrous feminine.

BRITISH GRAFFITI:

ME, I'M AFRAID OF VIRGINIA WOOLF

AND *SAMMY AND ROSIE GET LAID*

[Trevor] unrolls the picture of E. M. Forster. It has a moustache drawn on it, a little beard and a large cigar. He unrolls the picture of Virginia Woolf. This has been decorated with a large pair of tits.

—Alan Bennett, *Me, I'm Afraid of Virginia Woolf*

RAFI lies in bed in the half-lit room. He's asleep, having a nightmare. He cries out, then awakes. He lies there being stared at by Virginia Woolf, which becomes more horrible the more she looks at him.

—Hanif Kureishi, *Sammy and Rosie Get Laid*

In his review of Alan Bennett's television play *Me, I'm Afraid of Virginia Woolf,* first shown on London Weekend Television in November 1978, Michael Ratcliffe writes, "It is typical of Bennett's broad sympathies that whilst Trevor [Bennett's protagonist] is about to test the orthodoxies of Bloomsbury against the facts of his own experience, we are left feeling that in the end, despite the graffiti and the rude jokes about them, the old mentors will not fail." In contrast, Chris Dunkley feels that for most of the play "the text was actually contradicting" its "irresistible yet suspect" title: "the one thing that *didn't* seem to frighten Trevor Hopkins was the safely dead Virginia Woolf"; but "at the very end it turned out that Bennett's plot did fully warrant his piracy."[1] The contradictory readings of both the "graffiti" defacing Virginia Woolf in Bennett's play and, later, the poster of Virginia Woolf that so terrifies Rafi in Hanif Kureishi's 1987 film *Sammy and Rosie Get Laid* aptly summarize the deeply contradictory attitudes toward Virginia Woolf icon in Great Britain, attitudes that are rooted as much in class as they are in gender. Virginia Woolf's appearance as a visual icon in these studies of social and cultural mores, both of which include close-ups where her face and/or eyes dominate the screen, does more than underline the familiarity of her image, her star status, and/or the aristocracy, the cultural class, often read in or through it; it foregrounds the powerful intertexts, including her alignment with sexual and cultural destruction, that by this time are so deeply imbricated in her image that no graffiti can hide or erase them. Virginia Woolf has become as mythic and enigmatic as Medusa and the Sphinx, her shadowy alter egos.

My use of the term *graffiti* in the context of these two works needs some explanation. *Graffito,* the singular, defined by the *OED* as "a drawing or writing scratched on a wall or other surface; a scribbling on an ancient wall, as those at Pompeii and Rome," and by *Webster's* as "an inscription, slogan, drawing, etc., crudely scratched or scribbled on a wall or other public surface," has more recently been associated with "the spray-can brigades of the period since the 1960s," who, depending on your point of view, are either defacing or reclaiming public property. Part of the carnage wrought by these brigades, the 1996 edition of *Fowler's Modern English Usage* tells us, is the misuse of *graffiti,* the plural, as if it were a "mass noun requiring a singular verb." The implication is clear: more than public surfaces or grammatical rules are under threat; the graffiti-writing hordes or masses undermine the "distinction" between the singular and the plural that has provided clear boundaries and hence order in society and culture.[2] One is reminded here of the significant role played by popular genres such as T-shirts and posters in providing a space, a forum, for countercultural rearticulations of cultural signs or icons, a crossover reinforced by one of *Fowler's* examples of *graffiti*'s (mis)use as a singular: " 'I don't do drugs,' the T-shirt graffiti proclaims. . . ." One is reminded as well of the distinction drawn in the California courts between the singularity of works considered to be "art" and mass-produced objects such as T-shirts and posters that circulate within a more popular culture.[3]

The difference is that unlike the Historical Products Inc. T-shirt, the poster of Virginia Woolf defaced by the graffiti in Bennett's play is, as one of Trevor Hopkins's night students at the provincial Mechanics Institute where he teaches comments, "Council property," belonging to the state and its educational system.[4] Rather than being a countercultural icon, she becomes a sign of legitimate or official culture, and if not totally *of the* system, her suspect status resides more in her incarnation of Art, with a capital *A,* than in social rebellion. When combined with her class privilege, this designation would seem to render her work and perhaps her life alien if not meaningless to most of Hopkins's students. The conflict between Art and life enacted in Hopkins's classroom through Virginia Woolf is introduced in an aside made by the off-stage narrator, played by Alan Bennett, which appears in the script though not in the film. Responding to the insistence of Skinner, the most class-conscious and articulate of the students, that they debate whether Virginia Woolf's relationship with Vita Sackville-West was physical, Hopkins replies, "Would there be any point? I don't think any of us have precise information," to which the narrator adds, "Or were you crouching in your Leavisite underpants in the wardrobe at the time?" (58).

Enter F. R. Leavis, whose relegation of Woolf to a footnote in the great tradition of the English novel located in Jane Austen, George Eliot, Henry James, and Joseph Conrad, with a nod to Dickens and a sweeping endorsement of D. H. Lawrence as its inheritor, combined with his unremitting attacks on Bloomsbury and its ethos, had an enormous influence throughout the British educational system, doing more to shape British attitudes toward Virginia Woolf in Britain in the years following World War II than is currently recognized.[5] As Francis Mulhern argues in his 1979 study of Leavis, his intellectual colleagues, and his signature journal *Scrutiny,* by the 1950s "the literary canons established by Leavis became highly influential, his critical methods even more so; and the broad cultural themes of his journal became commonplaces of secondary education. Many accepted them literally and in their entirety; reformed or diluted, debased or syncretized, they became the faith of a whole profession, an inclusive vision of things that no other school subject and few university disciplines even attempted to match."[6] David Simpson attributes this success as much to Leavis's "immense personal influence upon generations of secondary school teachers" as to the role played by Cambridge English, founded in the years following World War I and Leavis's longtime base, in shaping the national agenda for English studies. As Simpson explains the Cambridge influence, "Through control of a major examining board in the secondary schools, and by sending generations of 'trained men' (as they mostly were) into those same schools to preach the gospel of the best that has been known and thought in the world, the orthodoxy in English (though not Scottish or Irish) literary education has been a creation of the Cambridge school."[7]

The success of one aspect of *Scrutiny*'s agenda proved particularly crucial to Virginia Woolf's image: its campaign "to mediate the introduction of a new, mainly petit bourgeois and self-consciously 'provincial' social layer into the national intelligentsia" (Mulhern, 320); in Simpson's terms, Leavis stood for a "lower middle (never a working) class ethic of vital human nature that, ever since the Augustans . . . had been disclaimed and displaced by polite culture and polite conventions" (253). Within this campaign, Virginia Woolf, both individually and as a representative of "the Bloomsbury ethos," becomes the emblematic representative of the "upper-middle class belle lettrists" and politeness that Leavis deplored (Simpson, 253). "Woolf," Mulhern writes, "was the main focus of *Scrutiny*'s pre-war campaign against Bloomsbury" during the 1930s, when the Leavisite canon and ethos were beginning to assert themselves, and part of the argument made against her was her "privileged amateurism" (123, 124). Q. D. Leavis's assaults in *Scrutiny* on "Woolf, [Dorothy] Sayers, and Gordon [G. S. Gordon, a disciple of Walter Raleigh, who ended his career as Oxford Professor of Poetry]," he adds, "were outstanding cases" of the attack on "haut-bourgeois predominance," an attack taken to heart by its younger "beneficiaries" such as Malcolm Bradbury, who participated in " 'the rise of the provincials' in English culture" (Mulhern, 320).[8] Bradbury's 1956 essay on the topic presents the challenge to Woolf and Bloomsbury as a central component of the change in taste that became part of the educational system: a " 'training in taste' " that "was qualitatively different from 'that Good Taste that one associates with the dons of Oxford colleges, with Virginia Woolf or E. M. Forster—it is far less dilettante and elite, involving rather a rigorous training in discrimination' " (cited in Mulhern, 320–21).[9]

When Mulhern published his book in 1979, the year following Bennett's play, he argued that the Leavisite canon and Leavisite critical practices were still very much in place in the English system, the latter challenged only recently by "alternative methodologies, derived largely from French and Russian semiotics" (328). Simpson concurs, although, as he points out, it's a story that did not necessarily apply to the new universities founded in the 1960s with a very different curricular organization and concept of education, especially in the humanities (258). Meanwhile "the turbulent younger generations in the 1960s and 1970s," Noel Annan writes, were far more likely to be influenced by the newly rediscovered Bloomsbury than by the Leavisite orthodoxy, finding in Bloomsbury "another group of young men and women [who] had mocked authority" and who shared their views on many matters, including sexuality. In Woolf's case, he writes, "the publication of Virginia Woolf's papers, diaries and letters established beyond question what the Leavises had denied: her claim to be one of the greatest writers of her age."[10] But this did not ensure her entrance into the university curriculum, an occurrence often dependent on the presence or nonpresence of Cambridge-trained faculty in the department; nor did it necessarily diminish the role of class in perceptions of the woman and the writing.[11] Talking at a 1982 centenary celebration at the University of Texas, Nigel Nicolson noted that "far more attention is given to Bloomsbury in your universities than in ours. At Cambridge, until a couple of years ago, Virginia Woolf was virtually ignored by the English Literature school," though at Oxford the situation was a little better.[12]

The situation at Cambridge, where the Leavisite attitude to what literature was and was not continued to hold sway,[13] also resulted in the opposition to those on the faculty working to construct a more comparativist, cultural, and/or materialist approach, endeavors linked variously at Cambridge to such figures as George Steiner, Raymond Williams, and Colin MacCabe. Again, Virginia Woolf and Bloomsbury play a role here, for MacCabe and many of the others involved in these intellectual and curricular initiatives were located in King's College, "very definitely a 'fashionable' college and . . . a particular object of scorn for F. R. Leavis himself, thanks to its Bloomsbury traditions," which had since the 1960s become "the most avant-garde intellectual community" in Cambridge (Simpson, 255–56). Given this background, the convening of the sole 1982 Virginia Woolf centenary celebration to be held in Britain at Cambridge becomes a stranger phenomenon than it first appears, bringing into open conflict the new critical/theoretical paradigms and the remnants of older Leavisite attitudes toward Virginia Woolf.[14]

While Hopkins's classroom in the Mechanics Institute is a long way from Cambridge and its tensions, Leavis's influence can be felt. Hopkins, with his attraction to both Woolf and Forster, seems at first distinctly un-Leavislike, although the title of the article he tells his mother he is writing, "Culture and Expropriation in the Novels of E. M. Forster," could imply a Leavisite stance; but his students show some very Leavisite attitudes toward Virginia Woolf's life and writings. What defined the great tradition of the novel for Leavis, and hence what Woolf lacked, was an interest in "form," yes, but never for its own sake: it had to be combined with or serve the interests of "truth to life," "interest in life," and "a marked moral intensity."[15] In this context Hopkins's desire to direct the discussion away from her life and onto her works seems a losing proposition. Skinner, the young, earringed man who at the end of the play will become Hopkins's lover, rescuing him for vitality and life, introduces the theme: "Take the novels of the lady in question, Virginia Woolf. Sensitive, yes. Poetic, yes. Gutsy? No" (52). Mrs. Tucker adds another element: "You see, she never had any children. If you've not had children you don't know what life's all about" (58).[16] Hopkins tries to defend her, pointing to her constant questioning of "What is life like?" "Listen," Skinner responds, "If Virginia Woolf had been born in Brighouse she'd never have got off the ground" (59). Mr. Dodds comments that he gets the feeling she "would have despised" him: "I know jolly well she'd have really looked down her snitch at me. Whereas it's funny I never get that feeling with Kipling" (60). At the end of the class, Skinner, addressing the "battered" picture of Virginia Woolf before throwing it away, sums the attitude up: "Well, love. Was it worth it? Look at the figures. Ten novels, five nervous breakdowns, no kids, one suicide. And this is where it's landed you, sweetheart: a further education class in the Mechanics' Institute, Halifax, on a wet Tuesday night in 1978. Let me introduce you, Virginia, old love. Here it is. Posterity. (*Puts her in the waste-paper basket.*)" (61–62).

Class conflict, then, as it intersects with Art and life, is central to Bennett's evocation of Virginia Woolf, as it seems to be to Bennett himself, who, by the way, went to Oxford; in the introduction to his collection *Writing Home* he transforms an actual encounter between his working-class mother and T. S. Eliot into a symbolic conflict between his two writing voices, in which Eliot "[represents] Art, Culture and Literature (all of them very much in the upper case) and my mother [represents] life (resolutely in the lower case)."[17] But other issues raised by Virginia Woolf play a role as well. Bloomsbury, for example: Hopkins finds it ironic that after struggling so hard in her writing to escape time and circumstances Woolf is now remembered almost primarily as the center of a group. And lesbianism: first in a painfully funny conversation between Hopkins and his mother, who tells him that she shared a bed with Aunty Phyllis during the war before asking euphemistically whether he is gay; and later in relation to Virginia's "very intimate relationship" with Vita Sackville-West (58), which might or might not have been physical. But lesbianism remains a hypothetical concept in view of the larger issue of Hopkins's sexuality, or lack thereof, and here perhaps Virginia Woolf is found most wanting. At the end of the play, after an unfulfilling sexual encounter with his horrid nongirlfriend Wendy, Hopkins remeets Skinner and realizes simultaneously his love for Skinner and his homosexuality; Virginia Woolf is present throughout. First, asked by Wendy, "What are you thinking about?" the frustrated Hopkins replies, "Virginia Woolf." On the bus home, still clutching the Virginia Woolf book he's been carrying all day, Hopkins watches a couple kiss; the man, angered, hits Hopkins, causing his nose to bleed, and this blood, staining Virginia Woolf's words at the moment of Hopkins's self-revelation, marks his entrance into life.

Virginia Woolf, you might think, would prove encouraging here, but no, and to understand why not, and why the plot fulfills the piracy of Albee's title, we need to return to the graffitied image of Virginia Woolf. Here we shift away from social and cultural class toward the more gendered, mythic anxieties Albee presented so well. The photograph is one of those taken by Lenare in 1929; the graffiti artist has added a white moustache and what the novelist Julian Barnes, reviewing the play, calls "pumpkin breasts," indicative of the "sexuality which an anonymous graphic critic held [her] to lack" (fig. 20).[18] (Recall here the scene in the early draft for the film version of Albee's play where Martha draws a moustache and a single eyebrow on her face: see Take 3.) Responses to the graffiti among Hopkins's students vary. One older woman, perceiving it as anarchy, demands Hopkins try to find the perpetrator, so he takes the photograph next door to the Mechanical Drawing class where, when told who she is, one student pronounces Virginia Woolf a "gormless-looking cow" (54). Later, during Hopkins's lecture, the picture hangs on the blackboard behind him; when Skinner approaches Hopkins after class, the breasts provide the backdrop for Hopkins's head. Just as Skinner is about to drop the picture in the trash can ("Here it is. Posterity."), the camera moves in to a close-up of Virginia Woolf's face.

And there is more. Before its circuit of the other classrooms and its trashing, the picture experiences yet another vital transformation: a young woman student, attempting to erase the graffiti, erases instead Virginia Woolf's nose (fig. 21). On one level clearly emblematic of her class status ("she'd have really looked down her snitch at me"), Virginia Woolf's nose, both Bennett and his audience would know, signifies as well the far more frightening power, the phallic power, attributed to women, strong women in particular. She might appear a "gormless-looking cow" once the nose has gone, but the visible lack of the nose, foregrounded during the close-up, remains a vivid marker of the uncanny threat posed by Virginia Woolf that no amount of erasing can undo. Whatever else "Virginia Woolf" may be in this play, her meaning never escapes her first representation: an exchange in which a bus conductress asks whether Virginia Woolf is funny and Hopkins replies, "Killing" (38).

At this level, Virginia Woolf once again becomes aligned with the monstrous, especially if one reads the image against the fear associated with noselessness, a state that returns us to the Sphinx—Egyptian, this time, rather than Greek, but frightening just the same. Harriet Martineau, the nineteenth-century Englishwoman abroad, provides a useful reference point in her description of the "nightmare" associated first with *not* seeing and then with seeing the Sphinx:

FIGURE 20. *Me, I'm Afraid of Virginia Woolf.*

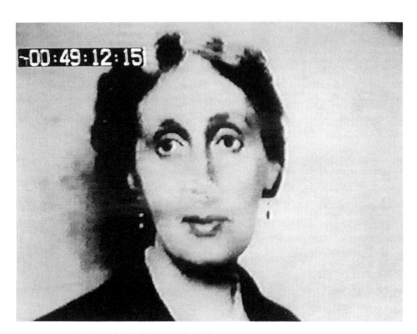

FIGURE 21. *Me, I'm Afraid of Virginia Woolf.*

When we first passed it, I saw it only as a strange-looking rock; an oversight which could not have occurred in the olden time, when the head bore the royal helmet or the ram's horns. Now, I was half afraid of it. The full serene gaze of its round face, rendered ugly by the loss of the nose, which was a very handsome feature of the old Egyptian face;—this full gaze, and the stony calm of its attitude almost turn one to stone. So lifelike,—so huge,—so monstrous,—it is really a fearful spectacle.

As John Barrell notes about the emphasis on missing projections in this passage (the helmet, the ram's horns, the nose), "we are positively invited . . . to discuss the Sphinx—a new Medusa's Head, the sign of an absence which can petrify—in terms of the crudest version of an anxiety about sexual difference."[19] Yes, although as Barrell argues it can also be read in terms of human/animal differences that have as much to do with race as with gender, a crossover that Cora Kaplan, looking at women's, even feminists', fears of feminism in nineteenth-century England, extends even further when she reads Martineau's Sphinx as

an aspect of monstrous femininity emerging in the 1840s as a figure of female excess, imagined as a vengeful black or brown woman. This figure which haunts a series of female narratives is a composite projection not only of what is unacceptable and transgressive in contemporary femininity, but in feminism itself—in women's resistance to dominant mores of gender, a resistance energised by a contradiction: for it involves the simultaneous recognition of her castration and her phallic power to resist. In threatening ways the sphinx and Martineau are dangerous doubles. . . .[20]

So too the Sphinx and Virginia Woolf.

Before leaving Bennett's play I want to record an extra-literary example of its representation of Virginia Woolf's uncanniness. When I first read the play I wrote to Bennett asking which photograph of Woolf appeared in the film; "the one by Man Ray," he replied, "with VW, with her fingers like this, indicating the size of something—what I don't like to think."[21] The accompanying drawing shows two moonlike crescents, top and bottom, with a space in between. Given the vividness and certainty of this response, with its playful sexual frisson, discovering that the picture was in fact the more benign Lenare photo becomes doubly intriguing. As we have seen, the Man Ray photo has a history of evoking strong responses from viewers,

and Bennett always enjoys playing the bad boy; but the absolute clarity of
the misprision suggests the eruption of a less playful fear.

Fear of what? becomes a central issue in *Sammy and Rosie Get Laid,*
which offers the most ambitious and ambiguous variations on the motif
established by Albee twenty-five years before, including the conjunction
of Virginia Woolf, the monstrous feminine, Medusa, and the Sphinx.
The recurrence of this motif at times of social crisis or change tells us a
great deal about Virginia Woolf as location and representation of cultural
anxieties; for if Albee's play appeared at a time when the phenomenon
of mass education and the demographics of who was being educated
raised the threats in the United States of the homogenization of culture,
the feminization/feminist-ization of culture, the intellectual or dominant
woman, and the refusal to reproduce, Kureishi's film conveys the fractures and contradictions in postmodern, postcolonial, Thatcherite Britain,
contradictions imbricated in the multifaceted, indeterminate image of Virginia Woolf.

How does Virginia Woolf perform this role? As in Bennett's play,
through a "fearful spectacle": the presence of a poster-size reproduction
of another of the Lenare photographs, this one presenting a more direct
gaze (fig. 5); as a result, Virginia Woolf looks silently out at the actors
and toward the viewers in many of the central scenes. Before turning to
the enigmatic quality of the poster, however, I want to back up a moment
and note the other major link between the two works: both were directed
by Stephen Frears, one of the British directors linked to the visibility and
vitality of British film during the Thatcher years. Between 1985 and 1987,
Frears directed three of the most highly praised and politically inflected
films of the period: *My Beautiful Laundrette,* also written by Kureishi;
Prick Up Your Ears, a film about gay playwright Joe Orton, with a script
by Alan Bennett; and *Sammy and Rosie Get Laid.*

The first thing one learns in reading about Frears, whether in interviews
or biographical and critical articles, is his long history of working in
television during the late 1960s and 1970s, a history that ties him firmly
to a tradition of documentary style, realism, and social criticism. Critics
often cite the last as the impetus for the class consciousness and interest
in marginal groups that characterize his subsequent cinematic films. But
Frears himself gives a slightly different reading, emphasizing that British
television's embracing of "social criticism, not at a particularly ferocious
level," was a function of its commitment to "giving an accurate account
of what it's like to live in Britain"; his television films, he has also said,
deal with "men and women who go to work and lead rather desperate
lives."[22] In other words, Frears's depiction of "what it's like to live in

Britain" necessarily involves class, as well as race, gender, sexuality, family, regional differences, nationalism, metropolitan London, capitalism, unemployment, and the politics that informs each and every one of the above. *My Beautiful Laundrette,* financed by Channel Four, the independent television channel whose mandate was, in part, to speak to and for a wide range of "minorities," necessarily carried this tradition into the cinema.[23] Gayatri Spivak describes Channel Four's function as "something like what Gramsci calls the formation of the intellectual, the preparation of viewership. . . . If part of this role is to educate the so-called minorities, part is to educate the so-called dominant viewership about the minorities as well. Stephen Frears's films fit this latter role more persuasively. . . . As such, they renegotiate the relationship between aesthetics and politics."[24]

Sammy and Rosie Get Laid, Frears has stated, made when the government's economic and social policies had led to a substantial deterioration of living conditions in a large number of regional and urban areas and the Conservatives faced an election it was thought they might lose, "was an attempt to bring Margaret Thatcher down"; "that film is entirely bound up in the politics of Britain," a politics as fractured as the film itself.[25] Characterized by multiple protagonists, multiple narratives and themes, and the extensive use of crosscutting, including "shock cuts," the film wants, in Kureishi's words, to show "what's happening in England," including the overlap of the personal and political "in a certain world of stress, tension, and pressure, of political realities." In the diary he kept while making the film, Kureishi describes the film as consisting of a "mixture of realism and surrealism, seriousness and comedy, art and gratuitous sex."[26]

Critics' responses to the everything-and-the-kitchen-sink approach varied enormously and often had little to do with their stated sympathy for the film's explicit political critique. A number of reviewers, most of them British, wrote the film off completely, arguing it was a distorted, leftist, view of Britain and not worth the effort necessary to follow it; as one reviewer put it, "Kureishi is so set on pushing every distempered social misfit into his purpose-built purgatory of 'Thatcher's Britain' that Sammy and Rosie & Co. are overlaid with the graffiti of the Loony Left. Characters are made into message-bearers; voices become mouthpieces; and the thesis that communal chaos is inherently more humane than order is so foolishly over-indulged as to be self-defeating."[27] Other reviewers, more sympathetic to its vision and its goals and loath to "report unfavourably" on the film, nevertheless wish it had the naturalness, the "easy handling of big themes" and understated, ironic quality—or what one critic called the "lucid realism"—of *My Beautiful Laundrette,* which these writers consider a better film.[28]

But for some reviewers, the fragmentation, the abrupt cuts, the mixture of styles such as realism and surrealism, the lack of a simple or single reading of the major figures and of easy alternatives for action or belief, become the point of the film. As one critic put it, "*Sammy and Rosie Get Laid* steps boldly out of categories, in an attempt to capture realities that its own characters can't comprehend. . . . It expresses the violence of cultural collapse"; in another's words, "this film's truths are not so easy to see. . . . Nothing comes easy . . . , certainly not answers." Writing of the "ambiguity and contradiction" built into the film, including an "ambiguous and ironic perspective" on its own characters, a third argues that this perspective keeps it from becoming "either politically didactic or schematic."[29] This is my starting point as well, but not my conclusion, for reasons that have everything to do with the representation of Virginia Woolf.

Within the framework of ambiguity and contradiction, Virginia Woolf's multifaceted, highly ambiguous role in the film can be read as a metonymy for the film itself. When I first wrote about this role in the context of the postmodern versioning of Virginia Woolf's texts, I posed the question of her "meaning" as follows: What is Virginia Woolf doing in Hanif Kureishi's self-consciously postmodern depiction of London in the late 1980s, and why is she presiding over a race riot and the burning of the inner city? The poster of Woolf hangs in the study of Rosie, social worker, feminist, sometime political activist; Woolf's writings, in their distinctive Hogarth Press covers, figure prominently in the center of her bookshelves. Rafi, Rosie's father-in-law, the Pakistani politician returned to the "Home Country" to escape death threats occasioned by the brutal persecution of his enemies, sees the flames from the riot superimposed on Woolf's image and experiences her gaze with horror. In a film where the text of T. S. Eliot's *Waste Land* covers the outside of a caravan parked on a waste ground reclaimed by a countercultural, multiracial community, the status of "high" modernism in the world of postmodern, postcolonial, metropolitan London is very much at stake, and Virginia Woolf seems to have become an icon representative of modernism itself. Yet has she? And if so, what do she and her gaze represent? Aloofness? A life and a writing style out of touch with the political realities of her own day, let alone those of the present? Or is her presence more contemporary, and perhaps more sympathetic? Does it evoke her feminism, including her insistence on the interconnections of the public and private spheres, and her elevation by modern-day feminists such as Rosie (whose political commitments within the film are highly ambiguous) to the position of "matron saint"? Given the history of the British perception of Woolf as the elite, snobbish Queen of Bloomsbury and, oh yes, minor experimental writer, what does the prominence of her image in this distinctly political film suggest? Does she preside over it as modernist, as feminist, as pacifist, as highbrow, as sapphist, as suicide, as failed liberal anti-imperialist? And how do we begin to decipher the film's construction of her enigmatic, silent, Mona Lisa–like stare?[30]

Later, returning to the film in the context of Virginia Woolf's representations in popular culture, I found myself inexorably drawn to the fact that the one reaction to the photograph explicitly specified in the script was horror. Whose horror is it, I began to ask, and is the film really as undecidable, at least in relation to fear, as I had originally thought? While I still believe that the "meaning" of the sign "Virginia Woolf" in the film is multiple and will shift, in a distinctly postmodern fashion, in accordance with the discourse in which it is located (feminism, modernism, lesbianism, suicide, etc.), the reiteration of the topoi generated by the Albee play, particularly those associated with fear, constitutes a pervasive subtext that crosses discursive boundaries and jumps out of the film's immediate contexts to construct Virginia Woolf in surprisingly familiar ways.

The central scene for this reading occurs in Rosie's study, where the newly arrived Rafi has been put to bed under the poster of Virginia Woolf. As described in the passage from the script used in the epigraph,

> RAFI *lies in bed in the half-lit room. He's asleep, having a nightmare. He cries out, then awakes. He lies there being stared at by Virginia Woolf, which becomes more horrible the more she looks at him. The noise from outside rises around him. It could be in his head or for real: he doesn't know. He sits up. On the edge of the bed he pulls cottonwool out of his ears. He covers his face with his hands.*[31]

In the film, the camera shifts back and forth from Rafi's startled stare to the photograph of Woolf, moving closer and closer until Woolf's eyes fill the screen. What looks like lace curtains cover the portrait; flames burn at the bottom of the frame (figs. 22–24). Woolf might be presiding over sacrificial rites, or she might be the sacrifice. At any rate, Rafi's reaction is terror; still wearing his nightclothes, he runs from the room and the house.

Few reviewers or critics address the poster per se or its powerful presence during this scene. Those who comment on the poster but not the scene tend to read it as a sign of Rosie's "political correctness," her making "all the right feminist and left-wing noises." (Ditto for the picture of Jacques Lacan; Pauline Kael is the only person to note the postcard of Vanessa Bell that appears as well.)[32] The writers who comment specifically on Virginia

FIGURE 22.
*Sammy and
Rosie Get Laid.*

FIGURE 23.
*Sammy and
Rosie Get Laid.*

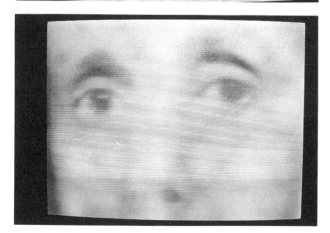

FIGURE 24.
*Sammy and
Rosie Get Laid.*

Woolf's fiery presence during Rafi's riot-inflected nightmare portray its meaning as self-evident and overdetermined, although they differ radically in their overall reading of the film. One commentator notes that the "shot of Rosie's photograph of Virginia Woolf seemingly enveloped in flames . . . is too obvious a bit of underlining," while another comments that "the *content* of [Frears's] images, for which Kureishi himself may be responsible, is occasionally redundant or excessive: see the shot that frames Virginia Woolf's photograph in flames." But underlining what? Redundant with respect to what? Virginia Woolf, the priestess of Bloomsbury and high culture, may be "burning," but does the film—do we—cheer or regret this? Moreover, the image itself is not as clear as these men think; Pauline Kael reads "the flickering fires in the street" during the riots as "spectral altar lights burning *for* Woolf" (my emphasis).[33]

If we look at this image through the motifs I have been tracking— fear and its monstrous incarnations in Virginia Woolf—the ambiguity both Frears and Kureishi insist is deliberate begins to acquire some edges; patterns begin to emerge. My first frame of reference is Bloomsbury, introduced into the discourse about the film by Gayatri Spivak, who reads Rosie as representing the difficult if not impossible position of "the old ideological subject of radicalism" at that political moment, particularly when the subject is British and white. Both terms are crucial, for as Spivak notes they connote a very different tradition of radicalism from that in the United States, even (or especially) in the sixties: a "whole mindset which was already established as a class producing its own radicalism from within." Rosie, Spivak argues,

> white, deliberately downwardly class-mobile, a social worker, het-
> erosexual, . . . seemed almost to embody the inherent orthodoxy of
> that position which Raymond Williams describes at the end of his
> wonderful essay entitled "The Bloomsbury Fraction": "The early
> confidence of the position [in the civilized individual], in the period
> before 1914 has, in its long encounter with all these other and actual
> social forces, gone, in Leonard Woolf's title, downhill all the way.
> For all its continuing general orthodoxy, it appears now much more
> often as a beleaguered rather than as an expanding position."[34]

In the essay cited by Spivak, Williams grants the Bloomsbury Group a significant role in the development of British culture. Although it remained a fraction of the ruling class, he notes, it was distinguished from it by its awareness of the contradictions in its class position and by its social and political critique, including its social conscience, its anti-imperial and anti-militaristic stance, and its desire for the equality of women. The limits of Bloomsbury's position, he continues, is contained in its basic premise, that of the "civilized *individual,*" which ultimately split the public from the private sphere and left class formations in place: "The social conscience, in the end, is to protect the private consciousness." Yet Williams does not diminish what the group stood for or the genuineness of its critique; its position, he argues, must be understood historically and distinguished from its naturalization as the far less politically radical construct—a "social conscience" or the "civilized" norm—in more recent stages of British culture.[35]

In her reading of Rosie's political position as indeterminate ("You cannot really be against Rosie, but she has no final determination"), Spivak also notes that the film presents "in a very unemphatic way the real representative of the old Bloomsbury fraction":[36] Alice, the character played by Claire Bloom, whose family had been in India for generations, who loved Rafi, and who, as the film progresses, ultimately rejects him. Oddly, Spivak ignores the portrait of Virginia Woolf, which not only brings Bloomsbury visibly into the film's political discourse but provides a visual counterpart to Alice, who bears a resemblance to the picture on the wall. As we've seen, it is Virginia Woolf who stares down at Rafi after his nightmare and who, later in the film, visibly witnesses the exchange where Rosie defends Rafi ("I don't hate him") against the two black women, Rani and Vivia, who want to confront him for his political crimes. Rani replies, "This is liberalism gone mad!"

The introduction of Rani and Vivia into the discussion also introduces a response to Rosie that finds her far less indeterminate and challenges Spivak's view that Rosie "loves all the right people. She's a white heterosexual woman who loves lesbians, loves blacks, is in an interracial marriage, etc., etc."[37] My source here is bell hooks, whose focus is Rosie's whiteness. Rosie, she writes, is "the quintessential white 'feminist.' When she is not having sex, she is bonding with white women and non-white women to critique masculinity. Conveniently, this bonding is not disrupted by sexual competition for men, since the two most visible black women are lesbians." Hooks's critique grows from her broader observation of the writing of black women out of the film, both as mothers and as the objects of desire for the nonwhite men; in the interracial heterosexual couples, all the women are white and all the men are black. Black women such as Rani, she adds, who show clearly "radical political beliefs," are "portrayed as 'hysterical,' one might even say as monstrous." However much Rosie might be a "symbol of failed modern radicalism," hooks concludes, her "cool, politically correct" attitude is indistinguishable from her presentation as "nurturing mother" to the Third World, where she duplicates "in a slightly inverted form the white male, imperialist, paternal position."[38] In this context, Virginia Woolf, standing in for Rosie, becomes emblematic of the whiteness of a "feminism" that looks on at but resists the political and sexual demands and actions of nonwhite women; her indeterminacy becomes a sign of a whiteness that gives her the privilege to move around denied to those marked by not being white.[39] Like the Virginia Woolf in Alice Walker's "In Search of Our Mothers' Gardens," this Virginia Woolf would need to be rewritten for a "womanism" defined in its own and not white terms.[40]

Kureishi and Frears, it should go without saying, are not Alice Walker, and their fears of Virginia Woolf, read through the British/Bloomsbury context with its ongoing, controversial imbrication of politics and sexuality (bisexuality, homosexuality), have a different valence. Here the older woman, Alice, becomes as much of a player as Rosie: Alice who, standing in for Virginia Woolf, finds immediate acceptance among the lesbians, even as she defends her own (hetero)sexual choices in terms of the social mores of her time. At the end of the film, having rejected Rafi and his politics, she makes up one of the group of women of disparate ages, races, and sexualities who sit around the kitchen table while Rafi, we later learn, hangs himself.

At this point, I want to separate the political from the sexual and suggest that however much the Rosie/Alice/Virginia Woolf configuration may be unreadable in the film's political discourse, its meanings in the sexual discourse are only too clear. In terms of Rafi's politics, that is, there appears to be no way to decide whether his horror of Virginia Woolf is justified or not. We are not meant to reject Rafi out of hand, despite his politics, just as we are not meant to reject Rosie or Alice. Given this undecidability, Bloomsbury and Virginia Woolf can be articulated either as moral outrage, in which case we have no empathy with Rafi when he runs in terror from her gaze (or when he commits suicide), *or* as the failure of the liberal British intelligentsia, represented by Virginia Woolf, to understand the complexity of both the colonial and the postcolonial situation. In the latter case, Rafi's fear of Virginia Woolf is justified, and we share it.

But the sexual fears read differently. Virginia Woolf may well mirror or reflect Rafi's worst nightmares, but his nightmares, as the film progresses, have as much to do with the breakdown of his expectations of "the family" and "home" as they do with his political past. And within this latter discourse the Virginia Woolf/Bloomsbury configuration is troped once again as a threat to manhood, heterosexuality, marriage, and the patriarchy: a threat to the family that Rafi had abandoned earlier but wants Sammy and Rosie to reproduce by having children. Both Rafi and Frears are explicit on this point, though Frears's comments have an ironic edge. "What about the sound of little footsteps," Rafi asks Rosie; "isn't it about time? . . . Eh? I know you're a kind of feminist, but you're not a lesbian too, are you?" Frears, writing that "Hanif put Virginia Woolf in both as an homage to Feminism (the poster would belong to Rosie) and as a reminder of the nightmare of Feminism (Sammy's life is made miserable by Rosie's liberation)," adds that Rafi, "a sentimental Asian torturer, is outraged to discover his beloved London gripped by race riots and filled with women confronting him with his crimes. How can he be haunted by a picture of a dotty upper-middle-class woman who walked into a river in 1941 and wrote about lighthouses in Cornwall?"[41]

Within the context of a (patriarchal) sexual discourse, then, Rafi has clearly defined fears of Virginia Woolf; Sammy shares at least some of them although he would never admit it. As almost all the reviewers agree (although none is as explicit as Frears is ten years after the fact), despite the "open marriage" and Sammy's sexual relationships it is clear he would like more from Rosie than she is willing to give, and many respond by writing nervously of Rosie's control of the situation; in one critic's telling, "She is the Free Woman with the Gioconda smile. Like her husband, she sleeps around: she is . . . sphinx-like, self-assured."[42] Spivak argues that *Sammy and Rosie* stages its broader political and cultural issues "in the break between father and son, and the general crisis of the legacy of heterosexism," but the "Oedipal parricide"[43] might well not occur without Rosie's strong presence and her resistance to both Rafi's and Sammy's desires. Ultimately the film's fear of Rosie and her sexuality becomes a fear of the powerful, potentially deadly woman, and I want to illustrate why by returning to the mythic figure of the Medusa, introduced into the film's discourse through the portrait of Virginia Woolf blown up to poster size and displayed so prominently in Rosie's room.

As noted above, the Lenare photograph featured in the poster is one of the few portraits of Virginia Woolf where she looks more or less directly into the camera and hence at the viewer. Elizabeth Richardson describes it as the softest of the three Lenare photographs; Kael writes that it portrays Virginia Woolf "at her most luminous."[44] This makes the role of the photograph particularly ironic, because staring in our direction, the portrait poses a series of questions associated with the female gaze: about what happens when women, traditionally positioned as the object of the gaze, look back. One answer, of course, is that she becomes Medusa. Here, Virginia Woolf, who herself had written "What does one fear?— the human eye," becomes the woman who looks, and in Stephen Heath's formula, "If the woman looks, the spectacle provokes, castration is in the air, the Medusa's head is not far off."[45] The provocation, the seductiveness, of Medusa's deadly gaze becomes even more powerful when read against her beauty, a doubleness brilliantly encapsulated by Jean-Pierre Vernant when he writes, "Superimposed on the mask of Medusa, as though in a two-sided mirror, the strange beauty of the feminine countenance, brilliant with seduction, and the horrible fascination of death, meet and cross."[46] When Sammy, asked by a Rosie who clearly fascinates him, "If you had to choose between sleeping with George Eliot or Virginia Woolf, who would you choose?" replies, "On looks alone, I'd go for Virginia," he too is drawn into her potentially deadly gaze. Beautiful but castrating, beautiful but deadly: looks can kill.

Rafi's experience of Virginia Woolf's gaze differs, reflecting another of Vernant's insights into the terror, the incarnation of "pure fright" located in Medusa: that Medusa's stare, always situated in front of you, reflects back to you, as in the mirror, your own image and your own impending death:

> Like the image of yourself reflected by the mirror that always sends back your own gaze, the head of the Gorgo—contrary to the artistic conventions of archaic art where characters are always painted in profile—is always represented frontally. The glimmer of its staring eyes beams down on its spectators, sending them its fascinating frontal gaze. Whoever sees the head of Medusa is changed in the mirror of its pupils, . . . into a face of horror: the phantomlike figure of a being who, in passing through the mirror and leaping over the boundary that separates light from darkness, has immediately sunk down into formlessness and is now a nothing, a nonperson.[47]

No wonder Rafi, pursued by the phantom of a torture victim and rejected by Rosie and Alice, fears Virginia Woolf's stare. When at the end of the film, having nowhere to go to escape from himself, he hangs himself in Rosie's study, Virginia Woolf, we know, looks on.

The image of Rafi as the hanged man introduces another recurring and powerful aspect of Virginia Woolf icon in the film: her presentation as a visual image, a "powerless, mute [sign]" that, particularly when read against the long history of distrust of spectacle and its associations with "Woman" or the feminine, threatens by its spectacular silence to devour or destroy.[48] Here, Virginia Woolf stands juxtaposed to the other literary/cultural modernist who intertextually haunts the film, T. S. Eliot, but who, in sharp contrast to the deadly Virginia Woolf, is represented through the creative power of words. The words are those of *The Waste Land*. They are written on the walls of the caravan where Rosie and Danny/Victoria, the androgynously beautiful young black man and pacifist who guides Rafi and the viewer through the film, make love; and they are brought to life by the countercultural inhabitants of the waste ground where the caravan is parked, who use the site to grow food, print texts, and play a game of chess. In this context, only Rafi, pursued by the one-eyed ghost of his tortured victims, unable to stay in the waste ground where he has taken refuge and returned to the realm of Virginia Woolf's stare, suggests the darker side of Eliot's poem.

My reading of Eliot's words, "graffitied" on the caravan as a sign of countercultural defiance, once again poses Virginia Woolf as a representation of official or high culture.[49] In an article that presents *Sammy and Rosie* as "a filmed version of [*The Waste Land*], . . . a poetic, symbolic, visionary presentation of Thatcher's England as Eliot's Waste Land," Colette Lindroth places the image of the burning "poster picture of Virginia Woolf" in the context of the destruction of Western culture, a destruction, she argues, that is linked to the redemption by fire written into Eliot's poem and promised at the end of the film through the "sympathy" Sammy and Rosie, locked in each other's arms, appear to offer each other after Rafi's death. But she does not explain why, or in what way, Virginia Woolf's and/or Western culture's fiery end become necessary to this redemption, or why Virginia Woolf represents that which is being burned away. Nor does her reading of the ending as a return to the heterosexual marriage and the implied end of the sterility she associates with Sammy and Rosie's childless marriage address the continued, deadly presence of Virginia Woolf after the flames.[50]

What strikes me finally about the juxtaposition of Virginia Woolf's eyes and T. S. Eliot's words is the asymmetry of their representations in relation to life and/or death and the push-and-pull effect of their interactions. Virginia Woolf's Medusa-like stare may win out over T. S. Eliot's life-promising graffiti, but it is a chimerical victory in a culture that continues to fight its class and gendered battles, including its battles over the nature of culture, both high and low, through the figure of Virginia Woolf. The 1994 film *Tom & Viv,* in which both Virginia Woolf and T. S. Eliot appear in their own persons, offers another take on the contours and ramifications of the struggle.

Outtake 1

Before leaving the conjunction of Virginia Woolf and T. S. Eliot in *Sammy and Rosie Get Laid,* I want to mention Peter Wollen's interpretation of the factors that kept Britain, in particular England, from producing what could be characterized as a "new wave" cinema until the 1980s; among the most significant was the absence of "an avant-garde section of [the] intelligentsia" that accepted and advocated "modernism" in its purer, European forms. In "literature and in taste-setting journalism," he argues, what England had instead of an avant-garde was "a bloodless transfer of power to the Bloomsbury group, within the traditional intelligentsia itself, and an increasingly emollient modernism was assimilated into the ongoing high culture with hardly a break. Indeed, the most effective protagonists of modern literature—Eliot and Leavis—argued for modernism in frankly traditionalist terms." As a result, before the "last new wave" could occur—and *Sammy and Rosie Get Laid* appears in Wollen's list of the films illustrating its existence—British cinema had to jettison both "the diluted modernism of the traditional intelligentsia, a decaying amalgam of Bloomsbury and Cold War pieties," and the romanticism and neoromanticism associated with Eliot. From this perspective, one assumes, both Virginia Woolf *and* T. S. Eliot would be equally problematic for a "new wave" oppositional filmmaker. Elsewhere, however, Wollen exempts Virginia Woolf; explicating Raymond Williams's "Bloomsbury Fraction," he adduces her feminism as the impulse for her entrance into the avant-garde and the source of the subversive residue that she, unlike others in the group, left to future generations.[51]

Outtake 2

While there are many (mainstream) films by Anglo-American directors that cite Eliot's words, Woolf's words are still few and far between, although that may be changing. *The Proposition* (1997), for example, whose working title was *Shakespeare's Sister,* explicitly evokes the room of her own belonging to the writer-protagonist, who, we are told, thinking of herself as Judith Shakespeare, quotes the words from the conclusion of Woolf's essay declaring that "the dead poet who was Shakespeare's sister will be born again" in a novel dedicated to Virginia Woolf; subsequently, she dies giving birth to twin sons.[52] But French directors have long used Virginia Woolf's words to mark significant moments in their films. One, Jeanne Moreau's 1976 *Lumière,* explores the complexities of mixing life and art for four actresses. Toward the end, as two friends of the older actress (Moreau) wait for her to wake before telling her an old friend has committed suicide, Woolf's words from *Between the Acts* are heard on the radio. The words come from two passages in the novel. The first, introduced by the question "Did the plot matter?" tells us that "the plot was only there to beget emotion. There were only two emotions: love; and hate." The second describes the playwright's agony when "the stage was empty," her "power had left her. . . . Illusion had failed. 'This is death,' she murmured, 'death.' Then suddenly, as the illusion petered out, the cows took up the burden."[53]

Another film, Jean-Luc Godard's fragmented, postmodern version of *King Lear* (1987), juxtaposes, in one of its multiple "plots," Shakespeare's play with other patriarchal stories and figures in an attempt to recover Shakespeare's words. During the moments preceding Cordelia's presumed off-screen murder by her father, a woman named Virginia is shown reading Woolf's *The Waves;* the novel had previously washed up on shore. A voiceover speaks the penultimate paragraph of the novel, which begins "And in me too, the wave rises" and ends "Against you I will fling myself, unvanquished and unyielding, O Death!"[54] After this we see Cordelia, dead.

In both citations of Woolf's novels, life, art, illusion, the construction of self, the dispersal of self, and death are twined and intertwined, although the emphasis differs. If *Lumière* uses Woolf's words to stress the gaps in life where illusion fails even the playwright or actor and death enters the scene, Goddard's *King Lear* evokes one of Woolf's strongest defiances of death, however inevitable. In both, gender plays a role: in terms of the films' concern with the situation of women in Western culture and art; and in terms of a woman writer's providing the words. In *Lumière* the words stand on their own, bridging a moment of silence; hearing them on the radio one character murmurs, "How strange." In *King Lear,* Peter Donaldson writes, Woolf's words "compete with and supplant those of Shakespeare," constituting "a restoration to voice of some part of [Cordelia's] story left unwritten by Shakespeare," speaking dispersal and a "terrible 'nothing.' "[55] In the works of French filmmakers, then, Virginia Woolf's words became part of "the secular canon in which we paradigmatically locate 'meaning' and 'culture,' " an ironic juxtaposition to her problematic cultural position as threatening visual icon in Anglo-American film.[56]

TOM & VIV & VIRGINIA & EDITH &

OTTOLINE & VITA & CARRINGTON...

Looking back at Alan Bennett's *Me, I'm Afraid of Virginia Woolf* in 1997, the director, Stephen Frears, commented that Virginia Woolf is present in the play "as a symbol both of high intelligence and literary genius and of the ridiculousness and futility and inappropriateness of high culture in the modern world (who deserves to be defaced since our sympathies are clearly with the defacing). Literature (Art?) is therefore both where you learn how to live and where you avoid living."[1] From Frears's added comment that "Virgina [*sic*] Woolf is now of course more honoured for her place in Biography and Literary Gossip," we might well feel that Bennett was prescient: that Art with a capital *A*, high art, has indeed ended up in the wastepaper basket of contemporary culture, which might or might not include films about such modernist icons as Virginia Woolf and T. S. Eliot.

Certainly a number of commentators on Brian Gilbert's 1994 film *Tom & Viv*, the chronicle of the poet's marriage to Vivienne Haigh-Wood, felt that the film trashed Art, loudly lamenting not only the film's focus on the man and the husband rather than the poet and his poetry, but the death blow it dealt to Eliot's literary, cultural stature. Writing in the *New York Times*, Richard Bernstein declared that after this film one will no longer be able to write, as Cynthia Ozick once did, that Eliot seemed " 'pure zenith, a colossus, nothing less than a permanent luminary fixed in the firmament like the sun and the moon.' " The Englishman Anthony Lane, writing in the *New Yorker*, put it even more strongly. Describing "the motives that fuel the film" as "[dramatized] envy, raising the dismal prospect that our age has become offended by genius," he offers the following prediction: "Devotees of the poet . . . will leave the theatre in suitably controlled fury; he is now so unfashionable that the act of reading him has itself become a monastic Eliot-like operation, and the film can only drive us deeper underground. . . . The movie is not just lacklustre but irresponsible, because it will foster more Eliot haters than there are Eliot readers; people will come away knowing for certain why they dislike him, without feeling the need to discover whether they like his work."[2]

The 1994 perception that *Tom & Viv* was demolishing the poet's stature challenges Jonathan Freedman's 1987 argument (the same year *Sammy and Rosie Get Laid* appeared) that popular culture, in its "search for cultural legitimacy," drew upon those figures and concepts that "official or high culture," including the academy, were in the act of abandoning; T. S. Eliot plays the starring role. Freedman's speculations hinge on his observation of a crossover between the academy and popular culture: that while academics had begun to teach and write about popular culture, popular culture was introducing into its productions both "those works which have been traditionally cited as being central to the Western literary tradition" and "the very notions that we in the academy have come to distrust most intensely—the privileging of irony, complexity, and ambiguity, the timelessness of works of art, the notion of the tortured genius of the poet, writer, or musician."[3] This had not been the case in the 1950s and 1960s, John Guillory notes; at that time the academy, functioning as the "social space" where literary culture, characterized as "minority culture," was "internalized as a *mode of consumption* in the graduate of the university," remained distinct from the social space of mass culture.[4] But even as it performed this function, it provided a basis for subsequent eruptions of Art into the popular realm. As Freedman describes this process, Eliot's "apotheosis" in popular culture, in particular his presence in Francis Ford Coppola's *Apocalypse Now,* embodies the dictum that "(academically) discounted poets, . . . immediately after their decline in the university," turn up in popular culture as a form of "autocanonization": as a way of saying that what we have here is "art."[5] The reiteration of lines from "The Love Song of J. Alfred Prufrock" in films such as James Brooks's *Mike's Murder* and Woody Allen's *Love and Death,* Freedman argues, indicates the stature achieved by Eliot during the 1960s when the directors were in college, the same stature that academics in 1987 were in the process of dismantling. Freedman's analysis is directed toward American culture, but given the ambivalence of British academics toward Virginia Woolf during the 1960s and 1970s, it could explain the vitality of T. S. Eliot's presence in *Sammy and Rosie* and the negativity of Virginia Woolf's.

If Freedman's reading of the time-lag between academic and popular attitudes toward high culture is accurate, the reincarnation of T. S. Eliot as "Tom" in *Tom & Viv* would seem to mark the end of high or literary culture, of Art, as a source of vitality or authority in either realm: academy or popular culture. No more wastelands as an emblem of life, however diminished. The same might be said for the appearance of Virginia Woolf in the film, but with a difference, the difference of gender, transforming her from the threatened artist/genius into the threat itself. Here, Virginia Woolf becomes the embodiment of a Bloomsbury that has undergone a significant refashioning for the worse. Rather than representing feminism or a tradition of rebellion, however limited, against her own class, Virginia Woolf now exemplifies a feminized elitism that destroys both genuine creativity and human beings. Read from this perspective, T. S. Eliot and the culture he represents are far from dead. Not only does he retain his authority and canonical status, he reigns supreme, and he does so at the expense of those women such as Virginia Woolf and Vivienne Eliot whose own claims as artists are either discredited or overwhelmed by the pervasive, destructive power of their material beings. In this way *Tom & Viv* proves a trenchant commentary on the intersections of cultural class and gender in the mid-1990s, in which Art, at least in its male figurations, remains alive and well despite the encroachment of the monstrous Other incorporated in the woman/artist.

Based on the 1984 play by Michael Hastings, who, with Adrian Hodges, adapted the play for the screen, *Tom & Viv* covers the period from the couple's courtship and elopement in 1915 to Vivienne's death in a private mental asylum in 1947.[6] By that time she had been in the asylum, committed, according to Hastings, by her brother and by Tom, who jointly controlled the considerable Haigh-Wood estate, for eleven years, during which period Tom neither wrote to nor visited her. As represented in the film, Vivienne's "madness," defined by the doctors as "moral insanity," may well have been related to the medicines prescribed for what today we would call a hormonal imbalance, which caused severe headaches, stomach pains, and incessant menstrual bleeding. The medicines led to erratic behavior, defined as antisocial and inappropriate, and illustrated in the film first by loud, "vulgar" talk and wild mood swings and later by such acts as pouring melted chocolate through the mail slot at Faber and Gwyer's when Tom's secretary refuses to let her in. Finally, in a gesture that is used decisively against her when she is committed, Viv threatens Edith Sitwell and Virginia Woolf with what turns out to be a toy knife. When, post-menopause and perfectly "sane," she is visited by an American psychologist who is horrified that no one has had her released, she in turn defends Tom—"T. S. Eliot is the greatest living poet in the English language"; "he has my undying love . . . and he knows it"—and walks away. The movie ends with an image of Tom's suffering face.

Among the many premises governing the film's representation of the relationship, two are particularly significant here. The first is that Viv was herself a talented writer, whose hand, quite literally, is all over *The Waste Land*. She provided, that is, not only the inspiration (the negative inspiration, some might say) for the poem but phrases, lines, and most important, the title. The second premise is that Tom's betrayal of Viv is inseparable from the influence of what Viv's mother, in a moving denunciation of Tom at the end, calls "those Bloomsbury types." Included in this designation are Bertrand Russell, who is (erroneously) presented as Tom's tutor at Oxford; Ottoline Morrell, at whose house, Garsington—at least in the European version of the film—Tom and Viv have one of their earliest fights about the snobbishness of Tom's friends (the fight, not the whole scene, is cut from the American version);[7] Edith Sitwell, who inspired Hastings's research on Viv by her comment, "At some point in their marriage Tom went mad, and promptly certified his wife";[8] and Virginia Woolf.

Indeed, one of the nastiest scenes in the film takes place at a dinner party at Virginia's house, where Virginia and Viv are seen to vie with each other for who can claim Tom, a struggle that consists in part of who can most successfully define the other as "mad." The scene includes a conversation between Virginia and Ottoline where Virginia says first, "There is nothing wrong with Tom that separation from his wife couldn't cure. She reeks of ether," and then, "If she had any conception of his real significance it would be less alarming. . . ." This is followed by a conversation between Tom and Virginia where he states, "I don't keep a line that Viv hasn't approved. I rely on her completely," and then, "She's a writer too . . . considerable talent. . . . I'll send you some of her things, shall I?" Virginia's response is to lean in, intimately, and say, "You do realise of course what she's doing to you? To your reputation? What she might do to your work?" Much to Virginia's surprise, Tom defends Viv. Meanwhile, at the other end of the table, Viv is getting more and more agitated; turning to her brother she says, loudly, "Of course Virginia wants Tom to leave me. She refers to me as 'a bag of ferrets'—my nerves, you see. Writer's insight. She ought to know—Leonard has her in and out of the loony bin every couple of months! They all hate me because I've got Tom and they all want him." Later, at the time of her committal, one rationale offered is "Mrs. Virginia Woolf's" complaint about the knife.

For those interested in the "facts" underlying the narrative representation of Virginia Woolf's relationship to Vivienne Eliot, a quick reading of the entries indexed under "Vivienne Eliot" and "T. S. Eliot" in the letters and diaries, which granted are never a guaranteed source of accuracy, reveals that yes, Woolf did in 1930 refer to Vivienne in her diary as a "bag of ferrets"; that Vivienne was heard, although not by Woolf herself, to have accused Tom of being in love with Ottoline "and me, but this Ott: threw in as a sop"; and that in 1933 Woolf reported the following anecdote to Quentin Bell: "Have you heard that Mrs Eliot is on the war path, said to have a carving knife with which first to skin Tom; then Ottoline; finally me? For she says Ott and I are Tom's mistresses."[9] One also finds some very harsh descriptions of Vivienne's appearance and behavior.[10] But we also read that Virginia encouraged Vivienne to write, that she took Tom to task about his treatment of his wife, that Vivienne continued to write to Virginia after her separation from Tom, and that she asked Leonard Woolf (who with the other men attached to the "Bloomsbury" women, Philip Morrell and the Sitwell brothers, is conspicuously absent from the film) to be her executor.[11] But my own interest lies less in the "facts" than in the cultural perceptions and attitudes suggested by two interrelated aspects of the film: the increasingly broad sweep of who or what is meant by Bloomsbury, particularly when the term carries negative connotations; and the (gendered) discrepancies in the representation and reception of male and female artists at a time when, as one reviewer commented, it is "open season on dead geniuses,"[12] discrepancies that make women a distinct part of the problem.

In *Tom & Viv* both aspects inform the assumption, unquestioned by most reviewers and commentators, that it was other women, lumped together as "those Bloomsbury types," who helped destroy the marriage, in part by not taking Viv seriously as an intellectual or writer, and that Virginia Woolf becomes a sign for this distinctly gendered cultural struggle. When Peter Samuelson, one of the producers, first showed me the film, he repeatedly asked why Virginia Woolf, that committed feminist and author of *A Room of One's Own*, would have taken Tom's side and not Viv's, and why she did not support Viv's writing.[13] But the film itself does little to privilege the authority of either of the women as *writers*. Although Tom mentions that Viv writes, we never see her engaged in her own work or hear from her about it; nor do we learn that some of her pieces were published in the *Criterion*. Woolf's writing enters only in Mrs. Haigh-Wood's critique of Bloomsbury: "It isn't such an achievement to turn gossip into art and write nasty novels about one's friends." As a result, the Virginia Woolf who appears in both the film and the reviews becomes little more than a sign of the corrosive snobbery associated with Bloomsbury and located squarely in its women.

Because this is a film, a spectacle, the visual becomes just as significant as the verbal in constructing Virginia Woolf's destructive self-absorption, and the primary visual marker resides in her clothes. Here, a slight digression is necessary. Woolf, we know, had a hard time buying clothes and was often self-conscious about the way she looked—or failed to look.[14] For the most part, judging by both the studio portraits and the more informal photographs we have of her, she dressed simply and comfortably, with little in the way of jewelry and little to no makeup; Man Ray, you might recall, felt compelled "to put some lipstick on her mouth" before photographing her (see Take 6). All of these facets of her appearance are evident in one of the photographs that I'm told contributed to the conceptualization of the film: a highly disturbing picture of Tom, Virginia, and Vivienne taken at Monks House in 1932 just before Eliot left for the States and what became his final separation from Viv. In this photograph, Tom and Virginia dominate; they stand close together, heads up, looking confidently outward; Viv stands off by herself, arms behind her back, looking down. Virginia is dressed as she often is in photographs: a dark skirt, her trademark long cardigan-jacket, a soft blouse, plain oxford-style shoes, a single strand of large beads, and a large but plain straw hat; Vivienne is dressed fashionably if somewhat oddly all in white.[15]

But in the film Virginia is virtually indistinguishable from "the women" at Garsington, who are described in an early version of the script as "garishly arrayed in a phantasmagoria of personal and eccentric styles."[16] The directions for the scene where Viv threatens Edith Sitwell and Virginia Woolf calls for them to be "outlandishly dressed and made-up," and in the film they certainly are, the Virginia figure a little less so than the others. During the dinner party scene, "Ottoline" is dressed so similarly to "Virginia"—they even wear more or less the same colors—and "Edith" looks so much like pictures of "Ottoline" that if the names weren't marked in the script it would be hard to know who was talking to whom. When I showed these scenes to a colleague who had not seen the film but who designs and teaches about costumes and knows the Bloomsbury period well, she was struck by how unusual it is for a realistic film to dress characters in such similar styles so many times running. She also noted that the intention, particularly in the knife scene where "Virginia" and "Edith" wear grays and browns that blend into the gray weather and gray stones behind them and Viv wears red, is to make Viv stand out. (Viv wears to-die-for clothing throughout the film, often punctuated by splashes of red.) When the scene at Garsington came on the screen my colleague had a hard time deciding who was who and didn't identify "Virginia" at all the first time she appeared. She is not alone. Reviewers were confused as well, often identifying the women in the knife scene as Edith Sitwell and/or Ottoline Morrell, apparently not recognizing what the script makes explicit: that one of them was Virginia Woolf. As one reviewer put it, "The settings are beautifully dressed and peopled with extravagant, arch and artistic characters whose significance is often suggested only belatedly in the credits."[17]

An article on Phoebe De Gaye, who designed the costumes, tells us that she did extensive research into the period after 1914 when "the Bloomsbury literary set," including such "eccentric figures" as Woolf, Sitwell, and Morrell, was in "high gear," and that she used the extensive photographs and portraits of these figures in her designs; but when De Gaye gets down to specifics, she mentions only the photographs of Edith Sitwell in "formal clothes" taken by Cecil Beaton.[18] I am told that her sources also included the photographs in Lady Ottoline's Album, which contains numerous shots not only of Ottoline but of her guests at Garsington, Virginia Woolf among them;[19] and De Gaye notes that Sitwell and Morrell, "when you saw them in the street, they should look quite outlandish." This latter comment echoes a statement about Ottoline in Lord David Cecil's introduction to her Album.[20] De Gaye also acknowledges Eliot's notably fastidious dress, referring to Woolf's well-known barb about his "four-piece suit," and the film portrays this fastidiousness well. Otherwise, Woolf is absent from her discussion.

The scene at Garsington seems to make some attempt to reproduce the clothing worn by Woolf in one set of Garsington photos, clothing that is more dressy, more festive, than her ordinary attire, although by no means "eccentric" or "garish." The look in the film, however, is far sleeker and more stylish than the summery look Woolf has in the photos, including layers of ornamented (lacy, beaded) tops, a straw hat sporting ribbons, at least three necklaces that are almost identical to those worn by Ottoline, who sits beside her, and makeup. I know of no pictures that match her depiction in the dinner scene, where she wears an elaborate brocaded evening dress, elaborate, heavy earrings and necklaces, and a great deal of makeup. The same is true of the knife scene, where she might have walked out of an advertisement for the sophisticated lady-who-lunches, with her elegant crocheted coat, long white gloves, sleek hat, and carefully tied packages in hand. In general, the "Virginia" in the film, while sharing certain characteristics with the "Virginia" captured in photographs, including those taken at Garsington, is more chic, more noticeably fashionable, more given to elaborate accessories and garments, and certainly more made up than one expects her, if not "Edith" and "Ottoline," to be.[21]

This representation not only blurs the vestimentary differences among the three women but erases the clear lines of demarcation that the original members of Bloomsbury drew between themselves and the artistic and social worlds centered on either Ottoline Morrell or Edith Sitwell, which equally saw themselves as distinct from the others, albeit with overlaps. The reviews make clear how general this erasure has become. Bloomsbury, it appears, now functions as an infinitely elastic category, particularly when the goal is disparagement. Part of this rewriting of cultural history, I suspect, reflects the reviewers' lack of specialist knowledge, particularly in the States; even so, I was surprised at how little people seemed to know about Woolf, Bloomsbury, or even Eliot. I can state with far more certainty that a great deal of this revisionary response reflects the generally negative connotation evoked by Bloomsbury in many cultural quarters today; Michael Musto captures this trope beautifully when he renames the film *Mrs. Eliot and the Vicious Bloomsbury Circle.* And a number of reviewers, both English and American, who otherwise do not have much good to say about the film, found "compensations" in its "quietly devastating demolition of the Bloomsbury Group," or commented with some glee that Virginia Woolf and whoever that second woman was were only too deserving of attack.[22]

Ironically but tellingly the most explicit example of this particular representation of Bloomsbury occurred on the *Charlie Rose* show, generally acknowledged to be one of the most intellectual of the American TV talk shows, during an interview with Miranda Richardson, who played Viv:

ROSE: Who was in the Bloomsbury Group?
RICHARDSON: Oh, God!
ROSE: No, I don't mean to ask—you know why I ask? I mentioned this earlier, I just saw—clearly, Vita Sackville-West was, along with—
RICHARDSON: And there's Ottoline Morrell, and the Sitwells, and Virginia Woolf, Lytton Strachey, yeah, all those people. I mean we don't—we don't concentrate on them for a lot of the film, but they—they were trying to move Tom away into their circle. He was very special, and as I say, they lionized him.
ROSE: Yeah.
RICHARDSON: And she just found them full of hot air, and false and sham and all show.
ROSE: Full of pretensions, and—
RICHARDSON: Yeah, and actually stuffy. You know, not too dissimilar from the stuff she was trying to get away from in the first place, you know, even though they purported to be in the new wave.[23]

Equally telling, one of the only commentators willing to defend Virginia Woolf and Bloomsbury, Richard Alleva, writing in *Commonweal,* seems just as hazy as to its members and merits; admitting it was "certainly snobbish and cliquish" if "hardly *the* cultural establishment," he rallies to write that Virginia Woolf was certainly not the "Margaret Dumont matron" the film made her out to be, and that " 'nasty novels about . . . friends' hardly describes the productions of Woolf, Vita Sackville-West, or E. M. Forster."[24]

The introduction of Vita into the company of Bloomsbury women also introduces my next point: that the clothing in *Tom & Viv* becomes even more significant when read against the discursive use of clothing in a number of recent representations of Virginia Woolf, *Vita & Virginia* among them. In the American production of the play (1994), which is a dramatization of Vita Sackville-West's and Virginia Woolf's letters to each other, Vanessa Redgrave played Vita and Eileen Atkins, building on her highly acclaimed dramatization of Virginia Woolf in the television and stage version of *A Room of One's Own,* once again played Virginia. Here, in stark contrast to the Virginia of Gilbert's film, Virginia is portrayed as frail, dowdy, "femme," and middle class, looking, in one reviewer's phrase, "like a bouquet of wilted violets"; another describes her as "dressed in an old-maidish faded-pastel dress."[25] Again, photographs of Woolf suggest individual pieces of the costume, but not the overall outfit or look. Vita, in contrast, is dressed to the hilt as the active, striding, sexual, "mannish" aristocrat Woolf's writings and extant photographs tell us she was. In this representation of Virginia Woolf, where Vita comments on how atrociously Virginia dresses and Virginia laments her lack of clothes sense, the point of the clothing is not Virginia Woolf's snobbish elitism but her personal and social vulnerability. Finally, it is worth noting that Atkins's costume here is a far cry from the tailored clothes she wore in the television version of *Room*—long skirt, shirt with vest-like tails worn over it, long scarf knotted loosely like a tie, long cardigan-jacket—a look so severe that it was softened before the play moved to the stage, and even then Atkins, who chose it, complained the outfit was "too butch."[26]

At one level the competing renditions of Virginia Woolf's clothing suggest the cultural contradictions within her star image that by 1994 threatened to shatter the image itself. But this discordant rendering also illustrates the long-held belief among costume designers that because "personality finds its direct manifestation in manner of dress," they can construct carefully coded systems for conveying characteristics such as "serious" (wool tweed), "wicked" or "decadent" (black satin), or "lighthearted" (tulle). As Jane Gaines argues in "Costume and Narrative: How Dress

Tells the Woman's Story," "a designer is using metaphors . . . every time
he or she translates a character trait—such as that of 'female' wickedness
or destructiveness—into an item of apparel."[27] Clearly, then, what Virginia
Woolf wears is inseparable from what she "means" in popular representations of her, playing as great a role as the words she speaks even when, as in
Vita & Virginia, the words are her own. From this perspective, Virginia's
appearance in *Tom & Viv*—her cool, sophisticated elegance, bordering on
the grotesque—and by extension the class- and gender-inflected cultural
status it signifies, incites not ridicule but terror; Virginia Woolf is dressed
to kill.

The refashioning of Virginia Woolf into a female grotesque suggested
by the visual images becomes explicit in the reviews, which draw clear connections between women's materiality, the woman artist, and monstrosity.
All of these are perceived to threaten the male artist/genius as much as if
not more than the contemporary cultural rejection of Eliot and high art,
and all of these suggest a frightening crossover between Virginia and Viv,
who become more like mirror images of each other than rivals.

This is not to say that everyone evinced outrage at the film's debunking
of Eliot and his art; many reviewers express what amounts to glee at seeing,
as Bernstein wrote, the artist with his "pretensions . . . stripped away."[28]
But this glee does not necessarily translate into an elevation of Viv. Few
share or even recognize Michael Hastings's view of the film as "a portrait of
domestic fascism in both marriage and art" or give credence to his rationale
for the film's discrediting of Eliot's stature as writer and modernist. Eliot, he
explains, was one of the "five great fascist artists" exported by America at
the beginning of the century (the others being D. W. Griffith, Walt Disney,
Frank Lloyd Wright, and Henry Ford), whose "profound influence on the
Modern movement has been, in my opinion, a malign and destructive form
of social change."[29]

The observation made by several critics that the real threat to Eliot's
stature lay less in the debunking than in his loss of star or celebrity
status, his lack of "well-knownness," also deflects attention away from
Viv. As one reviewer noted, "it's difficult to make exposés dramatic unless
the audience starts with the accepted myth, then sees it crumble," the
implication being that in Eliot's case the audience does not. This reviewer
would agree with the prediction made in *Variety* when the film opened
in Britain that it would suffer commercially from "the 'Tom & Viv . . .
who?' problem,"[30] a phenomenon that proved very much the case in the
United States, if not in Britain itself. There the film received a great deal
of pre- and post-opening publicity across the mainstream media, including
a highly informed discussion of its accuracy or lack thereof; even Eliot's

biographer, Lyndall Gordon, jumped into the debate. In contrast American viewers required not highly informed controversy but basic knowledge to pull them into the film. Hence, before *Tom & Viv* crossed the Atlantic it acquired a voiceover narration spoken by Vivienne's brother Maurice, which begins by identifying Bertrand Russell and Tom and explaining why Tom spoke in such an odd accent (he was American). This was not, one would think, a good omen for the success of the film—or for Eliot's status as artistic legitimator of popular culture.

But a further look at the film's reception reveals a very different picture of Eliot's—and hence high culture's—still powerful presence in the popular realm, one in which the poet's canonical eminence remains secure; as Mark Twain might have said, reports of the (male) genius/poet's death have been greatly exaggerated.[31] "Would 'Tom & Viv' be of interest if it didn't involve T. S. Eliot, the greatest English-language poet of the 20th century?" one reviewer asks; "probably not," he answers, and almost every reviewer who talks about Eliot as a poet reiterates not only his enduring greatness but the equation of his voice with that of Modernism itself.[32] More to my point, numerous reviewers and commentators on both sides of the Atlantic voice the desire to know a great deal less—if anything at all—about Eliot's marriage and more about his poetry. Even Caryn James, who calls the film "one of those reclamation projects in behalf of a woman almost lost to history," concludes that "however sympathetic to Vivien the film is, it cannot overcome the simple fact that Eliot, an enduring poet and a horrid individual, was far more interesting than his wife."[33]

Most reviewers skip the sympathy and go immediately for the kill, resurrecting Tom for Art by bluntly portraying Viv as a destructive force, whose dark powers lay in her female body. This attitude is particularly strong among (male) reviewers whose primary response is to Vivienne's bleeding, producing reactions as "hysterical" as Viv is often said to be. One depicts the film as a conflict between the "Living Hell Menstruation" and "the great American expatriate poet"; another speaks of the "famous poet 'who sticks his erect member into a cup of menstrual blood.'"[34] The American version exacerbated this reaction by stating in the narration that "Vivie suffered from what we used to call 'women's troubles,'" a phrase that appears with tiresome regularity in the American reviews. But as Claire Monk argues, even without the narration the film invites this response; the problem, she notes, is not the "insertion of gynaecology—the female body as messy, uncontrollable organism"—into cinematic representations of a more repressed past, which could be read as enlightened and genre-disrupting; the problem comes from not emphasizing Tom's equally chronic illnesses and neuroses, thereby pathologizing Viv alone.[35] Tom, the poet/genius, suffers and writes; Viv, the woman, bleeds.

If, then, we return to Anthony Lane's prediction that this film indicates the end of Eliot's reputation and by implication high art and literary culture, the reviews do not bear this jeremiad out. Film directors may not be as respectful—may not court the legitimation that figures such as Eliot once procured—but numerous reviewers, critics, and cultural commentators are more than willing to uphold the sanctity of Art and the authority of artists such as Eliot from what is now perceived to be the philistinism of both academics *and* the creators of popular culture. These critics still want their high cultural heroes, and they want them out of the domestic world associated with women, the world defined by one reviewer as "tedious domestic melodrama."[36] They want them, we could say, to be men.

Women artists, even when they are located in or have pretensions to high culture, need not apply; with the exception of Alleva, no one feels it necessary to mention, let alone insist on, Virginia Woolf's stature as a writer. To the extent that the film is perceived as addressing the social and cultural double standards that confronted Viv and other intelligent women (which its makers argue was its intent), it is accused of being "feminist"; when perceived as "an epic of loving feminine sacrifice and loyalty despite male unworthiness," it's reduced to a "romantic weepie," a " 'woman's picture,' " and dismissed.[37] Monk alone highlights this gender divide when she addresses what she sees as the major problem with the film's representation of Viv, her "embodying two contradictory discourses: the feminist reclamation of the woman artist written out of male history, and the misogynist conception of female creativity as intrinsically rooted in hysteria," neither of which ever mentions "the fact that she was a talented, and much admired writer independently of Eliot." By this point Hastings's original title for his play, *Tom's Wife,* despite the protest of his own wife that she "never heard of anything so outdated and reactionary," turns out to be exactly right.[38]

One other film needs to be introduced here, *Carrington,* a film that in bearing the name of its female protagonist promises a contradictory representation.[39] Not so. Based, we are informed in the opening credits, on Michael Holroyd's biography of Lytton Strachey (with no mention of her own published diaries and letters), it begins by informing the viewers that Dora Carrington was a prize-winning student at the Slade School with a great future before her, and that this is the story of her life. The next thing we see is the title of the first "chapter": "Lytton"; each subsequent chapter bears a man's name. None of the struggles Carrington experienced around her art and her place in the artistic world she inhabited, charted so powerfully by critics such as Mary Ann Caws, troubles the "story" of an emotional, domestic, and artistic life devoted to Lytton and the achievement of sexual satisfaction with other men.[40] Carrington's sexual relationships with women, we might add, have disappeared as well.

While I do not want to make pronouncements on the basis of one or even two films, *Tom & Viv* does lend itself to speculations about the intersections of gender, cultural class, and cultural contexts in the debates about popular culture's relationship to high art, speculations that highlight once again Virginia Woolf's power to disrupt categories and boundaries. Freedman provides one clue. If, as he argues, films, as a form of popular culture, legitimate themselves by appealing to the presumably higher culture absorbed while the directors were at college, women writers, with the exception of Virginia Woolf—and that is very recent—do not yet carry much cultural currency, or at least not *as writers*. They do not emerge from the directors' formative years with the authority to be serious players in the ongoing cultural wars or to evoke lamentations about the denigration of genius and Art.[41]

Freedman himself recognized the gendered nature of high culture in 1987: all the high cultural figures he cites are male, even when the performer, if not the writer or director, is female.[42] The gender of the poet who is portrayed in popular culture as the carrier of "the cultural authority of authorship" and the "potential social power of the writer's discourse," he writes, is "clearly masculine." This division reflects the tradition in literary studies that reinforced the high culture/masculine mass culture/feminine divide; as Guillory writes, "when the choice is between literary culture and mass culture . . . there is no question of 'both-and' ": "If mass culture can be stigmatized by association with the lurid taste of the female consumer"—"the woman absorbed in her confession magazines"—"literary culture . . . becomes the site of a certain kind of worship, . . . of its own version of transcendence, the experience to be found only in reading 'the greater poems of our tradition.' "[43]

Judging by the popular cultural works I've been exploring, this situation has not altered much; the woman writer, no matter how high cultural, has not yet overcome this distinction except by threatening, as Virginia Woolf so clearly does, to destroy it. What one feels in films such as *Sammy and Rosie Get Laid* and *Tom & Viv* is both fascination with and fear of Virginia Woolf's protean cultural status and powers. But whereas *Sammy and Rosie* acknowledges Virginia Woolf's authority in both literary and popular culture and edgily savors her ability to destabilize categories that the film also undercuts, *Tom & Viv* writes her out of high culture by associating her with a feminized Bloomsbury whose role is to lionize Tom and destroy Viv. The result is to leave male artists like Eliot occupying the site of literary authority.

The problem is, Virginia Woolf refuses to stay in her place, any place, having become a figure who stands in for women writers and women readers/consumers across the cultural board. Again, *Sammy and Rosie* illustrates this ability to break down the traditional cultural categories. The occasion is Sammy's Woody Allen–esque "We are Londoners" speech, meant, however tongue-in-cheek, to establish the eclecticism and sophistication of Rosie's and his cultural consumption: semiotics seminars at the ICA (Institute of Contemporary Art), plays at the Royal Court Theatre, political satires in pubs, going "to the bookshop and [buying] novels written by women." In this scenario Virginia Woolf, whose books occupy the center of Rosie's bookshelves, signifies neither a discredited high culture nor a culture of confession-magazine readers; instead she becomes the emblem of a vital women's literary culture that escapes categorization. Perhaps what these films illustrate, then, is not envy of genius among philistines, as Bernstein suggests *Tom & Viv* does, but envy of the success women writers have had among readers from all segments of society, invading even those preserves usually reserved for men and displacing the previous inhabitants. Given this premise, I am led to posit that the makers and reviewers of films in the mid-1990s continue to have a love/hate relationship with the genius and authority of dead male poets such as T. S. Eliot that motivates and legitimates their discourse, but that when it comes to the genius and the authority of women writers, particularly a women writer as culturally powerful as Virginia Woolf, the overriding emotion remains fear.

FASHION STILLS

Had the aliens in "Independence Day" succeeded in their conquest of the Planet Earth and set about investigating the world they'd just destroyed, . . . they might have concluded that . . . Virginia Woolf was a fashion designer working with Anna Sui. . . .

—Michiko Kakutani, "The Trickle-Down Theory," *New York Times Magazine,* September 22, 1996

When the makers of *Tom & Viv* decided to characterize the Blooms-bury women and the Bloomsbury ethos through their clothing, they were not alone; according to a July 1996 article in *W* magazine, "Bloomsbury Forever," Bloomsbury has long been a significant player in the fashion world, experiencing a revival about every five years. The article attributes the current revival to "last year's *Carrington* and this year's *Cold Comfort Farm*," whose protagonist, Flora Post, according to the costume designer, " 'was meant to evoke a sensible, well-ordered girl, loosely based on Rosamond Lehmann'—a writer on the fringes of Bloomsbury. 'Their look was rather eccentric. The whole concept was to appear creative rather than fashionable. Shoes like the one-strap, fringed brogue were vital, jewelry moved away from precious stones into more natural-looking jade, amber and coral, and closer-fitting hats like the knit cloche became popular. Beaded and embroidered bags and satchels were also important.' " The group itself, the article notes, "that Twenties' literary clique—which included Virginia Woolf, Vanessa and Clive Bell, Roger Fry and Lytton Strachey—and their arts-and-crafts-influenced style, is having a particularly strong impact on fashion and accessories."[1]

Virginia Woolf understood well the role of clothing in fashioning the person wearing it, in terms of both self-presentation and the perception of others; witness her brilliant use of it in *Orlando,* where the narrator acknowledges the way clothes "change our view of the world and the world's view of us[,] . . . [moulding] our hearts, our brains, our tongues to their liking," before arguing that "in every human being a vacillation from one sex to the other takes place, and often it is only the clothes that keep the male or female likeness, while underneath the sex is the very opposite of what it is above."[2] Sally Potter's film version of *Orlando* capitalized on Woolf's insights, presenting clothing so extravagant and so riveting that it often becomes the point of the scene, a feature that translated into extensive fashion magazine coverage and a collection at Bloomingdale's. Given that Woolf's model for Orlando was Vita Sackville-West, distinguished for her stylish mixture of clothes traditionally associated with men as well as women, Woolf would have appreciated Vita's appearance in British *Vogue* (December 1996) as one of four progenitors of a distinct style for women (the others are Marilyn Monroe, Jackie Kennedy, and Katharine Hepburn);[3] but I doubt she could have imagined or predicted the large role clothing would play in shaping her own persona and image.

Significantly, much of the attention paid to Virginia Woolf in the 1996 Bloomsbury revival (and I am limiting myself to this one moment) accrues to her name, not her dress, which was not particularly eccentric, arts-and-crafts, or fashionable; the name and with it her richly intertextual star image provides the recognition, the panache, used to sell the concepts and the goods.[4] The power of her name becomes all the more evident when we consider that it is her sister, Vanessa Bell, not Virginia Woolf, who usually appears in histories of clothing as an exemplar of the "bohemianism" attributed to Bloomsbury: Vanessa, who designed clothing for the Omega Workshop that was meant to be "gay and fashionable" but was so "far in advance of accepted taste," so "*outré,*" that it discouraged Omega clients and led Virginia to write that having had her eyes " 'wrenched . . . from the sockets' " by the colors, she would " 'retire into dove colour and old lavender, with a lace collar and lawn wristlets.' " Vanessa's designs, as well as her own "bizarre clothes made from stuffs bought in Italian rag markets,"[5] aligns her with an aesthetic or artistic style that Elizabeth Wilson, in her study of clothing, associates with "Oppositional Costume," with taking an anti-fashion stand: "At the time when Lucile [a fashionable designer] was putting Edwardian ladies into pastel chiffons and seductive silk, Vanessa Bell, Bloomsbury painter and sister of Virginia Woolf, was creating an alternative look as she searched through markets for exotic materials and old costumes." But Wilson also makes it clear that Chelsea, not Bloomsbury, provided the major locus of Bohemian style during the twenties and thirties.[6]

Nevertheless, Bloomsbury remains the referent in revivals of 1920s fashion such as the one in 1996 that led *New York Times* cultural critic Michiko Kakutani to lament the fall of the high cultural figure Virginia Woolf into a "fashion designer working with Anna Sui." For Kakutani, this slippage is just one example of the state of cultural degradation she defines as a "Classic Comics limbo, where it's hard to tell what's parody, what's rip-off and what's just user-friendly adaptation"; rather than high culture trickling down to the masses, she argues, mass or popular culture has triumphed, producing a marketplace in which "elitism has no value—money has become the only yardstick." Mass culture's use of "pretentious allusions" to figures such as Virginia Woolf, she adds, only exacerbates the dilution. Letter writers to the *Magazine* disagreed, stressing instead the value of border crossings; popular culture's borrowings from high culture, they respond, not only give it more "sophistication," but play a significant role in exposing and introducing kids to art and music and literature they otherwise might not know or like.[7]

Virginia Woolf's appearances in fashion magazines, then, do more than raise questions about how clothes make the person—or the icon; they also challenge those commentators and discourses that want to fix Virginia Woolf and her cultural meaning in any one style or place. To be in fashion is, we know, to be open to unending variety, perpetual change; it is to move, as fashion writers have increasingly described fashion itself as moving, into the realm of the postmodern, where dress codes and categories disappear and styles intermix. With this move, the "structured polysemy" characteristic of the star image intersects with the refrain "Virginia Woolf, like fashion, like postmodernism . . . ," suggesting the wide array of clothing adorning Virginia Woolf icon, the multiple cultural sites she marks. This multiplicity, however, has its perils, for the refrain also evokes feminism's uneasy relationship with fashion, postmodernism, and a "postfeminism" that is often presented as the only feminism for the 1990s. Although the complexity of the terrain makes it difficult to determine whether the construction of Virginia Woolf fashion icon signifies an act of subversion or containment, this indeterminacy, I believe, is preferable to clothing Virginia Woolf in a single, "authentic" costume or position.

If we begin by asking what images of Virginia Woolf emerge from the coverage of the 1996 revival, what "sophistication" she offers in her role as fashion icon, the first would be modernity, strength, and independence. W's table of contents tells us that "Fall accessories are not afraid of Virginia Woolf," and in the article Anna Sui, one of the figures most associated with the revival, states that "women of that time were really the forerunners of modern women. . . . They had just come out of corsets and Victorian confinement and could finally vote. Clothing became much more relaxed, with long skirts and fitted tops."[8] Virginia Woolf also promises bohemianism, British style; the table of contents in the September 1996 *Harper's Bazaar* offers us the "London Beat. The bohemian days of Bloomsbury—captured in velvet frocks, sweeping military coats, and eccentric accessories—give fall a catchy, offbeat feel." The article is more specific: "Eccentric, eclectic, and thoroughly English, the thrown-together, flea-market sensibility of a certain strand of fall fashion has its roots in the '70s, in London stores like Biba and Granny Takes a Trip, and earlier, in the intellectual artiness of the Bloomsbury group, in the '20s."[9] The clothing featured in the *Harper's* piece comes from such top designers as Donna Karan, Gucci, Martine Sitbon, Versace, Prada, and Chloé, as well as Anna Sui and the Italian designer Alberta Ferretti, who, like Sui, explicitly linked her line that season to the twenties and Bloomsbury. As Annabel Bryant of Ferretti explains in a (British) *Guardian Weekend* article "[welcoming] the return of opulent Twenties glamour: A Bloomsbury set sensibility, brooding sexuality, and a riot of velvet and lace," " 'There's a very androgynous feel to fashion at the moment. It's all very long, lean and clean, which is very much Twenties-inspired. . . . Similarly, there is an underlying, rather than overt, sexuality to the period which is perfectly suited to modern tastes.' " But the *Guardian* article also serves to distance the current styles from the past, arguing that while Anna Sui proffers "heavily beaded velvet dresses of which Vita Sackville-West would have been proud," if we "look closely at [her] tailoring . . . it is, in fact, more structured than anything Virginia Woolf would have worn." As Ferretti's Bryant warns, the revival should not be taken "too literally," because today " 'we can break all the rules.' "[10]

Not everyone welcomed the Bloomsbury connection, even if they welcomed the season's opulence, a predominant theme in American *Vogue's* treatment of the fall collections. In fact, it seems as if the Bloomsbury motif, as Susannah Frankel writes in the *Guardian Weekend Fashion Special,* is "a very London-girl look," not necessarily shared by those on the other side of the Atlantic; Katherine Betts's early report on the fall collections in *Vogue* (U.S.) puts Bloomsbury, associated here with Anna Sui, Prada, and Chanel, on the side of "dowdy chic." Prada's "Bloomsbury-style dowagers," she writes, "in calf-length skirts, oddball computer prints, and pony-skin pea-coats in a palette of forest green, burnt sienna, and purple" may have "an Edwardian feeling (although Miuccia [Prada] preferred to call them 'technical bohemians')," but to her they are "dumpy."[11] By the time Betts edited her "Vogue's View" for September's *Vogue,* she had abandoned any mention of Bloomsbury, emphasizing instead the flapper element in the twenties revival; elsewhere the issue includes an article called "This Side of Paradise" that tells us "the latest decade to inspire designers is the 1920s of Hemingway and Fitzgerald—think sultry slip dresses and bold accents of color, like the flash of the matador's cape"—even as it exhibits exactly the same designers and much of the same clothing that *Harper's* was simultaneously featuring as Bloomsbury.[12]

But whether the reference is to Bloomsbury or Fitzgerald, the appeal in the fashion magazines remains the same: the opulence, the richness of the fabrics and colors, the long, lean lines, the eclectic layering, and the offbeat, arty, for the most part decidedly urban, nature of the settings. Given this emphasis, the final evocation of Virginia Woolf in the fall 1996 fashion coverage I want to note comes as a surprise: her appearance in "Fashion Literate: Great Women Writers Dress in Clothes from the Fall Collections," a delightful series of drawings by Michael Crawford found on the last page of the *New York Times*'s *Fashions of the Times*. Here, in contrast to Jane Austen in Prada or Edith Wharton in Chanel or Emily Dickinson in Comme des Garçons or Gertrude Stein in Issey Miyake, Virginia Woolf, seated cross-legged with book in hands, wears the Gap white pocket T-shirt and jeans.[13]

As Richard Dyer might ask, what texts, what ideologies structure this polysemy? What is being foregrounded, what masked or displaced? From one perspective, the shifting meanings assigned to the signifier Virginia Woolf in this single fashion season can be read as a powerful example of her versatility, her usefulness as a marker for any one of a number of social or cultural positions, whether it be Bloomsbury elitism or Bloomsbury bohemianism; the luxury and elegance of velvet and beads or the elegant simplicity of T-shirt and jeans. From this perspective, little if anything seems to be masked or displaced, although, as we'll see, much is. The message seems to be that Virginia Woolf can be refashioned for almost every market. Most women, I suspect, find something here to attract them; some would identify with all the images except, perhaps, those characterized as "dumpy." I, for one, laughed when I saw Virginia Woolf among the "Fashion Literate": it seemed so right; but I lusted after one of the Anna Sui outfits featured in the *Guardian*, even though it wasn't my style, and I knew I would never buy it.

It is here that Virginia Woolf crosses with fashion, ceaselessly shifting, ceaselessly being presented in different guises that offer us "a double dream of identity and play—indeed, the invitation to play with identities"—that is distinctly postmodern.[14] Virginia Woolf becomes part of that discourse that has increasingly defined fashion as play or performance or masquerade, a discourse that occurs in both the industry and academic writing. The industry would not necessarily use the same terms as the academics, given its proclivity for presenting itself in declarative sentences about what it *is* at any one moment, even when the declaration is about multiplicity. (One fashion writer attributes this rhetorical style to Diana Vreeland, former editor of American *Vogue,* who announced in the 1950s that "Pink is the navy blue of India.")[15] But the characterization of the same clothing as both London/Bloomsbury and Fitzgerald/Hemingway, as simultaneously romantic and strong and androgynous, presents a distinctly postmodern scenario, where, as one journalist notes, "a jacket can be clever, witty, ironic, sexy, aggressive, feminine or masculine—it can even be all of these things at the same time. In the past few weeks [still fall 1996] we have been told that the clothes from next year's spring and summer collections could have been worn by a Jane Austen heroine, by a young Bianca Jagger, or by Morticia Addams. They harked back to the seventies, but were also futuristic."[16] The eccentricity and eclecticism attributed to Bloomsbury also come into play in its postmodern refashionings (creating one's own "look"), as does the intermixing of clothing from different decades, tying the Bloomsbury revival to retro, a genre or style described by Kennedy Fraser, if not by fashion designers and the fashion press, as "the desire to find style, but obliquely, and splendor, but tackily, and so to put an ironic distance between the wearers and the fashionableness of their clothes."[17] What we have here, then, is a discourse that produces, simultaneously, a distinctly postmodern fashion for the 1990s and a distinctly postmodern Virginia Woolf.

To understand the implications, it is useful to look more broadly at the postmodern groundings of fashion and its analysis, including their intersections with feminist critiques. While many in the industry would eschew such terms as "irony" or "parody" or "pastiche" to characterize their styles, announcing instead, as designer Jil Sander did about the contrasts in the 1996 fall styles, that they characterized "the 'rough and soft side of femininity,' "[18] for some designers and many writers on fashion, feminists included, postmodernism readily becomes a synonym for fashion itself. When *New York Times* fashion writer Holly Brubach brought together the French designer Thierry Mugler, "notorious for his theatrical runway shows—a cavalcade of Amazons, mermaids, angels, dominatrixes, space-age sex goddesses, vampires and other female stock characters," and feminist art historian Linda Nochlin, they shared a vision and a language. Nochlin begins by questioning the term *woman,* talking instead about a "femininity" that is a learned "condition of disguise"; Mugler responds, "Very true. There is only the person who chooses to play the feminine role, to experience different aspects of femininity." Later Nochlin expands her position, tying it "in to certain postmodernist ideas about the self—that there is no real self, even. That the self is a condition of disguise and that we can move back and forth in terms of sexualities, in terms of social being, in terms of all kinds of senses of who we are. And I think fashion helps us wonderfully in this. That's why, in a sense, I would say that fashion is *the* postmodern art, because it helps to destabilize the self in such a wonderful way." This makes Mugler nervous: "I don't really agree about fashion. I don't like it when it gets carried away with itself, when anything is possible," though he admits in response to a question about his use of drag queens and transsexuals that it is a "game open to everyone, not just women."[19]

Nochlin's claim of fashion for postmodernism is equally a claim of fashion for feminism and strikes a note heard in many feminist writers who, like Nochlin, "adore clothes" and can't imagine why any woman should feel "forced" to wear something she does not want to; nor can she "imagine not being interested in clothing. I guess if you're an intellectual woman," she adds, "you're not supposed to talk about how much pleasure you get out of clothing." She justifies her pleasure in part by describing fashion as "an art form that can be part of your body," but what interests me more is her feeling that she *needs* to justify her love of clothing and fashion. This feeling reflects the ambivalent position that Second Wave feminists, and to a lesser extent those identified as Third Wave, including— or particularly—academics, continue to find themselves in when it comes to what Valerie Steele described in 1991 as the "F-word."[20]

As those who have charted the cultural shifts that made fashion a topic of feminist study and practice document, the double binds confronting feminists in the early years of the movement were both concrete and historically grounded. For one thing, Wilson notes, they were faced with the long tradition of dress reform advocated by feminists and other social reformers that associated women's clothing with enslavement and/or display, "confining women to narrow stereotypes of femininity and the 'beautiful,' often even restricting their actual movements"; this view was reiterated by Simone de Beauvoir in *The Second Sex*. Capitalism also played a role in this analysis, leading feminists to argue that "femininity . . . was false consciousness," and fashion and beauty culture a form of commodification that not only harmed women physically and psychologically but could be read as playing a causal role in their history. The other prevailing view at the time, inherited from the 1960s, argued that "everyone now 'dressed to please themselves.' "[21] Feminists who were also lesbians and adopted the anti-fashion, anti-style "flannel-and-denim look" in the 1970s had still other explanations: that it provided both "a way for dykes to identify one another" and a way out of the butch-femme roles then considered "vestiges of a patriarchal past."[22]

In the early 1980s, however, scholars began to bring feminist theories and practices to the rethinking of fashion. A variety of reasons have been offered for this reassessment. The editors of *On Fashion,* for example, write that "fashion entered the academy by way of 'French theory,' whose stylish, wickedly witty, playful intellectualism made our heads spin"; they cite the summer 1982 issue of *Diacritics,* with its cover images of a headless, handless woman and disembodied, free-floating articles of clothing, as the starting point.[23] Others emphasize the rise of cultural studies, which not only made the study of popular cultural forms, including fashion and style, a central focus for the study of class, racial, gender, and power relationships, but, under the influence of British cultural studies, began to redefine the consumer's role as that of active agent in the construction of personal and social/political identities.[24] Here fashion and style become a form of resistance, a way for marginal groups to seize culture, "now understood as reinflecting signs already in circulation for their own political ends." Drawing upon the work of Angela McRobbie on the subversive styles of young working-class women, Jane Gaines asks, "What better site for disruption of the social order than the seeming scene of the origin of women's oppression," i.e., traditional femininity?[25]

Gaines also offers other explanations for the feminist reconsideration "of costume and body": changing attitudes toward women's sexuality (more pro-sex) and the role of pleasure within it, catalyzed by the 1982 Barnard Conference on sexuality; and the developments within feminist film theory that led it to explore the concept—and gratifications—of female spectatorship, including those associated with masquerade. One can also add here the development of a lesbian and later a queer analysis that challenged both the traditional view that women, trained to see themselves as men see them, dress for men and the presumed heterosexuality of the fashion system. Judith Butler's rendition of gender and identity as performative, produced as an effect of performative acts and hence open to disruption through the practices of drag, camp, parody, etc., also played a role. All of these explanations support the association of feminist interventions in fashion with the "aggressive postmodernism" perceived to characterize the recent fashion scene itself.[26] The result is a multiplicity of critical approaches that parallels the multiplicity of clothing styles; the hope is that this multiplicity will erode the ideological systems that have traditionally worked to naturalize gender and its roles.

The emphasis on eclecticism in the fall 1996 season, with its doubled dose of retro (the twenties read through the seventies or vice versa), would seem to bear this argument out. In June, just before Bloomsbury made its appearance, an article in W called "Opposing Forces" asks "Plain or done-up?" and answers, "It's fall's big question—and there are two right answers." August's W featured an article, "Trend Watch," in which buyers for a number of American stores explain what excites them about the season's clothes. One extols "a new free spirit emerging this fall with a host of creative choices. . . . What is most important is the mix that brings things together in modern new ways." Others point to the unusual pairings ("a classic peacoat with animal print pants"), the "multiplicity of shapes," and the fact that "it's no longer about just one look." September's W continues this theme, presenting London as the hot new place for fashion and style, signified, among other things, by the "constantly evolving . . . phenomenon" of its street style, which, one non-English designer notes, comes up " 'with the most unlikely mixes. Everything is too much, but it doesn't bother anyone at all—they love it. That's what makes London move.' " By October W feels confident enough to run a story called "The Thrill Is Back," chronicling the return of "the passion for fashion" among "gamines and grannies, street kids and CEOs[,] who just can't get their fashion fixes frequently enough." Even the dissenting opinion of the New York Times in August that "matters de la mode are of ever diminishing concern to women today" becomes for W writer Bridget Foley proof that what characterizes the current moment is a "celebration of diversity. As politically correct and edgy as the fashion world fancies itself, its exclusionary attitudes can veer toward the provincial. Too often," Foley continues, "the strength of a single direction has negated everything else in the eyes of the hip: If minimalism is in, then embellishment is passé. Now, however, the environment is such that not only can the anti-fashion of Prada or Jil Sander stand up against Lang's fashiony street chic and Galliano's lavish, quirky frills, or for that matter, Anna Sui's thrifty frivolity, but all can flourish at once."[27]

Looking back from this euphoric pronouncement of "diversity" as fashion itself rarely does except to evoke the names or periods such as Virginia Woolf or Bloomsbury that it claims inspired its expression of current desires, we can see that "the mix that brings things together in modern new ways" can itself be read in and through the cultural shifts that occurred from the 1960s on, including the rise of feminism. From this perspective, and Wilson charts this well, the rise of eclecticism and pastiche among youth cultures of the 1960s, often in the name of a defiant or oppositional expression of individual and group identity, anticipated the eclecticism and pastiche that began to appear in the fashion industry during the 1970s, where it acquired the label "retrochic." By the 1990s, Holly Brubach notes, fashion had been going through the decades at the rate of one every five years for at least twenty years and had begun the practice of doubling them.[28] This practice, so visible in the discourse of the fall 1996 Bloomsbury revival, would seem to support Kaja Silverman's 1986 argument that vintage dressing, retro, which deliberately cuts across historical periods and styles, can be a way of resisting fashion's dictate that things be if not new at least now. But it also points to another phenomenon central to fashion: the appropriation and commodification of subversive subcultural and street styles such as retro by the industry. This "double movement of containment and resistance" has increasingly become not only part of fashion but also part of the writing about it, where critics, who assume its presence, analyze particular instances for their cultural and ideological significance.[29]

At this point the refrain "Virginia Woolf, like fashion, like postmodernism . . ." intersects with versioning, juxtaposing the promise of diversity, democratization, and the free circulation of meaning with the constraints inherent in the processes of appropriation, commodification, legitimation, and containment. In this way the refrain becomes a case study in the possibilities and dangers of postmodern versioning itself, forcing us to ask again what we gain or lose by accepting or advocating an open-ended, mobile, continually refashioned Virginia Woolf. Equally important, what are the dangers of refusing this position, of advocating a singular or authentic Virginia Woolf?

The distinction between the "authentic" and the "modern"/postmodern governing Elizabeth Wilson's reading of attitudes toward clothing and fashion proves useful here. The authentic aligns itself with a "natural" or true body, self, or identity, that, it argues, clothing should emulate; the modern, modulating into the postmodern, aligns itself with a recognition of the constructedness of the body, self, identity: the role of images, representations, codes, or fashion at every level of our lives. The division, she argued in 1985, encompasses conflicts within feminism as well as fashion, suggesting "two radically divergent ways of seeing the world— and fashion—and two radically different kinds of politics. Is fashionable dress part of the oppression of women, or is it a form of adult play? Is it part of the empty consumerism, or is it a site of struggle symbolized in dress codes? Does it muffle the self, or create it?" Wilson supports the second perspective, illustrating throughout her study that clothing is never "natural" or "authentic": that even the clothing designed or advocated by the various reform movements over the centuries, however much they appeal to scientific rationalism and/or utilitarianism (and garner the support of feminists), is just as much an "unnatural" construction as any other clothing.[30] The etymological roots of *fashion* in the French *façon* and the Latin *factio,* from the verb *facere,* "to make," whose second definition in the *OED* is "make, build, or shape," supports this contention.

Undoing the binary between the "authentic" and the "[post]modern," one would think, would make any claim to the authentic untenable. This would seem particularly true in the contemporary period, when, Wilson argues, pastiche and retro have so permeated culture at large that it is impossible to see either a particular style or the deliberate attempt to eschew style as anything except "style"; at a time when "all styles are now self-caricatures," she argues, "we have all become so sophisticated about performance that we slily recognize the attempted sleight of hand that aimed to suggest the absence of effort or impression-creation. No longer do *any* fashions seem normal or 'natural.'"[31]

Having established that, however, Wilson, like others writing to re-claim and rearticulate the subject of fashion for feminism in the name of cultural studies, postmodern identities, and/or queer theory, does not endorse postmodernism uncritically, although she remains even warier of the alternatives. Committed to social change as well as cultural analy-sis, these writers often provide trenchant critiques of particular aspects of postmodernism, but they are unwilling to reject its role in undoing boundaries, categories, and power relations, including those associated with "identity." Nor do their very real reservations lead them to call for a return to a natural or "authentic" clothing and/or identity. As Su-san Bordo, writing of the love/hate relationship she and so many other feminists have with postmodernism, argues, the experience of being "de-centered," of multiple or fragmented identifications, is "part of the lived experience of acting, thinking, writing in fragmenting times" and cannot be theoretically or practically wished away.[32] Instead, what these critics advocate is a more self-conscious, more historically located examina-tion of the intersections of style, on the one hand, and art, social the-ory, social relations, politics, and the material, on the other, including an awareness of the conditions under which clothing is produced and by whom.

The debate takes a variety of forms. Julia Emberley, for example, reads the layerings of meanings and historical periods associated with a post-modernism/fashion defined as "life-style" as a false promise: a promise of "diversity, and the freedom of choice to create an individually unique style" that produces instead "alienation from self and one another."[33] Susan Bordo's concern is not so much fashion as the body fashioned by our cultural discourses: the medical, corporate, and advertising discourses that use "breezy analogies comparing cosmetic surgery to fashion accessorizing" to suggest that we can make our bodies anything we want them to be. For Bordo, the danger of the postmodern declaration that we can all freely play with our clothes, our bodies, ourselves in a world in which "anything goes" lies in the assumption that everyone participates equally: a position that, while accurate theoretically, "effaces the inequalities of social position and . . . historical origins" as well as the "practices that do not merely transform but *normalize* the subject." Critical analysis of this effacement, she adds, is further discouraged by the media that respond to any critique of current practices by calling the critic a "homogenizing and stifling . . . feminist dictator."[34]

For Arlene Stein, the concern is whether the deconstruction of the "old, perhaps overly politicized or prescriptive notion of lesbianism" by the new proliferation of styles "[depoliticizes] lesbian identity and [perpetuates] our invisibility by failing, frequently, to name itself to others." Danae Clark, building on Stein, concurs, especially when she looks at the discrepancy between the mainstream media's "postmodern, antiessentialist (indeed, democratic) discourse"—"homosexuals are not . . . inherently different from heterosexuals," e.g.—and the homophobia that it displaces and masks. Denying a homosexual identity, she and others argue, potentially undercuts the grounds for arguing against discrimination. "The issue," she writes, sounding a note that others caught in the postmodern double bind reiterate as well, "is not a matter of choosing between constructionism or essentialism, but a matter of examining the political motivations involved in each of these approaches—whether they appear in theory or media texts."[35]

Writing from the perspective of a "Third Wave" or second-generation feminist, Lucinda Rosenfeld has a different take. Having imbibed the feminist rearticulation of sexuality and style in her college courses and lived it in her defiantly sexual, revolutionary way of dress ("underwear as outerwear"), she found herself concerned about both local constraints and the translation of a (postmodernist) style into social change. Graduating in 1991, she soon discovered that "garter-belt feminism" had its limitations in both the world of work and the world of the streets; in the latter, she learned that "one girl's 'parodic recontextualization' is another's business attire" and that, much to her chagrin, she "did not want to be mistaken for a transvestite prostitute." Now age twenty-seven, Rosenfeld still wears black-lace slips as skirts, but she's "learned to appreciate the masquerade for what it is—a costume—and what it's not: an identity, a political platform, a life."[36]

While Jane Gaines might question the use of the term *identity* in Rosenfeld's moral, she would recognize the dilemma, having expressed as clearly
as anyone the difficulties of the postmodern position: the worry that the
"contention of postmodernist theory—the idea that the image has swal-
lowed reality whole—obliterates the problems endemic to comparisons
between images and society. If the image now precedes the real, engulfs it
and renders it obsolete as a point of comparison, do we any more need to
show how representation is ideological?"[37]

For Gaines, and for me, the answer is yes. I have no trouble accepting
that like fashion, Virginia Woolf and her "meaning" are permeable and
recombinable, open to reinterpretation. That like fashion, Virginia Woolf
will be repeatedly recycled, reappearing in shapes that, like Alberta Ferretti's, will be structured differently from those of the past, breaking all
the rules, in order to express the maker's vision. That like fashion, what
begins as a subversive gesture on the "streets" may well be recuperated by
the mainstream for its own ends. And that, like fashion, Virginia Woolf will
be evoked as a model for diverse, even conflicting, identifications, acting
out Wilson's contention that "fashion is a magical system, and what we see
as we leaf through glossy magazines is 'the look' " that we can make our
own.[38] Alberta Ferretti provides a case in point, returning, surprisingly, to
Virginia Woolf and "the women of the Twenties and Thirties" in her 1997
fall collection, because, she says, they are "very eccentric and very inspired
and very sophisticated women." Elsa Klensch, introducing Ferretti's collection on her television show *Style,* also emphasizes the "strong independent
women of the Bloomsbury period in England, women who helped change
the direction of British literature in the Twenties. . . . Ferretti says she was
especially influenced by Virginia Woolf and the characters in her novels."
This sounds straightforward enough, but Ferretti immediately complicates
the referent; Virginia Woolf might be "inspired and sophisticated," but the
collection, she says, represents "a new interpretation of romanticism and
femininity which is a very modern and very streamlined romanticism" appropriate for those on the verge of the year 2000. Her goal, she concludes,
is to "offer a wide variety for a wide variety of women"; we can take
our choice.[39]

However problematic the "variety" may be, I'd rather have Virginia
Woolf available as a source of multiple identifications and/or a spokes-
woman for exploring the conflicted meanings of fashion, including its
possibilities for experimentation, than to limit her to any single definition
of what an authentic "dress" for women should be. After all, as Holly
Brubach points out, it was Virginia Woolf who in the 1920s argued against
a system in which "it is the masculine values that prevail. Speaking crudely,

football and sport are 'important'; the worship of fashion, the buying of clothes 'trivial,'" anticipating—though Brubach does not add this—a feminist cultural criticism that has argued exactly this same point about the genres and arts associated with women and the feminine, including fashion.[40] It is also Virginia Woolf, journalist Linda Grant reminds us, who represents shops and shopping as life-affirming in *Mrs. Dalloway.* (Fashion reciprocated, depicting a pink-sweatered, sleeping Kate Moss with an open copy of *Mrs. Dalloway* in her hand.)[41] But like others committed to a postmodern multiplicity of meanings, I, too, would insist on the necessity of exploring the historical and social contexts of each and every manifestation of Virginia Woolf, of charting the patterns.

To this end I want to return to the 1996 representations of Virginia Woolf and Bloomsbury in the fashion discourse and focus on what is missing from the various lists of attributes and possibilities: feminism. This absence suggests that we have reached a point where fashion and fashion magazines reflect less postmodernism than "postfeminism," itself a construction of the media, where feminism, presumed to be a thing of the past, is no longer necessary for women who either know what they want, including what they want in fashion, or are quite happy to be told by experts what to wear without feeling this compromises their independence. Brubach, a journalist, raises this specter in the 1992 *New Yorker* article where she claims Woolf's authority for taking fashion seriously, but in the process she blames feminism for bringing about the "postfeminism" that, she says, it now laments.

Surprised by assertions that hemlines would drop next year, an indication that designers, after twenty years of working with rather than dictating to women, had once again taken control, Brubach turns to an executive from "a large American department store" who tells her that "her customers—intelligent women . . . accustomed to thinking for themselves—are again looking to designers and fashion magazines for guidance. The logic, as she explained it, is along the same lines as the reasoning behind what has lately been called the backlash against feminism: instead of allowing women to relax and worry less about their clothes, all the recent freedom in fashion has brought on a case of anxiety. The choices are overwhelming. After two decades of unprecedented free reign, she said, women once again want to be told what to wear."[42]

Confronted with this vision of what appears to be a retreat by or defeat of women, Brubach turns not on fashion but on feminism. This gesture illustrates once again the lack of exchange between the academy and the self-styled "intellectual" media; in this case even a cursory reading of the literature would have revealed the richness and wide variety of writing

among feminists (and others) on fashion that would have complicated if
not invalidated Brubach's argument. For someone who writes on fashion,
Brubach appears at this moment peculiarly out of date. Instead, ignoring
the diverse trends and published works that, crossing disciplines and critical perspectives, had by 1992 made the "F-word" more than the object of
moralistic rejection for at least ten years, Brubach blames the current state
of fashion on "feminist dogma [that] has always been hostile to fashion,
on the ground that it is nothing more than an instrument of oppression."
In this reading, it is "feminist dogma" that produced the "so-called postfeminist era," which seeks refuge in the past as recompense for the failure
of "the previous generation's revolution"; her example is a single book,
Susan Faludi's *Backlash: The Undeclared War against American Women*.
"Feminist dogma," Brubach writes, raises the wrong issues (oppression);
unlike Virginia Woolf, whose words she cites in opposition, it dismisses
fashion, "one of women's long-standing pastimes, as beneath the serious
consideration of intelligent people" rather than exploring "how women use
clothes to help them consolidate their identity and . . . how they choose to
present themselves to the world."[43]

What interests are served by setting a singular "feminist dogma" of
"oppression" against women's pleasure in fashion, and how does claiming
Virginia Woolf for your side help achieve this end? Clearly, who benefits
most are the media whose claim to speak in and for the public sphere
is premised on their *not* being feminist: media that seem to pride themselves on excluding the broad range of feminist perspectives from their
purview, as if any careful or nuanced examination of a topic such as
fashion would make it disappear; for which any one book, misrepresented
and misinterpreted, constitutes a "dogma." One begins to think that the
media are decidedly anti-intellectual, afraid of any genuine analysis or
discussion, afraid perhaps that "the public" would then demand more of
them than unsupported assertions of what "feminist dogma" holds and
how dangerous it is for people: as if an educated populace, capable of
analyzing opposing ideas and forming its own opinions, were not a desired
goal. Claiming Virginia Woolf in this context and using her to contradict
"feminist dogma" becomes as clear an example of the appropriation,
recuperation, and containment of subversiveness and resistance as one is
likely to find. Here Virginia Woolf and fashion, rather than being sites for
experimentation and change, are frozen into a monolithic position that
defines itself against an equally monolithic feminism. At this point one positively yearns for a postmodern unsettling of categories and oppositions.

Had Brubach, instead of blaming "feminist dogma," followed the example of feminist scholars and looked at the media itself, especially at fashion

magazines, and asked how they have represented women, feminism, and fashion, she might have concluded that her interlocutor's perception of feminism's decreasing role in fashion signals less a "postfeminist" reaction against the failures of feminism than an illustration of the way contemporary fashion discourse has simultaneously honored and buried women's self-assertion.[44] As Alice Gambrell argues of fashion magazines, once they deem something " 'of the moment' " it will inevitably soon be "declared 'over,' " the fate that befell "sexual politics" when, "following two decades of uneven, ambivalent coverage by the fashion press, [it] emerged in the early 1990s as an object of intense fascination among fashion journalists." Her example, occurring at the same time as Brubach's lament, is the so-called "bad girl" feminism connected with groups such as African American Women in Defense of Ourselves, Guerrilla Girls, the Women's Action Coalition, the Intelligent Black Women's Coalition, Riot Grrrl, and Women's Health Action Mobilization, which became visible in a wide range of public spaces at that time. These groups were actively engaged in "[negotiating] between female experience and feminist spectacle," "[testing] the limits of performance as a strategy for political resistance," but the representation of their activity within the magazines as stylized images served to contain this feminist activity, to "freeze" it. What followed was feminism's "inevitable . . . descent from valorization to obsolescence, from the display window to the bargain basement."[45]

But despite this act of journalistic disappearance, Gambrell is far more sanguine and optimistic about the complex intersections among feminism and style/fashion than Brubach, locked in a discourse she fails to interrogate, appears to be. Ignoring her own references earlier in the piece to the role of retro and pastiche in fashion, Brubach could never reach Gambrell's conclusion: that feminism's absence from fashion discourse, its descent to the bargain basement, makes it available once again for the strategic rearticulations, the "performative energies" and resistances, that are associated not only with the oppositional modes of the "street" but also with the play of identities Brubach advocates.[46]

Virginia Woolf's appearance in Brubach's essay also returns us to Nochlin's argument that intellectual women are not supposed to be interested in fashion. Here Virginia Woolf, troped as emblematic intellectual woman, appears on both sides of the debate, claimed both by those who want to undo the powerful cultural discourse that insists on separating intellect from fashion, body, and sexuality in women and by those who reiterate it. Linda Grant, a writer for Britain's *Guardian* whose beat "is the dark places of the human mind—child sexual abuse, rape in Bosnia, the forgotten sex slaves of the Vietnam War, the legacy of the Holocaust"—

presents one side when she calls upon *Mrs. Dalloway* to argue that even
the intellectually serious Virginia Woolf did not consider shopping and
by implication clothes "mindless trivia." But she also, inadvertently, introduces the other side by referring to the Virginia Woolf who is "so
engaged in the life of the mind that D. H. Lawrence accused her of having
'sex in the head.' "[47] Lawrence's comment signals not only the belief that
the intellect, the head, contradicts or eradicates the body and its pleasures,
including fashion and sexuality, in intellectual women, but the long history
of representing Virginia Woolf as the exemplar of the asexual, unerotic,
unfashionable, and, yes, frightening intellectual woman. In contrast to
recent fashion discourse, this history fixes or freezes Virginia Woolf into
a position or identity that threatens to close off the space for play or
experimentation, for strategic performances that might lead to change.
Gambrell associates this process of freezing or deactivation with elite
fashion when it appropriates the more mobile activities of the "street";[48]
but in the case of Virginia Woolf, elite fashion, at least in its 1996–97
guise, seems to offer a fuller range of alternative Virginia Woolfs than
other cultural forums.

Significantly, the detail that often announces the presence of the asexual,
intellectual, Virginia Woolf is an item of clothing: the cardigan. While
Virginia Woolf's identification with long sweaters has been used by fashion
designers to market "the Bloomsbury sweater,"[49] in its guise as cardigan,
particularly in its English manifestation as "cardie," it is more often
presented or read as a sign of the serious, asexual, unfashionable (read
unfeminine), and/or feminist woman. The "cardie" carries this meaning
even when Virginia Woolf isn't involved, although she often seems its
emblematic inscription. Grant provides a paradigmatic example when she
recounts a story told her by her friend Joan Smith, "novelist and author
of *Misogynies,* one of the most important British feminist books of recent
years," about a newspaper interview:

> "Joan Smith," the journalist wrote, "who looks younger than her
> age, was wearing for the interview no make-up and any old cardie."
> Joan rang me in a fury. Any old cardie had been a brand-new Sophie
> Gorton and she could do without much in life, but her Lancôme
> lipstick was not included.[50]

I am reminded here of James Watson's condescending descriptions in
The Double Helix of Rosalind Franklin, the crystallographer who, in
conjunction with Watson, Francis Crick, and Maurice Wilkins, discovered
the structure of DNA. Referring to her as "Rosy," as if, Mary Jacobus

argues, "she were a kind of scientific charlady," commenting on her lack of makeup and her unfashionable clothes ("Though her features were strong, she was not unattractive and might have been quite stunning had she taken even a mild interest in clothes. This she did not. There was never lipstick to contrast with her straight black hair, while at the age of thirty-one her dresses showed all the imagination of English blue-stocking adolescents"), labeling her a feminist and admitting she "had a good brain," Watson at one point finds himself thinking, "I wondered how she would look if she took off her glasses." Rosalind Franklin did not wear glasses; she did wear lipstick.[51] Joan Smith, feminist writer, wore fashionable clothing and lipstick. No matter; the cardie, the glasses, freeze the women, tell us all we need to know.

Anita Brookner's distinctly nasty and disturbing novel *Hotel du Lac,* which explicitly links Virginia Woolf to the cardigan, shifts the belief in a fixed, authentic, identity for intellectual women from the outside to the inside, complicating the question of what it means to fashion oneself on Virginia Woolf. On the second page, the narrator, Edith, a woman seemingly typical of the British "spinster," tells us "I am a serious woman who should know better and am judged by my friends to be past the age of indiscretion; several people have remarked upon my physical resemblance to Virginia Woolf." Shortly after this, remembering catching sight of herself in a mirror, she describes her "extremely correct appearance": a "mild-looking, slightly bony woman in a long cardigan. . . ."[52] Somewhat later, when an older woman comments, " 'You know, dear, . . . you remind me of someone. Your face is very familiar. Now who can it be?' " Edith unhesitatingly offers " 'Virginia Woolf?' . . . as she always did on these occasions." Mrs. Pusey's eventual recollection, " 'Princess Anne! . . . I knew it would come to me. Princess Anne!' " (63), proves devastating to the reader, leading us to wonder about the determined fixity and necessity of Edith's self-representation.

As Edith comes to wonder herself. Having acted out of character by deciding at the last minute she could not go through with a wedding that was about to begin, Edith finds herself, at her friends' insistence, resting and writing (she writes romance novels under a pseudonym) at a discreet Swiss hotel, where her self-identification is tested first by the women she meets who encourage her to buy new clothes and then by a suitor whose very name, Mr. Neville, presents him as a devilish seducer. Mr. Neville goes right to the heart of her self-identity in his attempt to enlist her in a marriage of convenience, loveless and selfish, which would preserve the façade meant to reestablish the loss of pride he suffered when his first wife left: " 'Now, Mrs. Woolf,' he said, 'I don't believe we've been properly introduced.

Philip Neville,' he added calmly" (75). He follows up this opening sortie by using her pen name, Vanessa Wilde. Edith laughs. But after amusing her by his astuteness, Mr. Neville uses this astuteness to shatter her self-possession. In a particularly unpleasant scene where he begins to break down her defenses, he attacks her evident loneliness, her seeming lack of sexuality, and her clothes: " 'If your capacity for bad behavior were being properly used,' " he tells her, " 'you would not be moping around in that cardigan' " (102). This particularly hurts, since by this time we know that the adulterous affair she's been having has not been as constant or as satisfying as we were originally led to believe and has almost certainly come to an end. During their final conversation, after which she decides she will marry him in order to have the social life, the opportunities, the pleasures she so clearly lacks and sees no hope of achieving, Mr. Neville begins by observing, " 'You are shivering. That cardigan is not warm enough; I do wish you would get rid of it. Whoever told you that you looked like Virginia Woolf did you a grave disservice, although I suppose you thought it was a compliment' " (158). Edith's response to his insistence that she can change returns us and her to Virginia Woolf: " 'I really don't see how. If all it involves is giving away my cardigan, I feel I should tell you that I have another one at home. Of course, I could give that away too. But I seem to be too spiritless for radical improvement. I am simply not fascinating. I don't know why' " (158–59).

At the end of the novel, having discovered a bathrobed Mr. Neville stealthily exiting the room of another woman and realizing she could not endure a loveless life, Edith changes her mind again; at this point, she might have repeated an earlier observation when giving way to her strong but repressed emotions: "I have taken the name of Virginia Woolf in vain" (88). Although she wires that she is "returning," not "coming home" (184), her future looks bleak, as bleak as the grayness that permeates the novel from the first page. Most people I know feel Edith's decision not to marry Mr. Neville is right, but the alternative, the Virginia Woolfian, cardiganed, existence, seemingly as unalterable and/or authentic as she claims her own nature to be, feels equally self-destructive.

Virginia Woolf's appearances on both sides of the authentic/postmodern dichotomy that still characterizes discussions of fashion and clothes illustrate once again her potential to deconstruct categories that limit women's self-perceptions and choices, signifying that one can be *both* an intelligent, serious, intellectual woman, even a feminist, *and* open to the pleasurable, seriously playful self-representation enacted through clothes: that one need not be fixed in any one position regardless of how one chooses to dress, or not dress; that the danger is refusing to recognize the pleasures and dangers of any choice one makes; that multiplicities, ambiguities, are the necessary name of the game if we are to be free to experiment and change. But not everyone, including feminists and Woolf scholars, has seen her equation with a postmodern fashion and the fashionable in this light. For those who want their categories and their Virginia Woolf in a single, avowedly authentic, recognizable place, Virginia Woolf's refashionings, her versioning, signal only a fashionable appropriation as harmful to women and feminism, as fashion itself is held by many to be.

One way out of this double bind is to return to Dyer's concept of structured polysemy: to his argument that "it is misleading to think of the [various media] texts combining cumulatively into a sum total that constitutes the [star] image, or alternatively simply as being moments in a star's image's career that appear one after the other." Instead, we need to think of the star image as a *"complex totality"* with a *"chronological dimension,"* in which "the possibilities of [a star's] meaning are limited in part by what the text makes available." Within this framework, new texts (or refashionings) present the possibilities for new meanings. Given the intersections of chronology and intertextuality at work in the *structured* part of structured polysemy, the question becomes, does the ongoing intertextuality reinforce a single image that legitimates "a certain way of being" a woman in society? Or does it introduce contradictions that in threatening to fragment the image open the space for illegitimate readings? Here Virginia Woolf's longevity as star becomes crucial, leading us to a slightly different question: Does the neverending proliferation of texts and readings serve to continue an overriding image, as happened, Dyer writes, with Marlene Dietrich when she became the emblem of "the alluring, exotic female 'other,'" the " 'Eternal Feminine' "? Or, as is true of the more volatile Jane Fonda, do the new texts shatter traditional concepts of femininity?[53]

This question is far from hypothetical or abstract when it comes to Virginia Woolf, for new texts are appearing all the time, and they are very much concerned with what it means to be a woman. Witness, for example, the numerous adaptations of Virginia Woolf's works that have appeared on television, stage, and in films over the past few years, producing debates about sexuality and gender. Or witness the Chapel Hill hybrid, which combined the head of Virginia Woolf with the body of Marilyn Monroe. How much do these texts and their reception reiterate a Virginia Woolf who legitimates traditional ideas of what a woman is and is not? And how much do they foreground the contradictions that Dyer argues are at the heart of not only star images but society itself?

At this point my narrative branches in at least two directions. One picks up on the postmodern versioning of Virginia Woolf, the proliferation of her meanings, using the adaptations of *A Room of One's Own* and *Orlando* to illustrate the politics of claiming to know and impose on others an authentic Virginia Woolf. The other focuses on the Chapel Hill hybrid, returning to the reiterated images of Virginia Woolf as monstrous feminine, exploring the ramifications of and resistances to representations that freeze her into myth. In both cases the categories of continuity and change, of proliferation and reiteration, at work in the construction of star images become as unstable, as permeable, as any other set of binaries when confronted with the figure of Virginia Woolf.

three

DOUBLED MOVEMENTS

THE POLITICS OF ADAPTATION;

OR, THE AUTHENTIC VIRGINIA WOOLF

At the end of his exploration of "what . . . we mean by authenticity, and what [we will] accept as evidence of it" when it comes to Shakespeare, Stephen Orgel concludes that the desire for authenticity is for something "behind" or "beyond" the text:

> The assumption is that texts are representations or embodiments of something else, and that it is that something else which the performer or editor undertakes to reveal. What we want is not the authentic play, with its unstable, infinitely revisable script, but an authentic Shakespeare, to whom every generation's version of a classic drama may be ascribed.[1]

Virginia Woolf, you may be thinking, is not on a par with Shakespeare, but you would be wrong. By the mid-1990s she was not only appearing alongside Shakespeare whenever a "canonical" woman writer was needed, but her novels, already subject to versioning for scholars and general readers, were increasingly being adapted—or versioned—for the stage and screen. These new texts, these performances, became part of that "*complex totality*" that characterizes the star image, in which "the possibilities of meaning" may be "limited in part by what the text makes available," but in which the text, or vehicle, is only one aspect of a distinctly polysemous and often contradictory construct.[2] In this way, each new text functions as a pretext for what is really at stake: not an authentic text, but an authentic

Virginia Woolf, whose representation can be used to support particular social, cultural, and/or political ends. Since authenticity, as Orgel notes, is always a "matter of authentication, something bestowed, not inherent,"[3] the authentic Virginia Woolfs that emerge from the "something else" behind the texts must be viewed as the effect of distinctly historical and political acts.

In the case of Patrick Garland's adaptation of A Room of One's Own for stage and TV and Sally Potter's film version of Orlando, the two performances that concern me here, the almost simultaneous appearance and popularity of the refashioned texts in the early 1990s speak directly to debates about feminism, gender, sexuality, and androgyny in what has been called, conflictually, a "postfeminist" or a queer moment. These debates, extensively played out in the media, mark areas of profound cultural tension, and Virginia Woolf was claimed for almost every position. Everyone seemed to have something to say about the performances and their broader implications, raising the question of what the authentic Virginia Woolf for that generation would be: would Virginia Woolf, that is, be contained within a "postfeminist" status quo where heterosexuality and a sameness/difference binary are the ideological norm, or taking on the trappings of the queer, would she subvert the sameness/difference binary itself?

Viewed from this perspective the versioning of A Room of One's Own and Orlando for popular consumption can be seen as a politics of adaptation: an intersection of text, adaptor, audience, and institutions of production and dissemination that is inseparable from the politics of gender and sexuality being played out at a time when the norms appear to be in crisis. Within this context the adaptations and their reception reveal the role of performance in the production of normative discourses about gender and/or sexuality, as well as the gaps or fissures or slippages that threaten or promise, depending on your point of view, to undo them.

My argument begins with performance itself, a concept that crosses, as versioning does, between textual editing and popular culture, between the performance of a play or film and performance as a discursive event or act with links to performativity.[4] My starting point is that made by critics, often writing of Shakespeare, who argue that all versions of a work, all its constituent texts including adaptations, can be understood as performances; rather than existing in a hierarchical relationship to each other—original and adaptation, for example—these versions exist in a fluid, shifting relationship, an intertextual cluster, with each new performance an encoding of a particular historical, cultural moment that alters the configuration.[5] Alteration is the key term here, suggesting both the element of choice at work in adaptations and the element of refashioning. Writing of Shakespeare, Laurie Osborne notes that "as with scholarly editing, performances also represent a kind of editing . . . that involves cutting, rearranging, and otherwise altering a play in important ways"; the choices made, she adds, tell us a great deal not only about the theatrical practices and performance possibilities of the period but also about the more intangible historical contexts and pressures, including attitudes toward gender and sexuality.[6]

With the element of "cutting, rearranging and otherwise altering" in place, we can see that the adaptations of Woolf's texts become more than "an activity of literary criticism" that "can throw new light on the original";[7] they themselves become "originals" whose construction and performance set the stage for assertions about Virginia Woolf. The fact that so many people today see the film or television versions of Woolf's works before they experience (if they ever do) the versions she wrote and published also undoes the binary, transforming the adaptation into the original against which other versions are then read and measured. (Publishers capitalize on this phenomenon when they reissue a novel-made-into-a-film such as *Orlando* with photographs of the film actors on the cover.) In this way the audience enters into the action, participating in what Peter Shillingsburg calls the "Reception Performance" at work in determining "the 'functional authority' " of a version and by extension the Virginia Woolf that lies behind it.[8]

Another way to frame the status and significance of the adaptations is to see them, as Shillingsburg suggests, as one of a variety of potential versions, variously constituted by their potential function ("Is it for a magazine; is it a chapter in a book; is it a play adaptation, a translation, a revised edition aimed at a new market?").[9] This allows us to argue that when a novel or an essay—*Orlando,* say, or *A Room of One's Own*—becomes a play or a film it is functionally translated from one medium to another, using the definition of *translate* that associates it with the tailor trade, with the taking apart and remaking of a garment.[10] When the novel or essay is translated, then, it is metaphorically "re-fashioned" or "re-dressed" in the clothes (stage practices, cinematic conventions) currently fashionable or possible for that medium. In this sense we can say that clothes make the version, and the determination of how it is marketed and what sells becomes a question of that moment's style.

Here we enter squarely into the realm signified by the refrain "Virginia Woolf, like fashion, like postmodernism . . . ," where performance and play problematize the concept of the authentic, once again suggesting an unending, unfettered, permutation or proliferation, although, once again, each specific instance has a clear historical grounding and resonance.

Textual scholars make this point when they argue that a "work" is a series of texts, "a series of specific acts of production," or that "the work is not equivalent to the *sum* of its texts," including performances, "but instead is an ongoing—and infinite—manifestation of textual appearances"; and their formulations intersect with Dyer's contention when writing about the star image that "it is misleading to think of the texts combining cumulatively into a sum total that constitutes" this image; "the image is a *complex totality* and it does have a *chronological dimension.*"[11] In both cases the possibility if not the assumption exists that this progression can be infinite: a situation in which a work or a star image can be represented as an infinite series of texts, and a specific text can be represented as an infinite series of performances that could, conceivably, produce an infinite series of fashionable Virginia Woolfs.

At this point I would set out my argument as follows. Garland's and Potter's adaptations of *A Room of One's Own* and *Orlando* for television, theater, and film, as well as the other adaptations of *Orlando* I'll introduce later, can be read as versions of a work that play a performative role not only in constructing what we understand when we talk about these works, but also in shaping cultural debates about feminism, androgyny, gender, and sexuality. It is no accident that many of these performances achieved mainstream attention and commercial success: they raise some of the most hotly debated issues of our time. In addition, the conflicting meanings attributed to these versions, including that of the authentic Virginia Woolf—meanings produced by the congruence of creative, production, and reception performances—suggest that the adaptations are more than interpretations of an original or authentic text; to the extent that all works are a series of texts and these texts are a series of performances, a work can be said to exist only in its performance. If this formulation sounds suspiciously like those put forward by theorists such as Judith Butler in their radical deconstruction of gender and sexuality—both in their argument that there is no original or foundational gender or sexuality, no original and copy but only copies, and in their argument that gender/sex and the gendered/sexed subject are produced by repetitive acts or performances—it is meant to; theories about texts, including adaptations, are no more immune to the cultural tensions of their moment than any other form of criticism or scholarship, involving, as Orgel writes, "basically doctrinal and political elements."[12]

But this vision of the unstable work as a series of texts or performances that produces a series of Virginia Woolfs should not be read as an endpoint: as an uncritical acceptance of a pluralism of versions, interesting only because they differ one from the other. For one thing, the various versions exist as materially as the bodies that, in Butler's terms, are performatively engendered and gendered/sexed through the process of reiteration or sedimentation that produces *"the effect of boundary, fixity"* or norms,[13] and the way these norms are enacted, received, and policed can have a material impact on the way we teach and write and live. However unstable or multiple the texts, however much they proliferate, to the extent that the authentic Virginia Woolf behind them is perceived to authorize or normalize prescriptive versions of art or gender/sexuality, she will be fixed and serve to fix others into a single position. As Orgel cogently comments, because "the history of realizations of the text," including adaptations, "is the history of the text," it is imperative to ask "what is being realized in such representations."[14]

What Ever Happened to Judith Shakespeare?

But Virginia Woolf, you may now be thinking, is still not Shakespeare; the analogy is not apt. Again, you would be wrong. While it was once fashionable to consider Virginia Woolf the reembodiment of Judith Shakespeare— William's "wonderfully gifted sister" imagined by Woolf in *A Room of One's Own,* who rather than writing plays and becoming Britain's greatest writer ended up pregnant and a suicide (for "who shall measure the heat and violence of the poet's heart when caught and tangled in a woman's body?")[15]— more recently she has become for many the embodiment of Shakespeare himself. The *New York Review of Books,* remember, featured Shakespeare and Virginia Woolf together before soloing Virginia Woolf. This suggests a transformation, an elevation, that shifts Virginia Woolf's iconic representation from the gendered body of Judith Shakespeare to the androgynous mind of William: a concept that, along with Judith, Woolf also imagines in her 1929 text. There are, we are reminded, as many Virginia Woolfs as there are Shakespeares, and the battles to assert which one is authentic are inseparable from battles over what constitutes a legitimate feminist critique or gender politics or literary canon: battles that have been fought through performances of her texts.

A Room of One's Own has long been a central work in these battles. It is no exaggeration to say that from the late 1960s on almost every work of feminist criticism and theory, at least in the United States, was more than likely to include a quotation from Woolf's essay in its epigraph, its introduction, and/or its text to support or authorize arguments of every conceivable persuasion. By the end of the 1980s, however, the nature of this inscription had begun to change. Challenged, on the one hand, from within feminist discourse for the limitations of its class and/or racial positions, *Room* was reclaimed, on the other, by non- or antifeminist critics who used it against what they insist on defining as a monolithic feminist project: in their version, the consideration of women writers as *women* and the field of women's studies that encourages this consideration. In the opinion of the conservative columnist Jeffrey Hart, writing in the *National Review* about a "feminist criticism" that in 1988 still consisted for his purposes entirely of Sandra Gilbert, Susan Gubar, and Elaine Showalter, if feminists had "let Woolf be Woolf," had listened to her words in *A Room of One's Own*, none of this—that is, feminist criticism—ever would have happened.[16]

The question is, which words? and more to my point, in which text?— a question that foregrounds the multiple extant versions of the work and the differences among them.[17] Ironically—or presciently—the version that most clearly enacts or performs the political and doctrinal elements at work in Hart's claim to the authenticity of Woolf's words appeared immediately after his piece: the version adapted by Patrick Garland and performed by Eileen Atkins both on television and the stage, first in London (1989) and then in the United States (1991).[18] Both the editorial choices made by Garland for the performance text and the play's reception illustrate how even the smallest shifts can alter the perception of Woolf's words and of Virginia Woolf and how closely aligned these perceptions are to politicized cultural agendas.

In the case of *Room,* where all the words spoken by Atkins during the play appear in Woolf's book, the alterations that cut a number of passages and changed the order of others produce a subtle but significant refashioning; reiteration is not seamless. As Joseph Grigely argues, glossing Jacques Derrida's "Signature Event Context," an utterance, once the original moment is past, is " 'grafted' " or "recontextualized: . . . language deceives us as to how its iterable presence (written words, marks, inscriptions) do [*sic*] not translate to an iterable intention, or meaning." The implication, he notes, is that editions are always "re:construct[ed]" texts, "texts that are a part of the social institution of professionalized literature . . . , and these texts serve all kinds of social, economic, and political purposes." When the text is a theatrical performance, meant to be heard once only, the potential impact of the agendas signaled by the choice and sequence of passages increases; "performance," Harry Berger, Jr., writes, "does not allow us the leisure to interrupt, challenge, or question. And since we can't flip the moments of a performance back and forth the way we can the pages of a book, we are prevented as spectators from carrying out central interpretive operations that presuppose our ability to decelerate the text, to ignore sequence. . . ."[19]

What we hear, then, is what we get: a version of *Room* that almost without exception the reviewers, despite or because of the alterations, declared to be not just "faithful" to the original but to represent the authentic Virginia Woolf. In the few reviews where critics acknowledge the cuts, they either shrug them off as inconsequential or prefer the new version; with one exception, no one analyzes *what* was left out. No one seems to have noticed one of the major editorial decisions made by Garland: the change of sequence that alters the last words of the play and hence its perceived meaning, although the effects of the change are apparent in almost every rendering of Woolf's message. Repeated performances in this case truly seem to create a depth and substance that present themselves as given or natural or authentic: Garland's version becomes the work itself. The result is the construction of a *Room* and a Virginia Woolf for the 1990s that recuperates them from the monolithic feminist criticism portrayed by Hart and the "intellectual"/mainstream media and returns them to their "proper" place in the realm of art.

The text achieves these effects by what it leaves out, excisions that elide the complexity and multiplicity of both the arguments in Woolf's version and the readings it has generated. The grounds for this multiplicity reside in Woolf's positing of a divided consciousness when it comes to gender and art. The narrator, that is, speculates, with Coleridge, that "a great mind is androgynous": that each of us has two powers in the soul, male and female, and that when a fusion, or marriage, occurs between them, "the mind is fully fertilised and uses all its faculties." Only then, perhaps, does it become "resonant," "porous," "incandescent," "undivided" (98)—and produce, as William Shakespeare did, great art. As another interrelated thread in this strand of the argument asserts, the best writers are not conscious of their sex when they write; it is, in fact, "fatal for any one who writes to think of their sex," whether that anyone is man or woman (104).

But, as strongly as the book posits the potential of the androgynous mind (and the concept itself has been interpreted in radically different ways as definitions of androgyny have changed), it also repeatedly asserts how and why women's writing, women's creativity, has been and will remain different from men's: that it has been, and will remain, no matter how unconsciously (and in fact the art is better when it *is* unconscious [93]), sex-inflected, and what a loss it would be if this were *not* the case. "For we think back through our mothers if we are women," the narrator states in one of the most widely cited passages (76); women's texts, she speculates, from their sentences to their genres, have "somehow to be adapted" to their bodies (78), and "it would be a thousand pities if women wrote like men, or lived like men, or looked like men" (88). Finally, much to the delight of recent queer theorists, the text also seems to be making an argument for dismantling the binaries that lead to either sameness or difference, men or women, for putting into play the categories that underlie gender not by embodying them in a single (androgynous) figure but by multiplying gender's permutations and possibilities: "for if two sexes are quite inadequate, considering the vastness and variety of the world, how should we manage with one only?" (88).

If this summary does not do justice to the complex counterpoint of seemingly dissonant motifs in the book, it is a great deal more inclusive than Garland's dramatized version; Garland's choices construct a text that gives us not a multiplicity of speculations that leave literature firmly, if lightly, attached to sex/gender and its cultural politics, but a single note: the transcendent universality of art. It gives us William, we could say, a William in whom Judith, his gifted sister, is subsumed, but not Judith herself. This is not to say that Judith is entirely absent: the story of her genius and death is told, and her ghostly presence permeates the play's exposition of the difficulties confronting women in the past who wanted to write. Her legacy is also felt in the more subtle representation of the difficulties confronting women who wanted to write in what was Woolf's present (1929): the inequalities within the educational system and the dominance of "experts" such as Professor von X who set out to define what women are. But Woolf's present is now our past, and the Judith who emerges from Garland's text as a model for women in the 1990s can be perceived either as already beyond the politics of gender and its discriminatory practices—to have entered, that is, into a disembodied, mental, "postfeminist" world of art—or as the recipient of an admonishment to do so as quickly as she can. The words, then, even the sentences of Garland's *Room* might be more or less identical to those in the 1929 book, but the "extralinguistic (dialogic) aspects" of the utterance, the historical and social circumstances in which they are uttered, alter the message.[20]

Taken as a whole, Garland's *Room* leaves intact those parts of the argument that posit androgyny as the erasure of gender-consciousness necessary for art even as it erases those parts of the argument that bring gender back into art. Audiences can hear the speaker, who is presented as Virginia Woolf herself,[21] say loudly and clearly that "it is fatal for a woman to lay the least stress on any grievance; to plead even with justice any cause; in any way to speak consciously as a woman"—the words that Jeffrey Hart cites in his article to illustrate the wrongheadedness of "feminist criticism," with its emphasis on women writing as women—but they won't hear any of the counterpoint that shows how gender permeates art, men's and women's alike. Gone are the descriptions of what it means to think back through one's mothers or what it means to write as a woman or even what it means to *be* a woman, with the multiple perspectives that entails. Gone are the text's construction of a female narrator whose explicit assumption of anonymity and multiplicity stands in direct contrast to the male authorial "I," and gone are the critiques of "virile" and fascist literature by men. Gone are the long passages detailing the marks of women's creativity; and gone are Chloe and Olivia, the two protagonists of the contemporary women's novel the narrator evokes, who for the first time in fiction not only like each other but in liking each other open the door for women to explore those areas of their experience for which no language yet exists. Also gone is the narrator's invocation of Sir Chartres Biron as the man lurking behind the curtain, who, if he heard her say that Chloe liked Olivia, might well censor her speech; what Woolf's audience in 1929 would have known immediately was that Biron was the presiding magistrate at the obscenity trial of *The Well of Loneliness*. In other words, gone is any reference to, any hint of, lesbianism.

In the end, though, it is the ending of the play that serves most effectively to assimilate Judith to William: not by erasing her but by rearranging the scenes to give her the penultimate rather than the final word. The book ends with a vivid image of Judith and her rebirth: the narrator's assertion that "the dead poet who was Shakespeare's sister will put on the body which she has so often laid down" if "we [women] worked for her" (114). In the play this vision of women's communal inheritance and struggle is followed by the reiteration of a passage already spoken in conjunction with the past: the narrator's assertion that "it would have needed a very stalwart young woman in 1828" to ignore the snubs and chidings of the male experts and to say "literature is open to everybody. I refuse to allow you, Beadle though you are, to turn me off the grass. Lock up your libraries if you like; but there is no gate, no lock, no bolt that you can set upon the freedom of my mind." Powerful as these words are, their sole appearance in the book (75–76) is followed immediately by the narrator's exposition of what she calls the more important impediment facing women writers in the nineteenth century—that there was no tradition of women's writing for them to look back to, no literary mothers—and they do not appear again. Taken out of context and placed at the end, these words give the play a structure different from that constructed by the book: a structure, and hence a meaning, that hinges on its ungendered, individualist, humanist last word.

Laurie Osborne has argued that changes in the sequence of scenes in late-eighteenth-century performance texts of *Twelfth Night* indicate as much an "anxiety or unease" about gender relationships (in that case the potentially homoerotic relationship between Sebastian and Antonio) as they do changes in theatrical conventions;[22] the same holds true for this translation from one medium to another. The changes in Garland's performance text of *A Room of One's Own* can be attributed as much to anxiety or unease about what happens when Judith Shakespeare is allowed to have a last word unmediated by William, as has been the case in much feminist criticism, for example, as it can to the need for the play to present a more focused narrative line. The implications were not lost on reviewers, whether or not they acknowledge that alterations were made. Thus Sylvie Drake, who, after noting that the play was a "faithful adaptation," concludes that "ultimately 'A Room of One's Own' the play, like 'A Room of One's Own' the book, celebrates the one thing we all possess: the inviolable freedom of the mind, the only region of our being to which we exclusively hold the key." Similarly, Sid Smith feels that the play "builds a passionate, cleanly logical argument for intellectual freedom. . . . In the end, Woolf magnificently argues that sex must be forgotten and humanity alone remembered to achieve any genuinely creative act."[23]

Even those who acknowledge the changes do not challenge the result. Rosemary Dinnage, for example, the long-standing reader and reviewer of Woolf's works, comments on what has been left out and why but then says that "it follows the main sweep of Woolf's leisurely but tightly controlled argument." The cuts comprise, she notes, "some digressions, and some sections that are perhaps not fashionable: the argument, for instance, that it would be a pity if women were, or wrote like, men (and that in fact we need a few more sexes). . . ."[24] "Fashionable" is the crucial word here, foregrounding the text's re-dressing of the earlier version and of its author in accordance with contemporary, "postfeminist," pressures and anxieties, although Dinnage, true to her ("intellectual") caste, seems out of touch with the countercurrents, the street styles, and the academic texts that were even then queering this "postfeminist" picture.

Others were more explicit and more vehement about what they perceive as the play's—and Virginia Woolf's—significance for current cultural battles, particularly those male critics in the United States who will go to any length to defend the text, the Virginia Woolf, and the meanings produced by Garland's editorial choices from those feminists who might claim to know otherwise. Stephan Kanfer makes no bones about his preference for Garland's version: "It hardly matters that adaptor-director Patrick Garland has omitted massive portions of the original work. Other than Woolf's long-suffering husband Leonard, the writer never had a more sensitive editor." The result is to transform what, he argues, should have been "relegated to the status of a charming but badly faded antique," whose theme, he says, "is being sung by more strident and effective voices" in the media and the academy today, to a statement for our times: "the freshest 63-year-old in town." Howard Kissel agrees, arguing that in his adaptation Garland "has done a splendid job of focusing on Woolf's sharpest ideas, her most pungent images" and insisting that "Woolf stresses that women must be able to take the large view generally associated with male writers. This concern with literature as something beyond special pleading," he adds, "is what raises Woolf above most of her feminist successors."[25] John Simon's enthusiastic review is more vehement still; asserting that Garland has "abridg[ed] and knead[ed]" the book without "betraying its essence and tone," he keeps his criticism for what he sees as Atkins's betrayal of Virginia Woolf:

> Under Garland's apt direction, this true-blue actress delivers that reddest of red jellies Woolf was after. The blood of all squelched, trampled-on women, writers and nonwriters, courses through this evening and keeps us, women and men, laughing blithely, compassionately, androgynously. At times Miss Atkins may be a shade too didactic, with effects a pennyworth or scruple too heavy, pauses a mite too conspiratorial. But this is only a mole on a beloved face, not so much black mark as beauty mark.
>
> Woolf knew what today's feminists don't: that humor and wit are more powerful polemics than shrillness and fanaticism.[26]

Ironically, had "today's feminists" (what Kanfer calls "the Sisterhood") not been so successful in making Woolf's works in general and *Room* in particular canonical, the struggle over who gets to speak for Judith, to define what her creator meant—to fix or contain her meaning by having the last word—would not be taking place.[27] The acclaim for Garland's version, indicated by positive reviews on both sides of the Atlantic and the awards it garnered, suggests the role of Garland's text in ratifying a "postfeminist" Virginia Woolf made in the media's own "postfeminist" image. This "postfeminist" Virginia Woolf can then be construed to rise above the politics of gender at the same time that, through its inclusions, exclusions, and rearrangements, the play creates a gender politics of its own.

But odd things happen in the reception performance so integral to the construction of a text's meaning, even when the creative and production performances would seem to be moving toward one conclusion only; slippages can and do occur. My own informal survey of those outside the media found distinctly mixed responses. Many viewers, most of whom knew Woolf's version, understood the effect of the alterations and found both the play and the reviews depressingly predictable; for them, it was one more example of an unacknowledged gender politics that reiterates and normalizes a supposedly "universal" realm of art and education, the same realm that produced and then dismissed the gender inequalities Woolf's text undertook to address in the first place. Others, particularly women, even if they noticed the elisions, felt empowered by the presence of a powerful woman talking about women and didn't worry about the fallout; they did not feel, as the (male) reviewers told them they should, that Virginia Woolf was protecting them from feminism.

Finally, even within the seemingly monolithic media reception, a subtle subversion occurred. Although the privileging of the androgynous (masculine) mind associated with William in Garland's text threatens to erase Judith's gendered body, this body, women know, cannot be left behind. Thus, despite the power of the final words of the play as Eileen Atkins performs them, with their emphasis on the freedom of the mind, and despite the status they gain from being the last word, a number of women reviewers, including Rosemary Dinnage, still present their readers with a text, a climax, and a message that ends with Judith Shakespeare "[putting] on the body which she has so often laid down" before.[28]

Refashioning Orlando

But I'm always true to you, darlin', in my fashion,
Yes, I'm always true to you, darlin', in my way.

                    —Cole Porter, "Always True to You in My Fashion," *Kiss Me, Kate*

If the gendered body constitutes the return of the repressed in the reception of Garland's *A Room of One's Own,* threatening an androgyny presented as a supposedly ungendered mental construct and linked to "great art," it is the ungendered, androgynous body—or multiply gendered/sexed body—that dominates recent performances of *Orlando,* threatening to undo both a mindset and social/cultural institutions that have traditionally been grounded in sex/gender difference and heterosexuality. The association of androgyny with a deconstruction of binaries that would make possible multiple genders and sexualities, present in Woolf's *Room* but excluded from Garland's, constitutes the central figure in *Orlando.* Woolf's texts were published within a year of each other (*Orlando* in 1928; *Room* in 1929) and have long been perceived as companion pieces. From this perspective *Orlando* becomes an exploration of what would happen if we extended the idea of androgyny from the mind of the artist to the body (in

terms of sexuality, not sexual organs): if we took seriously the speculation
put forward in *Room* that we could happily do with more than two sexes.

Given the interconnectedness of the two works, it is not surprising that
they should have generated a nearly simultaneous spate of adaptations,
especially of *Orlando*. The most visible version, at least in the United States,
is Sally Potter's 1992 film; having won raves at a number of festivals, it
became a box office hit in Europe and England before opening here, amid
great anticipation and publicity, in the summer of 1993.[29] Despite—or because of—the apparent sameness of the moment in which the adaptations
of Woolf's two texts appeared, the differences between the textual and
reception performances of Garland's *Room* and Potter's *Orlando* provide
vivid markers of the historical pressures at work in the claim to represent
the authentic Woolf.

For one thing, Potter's film is only one of several adaptations of *Orlando*
over the past two decades. Ulrike Ottinger's 1981 film *Freak Orlando,*
described in one filmography as "a history of society's 'deformed,' its
'freaks,' over five epochs, framed by the androgynous wanderer Orlando,"
portrays the protagonist variously as Orlando Zyclopa (Cyclops), Orlando
Orlanda, Orlando Capricho (here the setting is the Spanish Inquisition),
Herr Orlando, Frau Orlando, and Freak Orlando.[30] Robert Wilson's theatrical *Orlando,* which features a single actress and a radically pared-down
text, premiered in Berlin in 1989 before being extensively performed in
Switzerland and France in 1993–94; in 1996, Miranda Richardson played
the role at the Edinburgh Festival, its first English-language production (it
has not been performed in the United States).[31] Another theatrical *Orlando,*
Robin Brooks's adaptation, treats the novel as an autobiographical play-
within-a-play, placing Virginia Woolf, Vita Sackville-West, Violet Trefusis,
and Harold Nicolson on the stage in their own persons as well as in their
Orlando guises; it played at the Edinburgh Fringe Festival and in London
in the summer and fall of 1992. The earliest adaptation (1980), an opera
libretto by Angela Carter called *Orlando: or, The Enigma of the Sexes,*
remained unfinished at the time of Carter's death in 1992 but appears in
her collected dramatic works.[32]

What is it about *Orlando* that lends itself to such diverse performances,
not only in terms of texts but of gender and its realizations? Subtitled
A Biography and dedicated to Vita Sackville-West, *Orlando* has been
called "the longest and most charming love letter in literature";[33] its
connection with Vita, whose family history and ancestral estate bear a close
resemblance to Orlando's, has ensured from the beginning that *Orlando*
would have a following among those knowledgeable about its encrypted
lesbianism. But *Orlando,* like its title character, is never one thing only;

it is also an exploration, often ironic, of time, biography, history, English literature, literary criticism, imperialism, the "spirit of the age," and, as noted above, an androgyny that undoes rather than enforcing sameness by multiplying the genders. From this latter perspective the premise is fairly straightforward: Orlando begins the novel as a sixteen-year-old, a "he," an aristocrat and a would-be writer during the reign of Elizabeth I; sometime toward the end of the seventeenth century, age thirty, while Ambassador to Constantinople, he wakes after a long sleep to discover that he has become a "she." At the end of the novel Orlando the woman, now thirty-six, having married, borne a son, and published an award-winning poem, has arrived at Woolf's present, October 1928. Others in the novel prove equally mutable and hence uncategorizable; Orlando, particularly during the eighteenth century, pleasurably engages in relationships with both men and women.

During the course of the novel both Orlando and the equally central and unfixable narrator meditate on what it means to be a man or a woman, often tying the question of what constitutes our sexuality or gender to the role of clothes. The book, that is, explicitly evokes the cultural significance of clothing and its relation to subjectivity and to gender, whether in psychosocial or juridical discourses. It is not surprising, then, that *Lesbians Talk Queer Notions* (1992), to take just one example, places its widely cited passage—"In every human being a vacillation from one sex to the other takes place, and often it is only the clothes that keep the male or female likeness, while underneath the sex is the very opposite of what it is above"—immediately after the dictionary definitions of *queer*.[34]

Significantly, one of the central questions raised by the intersections of gender/sexuality and clothes—what, if anything, substantial or essential lies beneath or beyond this covering?—can be read as an apt analogy for the status of adaptations (clothes) and their relationship to the authentic text or the authentic Woolf. This is particularly true in the case of the *Orlando* adaptations, none of which is constructed solely from Woolf's words; with the exception of Wilson's version, few if any of the words in the adaptations are transcribed directly from Woolf's text, making translation rather than iteration the pertinent concept. Peter Shillingsburg speculates that adaptations, like translations, can be read in terms of George Steiner's "real presences": every word might be different, but there is a "real presence" that remains essentially the same.[35] But to the extent that translations themselves can be understood as a form of refashioning or re-dressing—the taking apart of a garment and making it anew—and to the further extent that the clothes make or define the essence or substance, then the adaptation, rather than capturing or preserving a prior essence, creates one by its fashioning of the body of the text. In this reading, the "something else" the performer or editor wants to capture or fix in his or her particular realization of the text is an effect of the representation or embodiment realized in the performance itself, not an origin or a cause, and tells us more about the values and politics of the historical moment of the performance than about an authentic Virginia Woolf.

For my purposes here, what characterizes this moment is the centrality of the questions posed by *Orlando* about the constitution of gender and/or sexuality and their relationship to "identity," questions that have generated acrimonious and far-reaching debates not only in the academic inquiries associated with women's studies, gender studies, gay, lesbian, bisexual, and transsexual studies, and queer theory, but in activist communities and organizations; in popular culture; in the medical profession; and in public policies governing the acceptance or restriction of gays and lesbians in the military, the government, and the public schools. (To cite just one example, Bill Clinton's promise and failed attempt in 1992–93 to make it acceptable for gays and lesbians to serve openly in the military, which evoked a form of mass hysteria among military and nonmilitary men alike, occurred during the period of the film's prominence in the United States.) Both the power of these issues and the stakes would be enough to explain why Potter's film enjoyed such widespread attention and why it generated so much controversy.

For unlike Garland's refashioning of *Room*, a refashioning that dresses antifeminism in the garb of androgyny for what has been called the "post-feminist" moment in gender politics, Potter's refashioning of *Orlando* projects it, potentially, into the arena of queer. Or, to put this somewhat differently, whereas Garland's refashioning evokes an intellectual androgyny that can be recuperated from "feminists" in the name of Virginia Woolf for a universality that leaves intact a sex/gender system grounded in difference, Potter's refashioning of *Orlando*, which dresses androgyny in the concepts of cross-dressing, gender-bending, masquerade, camp, and/or genderfuck, appears to undo not only the differences between the genders/sexes but the stability of gender itself. In this way the film's representation of gender could be read as a mirror image of its status as an adaptation: a performance that undoes any claim to stability, oneness, or an authentic text. Ironically, however, despite its potential to undo the concept of authenticity, Potter's *Orlando* and its reception illustrate how powerfully the desire for authenticity, both as trope and political strategy, continues to operate, even, or especially, in a queer age.

Both the extent and the nature of the film's reception testify to its timeliness. Everyone got into the act, from Ruth Bader Ginsburg to fashion magazines. Given the starring role of the parodic albeit accurate period-piece costumes in the film, the latter is not surprising, although rather than focusing on the clothing, the fashion magazines featured the film's evocations of "androgyny"; it was left to the mainstream press to talk about the costumes themselves.[36] This crossover occurred at all levels. *Marie Claire,* for example, the British fashion magazine, commissioned a diary from Quentin Crisp, repeatedly referred to by Sally Potter as "the *true* queen of England," who plays Queen Elizabeth I in the film, while the *New Yorker* printed Richard Avedon's nude photographs of Tilda Swinton, who performs Orlando, and trashed the film.[37] In a Britain that was distinctly unimpressed by Robin Brooks's autobiographical refashioning of *Orlando,* with its explicitly lesbian scenes between Virginia and Vita/Orlando, Potter's *Orlando* received almost nothing but praise, while the reception in the United States, where British films often tend to do better than they do at home, was far more mixed. One newspaper reported that the film was being marketed in the States to "women and homosexuals," but responses among gays and lesbians, in private if not in print, were decidedly ambivalent, with many lesbians declaring it was not a lesbian film.[38] Meanwhile, the harshest critiques of the film came from women writing in explicitly feminist publications on the one hand and from identifiably conservative journalists and journals on the other. When read through Eve Kosofsky Sedgwick's definition of queer as grounded in the concept of "across": *"across genders, across sexualities, across genres, across 'perversions,' "* this reception alone would seem to support the contention that this was a decidedly "queer moment."[39]

At the risk of reducing the film and its reception to their performance of gender/sexuality (a response Potter lamented even as many commentators accused her of doing the same to the novel), I want to focus on what should be the most unsettling moment—the transformation of Orlando from man to woman—as an illustration of the fractured politics inscribed in the constructions of an authentic Virginia Woolf. Sally Potter, interviewed extensively, has been unequivocal in her claim that her version is true to the "spirit" if not the details of Woolf's text: that her "translation," which several writers refer to as a "refashioning," retains its essence.[40] She is also clear about what this "essence" is: the "essential self," a self that transcends the false impositions of genders dictated by society that have nothing to do with the "essential human being." For her that essence is captured at the moment of Orlando's transformation when s/he looks at him/herself in the mirror and says, "Same person, just a different sex." When it comes to one of the major alterations Potter made—providing a motivation for the change of sex: Orlando's refusal to participate in the killing associated with war—she argues in part that it provides the "narrative muscle" necessary in the film (but not in the novel) to make the premise "psychologically convincing," and in part that, pushed to the limits of masculinity, Orlando rejects it, just as Orlando rejects the limits of femininity at the end. Potter is also clear about the choice she made when confronted with the need to have a person, with a body, visible on the screen: that is, not to try to make Tilda Swinton a convincing man, but instead to create a "suspension of disbelief." As she notes, and others confirm, this self-consciousness is reinforced in the opening scenes by the presence of Quentin Crisp as Queen Elizabeth I and of Jimmy Somerville, the gay pop singer known for his extraordinary falsetto, serenading the Queen. Finally, Potter is also quoted as saying that *Orlando* should not be seen as a "feminist" film, just as it wasn't an openly political novel; the word, she argues, has become too "debased" and dated, associated, at least in Britain, "with a movement with a rather limited appeal," and that men must struggle as well as women. In the same vein, she is wary of identifying the film with the current gay and lesbian visibility, which, she worries, apropos of "lesbian chic," is being represented "as if it were all just *fashion.*"[41]

Potter, of course, can no more fix the reception of her film than she can fix the definition of the "essential" Orlando or the authentic Virginia Woolf. The stakes were too high for too many people and deeply ideological, whether the responders were on the left or the right, gay/lesbian/queer or heterosexual, and they were not about to let the film, including its relationship to Woolf's novel and hence Virginia Woolf, go unchallenged. Writing in *Mirabella,* Ruby Rich offers one explanation for the strength of (some of) the responses when she attributes the popularity of Woolf's novel not only to "the centrality of sexuality to its story and the fillip of gender playfulness in its plot," but to the "eternal corps of Woolfians who preserve and celebrate everything by their author with near-religious fervor."[42] The last phrase, which recalls Orgel's evocation of the "doctrinal" aspect of authentication, seems particularly appropriate when listening to some of the critiques of how, in Jane Marcus's words, those involved in the production "desecrate" Woolf's novel, a denunciation that comes as strongly from those writing in recognizably conservative journals (John Simon in the *National Review,* e.g.) as it does from those writing in recognizably feminist journals (Marcus in the *Women's Review of Books,* or Robin Morgan in *Ms.,* who catalogues Potter's "disastrous" and "gratuitous" violations of the book). For Simon, as for Marcus and Morgan, the film fails for not being faithful to its source (it "is not even as faithful to its sources as Classic Comix are to theirs"). Stanley Kauffman, writing in the *New Republic,* takes a somewhat different tack when he links the desecration to the very attempt to adapt a novel by Woolf for the movies, a response that paradoxically claims Woolf for "high art" (the comparison is to *Finnegans Wake*) even as it insists that Woolf is not as good a writer as Joyce and dismisses the novel as "a lesser work than some claim." Potter, he asserts, "didn't quite grasp the inevitable. Woolf's work is in the form that it's in because that's what it *is.*" Marcus would agree, arguing that "Woolf has no claim to fame at all except in her words. . . . But the film rewrites all the words."[43]

The disconcerting conjunction of self-defined feminists and self-defined conservatives revealed by the assumption of—and claim to speak for—an authentic Virginia Woolf extends to their shared view of what, in addition to Woolf's words, is being desecrated: their reading of the film's undoing of gender categories as a challenge to the idea of "difference." Simon, for example, the same John Simon who so admired the androgynous mind in *Room,* balks when it comes to the androgynous sexual persona. While he acknowledges that Woolf's novel includes a "guarded plea for lesbianism" as a concomitant to the androgynous artist's "bisexual" amours, he wants his sexes clearly demarcated; Tilda Swinton, he writes (and he is not alone in this observation), "never made me believe her as a man, or respond to her as a woman," the assumption being that he (and his readers) know what a man and a woman *are.* Robin Morgan also laments the film's treatment of gender, its "trendy 'genderfuck' " message "that there really is no meaningful difference. The result is a sort of period-piece parody of *The Crying Game.*"[44] Morgan, though, attributes this as much to Potter's statement in the *New York Times* that women have hard lives but men do too—her "postfeminism"—as she does to battles over sexuality or sexual identity.

Given that a number of other critics either *lament* that the film does not go far enough in undoing gender stereotypes and difference ("Orlando's big moments fall along such classic gender lines"),[45] that it eliminates the lesbian sexuality, that it eliminates sexuality altogether (except for the straightest kind), that it is either too camp or not camp enough, too feminist or not feminist enough, or *praise* the film for its critique of gender politics and its daring portrayal of "the new androgyny," we can begin to assess the complexity of the cultural moment Potter's *Orlando* represents,[46] a moment in which the rhetoric of "anything goes" in the realm of gender and sexuality confronts the realities of large numbers of powerful groups and voices who have no intention of giving up their belief in an essential or authentic, not to mention differentiated, sex/gender system, just as they have no intention of giving up their Virginia Woolf.[47] Feminists and/or lesbians and gays and/or queers are just as enmeshed within this network of struggles as nonfeminists and/or heterosexuals, which is often presented as a question of individual and/or group identity or a challenge to that identity, sexual and political alike, a question that Potter's *Orlando,* despite her disclaimer, encourages us to consider in terms of fashion, style, clothes.

At this point we are back in the realm explored in "Fashion Stills," where the refrain "Virginia Woolf, like fashion" leads us to ask whether Potter's translation or refashioning is only a matter of the moment, a moment, as Sedgwick suggests about the "queer moment," that may already have exceeded itself "in the short-shelf-life American marketplace of images."[48] Is it, that is, only a question of style with no real social or cultural import, a diversion rather than a politics? I would say yes and no. Yes, to the extent that the film is an event, a performance, that enacts the cultural anxieties and desires of its moment and is no more fixed or fixable, even in terms of its reception, than any other performance. No, because it would be a mistake to dismiss this or any performance of Woolf's novel, as of Shakespeare's plays, as only fashionable performance. For one thing, performance and style can reveal and problematize established norms as well as reiterating them, opening the space for other possibilities. Moreover, because performance, in both its productive and its reception modes, establishes a text and hence meanings that become part of the cultural/social fabric and our self-representations, we would do well to understand what these meanings are perceived to be.

Returning, then, to the reception of Potter's *Orlando,* I want to tease out some of the intersecting strands. First, there is Ruth Bader Ginsburg, nominated in 1993 by President Clinton for a position on the Supreme Court. In an article about Ginsburg's legal philosophy, in particular the ways the law can mitigate gender inequities, Jeffrey Rosen defines it as premised on the concept of gender sameness and the equality of men and women rather than on gender difference(s): "a preference, in short, for equal rather than special treatment for women." Here, of course, he situates Ginsburg in one of the most divisive debates within feminism, both historically and in its current manifestations; the cover of the *New Republic* where the article appeared announces, "Judge Ginsburg vs. the New Feminism." As an illustration of Ginsburg's position, Rosen tells us that after reading Katha Pollitt's analysis and critique of difference feminism and its legal ramifications, "Ginsburg impulsively sent Pollitt a fan letter. (She enclosed a clipping about the movie *Orlando,* based on Virginia Woolf's novel about a man who becomes a woman.)"[49] For Ginsburg, Rosen notes, emphasizing difference or special treatment for women returns women to exactly where they were before the legal breakthroughs of the 1970s. In view of Ginsburg's identification of *Orlando* with sameness, the alignment of Robin Morgan with John Simon in defense of "difference" looks less odd. Ironically, the shifting attitude toward sameness and difference that surfaces in the reviews of the film, particularly when read against the reviews of *Room,* reveals the instability of the sameness/difference binary itself, but in the rush to claim the authentic Virginia Woolf for one side or the other no one seems to have noticed.

My second example concerns the contrast between the film's mainstream success in Britain and the United States and the reception of the other adaptations of the work, a discrepancy that highlights versioning's role not only in revealing conflicting cultural attitudes, but in the question of which ones have more social clout. Even when we recognize that Potter's vehicle, a commercially marketed film, ensured that it would reach a wider audience than Robert Wilson's avant-garde play or Ulrike Ottinger's avant-garde film, there is something else at work here: a something else that, using Orgel's formulation, we can attribute to the desire for self-authenticating realizations. Talking about his adaptation, Wilson makes a statement that appears to align him with Potter and should have made his version ideologically attractive to those who want to believe that we have achieved a positive "postfeminism": "The question of sexual difference has been overcome completely. Today, on an emotional level, men and women have too much in common to maintain the conflict between the sexes as the focal point of the interpretation of this text." Instead, he argues, "*Orlando*'s drama . . . is linguistic," and it is manifested in part by the two "I"s spoken by the figure as a young boy and after his/her transformation to a woman; the middle section, during which the transformation occurs, presents us with an unspecified "you." The result, in one commentator's words, is to eliminate the "fraught content" of Woolf's novel; instead we have a performance where the body, despite discrete changes of clothing, is at "degree zero" when it comes to functioning as a "sexual signifier."[50]

This is where the difficulties arise, because the British critics, who acknowledge openly that they have always differed from Europeans over the value of Wilson's work, want more than abstractions and a degree-zero body. Discouraged from discussing the gender/sexuality that they see as central to a novel described variously as "a camp fantasy," a study of how "gender determines your social role without necessarily taking your identity along with it," or an example of "freewheeling exuberance and postmodern pluralism," British reviewers describe the play's underlying message as an existential human aloneness and lament the change. Rejecting the cold brilliance of both Wilson's text and Miranda Richardson's performance, they want instead the fantasy and playfulness of Woolf's—

and by implication Potter's—"transsexual time-traveller," however problematic the social effects may be.[51]

Conversely, Robin Brooks's play ran into difficulties with British critics by being too explicit: by placing Virginia, Vita, Violet, and Harold on the stage and portraying lesbian sexual encounters. Here, the whole issue of sexual politics, androgyny, masquerade, and/or an essential self disappears into sexed bodies, and critics responded by treating it as just one more Bloomsbury romp (who cares?) and, ho hum, one more example of nudity on the fringe stage.[52]

But it is Ottinger's *Freak Orlando* that provides the most useful gloss on Potter's success. Like Wilson's play, Ottinger's film is located in the avant-garde, in this case art cinema; while distributed commercially in Germany, where Ottinger is a revered figure, it has been shown in the United States and Britain only in film festivals and retrospectives and been "reviewed" only in film journals. But even if the film had been commercially released (in the early 1990s, for example, when a retrospective of Ottinger's films traveled around North America), it is hard to imagine *Freak Orlando* garnering the kind of attention from the "general public" that Potter's film did. For at its center is not a playful, gender-bending androgyny, but an unrelenting display of physiological freaks: "ensembles of male, female, and male/female freaks" including Siamese twins, a double-headed woman, a black-and-white (Dalmatian) dwarf/dog combination, bearded women, and a child hermaphrodite, among others, as well as the "two-in-ones and split-selves embodied in the figure of Orlando." Comparing Ottinger's Orlando to Potter's, Mary Russo comments that Freak Orlando is "more like Tiresias" than "the integrated androgyne" played by Swinton; "only Quentin Crisp playing the old Queen Elizabeth in Potter's film, approaches the grotesque bodily representations of *Freak Orlando*."[53]

Unlike Potter's normalization of androgyny, that is, Ottinger's film presents the aesthetic and cultural process of "monstrification," a state in which, Susan Stewart notes, the "physiological freak represents the problems of the boundary between self and other (Siamese twins), between male and female (the hermaphrodite), between the body and the world outside the body (the *monstre par excès*). . . . Often referred to as a 'freak of nature,' " Stewart reminds us, "the freak, it must be emphasized, is a freak of culture." Although Russo contends that Potter's *Orlando*, "concerned with gender, politics, and social transformation," rightfully deserves the success it has achieved, she also notes that it is a far more "conventional film" than *Freak Orlando*.[54] However controversial Potter's film may seem in terms of gender/sexuality, it does not move beyond the implication that Orlando has an "essential self," however androgynous, and that this essential self is or can be independent of a socially and/or culturally produced gender that might restrict her legally (she loses her estate) but does not displace her from the mainstream of society, including its class privileges. Potter's Orlando is anything but a monster, a freak; s/he has not been banished to the margins, where s/he would provoke social crises and threaten deterritorialization.

Freak Orlando, in contrast, provides a powerful representation not only of Orlando's and the other freaks' marginalized status in society, their exclusion and persecution, but of their crossover with "normal" historical subjects, a move that undoes the concept of margins and center itself; as Ottinger said about the film, " 'The absolute outsider is the normal citizen, the conformist. This is another form of deformation.' " She is also clear, as are her reviewers, that these social processes are far from benign; talking of the exclusion of freaks throughout history, she notes that "today exclusion is effected inside the walls of prisons and psychiatric clinics." As Laurence Rickels notes about the film, "we watch the primal time combo of inquisition, fascism, and normative psychiatry working over time to assimilate—that is, efface—the freak, the other, reality, the future (you name it)."[55] Another major difference between the two films resides in the acknowledged status of *Freak Orlando* as a lesbian film, signified in part by its appearances in gay and lesbian film festivals and in part by its representations of lesbian experience through its body language. When Russo reads "the trope of the Siamese twins," one half of whom Herr Orlando marries and both of whom he later kills, as a sign of "a more radical female-female sexuality which is constrained and unrepresentable within the confines even of freak subculture,"[56] she aligns the film with a monstrous doubling of women associated with the female-desiring female that is absent from Potter's film.

The distance between Potter's *Orlando* and Ottinger's is apparent in the sparse references to freaks or monsters in its reviews; those who do introduce them represent them as embodying an asexuality that is neither frightening nor boundary-disrupting. Ella Taylor, for example, describes Orlando as freeing herself from "a couple of centuries of institutional sexism . . . by becoming her own kind of hybrid": an androgyne determined by gender, not sex; a hybrid in whom sexuality, both heterosexual and lesbian, is erased. "What happened to polymorphous perversity?" Taylor wistfully asks; "the beauty of androgyny is not that it does away with sexuality, but that it allows us to slither around inside it, to escape the fetters (and the safety) of a single gender. . . . When it comes to sexual freedom, we may end up leaving the 20th century prissier than we [and Virginia Woolf] found it." A more negative review skewers the "glazed hero(ine)" for being "such a conceptual freak, identity formed more by couture style than living experience," undercutting "any kind of sexual-politics analysis"; "still," this reviewer concludes, "a few hermaphrodites might weep."[57]

Reflecting, perhaps, Potter's statement that she wanted to return to Woolf's "gentle politics," leaving behind the violence of contemporary gender politics where "people have to hoist their sexuality up a flagpole to claim their identity,"[58] the film reiterates exactly that which Ottinger's film set out to undo: in Rickels's words, "the tolerant and integrationist manner in which we look past or overlook the freaks among us," trying to "assimilate" or "efface" them. In previous periods, Rickels adds, "even under the fire of persecution and exploitation, they had access, as sideshow attractions, to the center stage of visibility (and that means to some kind of inclusion of their otherness)."[59] The result of Potter's representation is the normalization Russo attributes to the women's movement in the United States: the "reassurances that feminists are 'normal women' and that our political aspirations are 'mainstream,' "[60] a stance that often leaves gender and class structures, not to mention heterosexuality, very much in place.

Similarly, Potter's emphasis on the androgyne effaces the body (although revealing Orlando/Swinton's body at the moment of the transformation reinscribes the female body as the sign of difference), even as it recuperates it for an asexuality that rather than undoing gender or multiplying the genders/sexes reduces them to one. The effect, as in Garland's *Room,* is to subsume the body into an androgynous mind/self that is beyond politics: a manifestation of the "postfeminist" refrain that we don't need feminism anymore, that we have transcended it just as we have transcended gender difference because women have achieved their goals. What gets lost is any vision of a discordantly multiple, experimental, and activist queer world in which such performances as masquerade, drag, die-ins, or kiss-ins draw attention to the ideological norms that police sexual/gender behavior; Potter's film does not provide the space for disruption, risk, or change. In an interview published in 1995, Potter appears to acknowledge the importance of such disruptive gestures, the "way in which the gay/lesbian/queer sensibility provides a much wider and more courageous, cutting-edge frame of reference for thinking about the connectedness between beings than the heterosexual frame of reference"; but when she describes the "camp sensibility" as an understanding "that all this masculinity/femininity stuff is really a dressing up of an essential self. They're identities you can choose or not choose,"[61] she undercuts not only the queer deconstruction of an "essential self," but the political aspects of these performances.

Fashion magazines, however, didn't mind their absence, publishing all those articles on androgyny and its multiple looks. Nor did advertisers miss the point; they were quite happy to contribute to a "dressing up" across the gender/sexuality board. As Danae Clark comments, by the beginning of the 1990s they were well versed in the marketing strategy known as "gay window advertising": the transmission of a doubled, encoded message that would appeal to gays and lesbians in the know without alienating their heterosexual audience. Fashion magazines and catalogues ranging from *Elle* and *Mirabella* to *Tweeds, J. Crew,* and *Victoria's Secret* began "capitalizing on a dual market strategy that packages gender ambiguity and speaks, at least indirectly, to the lesbian consumer market," at the same time that mainstream journals such as *Newsweek* were normalizing lesbianism under the rubric of "lesbian chic."[62]

Again the question arises: how to deal with the double binds raised by the intersections of fashion, gender/sexuality, and the versioning of Virginia Woolf, including the "double movement of subversion and containment" so central to it? On the one hand Potter's stylish refashioning projects Woolf's text and its challenges to gender/sexuality into the public eye and makes them visible; on the other hand the salability of the concept indicates that the style is on its way out. In this scenario what started as subcultural subversion—cross-dressing, for example, or queer activism—loses its political edge, its call for social change, and becomes style only. From this perspective, as Clark reminds us, the "postmodern, antiessentialist (indeed, democratic) discourse" adopted by the mainstream media—of individual choice, of no difference—can be seen as a homophobic response that erases difference in order, once again, to efface or push to the margins the "social and political issues that directly affect gays and lesbians as a group." But the answer, she argues, is not a renewed essentialism or insistence on a single group identity. For one thing, lesbians know from the differences among them that "a single, authentic identity does not exist"; for another, however much fashionable appropriation may be an act of containment, nothing can stop viewers or readers or consumers from reappropriating fashions or images or texts, recombining them, and using them for political ends.[63]

Whatever the realities of containment or appropriation or normalization effected by Potter's *Orlando* stylish refashioning, then, the possibilities for change offered by strategic deployments of style, performance, or theatricality remain a preeminent site for interventions in the processes that normalize gender/sexuality, whether in terms of heterosexuality or of what it might mean to be lesbian or gay or bisexual or transsexual or queer. However fashionable, Potter's version and the responses to it have the virtue of foregrounding the complexity of the cultural moment and the very real stakes involved, as well as the historically powerful relationship that, Butler illustrates, exists between politicization and theatricality for queers.[64]

To return to the fashion metaphor, then: just as younger lesbians and queers began to experiment with "fashionable" new looks as part of their perception of the changing political scene, thereby opening up spaces for a renewed political engagement, so adaptations, refashionings, however "trendy," can, by revealing the gaps and fissures in the social fabric and its norms, reveal the spaces where future actions might occur. Even those acts that reiterate the dominant norms, Butler notes, "cannot be controlled by the one who utters" them.[65] As I argued in the Introduction, we cannot stop the process of refashioning Virginia Woolf or the claims to authenticity/inauthenticity that accompany it, however much we might disagree with or be scared by the results, and this is, finally, a good thing. Instead we need to recognize and act on the recognition, as Ruth Bader Ginsburg did, that performances are acts or events that not only realize a particular historical moment and its social beliefs, but also have a substantive relationship to the structures that constrain or facilitate every aspect of our lives. For however unfixable, mutable, or unstable her texts may be, the politics of adaptation translates into a desire for an authentic Virginia Woolf whose performances create a material authority of their own.

THE MONSTROUS UNION OF

VIRGINIA WOOLF AND MARILYN MONROE

"By whom in history would you most like to be spanked?"
". . . Virginia Woolf does come to mind."

—Spalding Gray, in the *Chicago Tribune*

When the owners of the Hardback Café in Chapel Hill, North Carolina, created a six-foot cardboard photomontage that joined Virginia Woolf's head to Marilyn Monroe's body, they thought they were creating a playful image; instead, they created a monster. To its originators in the late 1980s the figure was just one of several high/low hybrids designed to elicit knowing smiles from their patrons (others included Shakespeare/Mick Jagger, Joyce/John Wayne, Eliot/ Fred Astaire, and Yeats/Gary Cooper); when pushed, they explained it combined brilliance and beauty, intellect and elegance, two ideals of what it was to be a woman. But not everyone saw it that way; according to my informants, a number of women were so horrified by the deracinated image of Virginia Woolf they demanded it be taken down.[1] My own experience confirms this reaction; regardless of the gender of the hearer—although gender produces different explanations—a description of the Shakespeare/Jagger hybrid is likely to produce a smile, but the Virginia Woolf/Marilyn Monroe hybrid evokes shudders. Rather than decorating the bookstore-café, then, the figure became a menace, threatening, as is the nature of monsters, to displace boundaries and unsettle categories traditionally held to be natural and inevitable. In the process, Virginia Woolf, aligned once again with spectacle, moves into the realm of the grotesque, providing a graphic illustration of the recurring, deeply embedded cultural fears imbricated in her mythic figurations and a spectacular instance of disruption, reincarnation, and the space for change.

The significance of this particular image of Virginia Woolf intensifies in urgency when we realize that the crossing of the two women embodied in the Chapel Hill hybrid has a traceable history going back at least as far as Norman Mailer's "biography" of Marilyn Monroe in 1973 and may well be present in Albee's 1962 play. Seemingly poised on opposite sides of every divide one might imagine, whether high culture versus popular culture, mind versus body, intellectuality versus sexuality, or aristocracy versus populace, the two nevertheless exhibit an uncanny, deterritorializing, attraction to each other, one that "dissolves all traditional . . . links and marks the entire social edifice with an irreducible structural imbalance."[2]

With this threatened dissolution in mind, I want to use the Virginia Woolf/Marilyn Monroe hybrid to ask a series of questions. For one thing, why do the women we love to look at—women such as Virginia Woolf and Marilyn Monroe—who are constructed as emblems of beauty, intellect, sex, and power, become at moments of cultural crisis increasingly indistinguishable in the eyes of (at least) the status quo from monstrous incarnations of the feminine associated with horror and death? When Virginia Woolf and Marilyn Monroe are crossed, is the fear that results generated by a hybridity that joins apparent opposites, or does it reflect a monstrous doubling? And, given this twofold potential, what does the monstrous union of Virginia Woolf and Marilyn Monroe tell us about the role of female icons in the recuperation and transgression of cultural borders and authority?

Finally, what does the Chapel Hill hybrid, when read through and against the repeated appearances of Virginia Woolf on the boundary between beauty and horror, beauty and death, signaled by the presence of her shadowy alter egos Medusa and the Sphinx, tell us about the role of reiteration in the construction of her image? Here, following Judith Butler's lead, construction ceases to be either a single act, event, or text or a "causal process" and becomes instead a "temporal process which operates through the reiteration of norms"; in this light, Virginia Woolf can be perceived or understood as "a sedimented effect of a reiterative or ritual practice," a "naturalized effect." But this process is not seamless; the same reiteration that produces Virginia Woolf as monstrous, scary, and naturalizes her place on the borders or boundaries, including the boundaries of what is human, also produces the gaps and fissures, the outsides and betweens, that destabilize the construction and prevent it from being fixed. Repetition, then, may produce or name Virginia Woolf by setting boundaries and inculcating norms, but it also destabilizes these boundaries and norms by putting them "into a potentially productive crisis."[3]

In order to address if not answer these questions, in order to tease out their implications for representations of Virginia Woolf and what these representations tell us about our cultural norms and crises, I want to return to several of the topoi I have been charting, particularly the central role of Virginia Woolf's face in constructions of her meaning. Often reproduced on its own, Virginia Woolf's face can be read as a metonym for her head, a head that is more often than not detached or divorced from its body, giving Virginia Woolf a decidedly disembodied nature. In his reading of portraits of "thinkers" or "geniuses" Richard Brilliant foregrounds the recurring presence of the large or prominent head, using as his prototype the portrait of Shakespeare on the First Folio: the "intelligent head and alert face" detached by the ruff from a "body too slight to bear its weight."[4] (From this perspective attaching Shakespeare's large head to the slight body of Mick Jagger would reinforce the image of the bard, not unsettle it or make it discordant.) The head, then, the intellect, characterizes men of genius; they become, in the terms of the New York intellectuals, *Luftmenschen,* airmen.

But what happens when the "thinker" is a woman? What happens when a woman, positioned in so many of our cultural discourses *as* body, appears as a head? Does she become, as Rosalind Franklin did in James Watson's biography, a "female grotesque"? Moreover, what does it mean when the image of the woman's disembodied head carries within it two contradictory meanings: that associated with the disembodied intellect and wisdom of Athena/Minerva, sprung full-grown from her father's head, which are put into the service of a system we can describe as patriarchal; and that associated with Medusa, whose disembodied, snake-encircled head, so beautiful and so frightening, can freeze and kill men? If she were re-embodied, if she were weighted down by a body, particularly the body of a woman often perceived to be "Woman" herself, the body of Marilyn Monroe, would she become less grotesque, less frightening, or more so?[5]

1. The Protagonists

"It has been nearly a quarter of a century since the death of a minor American actress named Marilyn Monroe. There is no reason for her to be part of my consciousness as I walk down a midtown New York street filled with color and action and life." But having made that statement,

Gloria Steinem proceeds to detail how everywhere she looked in 1986 Marilyn Monroe looked back. "These are everyday signs of a unique longevity," she concludes; "if you add her years of movie stardom to the years since her death, Marilyn Monroe has been part of our lives and imaginations for nearly four decades. That's a very long time for one celebrity to survive in a throwaway culture."[6] Four years earlier, on the centenary of Virginia Woolf's birth, Helen Dudar made a similar observation, albeit with more edge, when she catalogued the pervasive signs of Virginia Woolf's visibility and popularity, signifying her status as "cult" figure and object of consumption. "She has become," Dudar stated in one particularly biting moment, "the Marilyn Monroe of American academia, genius transformed into icon and industry through the special circumstances of her life and work." The "circumstances" are presented as follows: "the front-and-center seat in the Bloomsbury circle; the sieges of madness; the odd, sheltering marriage; the Sapphic attachments (to use her favorite term); the subtle and sinewy feminism; the thousands of pages of letters and diaries that tell us more about Virginia Woolf than we know of any major writer of our time; the moment, alas, in 1941 when, fearing the return of insanity, she loaded her pockets with rocks and walked into the river Ouse."[7]

Dudar's sarcasm was missed by Peter Watson when he translated her essay for his even more skeptical British audience in the London *Times*. "Virginia Woolf," he wrote, "is not a name one expects to see in the same sentence as Marilyn Monroe. But in America, in the centenary of Woolf's birth, anything and everything is possible. The author of *The Waves* and *Mrs. Dalloway* is described in the current issue of the *Saturday Review,* apparently without irony or any trace of humour, as 'the Marilyn Monroe of American academia.'" Extrapolating from Dudar's article, Watson describes the parallels as follows: "both had periods of neurotic madness; both made odd sheltering marriages; both evinced a subtle and sinewy feminism; both took their own lives. Perhaps," he concludes, "you find these parallels forced. But in a country which has embraced *Brideshead Revisited* so enthusiastically, is it really so surprising that Virginia Woolf has achieved cult status?"[8]

Nine years later, in January 1991, Angela Carter, appearing as a witness against Virginia Woolf on the British television program *J'Accuse,* introduced a note of dread into the comparison by limiting its range: ". . . it's like the dead Kennedys," she pronounced; "there's no greater morbid glamour than can accrue to someone who dies, you know, untimely, especially if they've been mentally unbalanced. She's become kind of like the Marilyn Monroe of feminist heroines; . . . she carries her martyrdom somehow around with her like a halo and it gets everywhere." While Carter speaks, the Beck and Macgregor photograph of Virginia Woolf in her dead mother's dress dominates the screen (fig. 13).[9]

Unlike the previous examples, which manifest varying amounts of contempt for both protagonists (and for those who have turned them into icons), Pamela Caughie's cover for the paperback edition of her 1991 book *Virginia Woolf and Postmodernism*—eighteen repetitions (six by three) of the seductive studio portrait of Woolf in a fur-collared coat—constructs a visual image of their crossover and claims it, approvingly, for postmodernism (fig. 25). "The suggestive parody of Andy Warhol's Marilyn Monroe seriograph," she notes, deliberately "[calls] attention to the many images of Virginia Woolf that have proliferated over the past decade and [confronts] her commodification as she has become the canonical female modernist as well as the preeminent feminist writer. . . . To acknowledge her status as a commodity in the academic marketplace and to affirm the multiple images that have been circulated by her critics is not to devalue Woolf as a woman or a writer," but "to reassess her status and significance."[10]

When I began to research the conjunction of the two women, I assumed it went one way only; I was wrong. Opening to the first chapter of the first book I read on Monroe, written by Cambridge sociologist Graham McCann, I found, "Virginia Woolf wrote that 'A biography is considered complete if it merely accounts for six or seven selves, whereas a person may well have as many as one thousand.' Marilyn Monroe always remembered this comment; her biographers rarely do."[11] (For one wild moment I thought Monroe had actually been reading Woolf; she hadn't, although she did read Rilke, Proust, and, perhaps, Joyce; Eve Arnold's photograph of Monroe reading *Ulysses* is the "evidence" for the latter [fig. 26].)[12] McCann's index shows two more references to Woolf; in these he quotes from *To the Lighthouse* and *A Room of One's Own* to make points about Monroe's relationship to men, the implication being that like Mrs. Ramsey and the looking-glass vision she embodies, Monroe served to bolster the male self-image and ego, often at a cost to herself.[13] In this instance, we could say, rather than Marilyn Monroe lowering Virginia Woolf, Virginia Woolf elevates Marilyn Monroe, and she does so as a writer, providing the words to explain or interpret the actress's performance.

When McCann introduces Woolf's statement about the limitations of biography into his text, he is following the example of Norman Mailer's 1973 fictionalized biography of Monroe, where the passage is preceded by the line, "It may be fair to quote another woman whose life ended in suicide," and is followed by the comment, "The words are by Virginia

FIGURE 25. Cover Photograph, *Virginia Woolf and Postmodernism: Literature in Quest and Question of Itself,* by Pamela L. Caughie.

Woolf." The context here is crucial; in the pages immediately before the passage from Woolf, Mailer details the contradictions surrounding both Monroe's self-presentation and the attitudes of others toward her. Anecdotes of her tenderness alternate with anecdotes of her narcissism and meanness and this in turn is followed by an entry from one of Monroe's notebooks:

> "What am I afraid of? Why am I so afraid? Do I think I can't act? I know I can act but I am afraid. I am afraid and I should not be and I must not be." It is in fear and trembling that she writes. In dread. Nothing less than some intimation of the death of her soul may be in her fear. But then is it not hopeless to comprehend her without some concept of a soul? One might literally have to invent the idea of a soul in order to approach her. "What am I afraid of?"
>
> It may be fair to quote another woman whose life ended in suicide. . . .

The similarity of this passage to Mark Schorer's rendering of Virginia Woolf in his review of *her* diary is striking: "Fear. This is what a stranger, who knew her face only from the many august and sometimes admonitory

FIGURE 26. Marilyn Monroe. Photograph by Eve Arnold. From *Marilyn Monroe: An Appreciation*, by Eve Arnold. Photograph copyright © 1987 by Eve Arnold. Reprinted by permission of Alfred A. Knopf Inc.

photographs, would least have expected to find in her. But fear, by which one means uncertainty about her own worth, was apparently among her first qualities."[14]

Here, then, in the earliest direct intertwining of the two women, we find the governing trope of fear. Although presented as a fear that Monroe and by implication Woolf ultimately enacted through their self-destruction (though many people doubt that Monroe killed herself), the trope is not that simple, crossing into the fear they evoke by their destructiveness of others. And this latter fear, whatever else it may be, is inseparable from their status as powerful women and by association their feminism. For Mailer, writing in 1973, when Monroe tells an assistant director on the set of *Some Like It Hot* to "Go fuck yourself" while she sits inside her dressing room reading Paine's *Rights of Man,* the incipient women's movement is not far behind: "Did she anticipate how a future generation of women would evaluate the rights of men?"[15]

While the grounds for crossing the two women and the implied ends vary, radiating outward in multiple and often contradictory directions, I want to focus on those aspects of their twofold conjunction—the yoking of opposites and the doubling—that link beauty and death, feminism and fear, desire and horror. This is not to deny either the haunting similarities between their lives or the iconization and commodification that followed their deaths; the similarities are certainly there, and one can imagine Andy Warhol adding Virginia Woolf to his gallery of dead and/or tragic "celebrities." Both experienced the early loss of a mother that left them with a need to be nurtured, by men and women alike. Both were subjected to childhood sexual abuse, generating questions about their ability to enjoy sex in later life. Both married men (Leonard Woolf and Arthur Miller) who took care of them or tried to take care of them—at least on the surface; both men have also been accused of trying to destroy them and vice versa. Both tend to be defined by their perceived vulnerability, fragility, sickness, and madness. Both wanted children, but were thwarted: Woolf by the doctors; Monroe first by abortions and later by miscarriages.[16] As a result, both developed close relationships with the children of family and friends. Both died in ways that link them to self-destruction. And both have been claimed and marketed by individuals and ideologies so diverse—not to say antagonistic—that the histories of their "reputation" function as paradigmatic case studies in struggles for cultural and critical authority over the past thirty years.

But what concerns me here is something other than what happens when people use the mantra "Like Marilyn Monroe" to describe Virginia Woolf, a mantra, according to McCann, "readily applicable to figures of glamour, femininity, fashion and tragic, early death"; what I am after can best be approached by reversing the direction, as Mailer did, by saying "Like Virginia Woolf" and shivering. McCann argues that the writings of Mailer (and Arthur Miller) on Monroe "have a wider significance as dedications to the 'masculine myth' which works to secure a meaning for Woman, to represent women as passive objects to be looked at and longed for";[17] yes and no. For "Woman," Mailer clearly believes and tradition supports, even when the passive object of the gaze, can also be deadly, not only to herself but to others.

2. Sexual Personae

Whatif, whatif a Beastji somehow lurked *inside* Beauty Bibi? Whatif the beauty were herself the beast? But I think he [the Great Poet] might have said I was confusing matters: "As Mr. Stevenson has shown in his *Dr. Jekyll and Mr. Hyde,* such saint-and-monster conjunctions are conceivable in the case of men; alas! such is our nature. But the whole essence of Woman denies such a possibility."

—Salman Rushdie, *Shame*

The Great Poet is, of course, wrong; Western myth and literature and art are filled with women who are both beautiful and beastly, beautiful and deadly. One need only recall Vernant's description of the Medusa: "Superimposed on the mask of Medusa, as though in a two-sided mirror, the strange beauty of the feminine countenance, brilliant with seduction, and the horrible fascination of death, meet and cross."[18] So powerful is this tradition, especially when it aligns Medusa with the femme fatale, that deadly provocateur of both male desire and discourse, that all beautiful women become potentially dangerous, a threat intensified when the woman is also intellectual. This conjuncture underlies the symptomatic crossings of Virginia Woolf with Medusa and the Sphinx, transforming her into a monster.

As we've seen, the transformation of Virginia Woolf—writer, intellectual, feminist, *and* beautiful woman—into an emblem of deadly female power occurs early in her career as public figure, as star. Witness Cecil Beaton's 1930 verbal portrait, accompanied by the drawing of Virginia Woolf in her dead mother's dress, where her beauty is inseparable from her ghostliness and she is "frail and crisp as a dead leaf."[19] With Edward Albee's play, the fear accruing to Virginia Woolf begins to acquire mythic attributes, takes on monstrous forms: both in the evocation of a riddling Sphinx associated with the "monstrous" Martha and in Robert Brustein's identification of the horror located in *Virginia Woolf* with the Medusa's head. By the time Hanif Kureishi put Virginia Woolf's photograph on the wall of Rosie's study, where her staring eyes propel a terrified Rafi out of the room and toward the suicide he commits under her silent gaze, the reiteration of her potentially deadly beauty has normalized both the iconography and the fear.

The doubling of beauty and horror identified with Medusa and reincarnated in Virginia Woolf receives a clear statement in Ovid's *Metamorphoses,* where Perseus, the heroic slayer, provides a history of the figure whose decapitated head rests beside him: her original beauty, in particular the glory of her hair; her rape by Poseidon within Athena's temple; and the punishment meted out by an Athena "shocked," as a later commentator puts it, "by the desecration of her holy place—or envious of Medusa's beauty."[20] By Ovid's time a number of the other attributes that recur in representations of both Medusa and Virginia Woolf were also firmly in place: her unusual frontal representation (true whether the full woman or just her head was present); the concentration of the figure and her powers into her head, severed from her body and surrounded by snakes; and the emphasis on her eyes as the locus of her deadly powers.[21] Whatever the emphasis, however reinterpreted over the succeeding centuries, these attributes remain central to renderings of Medusa and her power.

When the camera in *Sammy and Rosie* cuts back and forth from Rafi to the photograph of Virginia Woolf, depicting first her head and shoulders, then her disembodied head, and finally her disembodied eyes, we are in the presence of the Medusa's frightening powers, including her power to control the gaze. Most monstrous beings, Jay Clayton notes, drawing upon the etymological root *monstrare,* "to show," "represent something horrible to behold," but when the monster looks at you the horror is worse. This doubled horror manifests itself in Medusa's mythic ability to freeze or kill *both* by being looked at and by looking herself, and it multiplies again when we consider Medusa's power to convert the viewer's gaze into her own: to become a mirror in which the viewer sees his own face and his own impending death.[22]

To look at Medusa/Virginia Woolf, then, or to be looked at by her is to look death in the face, beauty and death. Deadly if she looks; equally deadly if she doesn't: a paradigm for the damned-if-you-do, damned-if-you-don't doubleness characteristic of so many renderings of Woman, including, to state the most obvious example, her relation to the phallus and fetishism within psychoanalytic thought. It is worth noting here that traditionally Medusa's "petrifying effect" and the fear it induces works only on men, "in a tête-à-tête between a male and the deadly gaze of the female";[23] women are not affected by either aspect of her look *except,* I would argue, through a mirror effect that produces the fear of being fixed or frozen into the position of female grotesque or emblematic figure of nightmares, including the nightmare of feminism Stephen Frears locates in Virginia Woolf. When Jeffrey Cohen writes that "the monster prevents mobility (intellectual, geographic, or sexual), delimiting the social spaces through which private bodies may move. To step outside this official geography is to risk attack by some monstrous border patrol or (worse) to become monstrous oneself," he points to the monster's role in securing and policing the naturalization of norms governing gender, sexuality, female behavior: female heads and female bodies.[24]

At this point a number of permutations of the fear associated with the disembodied head and eyes of Medusa/Virginia Woolf come into play, including the central role of visual imagery in constructing Virginia Woolf icon. For one thing, the fact that Virginia Woolf's eyes stare out from a photograph, itself often linked with death, intensifies their arresting power. For Susan Sontag, "all photographs are *memento mori*," emphasizing human "mortality, vulnerability, mutability," a theme Roland Barthes beautifully elaborates in his meditation on the impact of the photograph on the viewer. What obsesses Barthes is the photograph's ability to bring the subject, frozen in that moment of time, back to life. The image in a photograph, he writes, constantly "[protests] its former existence," clinging to the viewer like a "*spectre*" and haunting him (as Rafi, stared at by Virginia Woolf's photograph, appears to be haunted) both by "that rather terrible thing which is there in every photograph: the return of the dead" and by the "imperious sign of my future death." Barthes's added observation that "the Photograph has this power," particularly when it contains a "frontal pose, . . . of looking me *straight in the eye*," draws us compellingly, inevitably, into the purview of Medusa/Virginia Woolf's mirroring face.[25]

When Barthes expresses his desire to explore photography "not as a question (a theme) but as a wound: I see, I feel, hence I notice, I observe, and I think,"[26] he elicits the psychoanalytic discourse of wound, suture, the gaze, fetishism, fear, and death that leads Victor Burgin to argue that "the photographic look is ineluctably implicated in the structure of fetishism" and the fears it masks. If, he notes, the photograph " 'can be something you actually want to hold in your hand and actually press close to you,' " this imaginary relationship "may not be held for long. To look at a photograph beyond a certain period of time is to become frustrated: the image which on first looking gave pleasure by degrees becomes a veil behind which we now desire to see. . . . The image now no longer receives *our* look, reassuring us of our founding centrality, it rather, as it were, avoids our gaze."[27] Like Medusa, the image threatens by looking and/or by not looking; once drawn in, you might never escape: "Fascination means that man can no longer detach his gaze and turn his face away from this Power; it means that his eye is lost in the eye of this Power."[28] The result in both cases is alienation: a loss of authority and a loss of the imaginary self-coherence guaranteed by the look but "threatened by the look which comes from the other."[29] From this perspective, Virginia Woolf both escapes and challenges the authority of Rafi's (and the viewer's) gaze through the frozen blankness of her stare, anticipating or precipitating his alienation from family, home, and finally self.

If, as Christian Metz has argued, "the photograph is better fit, or more likely, to work as a fetish" than film, and film itself is "an extraordinary activator of fetishism" through framing, tracking, etc.,[30] to put a photograph of Virginia Woolf's face into a film is doubly to fetishize it. It is also to gender it. "At moments," Mary Ann Doane notes, "it almost seems as though all the fetishism of the cinema were condensed onto the image of the face, the female face in particular," which, when it appears in close-up, as it does in *Sammy and Rosie,* is transformed by the scale "into an instance of the gigantic, the monstrous." The fact that this face is veiled, an effect achieved in the scene with Rafi by a superimposition of lace window curtains over the photograph, translates Virginia Woolf into the emblematic veiled woman, associated, Doane argues, not only with the femme fatale but also with a "fear and envy of the feminine" that constitutes a basic strand of Western representations of the limits of knowledge.[31]

One other aspect of Medusa/Virginia Woolf's disembodied head/eyes has a place in this scenario: its status as *image* and hence its potential for subverting the power and authority of the word. For W. J. T. Mitchell, Medusa, particularly in her Romantic incarnations, "is the perfect prototype for the image as a dangerous female Other who threatens to silence the male voice and fixate his observing eye. . . . Beauty, the very thing which aestheticians like Edmund Burke thought could be viewed from a safe position of superior strength, turns out to be itself the dangerous force." But however dangerous Medusa/Virginia Woolf may be, however much she represents the "return of . . . [the] image," of the "graphic Other" repressed by language, she cannot speak or sing in her own right.[32] Unlike Orpheus's disembodied head, long the emblem of the (male) poet's undying voice, Medusa's (female) head is silent. There are, it seems, different kinds of disembodiment, and they are culturally inseparable from gender. This distinction is indicated further by the birth at the moment of Medusa's death of a son, Pegasus, the winged horse, who, flying off, becomes associated with both heroic exploits and the Muses; in the process, he leaves behind the world of heads, bodies, the material, nature. For Eleanor Wilner, the Pegasus/Medusa dichotomy speaks of our "culture's long bias in favor of flight, its angelic fantasies that gave virtue wings; its desire to disembody itself, to rise, to measure value by height and weigh perfection by loss of gravitational mass" that aligns Pegasus with the heroic and, with the exception perhaps of Athena, excludes women.[33]

By this point in the narrative one might well feel that the repetitions of the Medusean Virginia Woolf are overdetermined: that the figure too readily becomes an emblem of the fear and power associated with strong, rebellious, phallic women, including the rebellion staged under the name of feminism. Perhaps. But the question remains, what do these reiterations signify, particularly when they are used by groups with decidedly different ideological and cultural agendas? This was the case, Mitchell notes, during the French Revolution and its aftermath, when both sides evoked Medusa as the "emblem of the political Other": to the conservatives, she represented the "dangerous, perverse, hideous, and sexually ambiguous" forces that threatened a status quo defined in terms of its (Athenean) rationality; to the radicals, she was an "abject hero" whose unfair punishment and exclusion they were fighting to redress.[34] In both versions, the figure proves either frightening or exhilarating, depending on your perspective. The Medusean Virginia Woolf, conceived along the lines of Hélène Cixous's Medusa in the early days of the Second Wave, reverses and rejects the conservative attribution; "beautiful and . . . laughing," she uses her dangerous perversity and her eyes to look out for herself, watching Perseus creep up on her and escaping in time. Rather than freezing or being frozen, this Medusa/Virginia Woolf teaches women to fly, a verb that in French (*voler*) also means to steal.[35] But the "abject hero" can be equally effective in challenging the norms that keep women in their place; situated by contemporary critics at the borders where monsters reside, the abject marks that which has been excluded or erased or foreclosed for women within the sociality, but which can also return[36]—just as Virginia Woolf must have seemed to have done with a vengeance when her face and her words began to appear everywhere during the 1970s.

Overdetermined as it may be, then, the reiteration of the Medusean Virginia Woolf over the past thirty-five years cannot be separated from its normalizing functions and the slippages that ensue, both of which operate through and against her status as popular icon: the "double movement of containment and resistance" posited by Stuart Hall. In one guise this movement produces effects that appear to be always already given, a sedimentation of previous moments that draws on the authority of citation: Who's afraid of Virginia Woolf? or Lani Guinier? or whomever the outspoken, change-demanding woman happens to be at the time. In another, it functions as "apotrope, a gesture," Craig Owens argues in an essay exploring "The Medusa Effect," "executed with the express purpose of intimidating the enemy into submission" by creating stereotypes that "reproduce ideological subjects that can be smoothly inserted into existing institutions." "To be effective," Owens adds, "stereotypes must circulate endlessly, relentlessly throughout society."[37]

In the case of Virginia Woolf, the visual icon that threatens to seize the power of the word, the effect or stereotype produced is the monstrous nature of women when they begin to speak or act outside of society's scripts, marking the deterritorialization associated with the end of an era; the circulation of this stereotype runs the gamut from high culture to low. Those populating the more popular realm of film, for example, like Kureishi and Frears, go for the beautiful but deadly Medusa, exploiting the seduction and the dangers, the titillation, of social disruption and change, however much they want to keep *some* things in place. Those claiming the high ground contain her through a reversal, transforming her into her alter ego Athena, so rational, so supportive of our worldview and categorical distinctions, so much more like us. Let's turn Virginia Woolf, they seem to say, into an honorary *Luftmensch;* let's put her on our T-shirts and tote bags (*New York Review of Books*) as Athena put Medusa on her aegis to shield us from our enemies, in this case feminists. And, let's make sure that when she does appear in her more aggressive Medusean mode, she represents everything that we want to exclude or push to the borders of our social/sexual structures—that she is too monstrous to be seductive. The two hundred years since the French Revolution seem to have made little difference here. "Change is real," Wilner notes, "but much slower than impatient hope leads us to believe. Old emblems die hard."[38]

When we turn from Medusa to the Sphinx, we find ourselves in a discourse that, starting from different premises, ends at the same place: on the borderline of beauty and horror located in Virginia Woolf's face. As we've seen, the Sphinx, like Medusa, shares a history that represents her as the embodiment of the revolutionary, feminine, mob, threatening the social order; she is also silent, still, "a symbol of the unknown and unknowable." Although male in its original incarnations in Egypt, by the time of the Oedipus story it had been transformed into a female figure, whose attributes, elaborated in the centuries that followed, associated it variously with evil, "disease of the mind (ignorance, forgetfulness, thought-crippling fear) and death" as well as an enigmatic, terrible beauty. By the beginning of the seventeenth century, one writer commented, "whatever is enigmatic and disquieting has at one time or another . . . been compared with the famous woman-headed monster."[39] Albee's riddle, Rosie's enigmatic face, Virginia Woolf's disquieting question to Rafi—"Who are you?"—belong to this tradition.[40]

But the fear I want to trace out here returns us to the Sphinx's missing nose, or rather the now-you-see-it-now-you-don't horror that leads, via the doubling of absence and presence associated with fetishism and sexual difference, to Virginia Woolf, whether in Alan Bennett's *Me, I'm Afraid of Virginia Woolf,* where her otherwise prominent nose is erased from its pictorial representation (Take 7), or Slavoj Žižek's Lacanian reading of monsters in Hollywood film ("Why does the *Phallus* appear?"). Considering the question of what constitutes "the repulsive horror" of the phantom of the opera's face in Gaston Leroux's version of the story, Žižek comments, "His nose is so little worth talking about that you can't see it side-face: and *the absence* of that nose is a horrible thing *to look at.*" But its presence is equally horrifying, illustrated by another version where the phantom's nose becomes "an excessive phallic protuberance, repulsive to a 'normal' gaze" but attractive to his mother, who experiences it as "her missing phallus." This "excessive phallic protuberance" crosses with another aspect of the monster's horror: the "amorphous distortion of the face," as if it had "undergone an anamorphotic deformation." But true to both Lacanian logic and mythic paradigms of the (female) monster, the horror becomes inseparable from "an effect of sublime beauty. Let us just recall the face of Virginia Woolf," Žižek declares, providing a visual image (fig. 27), the same Lenare portrait, cropped to show the head only, that is defaced in Bennett's play but returns through another Lenarean image to exert its uncanny power in *Sammy and Rosie Get Laid:*

> Its ethereal, refined sublimity pertains to its anamorphotic extension, as if the reality of her face itself were protracted by a crooked mirror. To ascertain this link between anamorphosis and sublimity, it suffices to "retrench" this face to its "normal" measure by means of a simple computer treatment. . . . [W]hat we get is . . . a "healthy," chubby face without any trace of the unretouched photo's sublimity. [Fig. 28.]

Situated by Žižek on "the boundary that separates beauty from disgust," Virginia Woolf's face signifies a monstrous destabilization of the "entire social edifice."[41]

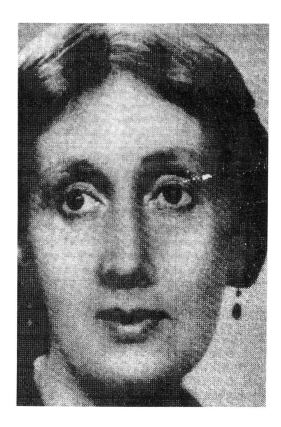

FIGURE 27. (left)
Virginia Woolf: "Sublime."
Copyright © 1992. From
Enjoy Your Symptom!
by Slavoj Žižek. Repro-
duced by permission of
Routledge, Inc.

FIGURE 28. (below)
Virginia Woolf: "Normal."
Copyright © 1992. From
Enjoy Your Symptom!
by Slavoj Žižek. Repro-
duced by permission of
Routledge, Inc.

3. Two-Sided Mirrors: Like Virginia Woolf...

At this point I want to make an intervention in the reiterative process, shifting the location and meaning of the "two-sided mirror" where "the strange beauty of the feminine countenance, brilliant with seduction, and the horrible fascination of death, meet and cross" from Medusa/Virginia Woolf to Virginia Woolf/Marilyn Monroe. My starting point is Mario Praz's rendering of the Romantics' Medusa: "to such an extent were Beauty and Death looked upon as sisters by the Romantics that they became fused into a sort of two-faced herm, filled with corruption and melancholy and fatal in its beauty."[42] For the concept of woman as two-sided mirror or two-faced herm, so common in representations of Virginia Woolf, surfaces in those of Marilyn Monroe as well, a doubling that demands a reconfiguration of the Virginia Woolf/Marilyn Monroe hybrid. In this reconfiguration, the figure ceases to be a single face or a single head (Virginia Woolf) on a single body (Marilyn Monroe) and becomes instead a two-faced figure with a shared (female) body. And rather than being opposites, the two faces mirror each other. To the extent that each face separately bears the inscription of the "two-faced herm" that makes beauty and death one, the twice-doubled figure potentially unsettles more boundaries than that between the women themselves.

A central aspect of this reconfiguration resides in Marilyn Monroe's status as iconic representation of the female body, a body whose history renders it as monstrous as the face/head in terms of its crossing of beauty, seductiveness, distortion, and death. One need think only of Aristotle's definition of the female body as a "deformed or incomplete man," a sign that, by virtue of its difference from and hence production of the male norm, becomes aligned with the monstrous.[43] Or listen to Simone de Beauvoir's history of woman's bodily degradation: "Since the Middle Ages the fact of having a body has been considered, in woman, an ignominy. Even science was long paralyzed by this disgust. Linnaeus in his treatise on nature avoided as 'abominable' the study of woman's sexual organs. The French physician des Laurens asked himself the scandalized question: 'How can this divine animal, full of reason and judgment, which we call man, be attracted by these obscene parts of woman, defiled with juices and located shamefully at the lowest part of the trunk?'" Jeffrey Cohen provides a way of reading this history when he notes, "The monstrous body is pure culture. A construct and a projection, the monster exists only to be read: the *monstrum* is etymologically 'that which reveals,' 'that which warns,' a glyph that seeks a hierophant."[44]

This history of woman's body, in which the "female body shares with the monster the privilege of bringing out a unique blend of *fascination* and *horror*," a "logic of attraction and repulsion,"[45] transgresses the "natural" boundary between head and body, defiling the head's autonomy; this holds true whether the head belongs to Marilyn Monroe or Virginia Woolf. Both head and body are implicated in woman's categorical threat. Turning to Marilyn Monroe, then, I want to explore some of the ways in which, like Virginia Woolf, she embodies the deadliness of the beautiful woman before turning to the ramifications of the Virginia Woolf/Marilyn Monroe head/body configuration exemplified by the Chapel Hill hybrid.

"Like Virginia Woolf . . ." At first glance it might seem that Marilyn Monroe could never be as scary, especially since the term most often used to describe her is "vulnerability."[46] For Diana Trilling, for example, one of the first women to write on Marilyn Monroe, her vulnerability made her "safe," contributing to her sexuality at the same time that, along with her innocence, it spurred both men and women to want to save her: "She glamorized sexuality to the point at which it lost its terrors for us; and maybe it was this veil that she raised to sexual reality that permitted women, no less than men, to respond to her so generously. Instinctively, I think, women understood that this seemingly most sexual of female creatures was no threat to them." This reading stands in direct contrast to the veiled woman as femme fatale or figure of fear and envy found in male theorists and film, suggesting a modesty, a femininity, even a domesticity in Marilyn Monroe that, in Trilling's telling, the sensitive but also fiercely "feministic" and intellectual Virginia Woolf arrogantly tore to shreds (see Take 6). For Trilling, Marilyn Monroe only began to incite "fear" in the nude photographs taken just before her death, when even the beauty of the face couldn't hide the signs of her suffering and her impending death: "her body looked ravaged and ill, already drained of life."[47]

But not everyone has shared Trilling's view. The teenage Gloria Steinem, the older woman tells us, felt extremely threatened by Marilyn Monroe's body: by "the vulnerability of the big-breasted woman in a society that regresses men and keeps them obsessed with the maternal symbols of breasts and hips."[48] And for many heterosexual men (gay men react differently), even as they adored her and agreed with Trilling that she made sexuality seem joyful and safe, the vulnerable body also had its threats; they didn't need to wait for her end to perceive her deadliness, and her deadliness, like Virginia Woolf's, can be monstrous.[49] Mailer, to take one well-known example, eulogizes her in the beginning of his "biography" as "our angel, the sweet angel of sex," but he also depicts her as a "queen of a castrator" and a "murderous emotional cripple"; one chapter is called "Ms. Monroe." On the screen, Wendy Lesser argues, in her reading of male representations of

Marilyn Monroe, she "seems to represent Fate personified—the fate of a doomed woman, or else the doom wielded by a beautiful woman when dealing with men."[50] The doomed woman dominates in Norman Rosten's description of Marilyn Monroe as potential sacrificial victim for her fans: "The crowd . . . moves around her, moves away and closes in behind as she passes, a tide of living men and women who smell out the one they will later crucify. They invariably pick a magical talisman: contradictory, all-embracing wife-mother-mistress, the mysterious link between sex and death. For as certainly as they adore her, they could also destroy her."[51] When Marilyn Monroe appears as the wielder of doom, Medusa, the mirror of one's impending death, appears as well. As Arthur Miller writes in *After the Fall,* his postmortem on his ex-wife, "a suicide kills two people, Maggie, that's what it's for!"[52]

These deadly attributes become even clearer when Lesser, who titles her essay "The Disembodied Body of Marilyn Monroe," argues that despite the fact that Monroe seemed to exist to be photographed, to exist as a body, what we see when we look at her is really an emptiness. Using as a source one of Cecil Beaton's photographs of Monroe, sunk into a chair and looking up at the camera (fig. 29), Lesser provides a reading that not only stresses the "distorted body parts," but also the sense of fright: Monroe's eyes, she writes, "are beautiful, but they are also frightened of their own beauty. . . . Beaton's portrait gives us a Marilyn Monroe who is retreating behind her own body, using it as a screen with which to hide from us." Lesser's language here directly echoes Beaton's description of Virginia Woolf as a ghost scared of her own beauty. In this reading, Marilyn Monroe's distorted body becomes a surface with no depth, nothing beyond; like Virginia Woolf, she is "frail and crisp as a dead leaf" and equally as frightening to others as to herself.[53]

Even those who argue for Monroe's control of her photographic image and her artistry—that is, her head—reach the same conclusion: the disappearance of the body. Using Bert Stern photographs where Monroe holds a large, transparent, striped scarf before her nude body (part of the series that frightened Trilling), Kathryn Benzel sees Monroe creating abstract artistic compositions that seem "to diminish altogether her body, even to erase her always anticipated face." In the pose that interests her most (fig. 30), Monroe "is almost decapitated; her head (mind/intellect) and body are separated, and even the profile of her body is refracted and distorted." The result takes us back to familiar territory, where Marilyn Monroe's "mind or intellect or spirit becomes the theme. We can almost imagine Monroe portraying a classic goddess; perhaps Athena, the goddess of wisdom and the arts." But rather than "Zeus giving birth to Athena in

FIGURE 29. Marilyn Monroe. Photograph by Cecil Beaton. Courtesy of Sotheby's London.

the heavens, the heavens are literally borne out of Athena/Monroe's mind. This last still suggests the essence of Monroe's art and, seen retrospectively, its message is foreboding in its portrait of Monroe's femininity." By turning her (naked) physical body "into an expression of artistic imagination," Benzel concludes, "something is made of nothing," but it is the nothingness of death.[54]

Ultimately the sexual body we see when we look at Marilyn Monroe becomes indistinguishable from a corpse, either Monroe's or the spectator's; it becomes uncanny. For Paige Baty, in her study of "mass-mediated" representations of Marilyn Monroe, the dead body of Marilyn Monroe, the body in the postmortem condition, becomes not only a representational site of social anxiety and control, but a defense against the monstrous threat

FIGURE 30.
Marilyn Monroe.
Photograph by Bert
Stern. Copyright © Bert
Stern.

the body poses. Using as her sources the photograph of Monroe after her autopsy and accounts of the autopsy itself, Baty's presentation of this body reiterates the thematics so familiar from representations of Virginia Woolf: like Virginia Woolf's face as described by Žižek, Marilyn Monroe's dead body becomes a mark of "the monstrous female who threatens the cultural order. The dead Marilyn doubles as a deified, holy, and iconic body *and* a defiled, horrific, and seamy body"; she becomes a "beautiful grotesque."[55]

We are faced with a seemingly no-win situation, signified by the horrified reactions to the Chapel Hill hybrid. Instead of combining two ideals of what a woman could be, the figure becomes a doubled image of horror, in which head *and* body, intellect *and* sexuality, whether on their own or together, prove multiply monstrous. Mary Russo provides one insight into this doubling in her study of the female grotesque; her example is Michael Balint's description of the configuration of participants in aerial acts or sideshows: " 'One type of showpiece is either beautiful, attractive women, or frightening, odd, and strange females; the other type is powerful, boasting[,] challenging men.' " This proximity, she writes, the "or," suggests that the " 'beautiful, attractive' and the 'odd and strange' female finally belongs to the same 'type.' " This doubled "type," associated with an economy of distraction/attraction, suggests in turn one of the earliest manifestations of the grotesque: "unnatural, frivolous, and irrational connections between things which nature and classical art kept scrupulously apart. It emerged, in other words, only in relation to the norms which it exceeded."[56]

What does this concept of the grotesque suggest about the fear evoked by the Virginia Woolf/Marilyn Monroe hybrid? What norms are at work here? For the women who saw it in Chapel Hill, the horror lay in the vulnerability of Virginia Woolf's head when appended to Marilyn Monroe's powerful body, suggesting an embodiment, a sexualization that denies the viability of head on its own. Men's reactions to the intellectual woman take a different turn. First, if a woman is intellectual, beautiful, and/or apparently asexual as, judging by the recurring references to her as ethereal, austere, chaste, was the perceived case with Virginia Woolf, she can pose a direct challenge to the male head/intellect. One response is to further desexualize the figure, to transform her perhaps into Beaton's village schoolmistress, a trope that still recurs with depressing regularity in our culture; at its most extreme, it denies the figure any beauty or attraction. James Watson illustrates this move in *The Double Helix* when he turns "fellow" scientist Rosalind Franklin into an "unattractive, dowdy, rigid, aggressive, overbearing, steely, 'unfeminine' bluestocking," one version of "the female grotesque";[57] writing of a lecture in which Franklin, "a woman," told him "to refrain from venturing an opinion about a subject for which [he was] not trained," he notes that "it was a sure way of bringing back unpleasant memories of lower school."[58] Simone de Beauvoir, the "emblematic intellectual woman of the twentieth century," proves equally vulnerable; analyzing this phenomenon in responses to Beauvoir, Toril Moi sees the obsessive discussion of her femininity—and lack thereof—by her critics as a way of countering her intellectual status. Beauvoir's recurring representations as "the priggish schoolgirl or the stuffy schoolmarm," "desexualized . . . , rigid, predictable and *confined* in [her] knowledge," Moi argues, bring with them a suggestion of the " '*monstre sacré*, a Minerva sprung fully armed from the brains of the god of philosophy, or perhaps emerged by spontaneous generation!' "[59]

But if the absence of a (feminine) body makes the head a sign of the (excessive) grotesque, the presence of the woman's body, particularly the sexual body, does not necessarily cancel or reduce the threat. If a woman is intellectual, beautiful, *and* sexual, whether heterosexual, homosexual, or bisexual, she introduces a threat that is potentially less containable than that posed by the head alone and elicits a more terrified response; crossing boundaries has its price. Ironically, the terror is often self-produced, the result of a desire to undo the threat of the intellectual woman by sexualizing her. Alan Bennett enacts this gesture when he adds breasts to Virginia Woolf's schoolroom image, and the Chapel Hill hybrid repeats it by giving her Marilyn Monroe's body. This gesture undercuts the woman's ability to fly, to be a *Luftmensch,* by weighing her down. The effect of this embodiment is to feminize the figure, whether male or female, a feminization inseparable from the embodied figure's status as spectacle; "embodiment *itself,*" Majorie Garber notes, "is a form of feminization."[60] I have come to associate this embodiment with the addition of the missing line in my notational representation of the Virginia Woolf/Marilyn Monroe hybrid as VW/MM: an upside-down reversal in which VW, without MM to weigh her down, signifies a frightening lack.

Initially this move can titillate rather than freeze desire, as Spalding Gray illustrates vis-à-vis Virginia Woolf when he playfully converts the schoolmistress trope into its erotic counterpart. Nor is she alone; other highly visible intellectual women have experienced similar transformations, often by crossing them, like Virginia Woolf, with figures from film or fashion. A 1992 article on Susan Sontag in a London newspaper, for example, headed "The Life of a Head Girl," reminds readers that in the 1960s, when Sontag was "still a relatively new star in New York's intellectual firmament," she was labeled "the Dark Lady of American Letters," "the *belle dame sans merci* of the literary world," and "the Natalie Wood of the avant-garde." In the 1970s, Gloria Steinem became the thinking man's [Jean] Shrimpton. And François Mitterand once observed that Margaret Thatcher had "the eyes of Caligula and the lips of Marilyn Monroe." These epithets, the writer on Sontag comments, "[function] as code for *this woman is brainy, but, guys, she's a looker, too*"; what the writer misses is the trope that turns Sontag into the femme fatale: beautiful but deadly.[61]

If crossing the head with the sexualized body can, at first sight, titillate, it can also frighten, whether the hybrid seduces men or ignores them: a distinct possibility when the head is Virginia Woolf's. This latter threat resides in the uncanny attraction of Virginia Woolf and Marilyn Monroe to each other, an attraction that distinctly queers the figure, drawing attention to the unacknowledged homoerotic identification and desire that theorists such as Diana Fuss have used to explain why women like looking at other women, in fashion magazines for example.[62] For many, this queered figure functions as a (grotesque) object of fascination and fear, a reaction apparent in one writer's description of the protagonists in *Vita & Virginia* as "hybrid of hybrids, Freakish Sex Queens of the Turn-of-the-Century London Beau Monde."[63] (We are back in the realm of *Freak Orlando*'s Siamese twins' radical female/female sexuality.) For the queered hybrid hints that what Virginia wanted all along was Marilyn and, even more disturbing, especially if you are a heterosexual male, what Marilyn wanted was Virginia: a desire that rather than separating head from body once again doubles them. From this perspective, the male desire to sexualize Virginia Woolf might well be the desire to turn her eyes from the other woman, to prove oneself the special man capable of making her desire him.

With this queered figure in mind, we can see that the gesture that sexualizes Virginia Woolf by giving her Marilyn Monroe's body might become even more transgressive when reversed: when the sexualized body gains Virginia Woolf's head and with it perhaps her feminism and sapphism. The category crisis signaled by the monstrous union of the two women achieves one of its most frightening and potentially disruptive aspects here; little in our culture suggests that men really want this particular combination of powers. Instead, the desired situation has been that expressed by a newspaper headline when Monroe married Arthur Miller: "EGGHEAD WEDS HOURGLASS."[64] When McCann grafts Virginia Woolf's head onto Marilyn Monroe's body by reading the actress through the writer, he may feel this strengthens her, but this strength is just what most men fear in beautiful, sexual women. Instead, most attempts to move Marilyn Monroe outside of her body bypass the head and posit, as Mailer said it might be necessary to do, a transcendental soul, which inevitably anticipates her death. Alexander Walker illustrates this move in a 1966 essay called "Body and Soul: Harlow and Monroe," where he argues that, unlike Harlow, Monroe "developed a way of taking the sexual appeal she at first crudely projected and turning it into something nearly transcendental," an act that proved deadly to herself and destructive to men. His example of the latter is *The Misfits*, where the Marilyn figure destroys the character played by Clark Gable, "[breaking] his spirit in the way he once broke the wild horses," a cinematic representation of the destructiveness that Arthur Miller, who wrote the script, experienced in life. With hindsight, Walker argues, the film can be read as Miller's attempt to "exorcise" his wife's destructive "spirit"; "the moral appears to be that in the films it is far less harassing to live with a 'body' than to settle for marriage to a 'soul.' In life, too, the same perhaps applies."[65]

There is still one more aspect of the monstrous doubling of Virginia Woolf and Marilyn Monroe to consider, that suggested by Walker's reference to Monroe's destruction of Miller: fear of the childless woman. More than the head comes into play here, although that too is an element; "like Virginia Woolf," Moi writes, "Beauvoir pays dearly indeed for the sin of not being the incarnation of the ultimate non-writing woman, the Angel in the House." Instead, she is represented as "cold, selfish, egocentric and uncaring, and above all as *non-maternal*."[66] As we've seen, fear of the childless woman has a number of roots, speaking powerfully to threats that are social as well as personal. When the childlessness is chosen, it threatens male power and a patriarchal system, leading Albee's George to accuse Honey of "little murders" and Kureishi's Rafi to ask Rosie if she is a lesbian as well as a feminist; in both cases the childless woman is linked to the nightmare of feminism and the threat of homosexuality, male and/or female. But the threat is equally strong when the woman, like Albee's Martha and her alter ego Virginia Woolf, wants a child that, for whatever reason, she does not have.

Where does Marilyn Monroe fit into this history of murderous childlessness? As Martha's double. The more I read about Monroe the more I begin to wonder whether Albee, in depicting his destructive and self-destructive marriage from hell—the intellectual man married to the sexual *and* childless woman—was reproducing, however unconsciously, the highly visible marriage and breakup of Marilyn Monroe and Arthur Miller, including Monroe's well-publicized affair with Yves Montand. It is not just the conjunction of Martha and Monroe as castrating women that prompts this speculation: the subtext of Albee's play, its reviews, and descriptions of Monroe's hatred of Miller all link the women's destructive behavior to the thwarted desire for a child. Mailer minces no words here, moving directly from Monroe's supposed miscarriages (or hysterical pregnancies), which made her a "sexual freak," to her overdose of drugs to her temporary gratitude to Miller for saving her; the latter leads Mailer to ask, ". . . has her hatred been put to rest by the look of relief in his eyes that she is still alive?" But the respite, in his telling, is short-lived, and it is downhill for the marriage from this point on. By the time he describes their relationship just before her affair with Yves Montand, using Miller's own depictions from *After the Fall,* it is hard to distinguish Monroe/Miller from Martha/George: "Miller has had to pay an increasing price—each year she speaks more rudely to him in public. . . . Marilyn is beginning to sound like many another drunken blonde. She is throwing herself at Montand."[67]

When the overwhelmingly male reviewers of Albee's play in the 1960s unequivocally asserted that the creation of the fantasy child was unbelievable, exhibiting an extraordinary blindness to the pressures that childless women knew only too well, their denial marginalized the stories Steinem heard after publishing an essay on Marilyn Monroe in an early issue of *Ms.* (1972); the responses, astounding both in their number and their expressions of empathy, highlighted the pain of not being able to have children in a society that defined women in one way only.[68] Instead, Albee's reviewers, like the play, perceive and send a different message: that women who are deprived of a child, whether Martha, Virginia Woolf, or Marilyn Monroe, turn against men. In this construction, the crossing of Virginia Woolf and Marilyn Monroe once again ceases to combine opposites and produces a monstrous double.

4. High Brows/Low Blows

Although the Virginia Woolf/Marilyn Monroe hybrid was one of several high/low combinations, it was the only female figure. While this singularity suggests the lack of women readily identified with high culture, it suggests more strongly the particular dangers of female infringements of the borders dividing high and popular culture. At first glance the union of the two women might seem to frighten by bringing together categories that until recently could be considered distinct from one another. Virginia Woolf, after all, by her own admission, was a self-identified highbrow, a view supported by others' perception that she represents the aesthetic detachment that distinguishes "art" from the " 'vulgar' surrender to easy seduction and collective enthusiasm" associated with more popular entertainments.[69] Even Diana Trilling, we know, despite her misgivings, claimed Virginia Woolf for high culture in the early 1960s when she found herself confronted with the seemingly endless encroachment of popular culture into high culture exemplified by Albee's play.

In contrast, Marilyn Monroe, like so many female icons, readily signifies the degradation and "femininity" of a mass/popular culture. Richard Schickel, for example, pairing her with Marlon Brando in a chapter called "Super Hero, Super Victim," reduces her to the "dumb blond done wrong," the "bimbo" with pretensions to transcendence in a celebrity culture that threatens to emasculate its male stars as well. The cover illustration on John Ralston Saul's critique of post-enlightenment culture, *Voltaire's Bastards,* makes a similar move, joining Marilyn Monroe's head to that of Voltaire in a two-faced herm (fig. 31). The image stands as an apt introduction to the author's contention that the revolution in cultural and political mores we associate with Voltaire—i.e., reason and the Enlightenment—has failed, bequeathing us, to take just one pertinent example, leaders defined not by their exercise of power with public responsibility but by their fame as stars.[70]

But despite the apparent fixity of the two women on opposite sides of the cultural divide, each on her own also threatens to undo it. Virginia Woolf, as I've argued throughout, throws into question one of the central boundaries in the construction of cultural class: the boundary that divides modernism, high culture, and maleness—not to mention fear of feminism and feminization—on the one side, from women, the mob, mass culture, and consumption on the other. Similarly, Marilyn Monroe performs an equally destabilizing role, one premised, in Dean MacCannell's telling, on the "density and diversity" of her "social network" ("She knew, and brought together, hundreds of individuals from sports, politics, letters, entertainment"); this places her "or her image," he argues, in "the same space as the deconstructionist critique of Western science and culture." Diana Trilling again provides a telling illustration, noting that her essay on Marilyn Monroe was the only one to appear in both "a popular journal" (*Redbook*) and "a literary magazine" ("the distinguished Anglo-American journal *Encounter*"); "it was Marilyn Monroe, not I, who bridged the gap between the two periodicals."[71]

By the end of the 1980s, when the Chapel Hill hybrid appeared, the fault lines in the high/low topography had themselves begun to alter; by then, worried commentators argue, both sides (high and low) had turned to (or appropriated) the other for self-legitimation. Jonathan Freedman made this point in 1987 when he argued that "the intellectual's discourse about popular culture" and "culture itself" are "spectral doubles of each other; mirrors in which they attempt to shape themselves into the image they imagine of the other's image of them, if only in [an] attempt to deny the resemblance." Daniel Harris concurred, declaring in 1992 that "mainstream reviewers are gradually assuming the mantle abandoned by academics, that of custodian of High Art," while academics are "wrapping themselves in a populist flag."[72] Under these circumstances, the issue is not so much the border crossings per se (are there any borders left?), but who has the power to decide their legitimacy. Or, to put this somewhat differently, if cultural productions by the early 1990s were always already a high/low hybrid, what boundaries were really being threatened or unsettled by Virginia Woolf's Marilyn-like iconization, signaled by her pervasive popular appearances, on the one hand, or, on the other, by Graham McCann's use of Woolf's feminist writings to explicate Marilyn Monroe's intelligence and relationships with men: cultural class or gender?

FIGURE 31.
Cover, *Voltaire's
Bastards: The
Dictatorship of
Reason in the West,*
by John Ralston
Saul.

I suggest the latter, and not only in the case of Virginia Woolf. When Harris, to take just one example in a far wider debate, mounts his critique of the "appropriation" of that archetypal popular cultural figure, Madonna, by "a marginal group" within the high cultural camp, academics, the sarcasm he brings to what, he writes, "mass-media pundit E. Ann Kaplan identifies in all seriousness as the 'MP,' the 'Madonna Phenomenon' "[73] distinctly echoes Helen Dudar's sarcasm about the "Virginia Woolf cult" among (women) academics and her equation of Virginia Woolf with Marilyn Monroe. In Harris's rendering of this recurring scenario of illegitimate crossover, the union of Kaplan (head/brains) and Madonna (body/sex) becomes as monstrous as that between Virginia Woolf and Marilyn Monroe. In both cases, it could be argued, the sarcasm is aimed at behavior deemed inappropriate for academics and high culture; "cults" and "wannabes," after all, are associated with popular cultural figures, with "stars." But when the figures involved on either side of the cultural divide are male, not female, the word *cult* does not appear. Would Harris, for example, have written the same piece about the academization of Bob Dylan? Would Dylan, but not Madonna, be allowed to cross the divide safely because he represents "brains," not "body"? (As Freedman notes, Dylan "legitimized" himself by claiming to be influenced by Rimbaud; Madonna's highbrow borrowings are belittled in Harris's account.) Or is it that Dylan being male, his place in high culture is inherently less problematic? Considering this question in light of my perception that the Shakespeare/Jagger hybrid usually evokes a smile but the Virginia Woolf/Marilyn Monroe hybrid provokes bewilderment if not horror, I am led to reiterate: how much are we dealing with cultural class warfare and how much with gender?

Before leaving "wannabes," I want to recall the image of the woman in the television program *J'Accuse* buying a slew of Virginia Woolf books, almost as if they were romances purchased compulsively for a pleasure that men not only don't understand but rightly scorn. Tom Paulin, the prosecutor-narrator, has a hard time deciding what to do with this popularity. First he tells us we need to see Virginia Woolf not as a pop star or feminist icon but as a writer of serious literature; but once he has located her in high culture, he sends her right back to the popular, describing her writing as "copywriter's prose," which "belongs in *Homes and Gardens;* it has all the self-conscious glossiness, the atmosphere of wealth, leisure, taste and consumption such periodicals ask us to identify with." Despite this, he says, he can't get his students to stop being "personally offended" if he makes "the slightest criticism of her work"; they just don't want to hear him. Whew! Such popularity for a woman supposedly as high cultural, elitist, and retrograde as the rest of the program makes her out to be must be really hard to take.

5. A Proliferation of Monsters

The political struggle is to see from both perspectives at once. . . . Single vision produces worse illusions than double vision or many-headed monsters.

—Donna Haraway, "A Cyborg Manifesto"

When I first wrote about the Chapel Hill hybrid, I had no visual image of the figure; I did not know which of Virginia Woolf's heads was attached to which of Marilyn Monroe's bodies. What I did know was that the body wore a bathing suit and heels and was clearly Monroe's, not just an anonymous body, suggesting that the figure relied on its particularity for its point.[74] Starting from that absence, it was easy to argue that we don't need to see the figure for it to "work"; on the contrary, the lack of a specific visual image multiplies the possible permutations implicit in the union of the two women, including those that would reclaim the hybrid's monstrosity for creative subversion, for social change. Increased awareness of which head (more or less) and which body has not altered my perception of the figure's disruptive polymorphism, its location on the borders where the monsters and the (im)possible reside.[75] This is the realm of the nonbinary, of category crises—what Jeffrey Cohen calls the "and-or"—where we can imagine the excessiveness called for by Donna Haraway. The speculations on the figure's potential transgressiveness that I turn to here begin with the premise that the Virginia Woolf/Marilyn Monroe hybrid, whether conceived as a combination of opposites or as a doubling of like and like, may destabilize established boundaries, but a multiplication of the doubled figure holds the greatest promise for deterritorialization. In this configuration, a proliferation of monsters covers the cultural landscape.

The question is how to shift the reiterative patterns, the sedimentation of images, that fix and contain women, even or especially iconic women, in their stereotypical roles. As Wilner so succinctly stated, "old emblems die hard," and one of these is Virginia Woolf as emblem of the frightening intellectual woman. Even when the evocation is seemingly positive, the point of crossing a woman with Virginia Woolf, of labeling her as an intellectual, remains fear; thus, an article that begins by noting that Katha Pollitt, feminist "writer and outspoken cultural critic . . . bears an eerie resemblance to Virginia Woolf. She turns her head slightly and her profile is Woolf's," goes on to show how she is intellectually scarier than her predecessor.[76]

Nor has the pattern of either desexualizing or sexualizing the intellectual woman and then fearing her disappeared. When Janet Reno, repeatedly characterized in the media as unmarried, childless, and independent, became the first woman Attorney General of the United States, a cartoon depicted her holding a ruler as she towers above the small, frightened, boys in the "Justice Department Day School"; the caption reads, "Good morning, class. I'm your new teacher—are there any questions?"[77] Or look at Hillary Rodham Clinton. Both before and after her husband's election to the presidency of the United States in 1992, her image seemed to be everywhere, prompting Katha Pollitt to write that "H.R.C." has "become a quasi-pornographic obsession."[78] This phenomenon is graphically illustrated by her appearance on the cover of the February 1993 *Spy* magazine, where, in a gesture reminiscent of both Spalding Gray and the Chapel Hill hybrid, her head is appended to the body of a dominatrix (fig. 32).[79] Three years later (October 1995) *Spy* returned to the visual attack, putting Rodham Clinton's head on top of a body that cites the photograph of Marilyn Monroe standing on top of a subway grate, her white skirt billowing around her waist. In the *Spy* image, the dress is black, and underneath "Hillary" shows a distinctly male bulge in distinctly male underpants. Surveying Rodham Clinton's monstrosity through the "collective fears and anxieties" about women in power that he calls the "Marie Antoinette syndrome," Pierre Saint-Amand characterizes it as a prototypical example of the "demonization and cloning of the [power-ful] woman's influence," which manifests itself visually in grotesque and monstrous images of her seductive beauty and sexuality, often associated with lesbianism. These images place her at "the center of a prolific *ars combinatoria,* which assembled monsters, hybrid creatures, and whole processions of deformed beings."[80]

The question of how intellectual women have been represented since the end of the nineteenth century led Griselda Pollock to posit that we suffer from a "semiotic inadequacy" that blocks or hinders the representational integration of sexuality and intellectuality in women. Presenting her ma-terials at a conference in 1993, she used a photograph of Marilyn Monroe wearing a strapless gown, arms raised, entertaining the troops in Korea, to illustrate the clarity of representations of the sexual woman, the body; the more opaque image of the intellectual woman, the head, juxtaposed to it on the screen was the Beresford profile of Virginia Stephen.[81]

Pollock's question raises yet another one: given the major role that visual images play in the construction of both Virginia Woolf and Marilyn Monroe as icons and the locations assigned to "Woman" in theories and practices of the visual field, can these women ever be anything but frightening? If, as feminist critics have argued, the theories we have all seem to locate the doubled horror associated with fetishism in the woman's face, if "we are surrounded by the image of the woman's face, the obsession of the portrait and the cover girl alike,"[82] and if "Woman" remains the feared and envied trope of enigma and boundary disruption, how can these figures help but be monstrous?

This is a big question, as big as Virginia Woolf's face in Kureishi's film or Žižek's essay, and one that calls for a shift in perspective: a shift that would use women's perceived monstrosity consciously and performatively to dissolve the "traditional . . . symbolic links" that support our social structures. As Butler and others have argued, the reiteration that produces norms through a series of exclusions, taboos, and banishings that in turn make certain attributes or actions monstrous, also produces "that which escapes or exceeds the norm, . . . that which cannot be wholly defined or fixed by the repetitive labor of that norm." In this way, the reiteration provides the potential for a "productive crisis." Monstrosity,

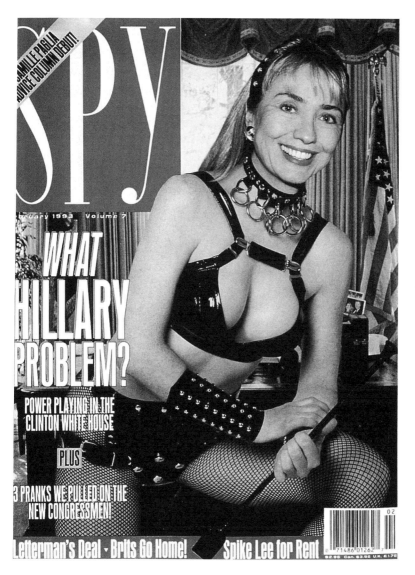

FIGURE 32. Cover, *Spy* Magazine, February 1993.

then, associated with the borders, marks the place where the dislocations and rearticulations that allow for other possibilities occur.[83]

When women in the 1970s wore Virginia Woolf's face on T-shirts or when in the 1980s men and women carried her face on placards at ACTUP anticensorship rallies, they were claiming her Medusean powers for deliberate acts of defiance and transgression, an apotropaic gesture performed not to freeze the spectators but to mobilize and change them. They accepted Cixous's challenge to women not only to look at Medusa with new eyes but to make her eyes their own. But looking back, reversing the gaze, may not be enough; as Doane points out, when the veiled woman in film looks back, the effect is to disintegrate her by reinscribing her into the weave or narrative of the screen or discourse on or in which she is represented. "It would be preferable" she adds, "to disentangle the woman and the veil, to tell another story."[84]

One such story, Doane notes, accrues to the mythic figure of Baubo, identified by Vernant as that aspect of Medusa's visage that makes it look "more like a grimace than a face" and produces an effect that oscillates between "the horror of the terrifying and the hilarity of the grotesque"; this doubling provokes "both sacred fear and liberating laughter," and Baubo falls on the side of the grotesque and laughter.[85] In some versions of the Demeter/Persephone myth, she uses her hand to make the face drawn on her pudenda into a grimace, thereby causing Demeter to laugh; by showing rather than telling she also represents the spectacle associated with the grotesque, which has, we know, its own discursive powers. Reading the figure of Baubo as represented in statuettes at Pyrene, where "the mouth above is juxtaposed with the mouth below," giving it "two heads that are both in the wrong place," Maurice Olender associates it with Priapos and Hermaphroditos; all of these figures, he argues, represent an exploration of the excesses that occur within and challenge the limits of human sexual categories. Situated on the borders, Baubo thus becomes a transgressive spectacle that "dramatize[s]" anxieties about sexuality, the human body, and reproduction.[86]

Perhaps, then, we need to return to the Virginia Woolf/Marilyn Monroe hybrid, seeing it this time as a productive marker of the laughter, the spectacle, the grotesque that, Russo argues, provides a space for change "within the very constrained spaces of normalization." Importantly, this space is not transcendent; it is not achieved by a flight that leaves behind (as if one could) the body in all its weightedness, particularity, grotesqueness, monstrosity. Instead, it's the "noise, dissonance, or monstrosity" that performs this role. Rejecting those aspects of the women's movement in the United States that have wanted to argue that "feminists are 'normal women,'" a stance that in addition to being class-based repeats society's misogynistic views of women and "leaves uninterrogated the very terms and processes of normalcy," Russo begins her study "on the side of the freak and the uncanny."[87]

Here we arrive with Donna Haraway at yet another possibility, one that resides in the figure of the hybrid itself: the cyborg, that vivid marker of boundary violations. In "A Manifesto for Cyborgs," Haraway makes one of the strongest arguments still for the creative destabilization embodied by the hybrid. "Monsters," she writes, "have always defined the limits of community in Western imaginations. . . . Cyborg monsters in feminist science fiction define quite different political possibilities and limits from those proposed by the mundane fiction of Man and Woman," and with it, I would add, the splits between head and body, intellectuality and sexuality, high and low, image and word. Haraway's cyborg does not fit into any concept of gender or sexuality based on singleness or doubleness: no two-sided mirror or two-faced herm. Instead, it multiplies itself into infinite possibilities; "a creature in a post-gender world," the cyborg "has no truck with bisexuality, pre-oedipal symbiosis, . . . or other seductions to organic wholeness." Nor is the cyborg fixated on childbirth, on heterosexual reproduction, being aligned, variously, with replication and regeneration; "sexual reproduction," she notes, "is one kind of reproductive strategy among many." And it recognizes other configurations of the body than those bounded by our skin; "it is not clear," she writes, "what is mind and what body in machines that resolve into coding practices." The drawing that accompanies one appearance of Haraway's essay shows a reconfiguration of the Sphinx.[88]

By the time Haraway turned to cyborgs in feminist science fiction as a way of imagining otherwise, Virginia Woolf already marked the possibilities of the genre. Two novels by Jody Scott, *Passing for Human* (1977) and *I, Vampire* (1984), feature a creature from outer space, the multisexual Benaroya, whose shape on her home planet resembles that of a dolphin but who can slip in and out of human bodies as need be; in both novels she spends substantial time in the body of Virginia Woolf. Recruited by Virginia Woolf for a project to change human behavior, the vampire-narrator of *I, Vampire* recalls a meeting with the writer in 1923, describing her variously as "beautiful, at once virginal and sensual," "the snooty, fashionable Mrs. Woolf," and "high strung, neurotic, desirable." Soon the narrator realizes that Benaroya "wasn't the 'real' Virginia Woolf," but it no longer matters; Virginia Woolf proves equally as erotic, exciting, and fulfilling in her new incarnation. The cover depicts the two women,

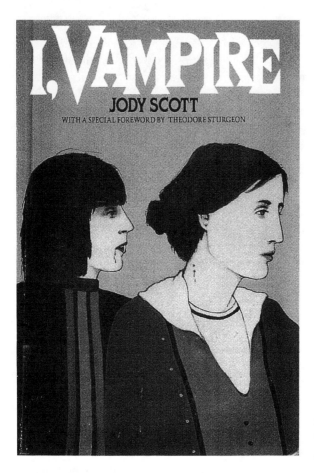

FIGURE 33.
Cover, *I, Vampire,* by
Jody Scott.

the vampire and Virginia Woolf, as two profiles, bodies distinguished but not distinct (fig. 33).[89]

Having reached this point in my argument, I want to return to the Virginia Woolf/Marilyn Monroe hybrid and posit two readings that break free of the single head on a single body or the doubled, two-faced herm, opening up spaces for chance and change. The first contemplates a scenario where the possibilities inherent in mimicry, masquerade, parody, cross-dressing, and spectacle can be mobilized to undo the power invested in stereotypes to fix individuals in gender and cultural class positions by terrorizing them through its (female) icons, Virginia Woolf and Marilyn Monroe included. "Whatif," to paraphrase Rushdie, we claim the monstrosity of the Virginia Woolf/Marilyn Monroe hybrid not only for a productive rather than destructive union of beauty and the beast, but for the disruptive/creative performance of gender, sexuality, and even the body that has been so ambitiously retheorized in a number of fields? "Whatif" we acknowledge women, including Virginia Woolf, as desiring subjects whose desires queer the split between heads and bodies? "Whatif" we reconfigure the image to include multiple heads and bodies: to suggest a multiplicity that unsettles the boundaries and distinctions so dear to the status quo, including those between women's heads and women's bodies? Although the normalizing process remains strong, as the recurring representations of Virginia Woolf and Marilyn Monroe illustrate so clearly, and we can never be either outside it or sure how our acts will turn out, the impetus to make monstrous interventions remains strong. When Russo writes that "the extreme difficulty of producing lasting social change does not diminish the usefulness of these symbolic models of transgression," and Butler asks, "How will we know the difference between the power we promote and the power we oppose?" adding that "the incalculable effects of action are as much a part of their subversive promise as those that we plan in advance," they reinforce the importance of posing other possibilities.[90]

The second reading grows from yet another example of the uncanny attraction between Virginia Woolf and Marilyn Monroe: Elizabeth Bronfen's juxtaposition of the two women in *Over Her Dead Body: Death, Femininity, and the Aesthetic,* creating at first glance what appears to be an opposition of head and body, word and image. On the one page we have the writer, who in *A Room of One's Own* brings the dead Judith Shakespeare, her Muse, to life through the power of her words. On the facing page, we have an image of the actress: one of Bert Stern's last nude photographs of Monroe, head and body crossed by lines she herself drew; the caption for the photograph, in which she seems to be *on* the cross, reads, "Photograph of Marilyn Monroe, crossed out by herself" (fig. 34). This opposition would seem to position Virginia Woolf and her strong words on the side of the head, the intellect, the flight of the mind: of a disembodiment that would "liberate" her for flight from the normalizing representations that have located woman as body, image, spectacle, sexuality, the material. But Woolf herself undercuts the opposition. In the passage cited by Bronfen, she calls upon women writers to ensure that "the dead poet who was Shakespeare's sister will put on the body which she has so often laid down . . . she will be born." For this act to challenge the reiteration of what has been, it needs to make raids upon the " 'outside,' a domain of unlivability and unintelligibility that bounds the domain of intelligible effects," the domain of "unthinkable, abject, unlivable bodies."[91] It needs to turn, as Woolf herself did when she turned to Judith Shakespeare, who

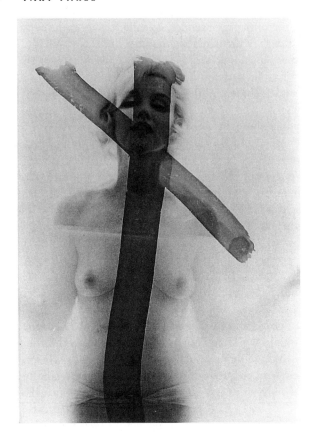

FIGURE 34.
Marilyn Monroe.
Photograph by Bert
Stern. Copyright ©
Bert Stern.

was buried, as suicides and monsters so often are, at the crossroads, to the boundary-haunting monsters, rewriting, revisualizing them, whether in our academic work or in popular culture, again and again. This boundary-defying monster allows us to see and think and speak and act differently, to become, like Virginia Woolf icon and star, a multiple, intertextual, proliferation of always partial images, acts, and words.

VIRGINIA WOOLF EPISODES

I

October 6, 1997. An editorial in the *New York Observer* headed "Top Colleges Teach P.C. Pulp" decries the academy's rejection of Virginia Woolf: "One can probably assume one won't be in any danger of encountering such fuddy-duddies as Shakespeare, James Baldwin or Virginia Woolf" in a course on Chicana lesbian literature they target for attack.

2

June 1997. Presentations at the Seventh Annual Virginia Woolf Conference, while illustrating a wide range of critical perspectives, lean toward cultural studies, popular culture, and a growing interest in technology. The media respond in kind, transforming Virginia Woolf and her writings into public events. When Hermione Lee talks at the conference about her new biography of Virginia Woolf, C-Span is there, and the talk is subsequently broadcast on their program *Booknotes*. The film version of *Mrs. Dalloway,* starring Vanessa Redgrave with a script by Eileen Atkins, has two showings and a panel devoted to it, anticipating its release later in the year. In December 1997 one of the panels offered by the Virginia Woolf Society at the Modern Language Association Convention features Virginia Woolf as public intellectual.

3

September 1998. *Lingua Franca,* the journal that calls itself "The Review of Academic Life," features on its cover an article called "Who's Afraid of Elaine Showalter?" The cover image, printed on a red background, is a close-up of Virginia Woolf's eyes. Showalter was president of the Modern Language Association at the time. The article details criticism of her, much of it by graduate students, not for being too intellectual but for not being intellectual enough: for writing in popular journals, for example, including fashion magazines.

4

1995. When Kathy Bates, playing the mother in the film *Dolores Claiburn,* discovers large quantities of pills in her daughter's suitcase and begins to have flashbacks to the past, the camera follows Bates's gaze to her daughter's wall, left untouched since her departure; the first thing we see is a photograph of Virginia Woolf. The flashbacks tell the story of the daughter's sexual abuse by her father. Contrary to what one might expect, however, the photograph is not the Beresford portrait of the young Virginia so often associated with her vulnerability; instead it displays the jaunty older woman in her fur-collared coat, looking confidently out at us (fig. 17). This woman is a fighter.

5

Virginia Woolf, it is clear, remains a favored iconic figure in debates over what constitutes culture across the academic, "intellectual," and popular realms, revealing through the diversity and assertiveness of her appearances the contradictory nature of culture itself. The issues of gender/sexuality and of cultural class enacted through Virginia Woolf remain as undecided as ever, often marking sites of cross-generational tensions that cause us to ask what the future holds and what we can take from the past.

6

September 1996 (U.K.), June 1997 (U.S.): Hermione Lee, practicing academic *and* journalist, a doubling still more common in Britain than in the United States, publishes her biography of Virginia Woolf, described by one of the few hostile reviewers as "this latest instalment of what has long since become the most upmarket of real-life supra-national soap operas."[1] In Britain, despite a smattering of some "too academic," "too feminist," "Quentin Bell's is still better," or "all those posters!" responses, the book received enormous praise; in the States, the enthusiasm was equally widespread and strong, and only the occasional reviewer in the self-styled "intellectual" press felt the need to assert that Lee wrote "without recourse to the politicized agendas of the academy or special pleading."[2] One striking aspect of the reviews is their acceptance of Lee's premise that every generation has its own Virginia Woolf and that hers, while committed to certain renderings, is no more "true" than any other:

> Virginia Woolf's story is reformulated by each generation. She takes on the shape of difficult modernist preoccupied with questions of form, or comedian of manners, or neurotic highbrow aesthete, or inventive fantasist, or pernicious snob, or Marxist feminist, or historian of women's lives, or victim of abuse, or lesbian heroine, or cultural analyst, depending on who is reading her, and when, and in what context. In the quarter-century since Bell's biography, her status has grown beyond anything that even she, with her strong sense of her own achievements, might have imagined. And the disputes she arouses—over madness, over modernism, over marriage—cannot be concluded, and will go on being argued long after this book is published.[3]

Here, Lee aligns herself with critics such as Rachel Bowlby and Pamela Caughie who have argued for a postmodern Virginia Woolf, continually in motion in both her own writings and the critical/theoretical marketplace. Yet this does not stop some reviewers, having acknowledged Lee's stance, from writing that the "truth" of the writer has "never been so carefully presented," or declaring that Lee has captured "the true Virginia."[4]

7

What most characterizes Lee's biography for her reviewers are her "judicious," "even-handed" approach to all aspects of Virginia Woolf's life and her description of this life as heroic. Characterizing Virginia Woolf in a widely cited passage as "a sane woman with an illness," "often a patient, but . . . not a victim," noting that we will never know "what 'caused'" her mental illness, Lee argues that "we can only look at what it did to her, and what she did with it. What is certain is her closeness, all her life, to a terrifying edge, and her creation of a language which faces it and makes something of it. This is a life of heroism, not of oppression, a life of writing wrestled from illness, fear, and pain."[5]

8

To illustrate her point, Lee wanted for her cover an image of Virginia Woolf that portrayed "a face with a life in it." The British edition features a portrait based on the Gisèle Freund photographs; the American edition features Gisèle Freund's portrait of the older writer with manuscript in lap and cigarette in hand (fig. 9).[6]

9

Heroism. How are we to read this in the late 1990s? Some responses, both real and imagined.

10

Cynthia Ozick, New York intellectual that she is, might well say, at last! Lee's evocation of Virginia Woolf's heroism can be read as a response to Ozick's analysis twenty-four years earlier of why Bell's biography failed to present the writer as a heroic figure. It is not just that Virginia Woolf's death could be considered heroic or not "depending on one's view of suicide by drowning"; it is more that "if Virginia Woolf is to be seen as a heroine, it must be in those modes outside the manner of her death and even the manner of her life as a patient in the house. If she is to be seen as a heroine, it must be in the conjuring" of a Bloomsbury photograph "that does not exist. The picture is of a woman sitting in an old chair holding a writing-board; the point of her pen touches a half-filled page. . . . A writer's heroism is in the act of writing; not in the finished work, but in the work as it goes."[7]

11

An interjection from the popular front. As if to illustrate the point that you should be careful what you wish for, we might compare the determinedly high cultural Ozick's imagined photograph and the covers on Lee's biography to the latest Virginia Woolf T-shirt, sold by Largely Literary Designs in the United States: a wittily drawn caricature of a Gisèle Freund profile of Virginia Woolf, pen in hand, tears falling into her ink pot as the ink drops onto the page.[8]

12

Jacqueline Rose, noted writer on psychoanalysis and culture, while praising Lee's biography, responds directly to both Lee and Ozick. Rose is concerned about what "goes missing" in the image of the heroic writer: the madness; "Woolf," she writes, "is never allowed to go missing from herself." This construction, she argues, denies the insight proffered by both Freud and Woolf in their writings: that madness is "something to which we all have a relation." When Lee rationalizes the madness by presenting it as a temporary interruption, when she "keeps Woolf sane . . . as her gift and tribute to Woolf's writing life," we lose sight of madness's integral relation not only to Woolf's writing, but to "a collective history that was no less dark" than her personal history, and to her suicide. Rose attributes this disappearance to a more general cultural discrediting of Freud; in contrast, she wants to restore Thanatos to the picture, to insist, as she argues Freud and Woolf insisted, that we cannot marginalize madness and death, whether individual or social, or will them away, without diminishing Virginia Woolf.[9]

13

Flashback. A number of letters to the *New York Times Magazine* about its 1996 "Heroine Worship" issue lambasted the overrepresentation of "models, entertainers and tragic victims" and the absence of "scientists, doctors, Nobel Prize winners, philosophers or mathematicians. A girl could be forgiven for doubting that there ever *was* a women's movement." Others criticized the use of the term *icon* in the title and introductory text, arguing it is not the same as *hero* or even *heroine*.[10] Meanwhile, *Life*'s 1997 issue "Celebrating Our Heroes" made a point of including a wide array of politically and socially active women (Eleanor Roosevelt, Margaret Sanger, Harriet Tubman, Susan B. Anthony, Jane Addams, Helen Keller, Amelia Earhart, Rachel Carson), but the only women who appeared on their readers' lists of heroes seem to be Mother Teresa and "Mom."

14

Maybe we need to give up the concept of the "hero" altogether. Virginia Woolf's appearances in two 1998 books that set out to honor *Legends: Women Who Have Changed the World through the Eyes of Great Women Writers* and *Icons of the 20th Century: 200 Men and Women Who Have Made a Difference* suggest this may be happening, even as they feature a wide variety of women (and in the case of *Icons,* men) from across the professional, political, and cultural terrain. For the record, Anjelica Huston's introduction to *Legends* once again pairs Marilyn Monroe and Virginia Woolf, presenting them as her first examples of women who changed the world, "women to be thankful for"—Marilyn Monroe for her "assault on the world's sexual myopia" and Virginia Woolf for pioneering "a whole movement in literature"—before commenting that "not all of the women gathered here have reached the status of Monroe and Woolf. . . ."[11]

15

Then there are those posters hanging on bedroom walls. They obsess British reviewers of Lee's book, seeming to signify everything wrong with the contemporary cultural world. But as one woman comments, when she "bought the Beresford poster, . . . it wasn't just the suicide romantic thing but the fact that Woolf did express what hadn't been expressed before— that the inner life is important. A lot of women find that cheering."[12]

16

The view from the National Portrait Gallery, London, courtesy of Robert Carr-Archer, Head of Retailing and Publications, March 1997, where the Beresford photograph of Virginia Woolf was "the most popular postcard this year in the Gallery" and, he estimated, had "sold upwards of 25,000 loose cards during the past five years. . . . The Beresford has a year-on-year consistency unlike any card outside the range of historical favourites and even then has generally outsold them." Given the portrait's comparatively obscure position in the gallery until recently, and the "c.400 other post-cards, this is a remarkable achievement." The gallery has "also developed a small range of other products around the image including a bookmark, paperweight, fridge magnet, greeting card, and . . . mug," which "items have sold more than 2000 pieces this year through the Gallery alone.

Of these it is perhaps the fridge magnet that best exemplifies the iconic status of Virginia Woolf. No product has come closer to representing the 'demystification' of works of art nor indeed the transformation in attitude towards commerce by galleries and museums." Non-Beresford items are available as well: postcards with other images (a Vanessa Bell painting of her sister, for example), books on Virginia Woolf, books "by her or based on her sayings and writings and almost 20 different products," including mousepads. "Virginia Woolf is not unique in inspiring sales of serious as well as more frivolous products; Jane Austen and one or two other writers do the same as do many historical figures, but she is by far and away the most varied and 'commercial' both as a fashionable icon and as a serious subject of study. Sadly I have no evidence to show that Woolf mousemats and literary critiques sell to the same customers. . . ."[13]

17

Given this history, Virginia Woolf readily joins Jane Gaines's list of those figures who, like "King Tut, the Statue of Liberty, the New York subway token, the pope, and images of Albert Einstein and Sigmund Freud," have "moved from public history to private . . . property and back again to public figure"; in this way she enacts once again the ongoing tension between the desire to maintain cultural boundaries asserted by high culture and subcultural forms of trespass and rearticulation. The National Portrait Gallery's seeming transgression of previously well-defended boundaries foregrounds the continual "shuffling" and reshuffling of the "deck" of culture so often inscribed through Virginia Woolf.[14]

18

One more reshuffle and we find ourselves back in the realm if not of soap opera, where one British reviewer of Lee's biography so snottily placed the Virginia Woolf story, at least of television sitcoms: Virginia Woolf has had her share of appearances in these as well, illustrating her ongoing power to shift cultural boundaries on both sides of the Atlantic. In what may be some of the most popular shows in contemporary popular culture, Virginia Woolf marks the complexity—and the generational anxieties—of the moment.

19

On *Beverly Hills 90210,* in an episode during the characters' senior year of high school, Dylan, the James Dean figure, begins his recovery from the trauma of his father's death by writing about it with the encouragement of Andrea, the writer/intellectual. "All I can think," Andrea comments as she watches him, "if I had a house like this to myself I could write and write and write." Dylan: "You sound like Virginia Woolf." Andrea: "You read *A Room of One's Own?*" Dylan: "Oh, yeah." Andrea: "Well, we just read that in AP English class." Subsequently Dylan joins the class.[15]

20

Murphy Brown returns us to Virginia Woolf visual icon, to the Beresford photograph reproduced as a poster hanging on a college student's wall, this time American, not English. In this episode Murphy, second-wave feminist and a founder of the women's studies program at her college, as she tells us, a woman who likes to consider herself in touch with social attitudes and struggles, returns to her alma mater to receive an honorary degree. Expecting adulation and awe from the women's studies students and faculty, she finds instead a professor who corrects her for using "seminar" instead of "ovular," a "p.c." curriculum where a feminist consciousness is described as being aware that one is a victim, and students who attack her for selling out: whether by giving in to the patriarchy or by giving up her femininity. Every negative stereotype of women's studies in the 1990s finds its way into this scene, in which Murphy identifies feminism with equal rights, equal pay, and reproductive freedom, and tells the students they are missing the point: that while they are arguing about the differences among women, the religious right is organizing to take away their rights. Returning to the dorm room where she had lived while a student, she muses on the generational differences; a giant poster of Virginia Woolf looks on (fig. 35). "Ungrateful turncoats," she begins; then, "Maybe, it's me; maybe I forgot to fight"; then, "I get the feeling my time is past. I have no relevance to this next generation, and they're the ones who are going to be framing the debate. It's time to be handing over the bullhorn."[16]

21

Sharing the screen with Murphy during this speech, Virginia Woolf would seem to back her up, although we know that the room's temporarily

FIGURE 35. Murphy Brown and Virginia Woolf, from *Murphy Brown.*

displaced occupant, an art history major dating an African American man and yet another model of the "young woman," might wonder what Murphy's going on about. This raises the question, whose room, whose Virginia Woolf, is this? Does Virginia Woolf "belong" to the young, who will necessarily fashion her to their own aspirations and ends? or to Murphy? Are we meant to see the poster as a sign of how women's studies, if not feminism, has failed, and Virginia Woolf as the sign of what we have lost and need to get back to? Or is Virginia Woolf the sign of feminist movement redefining itself? Or (and this may be the most important) does Virginia Woolf provide a space where debates such as these can constructively occur? I would answer yes to the last possibility.

22

Then there is *Ab Fab,* the wildly popular 1990s British comedy that features three generations of women in its satire of contemporary culture. In its Virginia Woolf episode, the last episode made, Saffie, the college student, who has spent years rebelling against her 1960s–70s drinking,

smoking, drug-taking, clothes-buying, sexual mother Edie and her inseparable friend Patsy by being responsible, studious, and sober—not
to mention sharing her generation's commitment to feminism, ecology,
etc.—has the Beresford photograph hanging on her bedroom wall.[17] At
the beginning of the episode, Saffie agrees to marry a rich, beautiful
young man who clearly wants a housekeeper and not a partner, sexual or otherwise (she is ironing his shirt when he proposes); we assume
he will find his companionship elsewhere. The engagement occurs despite Saffie's uttering some of the most explicitly feminist rhetoric about
women's independence heard on the show. Later, in a parody of maternal solicitude preceding a daughter's wedding, Edie lulls Saffie, lying in her bed, into a conversation; Patsy runs in with a hair-removing
strip that she applies to Saffie's moustache while Virginia Woolf looks
on. Saffie yells with pain, and the two older women run chortling from
the room.

23

There is more. When at the last minute Edie decides to stop the wedding,
it is not Virginia Woolf urging her on; it is Marianne Faithfull who,
appearing as God, provides the impetus, just as in the previous episode
she had sent a nearly dead Edie back from heaven because her time
hadn't come yet. At the time the episode was made, Marianne Faithfull,
an icon of the 1960s and early 1970s, and hence of Edie and Patsy's
generation, was experiencing a comeback, but my interlocutors in England
with teenage daughters tell me she means nothing to them, just as Virginia
Woolf, beginning her comeback in the United States but not Britain,
would have meant nothing to Edie and Patsy when they were Saffie's
age. By 1996, of course, that had changed, and Virginia Woolf was, as
commentators never stop telling us, young woman's icon extraordinaire,
but one who seems unable to help Saffie when, we might think, Saffie
needs her most. Is it because Virginia Woolf has become so "vulnerable"
or "p.c." that she has lost her fighting spirit, her disruptiveness? Or,
rather than Virginia Woolf's forsaking Saffie, has Saffie forsaken Virginia
Woolf, the Virginia Woolf who played so different a role in Rosie's life
in Sammy and Rosie Get Laid? Do we have here a battle of the icons
that pits generation against generation? Or a space where we can explore who or what works for us as we make decisions at every level of
our lives?

24

Nothing is fixed; nothing is frozen. Virginia Woolf and Marilyn Monroe; Virginia Woolf and Marianne Faithfull. Female icons mutate and proliferate, undoing stereotypes, putting us into motion. There is no stable place.

25

One final image, this one a poster sold by a local branch of the Communist Party in Rome, a city once home to a women's center named for Virginia Woolf. Featuring a drawing based on the Beresford profile, the poster also includes words from Woolf's last novel, *Between the Acts: "Che mi ricoprano le acque; le acque del pozzo dei desideri"* ("That the waters should cover me, . . . [the waters] of the wishing well").[18] Spoken by a woman the same age as the century (thirty-nine), wife, mother, and would-be poet, spoken at a moment when Europe was about to embark on another devastating war, the words would seem to suggest the desire for death that soon overtook their writer; Woolf drowned herself shortly after completing the novel. But when they appear on a poster sold during the last decade of the century by an organization that represents political activism, hope, and a future, the words, like Virginia Woolf icon, become unstable: both a warning about what political despair can do to a great writer, and a repository of dreams, a place of wishes. Evoking the realm of the uncanny, where fears and desires are submerged but not erased, the poster presents a Virginia Woolf whose appearances within and between the acts of our cultural performances bestow both a challenge and a promise.

Introduction

1. Lani Guinier, "What I Would've Told the Senate Hearing . . . ," *Houston Chronicle,* 16 June 1993, B11ff.

2. "Strange name, strange hair, strange writings, she's history," was one widely reported headline; other labels included the "Morticia of the legal profession" and "madwoman." She was also reported to be six feet tall. See, e.g., Dale Russakoff, "Lani Guinier Is Still Alive and Talking," *Washington Post Magazine,* 12 December 1993, 14ff.; and Sheryl McCarthy, "SI Finds Wisdom in 'Madwoman' Plan," *Newsday,* 2 March 1994, 26.

3. See Daniel J. Boorstin's definition of the celebrity as a person "known for his well-knownness": *The Image; or, What Happened to the American Dream* (New York: Atheneum, 1962), 57.

4. I am relying on published articles and reviews in this study, rather than audience response surveys. While it would be fascinating to know whether viewers other than reviewers, journalists, and critics recognize Virginia Woolf when she appears, and how they read the presence of her face or her name, that is another project.

5. Wayne Koestenbaum, *Jackie under My Skin: Interpreting an Icon* (New York: Farrar, Straus & Giroux, 1995); Ramona Curry, *Too Much of a Good Thing: Mae West as Cultural Icon* (Minneapolis and London: University of Minnesota Press, 1996); Claudia Roth Pierpont, "The Strong Woman," *New Yorker,* 11 November 1996, 106–18; Paige Baty, *American Monroe: The Making of a Body Politic* (Berkeley: University of California Press, 1995); Michiko Kakutani, "The Commodified Blonde, or, Marilyn as Text," *New York Times Book Review,* 1 August 1995, C17.

Since then other figures have garnered similar attention; the phenomenon is certainly not at an end. In 1998, for example, the *New York Times* noted that "about two dozen scholars across the United States and Canada have trained their gaze" on Martha Stewart, the subject of three books then being considered by academic publishers and, the writer adds, an inheritor of academic attention previously focused on Madonna: Margalit Fox, "In Martha 101, Even Class Anxieties Get Ironed Out," *New York Times,* 1 August 1998, B7, 9.

6. Thomas Hine, "Notable Quotables: Why Images Become Icons," *New York Times,* 18 February 1996, sec. 2, pp. 1, 37.

7. Holly Brubach, "Heroine Worship: The Age of the Female Icon," *New York Times Magazine,* 24 November 1996, 55.

8. William Safire, "Many Icons, Few Iconoclasts," *New York Times Magazine,* 24 November 1996, 42–44.

9. Russell Baker, "The Blathery Gibberish," *New York Times,* 29 April 1997, A23.

10. Brubach, "Heroine Worship," 55. The only other writer to receive an individual entry is Gertrude Stein; the only artist is Frida Kahlo, though there is an entry on the Guerrilla Girls, who "assume the names of dead female artists and writers in their crusade against discrimination in the art world" (97).

11. Russell Baker, "Icon Epidemic Rages," *New York Times,* 24 June 1997, A19.

12. Boorstin, *The Image,* 57.

13. This is both similar to and different from Vincent Cheng's definition of the *"Joycean Unconscious*—a culturally constructed consciousness of Joyce and his texts in the psyche of our mass culture; a collective Joycean Unconscious that exists and operates even within those who . . . have never heard of James Joyce and his works at the conscious level," since it does include Virginia Woolf's name; when people apply the question "who's afraid of . . . ?" to others like Lani Guinier, however, it does constitute a Woolfian cultural unconscious: "The Joycean Unconscious, or Getting Respect in the Real World," in *Joyce and Popular Culture,* ed. R. B. Kershner (Gainesville: University Press of Florida, 1996), 182.

14. Michael Holroyd, *Lytton Strachey: A Critical Biography* (London: Heinemann, 1967; New York: Holt, Rinehart & Winston, 1968).

15. See "Another Version of Virginia Woolf," ed. Madeline Moore, *Women's Studies* 4/2–3 (1977); the essays included came from two conferences: the Virginia Woolf Symposium held at the University of California, Santa Cruz, in November 1974, and the December 1974 Modern Language Association panel called "Another Version of Virginia Woolf: Political, Social, and Feminist Concerns." Olivia Records, a record company founded to produce records by women, provides one nonacademic example of her pervasive presence; the name comes from the statement in *A Room of One's Own* that Chloe liked Olivia.

16. Jeffrey Jerome Cohen, "Monster Culture (Seven Theses)," in *Monster Theory: Reading Culture,* ed. Cohen (Minneapolis and London: University of Minnesota Press, 1996), 4. The concept of the border has other histories besides those I evoke here, recognized by immigrants and articulated by poets, novelists, and academics, including feminist academics, as central to their lived existence.

17. Slavoj Žižek, *Enjoy Your Symptom! Jacques Lacan in Hollywood and Out* (New York and London: Routledge, 1992), 139.

18. The entrance of women into the workforce during the two world wars also contributed to perceptions of and reactions against a feminized society.

19. The launching of Sputnik, the Russian satellite, in 1957 set off shock waves in the West, providing an impetus for the expansion of higher education that occurred during the 1960s; in the United States, National Defense Fellowships sent numerous women through graduate school. For the history, see Barbara Solomon, *In the Company of Educated Women: A History of Women and Higher Education in America* (New Haven: Yale University Press, 1985), 198ff. For an example of the fear, see Walter Ong, *Fighting for Life: Contest, Sexuality, and Consciousness* (Ithaca: Cornell University Press, 1981), 119–48. For the definitions of *feminization* I am acknowledging if not accepting here, see Ann Douglas, *The Feminization of American Culture* (New York: Knopf, 1977); and David Simpson, *The Academic Postmodern and the Rule of Literature* (Chicago and London: University of Chicago Press, 1995), 92–110ff. Simpson associates feminization with literature and its study.

20. Margaret Ferguson and Jennifer Wicke, "Introduction: Feminism and Postmodernism; or, The Way We Live Now," in *Feminism and Postmodernism,* ed. Ferguson and Wicke, Special Issue of *Boundary 2* 19 (summer 1992): 2.

21. While race is often implicit in the construction of the monstrous other, even when couched in terms of gender/sexuality or class, race is the absent term in most readings of Virginia Woolf's iconic meanings, surfacing mainly in analyses of her relationship to imperialism and to "Jewishness." Alice Walker provides one striking exception, rewriting Virginia Woolf's *A Room of One's Own* for "womanism" in the title essay in *In Search of Our Mothers' Gardens* (San Diego: Harcourt Brace Jovanovich, 1983), 231–43. For the overlap of categories in the figure of the monster, see Cohen, "Monster Culture (Seven Theses)," 7–12, 15; and Judith Halberstam, *Skin Shows: Gothic Horror and the Technology of Monsters* (Durham and London: Duke University Press, 1995), 6–7ff.

22. Andreas Huyssen, "Mass Culture as Woman: Modernism's Other," in *Studies in Entertainment: Critical Approaches to Mass Culture,* ed. Tania Modleski (Bloomington: Indiana University Press, 1986), 198. See also Tania Modleski, "Femininity as Mas(s)querade," in *Feminism without Women: Culture and Criticism in a "Postfeminist" Age* (New York: Routledge, 1991), 23–34.

23. R. B. Kershner, "Introduction," in *Joyce and Popular Culture,* 6. Recently scholars have begun to question this distinction within modernism. For revisionary readings of Woolf and the gender/culture divide, see, e.g., Lois Cucullu, "Retailing the Female Intellectual," *differences* 9 (summer 1997): 25–68; and Jane Garrity, "Dodging 'Intellectual Harlotry': Virginia Woolf in 1920s British *Vogue,*" in *Virginia Woolf in the Age of Mechanical Reproduction,* ed. Pamela Caughie (New York: Garland, 1999).

24. Stuart Hall, "Notes on Deconstructing 'The Popular,' " in *People's History*

and Socialist Theory, ed. Raphael Samuel (London: Routledge & Kegan Paul, 1981), 228.

25. Donald Reiman, *Romantic Texts and Contexts* (Columbia: University of Missouri Press, 1987), 169.

26. D. C. Greetham, *Textual Scholarship: An Introduction* (New York: Garland, 1992), 341–42.

27. Nathaniel Mackey, "Other: From Noun to Verb," *Representations* 39 (summer 1992): 52.

28. Dick Hebdige, *Cut 'n' Mix: Culture, Identity, and Caribbean Music* (London and New York: Routledge, 1987), 12, 11, 14.

29. Mackey, "Other," 53, 52–53, 51–52. Building on Mackey's work, Alice Gambrell has explored what it meant for women intellectuals during the 1930s and early 1940s "to work within the boundaries of schools, movements, or disciplines in which, under more usual circumstances, they would have occupied the position of 'Other.' " Her emphasis is on the versioning produced by the continual acts of textual self-revision practiced by Frida Kahlo, Leonora Carrington, Ella Deloria, Zora Neale Hurston, and H.D., a sign of "the overbearing presence of powerful determining forces" that versioning both registers and partially undermines: *Women Intellectuals, Modernism, and Difference: Transatlantic Culture, 1919–1945* (Cambridge: Cambridge University Press, 1997), 1, 33–34.

30. Hall, "Notes on Deconstructing 'The Popular,' " 235, 228.

31. Michel Foucault, "What Is an Author?" trans. Josué V. Harari (1979), in *The Foucault Reader,* ed. Paul Rabinow (New York: Pantheon, 1984), 119.

32. Jane M. Gaines, *Contested Culture: The Image, the Voice, and the Law* (Chapel Hill: University of North Carolina Press, 1991), 178, 202.

33. Richard Dyer, *Stars* (1979) (London: BFI, 1990), 1–3. In contrast to this distinctly textual and conflictual rendering of the star, Wayne Koestenbaum's introduction to "icon Jackie" presents her as a fact of nature: "We called Jackie an icon because she glowed, because she seemed ceaseless, because she resided in a worshipped, aura-filled niche. We called Jackie an icon because her image was frequently and influentially reproduced, and because, even when she was alive, she seemed more mythic than real. We called Jackie an icon because her story provided a foundation for our own stories, and because her face, and the sometimes glamorous, sometimes tragic turns her life took, were lodged in our systems of thought and reference, as if she were a concept, a numeral, a virtue, or a universal tendency, like rainfall or drought" (*Jackie under My Skin,* 4).

34. Dyer, *Stars,* 72. For queer readings, see, e.g., Alexander Doty, *Making Things Perfectly Queer: Interpreting Mass Culture* (Minneapolis: University of Minnesota Press, 1993); and Corey K. Creekmur and Alexander Doty, eds., *Out in Culture: Gay, Lesbian, and Queer Essays on Popular Culture* (Durham: Duke University Press, 1995).

35. Dyer, *Stars,* 72; *Heavenly Bodies: Film Stars and Society* (New York: St. Martin's Press, 1986), 3.

36. Dyer, *Stars,* 38.

37. On the historical dichotomy of word and image, see W. J. T. Mitchell, *Iconology: Image, Text, Ideology* (Chicago: University of Chicago Press, 1986); on the association of women and/or the feminine with spectacle and the grotesque, see Mary Russo, *The Female Grotesque: Risk, Excess and Modernity* (New York: Routledge, 1994).

38. In Boorstin's definition, "the hero was distinguished by his achievement; the celebrity by his image or trademark. The hero created himself; the celebrity is created by the media. The hero was a big man; the celebrity is a big name" (*The Image*, 61).

39. Michael M. Thomas, "Once We Had Real Heroes; Now There Are Only Stars . . . ," *New York Observer*, 22 September 1997, 1, 34.

40. Quoted in *Celebrating Our Heroes, Life: Collector's Edition*, 1997, 6.

41. Theodore L. Gross, ed., *Representative Men: Cult Heroes of Our Time* (New York: Free Press, 1970); Richard Schickel, *Intimate Strangers: The Culture of Celebrity* (New York: Fromm International, 1986), 118–79; Marshall Fishwick, "Introduction," in *Icons of America*, ed. Ray B. Browne and Marshall Fishwick (Bowling Green: Popular Press, 1978), 3–12.

42. John Rodden, *The Politics of Literary Reputation: The Making and Claiming of 'St. George' Orwell* (New York and Oxford: Oxford University Press, 1989), 9–10.

43. Ibid., 225; Joanna Russ, "What Can a Heroine Do? Or Why Women Can't Write," in *Images of Women in Fiction: Feminist Perspectives*, ed. Susan Koppelman Cornillon (Bowling Green: Bowling Green University Popular Press, 1972), 8. For another now classic treatment of this subject, see Teresa de Lauretis's chapter "Desire in Narrative" in *Alice Doesn't: Feminism Semiotics Cinema* (Bloomington: Indiana University Press, 1984), 103–57.

44. Toril Moi, *Simone de Beauvoir: The Making of an Intellectual Woman* (Oxford: Blackwell, 1994), 10–12, 74–75.

45. See, for example, Dyer's reading of stars as social types, premised on Orrin E. Klapp's *Heroes, Villains and Fools* (*Stars*, 53ff.). Dyer's comments on Klapp's typography anticipate my reading of where women appear in such studies: not as heroes but as pin-ups (57).

46. See Judith Butler, *Bodies That Matter: On the Discursive Limits of "Sex"* (New York: Routledge, 1993), 2–3 and ff.

47. Dyer, *Heavenly Bodies*, 5; *Stars*, 184.

48. Rodden, *The Politics of Literary Reputation*, 69.

49. Susan Koppelman Cornillon, "Introduction," in *Images of Women in Fiction*, ix. The contributors, she adds, range from those who "haven't gone in formal education beyond high school" to those with Ph.Ds; and the articles are drawn from academic journals as well as countercultural feminist journals. For a reading of the significance of this anthology, see Jane Gallop, "Heroic Images: Feminist Criticism, 1972," *American Literary History* 1 (fall 1989): 612–36.

50. Helen Dudar, "The Virginia Woolf Cult," *Saturday Review*, February 1982, 32.

51. Boorstin, *The Image,* 162, 13, 50. For one pertinent reading of the ambiguous desire for European models, see Andrew Ross, *No Respect: Intellectuals and Popular Culture* (New York: Routledge, 1989), 42–64.

52. On the *Luftmensch* and his opposite, see Bruce Robbins, *Secular Vocations: Intellectuals, Professionalism, Culture* (London and New York: Verso, 1993), 7–10; see also his introduction to *Intellectuals: Aesthetics, Politics, Academics* (Minneapolis: University of Minnesota Press, 1990), ix–xxvii. Among the works he is responding to is Russell Jacoby's *The Last Intellectuals: American Culture in the Age of Academe* (New York: Basic Books, 1987). When women transcend their bodies, it has traditionally been not through their intellects but through their souls, and the result is usually death; see, e.g., Marianne Hirsch, "Spiritual *Bildung:* The Beautiful Soul as Paradigm," in *The Voyage In: Fictions of Female Development,* ed. Elizabeth Abel, Marianne Hirsch, and Elizabeth Langland (Hanover, N.H.: University Press of New England, 1983), 23–48. For the issues raised by women as aerialists, including Amelia Earhart, and the larger question of transcendence and weightedness, see Russo, *The Female Grotesque,* 17–51.

53. Robbins, *Secular Vocations,* 13. See also Lynn Garafola's review of *The Last Intellectuals* in *New Left Review* 169 (May–June 1988): 122–28.

54. See Robbins, *Secular Vocations,* 23.

55. For Rachel Bowlby's original formulation of a mobile Virginia Woolf, see *Virginia Woolf: Feminist Destinations* (Oxford: Blackwell, 1988), 12–14; for her reading of its association with French theory, see "Preface," in *Feminist Destinations and Further Essays on Virginia Woolf* (Edinburgh: Edinburgh University Press, 1997), vi. On the dangers for feminist criticism of fixing Virginia Woolf into any single position, see Bette London, "Guerrilla in Petticoats or Sans-Culotte? Virginia Woolf and the Future of Feminist Criticism," *Diacritics* 21/2–3 (summer–fall 1991): 11–29.

56. Bowlby, *Feminist Destinations and Further Essays on Virginia Woolf,* vii; Hall, "Notes on Deconstructing 'The Popular,' " 235.

57. Gaines, *Contested Culture,* 33.

58. Baty, *American Monroe,* 13, 38.

59. Gaines, *Contested Culture,* 35.

60. For the evocation of barbarism and its various manifestations in these battles over critical standards, see Barbara Herrnstein Smith, *Contingencies of Value: Alternative Perspectives for Critical Theory* (Cambridge: Harvard University Press, 1988), 40–41.

61. See Brenda R. Silver, "The Authority of Anger: *Three Guineas* as Case Study," *Signs* 16 (winter 1991): 340–70, which tracks the shift from the 1960s denigration of Woolf's anger to the denigration of her feminist critics.

62. I have made no attempt to include all of her appearances in mass/popular cultural productions or all of the cultural productions based on her writings or her life. She has, for example, an entirely other existence in the music world—ranging from Dominique Argento's oratorio based on *A Writer's Diary* and the opera *Mrs. Dalloway* by Libby Larsen and Bonnie Grice to jazz singer Patricia Barber's song

based on a phrase from "The Mark on the Wall" to Indigo Girls' songs—that is absent from this study. A wide array of Virginia Woolf sightings across the media appears in the *Virginia Woolf Miscellany* (see, e.g., 41 [fall 1993]), and on the website "Passing Glances," <http://metalab.unc.edu/sally/passing_glances.html>.

63. Dyer, *Stars,* 68.

64. The figure was created for the opening of the Hardback Café in Chapel Hill, North Carolina, during the late 1980s.

Part One

1. "Leading Feminist Critic Quits Post at Columbia University," *Chronicle of Higher Education,* 20 May 1992, A13.

2. On June 14, 1994, Limbaugh called Christina Hoff Sommers's *Who Stole Feminism? How Women Have Betrayed Women* (New York: Simon & Schuster, 1994) a "brave and courageous book," one of many plugs. Sommers herself acknowledges "the gracious and generous support" (8) of several conservative foundations for the writing of her book; according to their records, she received at least $164,000 between 1991 and 1993. Sommers is also active in the Boston chapter of the National Association of Scholars (NAS), funded by these same organizations, whose agenda is to undo what they see as the negative effects of multiculturalism and feminism on scholarship and the curriculum. For the Limbaugh quote and the figures, see Laura Flanders, *Real Majority, Media Minority: The Cost of Sidelining Women in Reporting* (Monroe, Maine: Common Courage Press, 1997), 144–47; on Sommers and/or the NAS, see Elaine Ginsberg and Sara Lennox, "Antifeminism in Scholarship and Publishing," and Moira Ferguson, Ketu H. Katrak, and Valerie Miner, "Feminism and Antifeminism: From Civil Rights to Culture Wars," in *Anti-Feminism in the Academy,* ed. Vèvè Clark, Shirley Nelson Garner, Margaret Higonnet, and Ketu H. Katrak (New York: Routledge, 1996), 186–89, 53–56.

3. Sommers, *Who Stole Feminism?* 19–22.

4. Daniel Cottom, "The War of Tradition: Virginia Woolf and the Temper of Criticism," in *Ravishing Tradition: Cultural Forces and Literary History* (Ithaca: Cornell University Press, 1996), 147; hereafter cited in text.

5. For the phrase "media spectacle," see Dana Polan, "The Spectacle of Intellect in a Media Age: Cultural Representations and the David Abraham, Paul de Man, and Victor Farías Cases," in *Intellectuals,* ed. Robbins, 343–64. I make no attempt here to rehearse in their entirety the debates surrounding the "culture wars" that raged during the late 1980s and early 1990s, or the more insidious attacks on the economic accountability of colleges and universities that followed. My focus remains Virginia Woolf's symptomatic appearances within them.

6. Lynn Garafola, "The Last Intellectuals," *New Left Review* 169 (May–June 1988): 125; the term "influential" comes from Jacoby's *The Last Intellectuals.*

7. Writing of statistics gathered by the monitoring group Women, Men, and Media on "the symbolic annihilation of women" in the media, Flanders notes,

"When the question 'how many women' is followed by 'which ones,' it's clear that some women are more 'symbolically annihilated' than others"—i.e., progressive, often feminist women: *Real Majority,* 132–33.

8. Ellen Rooney, "What's the Story? Feminist Theory, Narrative, Address," *differences* 8 (spring 1996): 1–30; hereafter cited in text.

9. The left media are as implicated in this process as those on the right; see, e.g., Flanders, *Real Majority,* 202–5; see also the exchange between Katha Pollitt et al. and Victor Navasky in the *Nation* over a special issue on travel that included no women writers: 27 October 1997, 2.

10. Carolyn G. Heilbrun, *Toward a Recognition of Androgyny* (New York: Knopf, 1973); *Writing a Woman's Life* (New York: Norton, 1988).

11. For Polan, see n. 5 above. With the exception of the *New York Times,* the *Chronicle of Higher Education* is the one publication that covered both Heilbrun's resignation and the conference: see n. 1 above and Courtney Leatherman, " 'Isolation' of Pioneering Feminist Scholar Stirs Reappraisal of Women's Status in Academe," *Chronicle of Higher Education,* 11 November 1992, A17–18. A Nexus search on the topic retrieved an article in the *Los Angeles Times Magazine* and short pieces in the *Washington Post,* the *Guardian,* and *U.S. News and World Report.*

12. For a history of the intersecting attacks on feminism and multiculturalism in the academy and out, see Ferguson et al., "Feminism and Antifeminism," 35–66.

13. David Denby, *Great Books: My Adventures with Homer, Rousseau, Woolf, and Other Indestructible Writers of the Western World* (New York: Simon & Schuster, 1996), 450, 456. Denby does acknowledge the broader historical resonances of *To the Lighthouse* but does not explore the range or specificity of its social/cultural critique or the ways in which for Woolf the private and public spheres are always already inseparably connected.

14. Ibid., 445–46.

15. John Guillory, *Cultural Capital: The Problem of Literary Canon Formation* (Chicago and London: University of Chicago Press, 1993), 40–41.

16. Virginia Woolf, *A Room of One's Own* (1929) (New York: Harcourt Brace Jovanovich, 1981), 32.

17. For Michael Rosenthal's diatribe, see *Virginia Woolf* (New York: Columbia University Press, 1979), 36, 242–43; on Heilbrun, see Kay Mills, "Life after a Tenured Position," *Los Angeles Times Magazine,* 19 July 1992, 13. Robert Hanning, also a member of the Columbia English Department, provides this comment: "Columbia has always been very, very, very male. If you were the good son, you got ahead, you received the mantle of power. The model allows no room for women, and to suggest it might has always elicited varying degrees of Olympian disdain and scorn. Yes, feminism threatens all that": cited in Anne Matthews, "Rage in a Tenured Position," *New York Times Magazine,* 8 November 1992, 73.

18. Timothy Cross, *An Oasis of Order: The Core Curriculum at Columbia College* (New York: Trustees of Columbia University, Office of the Dean, 1995), 110, 116. Woolf's admission in 1990 owes as much to the decision to include twentieth-century writers as to gender; she is one of several options.

19. Carolyn Heilbrun, "The Politics of Mind: Women, Tradition, and the University," in *Hamlet's Mother and Other Women* (New York: Columbia University Press, 1990), 213; Mills, "Life after a Tenured Position," 14.

20. Nancy K. Miller, "Parables and Politics: Feminist Criticism in 1986," in *Getting Personal: Feminist Occasions and Other Autobiographical Acts* (New York and London: Routledge, 1991), 61.

21. Ibid., 70.

22. Quoted in Miller, "Parables and Politics," 70.

23. On the subject of the continued existence of antifeminism in the academy, including that directed toward feminist scholarship, see Clark et al., *Anti-Feminism in the Academy.*

24. Sven Birkerts, *The Gutenberg Elegies: The Fate of Reading in an Electronic Age* (New York: Fawcett Columbine, 1994), 11.

25. Guillory, *Cultural Capital,* 340. In his preface Guillory explains his choice of topics as an attempt to redirect the debate from "who is in or out of the canon to the question of the canonical *form* in its social and institutional contexts," an argument that then separates "social bias" from "aesthetic judgment" and comes down in favor of the latter (xiii).

26. Helen Vendler, "The Booby Trap," *New Republic,* 7 October 1996, 34–40.

27. In 1992 Gerald Graff suggested that the negative publicity could "create an opportunity . . . for the accused to tell their side of the story to an audience that otherwise would not hear it," that it might create "a new public scene": "Academic Writing and the Uses of Bad Publicity," *South Atlantic Quarterly* 91/1 (winter 1992): 5–17. For the backtalk, see, e.g., Scott Heller, "Humanists Renew Public Intellectual Tradition, Answer Criticism," and "In Effort to Reach Broader Audience, Scholars Ask: What Is the Public?" *Chronicle of Higher Education,* 7 April 1993, A6–7, 12–13; Michael Bérubé and Cary Nelson, *Higher Education under Fire: Politics, Economics, and the Crisis of the Humanities* (New York: Routledge, 1995); and the essays in *Profession 1996* (New York: Modern Language Association of America, 1996).

28. Joyce Carol Oates, "Back to School," *New York Times Book Review,* 1 September 1996, 10. Christopher Lehmann-Haupt comments that if literature were all that were at stake, the title would be followed by an exclamation point, and that Denby ends up "moderately to the right" in what are political, not literary, battles: "Book of the Times," *New York Times,* 16 September 1996, C14. See also Norman Podhoretz, "Liberalism and the Culture: A Turning of the Tide?" *Commentary,* October 1996, 25–32.

29. Oates, "Back to School," 10; Roger Kimball, "David Denby Goes to School," *New Criterion,* November 1996, 14. See also Podhoretz, "Liberalism and the Culture," 28.

30. Robbins, *Intellectuals,* xiii, xvii.

31. Many writers make this point; see, e.g., W. J. T. Mitchell, "The Violence of Public Art: *Do the Right Thing*," *Critical Inquiry* 16 (summer 1990): 886–87; and Nancy Fraser, "Rethinking the Public Sphere: A Contribution to

the Critique of Actually Existing Democracy," *Social Text* 25/26 (1990): 59–69.

32. Fraser, "Rethinking the Public Sphere," 58–59.

33. Mitchell, "The Violence of Public Art," 886.

34. Janice Radway, "On the Gender of the Middlebrow Consumer and the Threat of the Culturally Fraudulent Female," *South Atlantic Quarterly* 93 (fall 1994): 884; Radway is quoting Michael Warner, "The Mass Public and the Mass Subject," in *Habermas and the Public Sphere,* ed. Craig Calhoun (Cambridge: Harvard University Press, 1992), 382.

35. Garafola, "The Last Intellectuals," 125.

36. Harvey Teres, *Renewing the Left: Politics, Imagination, and the New York Intellectuals* (New York: Oxford University Press, 1996), 173–77. Teres does an extended analysis of both the role of women within the group—including Hannah Arendt, Tess Schlesinger, Diana Trilling, Mary McCarthy, Susan Sontag, and Midge Decter—and the absence of any consideration of women and/or gender in writings about the group. The latter is grounded in a numerical analysis of how many times women appear and in what contexts in books written about the group (e.g., how many get chapters of their own: none), as well as their appearances in the indexes of *Partisan Review* and the *New York Review of Books.*

37. Ibid., 177.

38. Edwin McDowell, "Women at PEN Caucus Demand a Greater Role," *New York Times,* 17 January 1986; quoted in Elaine Showalter's analysis of the Dark Lady in *Sister's Choice: Tradition and Change in American Women's Writing* (Oxford: Clarendon, 1991), 23.

39. Teres, *Renewing the Left,* 177.

40. Quoted in Alan M. Wald, *The New York Intellectuals: The Rise and Decline of the Anti-Stalinist Left from the 1930s to the 1980s* (Chapel Hill: University of North Carolina Press, 1987), 40.

41. Teres, *Renewing the Left,* 178.

42. In an interview published in *Playboy,* Oates talks disparagingly of appearing in lists of " 'women's novels' . . . along with women who write about romantic experiences or domestic life or children. And my real kinship would be with someone in the realistic-novel category who's a man": "Playboy Interview: Joyce Carol Oates," *Playboy,* November 1993, 66.

43. Leslie Fiedler, "The New Mutants," in *The Collected Essays of Leslie Fiedler,* vol. 2 (New York: Stein & Day, 1971), 386, 390, 391, 393, 395, 397; the essay originated as a talk given at a conference sponsored by *Partisan Review.*

44. Jacoby, *The Last Intellectuals,* 14, 141.

45. Robbins, *Secular Vocations,* 11; for the Woolf quote, see *Three Guineas* (1938) (New York: Harcourt Brace Jovanovich, 1966), 86. Robbins arrives at Woolf through his argument that to separate the debased world of "work" from the "home," the site of the disembodied *Luftmensch,* is to ignore the gendered realities of who does the work at home; Woolf, he says, recognized that those inside and outside the home were equally embodied and grounded.

46. Frank Kermode, "The Pleasure of the Text," *NYRB,* 19 September 1996, 31–33.

47. Nicolas Von Hoffman, "Q: Who's Not Afraid of Virginia Woolf?" *New York Observer,* 11 October 1993, 17.

48. The history of the *NYRB* has been told repeatedly. In 1973, ten years after its beginnings, Philip Nobile wrote *Intellectual Skywriting: Literary Politics and the New York Review of Books* (New York: Charterhouse, 1974); another good source is Stephen Fender, "The New York Review of Books," *Yearbook of English Studies* 16 (1986): 188–202.

49. Joseph Epstein, "Thirty Years of the 'New York Review,' " *Commentary,* December 1993, 43; hereafter cited in text.

50. Fender, "New York Review," 189.

51. Epstein is not quite accurate about the noncoverage of popular culture; Miriam Horn's article on the thirtieth anniversary notes that it has recently included "David Remnick on John le Carré, Stephen Jay Gould on *Jurassic Park* and an upcoming piece on Nintendo. 'We should be doing a much better job covering mass culture,' worries [Robert] Silvers," its coeditor: "The Aging of a Literary Firebrand: Does America's Leading Intellectual Journal Still Influence Attitudes and Public Life?" *U.S. News and World Report,* 25 October 1993, 60.

52. "Gay or gay," one friend commented about this ad, indicating how close queer readings are to our cultural surface, despite conservative policing.

53. According to a longtime editor at *NYRB,* the ads were a response to what proved most effective in attracting subscribers at any particular moment; even in Virginia Woolf's heyday, other figures were used as well.

54. Tom Wolfe, "Radical Chic," *New York,* 8 June 1970, 54.

55. Quoted in Von Hoffman, "Q: Who's Not Afraid of Virginia Woolf?" 17. Fender argues that the British reviewers were consigned to "a sort of 'back of the book,' " where they wrote about "subjects deemed (by many American readers, anyway) to be safely uncontroversial: the classics, European history, the history of art, English literature, and literary biography" ("New York Review," 193).

56. Jacoby, *The Last Intellectuals,* 219; according to another source, the editors explained this preference by noting "that the British are particularly talented at writing intellectual essays for a popular, well-educated audience": David Blum, "Literary Lotto," *New York,* 21 January 1985, 40. In 1998 John Updike's alter ego Bech recalled a negative review by the English critic Featherwaite in "the ravingly anglophile *New York Review of Books,*" as Updike's English reviewer noted in his *NYRB* review: David Lodge, "Bye-Bye Bech," *NYRB,* 19 November 1998, 10.

57. Fender, "New York Review," 198.

58. Noel Annan, *Leslie Stephen: The Godless Victorian* (New York: Random House, 1984), 3.

59. Von Hoffman, "Q: Who's Not Afraid of Virginia Woolf?" 17.

60. Quentin Bell, "Who's Afraid for Virginia Woolf?" *NYRB,* 15 March 1990, 3–4, 6. The journal's practice was apparent from the beginning; see, e.g., Nobile, who records the scarcity of women writing regularly for the journal in its early

years and the habit of getting men to review works by women and/or feminists
(*Intellectual Skywriting*, 189, 119); and Teres, who estimates that only 8.9 percent
of the articles written between 1963 and 1992 were by women (*Renewing the Left*,
177).

61. Stuart Hampshire, "In Praise of Virginia Woolf," *NYRB*, 22 September
1966, 3.

62. Elizabeth Hardwick, "Bloomsbury and Virginia Woolf," *NYRB*, 8 February
1973, 15–18. Hardwick's slighting of Bell's biography stands in sharp contrast to
its eager anticipation in earlier *NYRB* essays.

63. For a fuller view of Hardwick's ambivalences, see her collection of essays
on women writers and characters, *Seduction and Betrayal: Women and Literature*
(New York: Random House, 1974), where the essay on Woolf is reprinted in the
section titled "Victims and Victors."

64. Both passages are quoted in Teres, *Renewing the Left*, 179, 178.

65. Noel Annan, "Virginia Woolf Fever," *NYRB*, 20 April 1978, 16–28; Frank
Kermode, "Yes, Santa, There Is a Virginia," *NYRB*, 21 December 1978, 31–32.

66. Annan, "Virginia Woolf Fever," 16, 27.

67. Rosemary Dinnage, "The Last Act," *NYRB*, 8 November 1984, 3.

68. Noel Annan, "A Very Queer Gentleman," *NYRB*, 6 June 1968, 11.

69. Annan, "Virginia Woolf Fever," 28.

70. Gertrude Himmelfarb, *Marriage and Morals among the Victorians* (New
York: Knopf, 1986), 3.

71. Jonathan Arac, "Peculiarities of (the) English in the Metanarrative(s) of
Knowledge and Power," in *Intellectuals*, ed. Robbins, 190.

72. For one version of this argument, see would-be *Luftmensch* James Atlas's
lightweight contribution to the culture wars, *Battle of the Books: The Curriculum
Debate in America;* in his penultimate chapter, "The End of Tradition," he adduces
envy of the self-enclosed structure of British "cultural inheritance," says that it's
harder in America, where "our literature, like our political tradition, is essentially
democratic," and then delineates an American tradition that consists entirely of
writers and works located squarely within a white, male, European tradition ([New
York: Norton, 1990], 103ff.).

73. Quoted in Fender, "New York Review," 191–92; Vonnegut attributes the
distinction between artists who respond to either history or life to Saul Steinberg.

74. Diana Trilling, *Claremont Essays* (New York: Harcourt, Brace & World,
1962), vii–ix. In her critique of Jacoby's *The Last Intellectuals*, Garafola notes
that he is less interested in ideas than in "the geography of intellect" ("The Last
Intellectuals," 128), a term that might well apply to Trilling and the New York
intellectuals in general.

75. Nicolas Lemann, "America's Bloomsbury," *Washington Monthly*, November 1986, 51.

76. See, for example, Fraser, "Rethinking the Public Sphere," 60–61. The question is, where to find them. Some, including Garafola, note that it's partly a question
of what journals you evoke; her offerings in 1988 included the *Village Voice, Mother*

Jones, Commonweal, the *Progressive, In These Times, Cineaste, October, Art in America, Dissent, Grand Street, Raritan, Signs, Ms.,* the *Advocate,* the *Drama Review,* and *Performing Arts Journal* as places to look for writers and topics other than those traditionally considered "intellectual" (125). Others, like Rita Felski, have argued that the university today constitutes—or should constitute—a major counter-public site: *Beyond Feminist Aesthetics: Feminist Literature and Social Change* (Cambridge: Harvard University Press, 1989), 164–74. See also the essays in Bruce Robbins, ed., *The Phantom Public Sphere* (Minneapolis: University of Minnesota Press, 1993); and Amitava Kumar, ed., *Class Issues: Pedagogy, Cultural Studies, and the Public Sphere* (New York: New York University Press, 1997).

77. Heller, "In Effort to Reach Broader Audience . . . ," A13.

78. J. Hillis Miller, "Forum," *PMLA* 112/5 (October 1997): 1138; for the full discussion, see 1121–41, noting in particular the letters grouped under the heading "Today, Tomorrow: The Intellectual in the Academy and in Society."

79. Conversation with Linda Gardiner, editor of the *Women's Review of Books,* March 1997; her goal was to reproduce the livelier and more opinionated London journal, with its broader mix of academics and nonacademics. For an analysis of the different positions occupied by academics and/or intellectuals in the United States and Britain, see David Simpson, "New Brooms at Fawlty Towers: Colin MacCabe and Cambridge English," in *Intellectuals,* ed. Robbins, 245–71, esp. 266ff.

80. Michael Holroyd, "Mrs Webb and Mrs Woolf," *LRB,* 7 November 1985, 17–19; Peter Wollen, "Wild Hearts," *LRB,* 6 April 1995, 28–29; Jacqueline Rose, "Smashing the Teapots," *LRB,* 23 January 1997, 3, 6–7.

81. Virginia Woolf hasn't totally gone; one omnibus ad offered T-shirts of Freud, Bill Clinton, Hillary Clinton, Virginia Woolf, Shakespeare, Bandit, and Beatrix Potter (19 September 1996).

82. Rose, "Smashing the Teapots"; Carolyn G. Heilbrun, "A Life of Heroism," *WRB,* June 1997, 1, 3–4.

83. Dinnage, "The Last Act," 3; "The Whirr of Wings," *NYRB,* 29 May 1997, 4. Dinnage ignores the fact that the *NYRB* was already selling its own T-shirts by 1984.

84. The quotation, attributed to Kenneth M. Harden, who took over sales of *GBWW* in 1954, is cited by Dwight MacDonald in "The Hard Sell," an appendix to his essay on *GBWW,* "The Book-of-the-Millennium Club," in *Against the American Grain* (New York: Random House, 1962), 259.

85. For an analysis of the scarcity of progressive women in the media, see Flanders, *Real Majority,* 132–34.

86. Katha Pollitt, "Why We Read: Canon to the Right of Me . . ." (1991), in *Reasonable Creatures* (New York: Vintage, 1995), 16, 19, 17, 19–20.

87. Ibid., 18.

88. Guillory, *Cultural Capital,* 7–8.

89. Joan Shelley Rubin, *The Making of Middlebrow Culture* (Chapel Hill: University of North Carolina Press, 1992), 175; Rubin's chapter "Classics and Commercials: John Erskine and 'Great Books' " explores the social/cultural factors

at work in the construction of Columbia's core curriculum, including class, and the cultural capital it granted (164–78).

90. Denby, *Great Books,* 14.

91. Virginia Woolf, "Middlebrow" (1942), in *Collected Essays,* vol. 2 (New York: Harcourt, Brace & World, 1967), 203.

92. Russell Lynes, "Highbrow, Lowbrow, Middlebrow" (1949); reprinted in *The Tastemakers* (New York: Harper and Brothers, 1954), 310–33, esp. 320. For the history that links Woolf to later discussions of the middlebrow, see Rubin, *Making of Middlebrow Culture,* xvi.

93. Woolf, "Middlebrow," 196, 197, 199.

94. MacDonald, *Against the American Grain,* 37, 255, xi–xii, x.

95. Ibid., 20, 62–63, 70. See also Ross, *No Respect,* 55–64.

96. Lynes mentions only Edith Wharton and Maggie Teyte, a singer of French " 'art songs' " (316). In contrast, Pierre Bourdieu uses Woolf's essay "Mr. Bennett and Mrs. Brown" to illustrate the aristocratic concept of "aesthetic distancing" associated with high art and high culture: "The Aristocracy of Culture," in *Distinction: A Social Critique of the Judgement of Taste* (Cambridge: Harvard University Press, 1984), 34–35.

97. Radway, "Gender of the Middlebrow Consumer," 881, 883. For a reading of Woolf's own deconstruction of the masculine versus feminine, producer versus consumer divide, see Cucullu, "Retailing the Female Intellectual," 25–68, esp. 43–48.

98. Radway, "Gender of the Middlebrow Consumer," 884, 883.

99. Marjorie Garber, *Symptoms of Culture* (New York: Routledge, 1998), 17–43; on the ideology of greatness, see also Ross, *No Respect,* 59ff. My reference to the "curtain of objectivity" comes from Garber's reading of *The Wizard of Oz;* other sites where she explores "greatness" as "an effect of mimesis" include baseball, presidential elections, and *GBWW.* Garber has no illusions about the "prize giving" aspect of such lists, wherever they occur, illustrating in detail how "the ideology of 'greatness'—an ideology that claims, precisely, to transcend ideological concerns and to locate the timeless and enduring, the fit candidates, though few, for a Hall of Fame, whether in sports or in arts and letters—is . . . secured" (27).

100. Quoted in Garber, *Symptoms of Culture,* 29, 31.

101. Mortimer Adler, *Reforming Education: The Opening of the American Mind,* ed. Geraldine Van Doren (New York: Macmillan, 1988), 320. When the revised edition appeared in 1990 with four women and no writers of color, Adler went on the offensive, defining his criteria: that it be "pertinent to contemporary life, . . . worth rereading many times and . . . contain a certain number of ideas"; that it be " 'contemporary in any century, endlessly rereadable, and relevant to the Great Ideas' "—i.e., the Syntopicon of "Great Ideas" that introduces and dominates the work. See Elizabeth Venant, "A Curmudgeon Stands His Ground," *Los Angeles Times,* 3 December 1990, E1; and John Blades, "Expanded 'Great Books' Sure to Open Great Debate," *Chicago Tribune,* 25 October 1990, C1. Having established this tautological definition, Adler then argues that "there are no 'Great Books' by

black writers before the 1955 cutoff"; "there are good books by blacks—about 10—that are worth reading for one or two ideas and they are in the Syntopicon" (quoted in Blades). See also Michelle McCalope, "Blacks Furious over Exclusion from New Great Books of the Western World," *Jet,* 19 November 1990, 14.

102. Boorstin, *The Image,* 163–64.

103. In 1998 Boorstin was one of the selectors of the Modern Library's list of the one hundred greatest English-language books of the twentieth century, a list that even its sponsor, Random House, which publishes the Modern Library, acknowledged had commercial origins (it supplied the longer list to choose from and planned to issue all one hundred books in the Modern Library). As numerous articles revealed, the selectors were 100 percent white, 90 percent male (one woman), and had an average age of 68.7; not surprisingly, the list included only nine books by women and four published after 1975. Woolf's *To the Lighthouse,* the highest-ranking novel by a woman, was number fifteen. See David Streitfeld, "How the '100 Best Novels' Got on the List," *Valley News,* 6 August 1998, A1, 6; Louis Menand, "Novels We Love," *New Yorker,* 3 August 1998, 4–5; Katha Pollitt, "Masterpiece Theatre," *Nation,* 24–31 August 1998, 9.

104. Adler, *Reforming Education,* 346–49.

105. On *Flush*'s history and its (postmodern) undoing of cultural categories, see Pamela L. Caughie, *Virginia Woolf and Postmodernism: Literature in Quest and Question of Itself* (Urbana and Chicago: University of Illinois Press, 1991), 143–68.

106. For a history of the *New York Herald Tribune Books* section and the *New York Evening Post*'s *Saturday Review of Books,* the two venues most associated with this middle ground, see Rubin, *Making of Middlebrow Culture,* 35–42.

107. Stuart P. Sherman, "An Uncommon Essayist to the Common Reader," *New York Herald Tribune Books,* 5 July 1925, 1–2.

108. Virginia Woolf, "Poetry, Fiction and the Future," *New York Herald Tribune Books,* 14 August 1927, 1, 6–7, and 21 August 1927, 1, 6. Earlier Woolf had published the first version of her influential essay "Mr. Bennett and Mrs. Brown" in the *Evening Post* (17 November 1923) and a revised version in the *Tribune Books* (23 August 1925, sec. 5, pp. 1–3, and 30 August 1925, sec. 5, pp. 1–4). These were Woolf's two major middlebrow outlets in the United States; more often she appeared here in "highbrow" journals such as the *New Republic,* the *Yale Review,* and *Atlantic Monthly.*

109. An entry for *The Years* in a 1998 rare-book catalog described it as a "potboiler": Ulysses. *Catalogue Seventy: Modern First Editions.* London (October 1998): 100, item 683.

Part Two

TAKE ONE

1. Robert T. Elson, *Time Inc.: The Intimate History of a Publishing Enterprise, 1923–1941,* ed. Duncan Norton-Taylor (New York: Atheneum, 1968), 166.

2. "How Time Passes," *Time,* 12 April 1937, 93–96; subsequent references are to these pages.

3. Hall, "Notes on Deconstructing " 'The Popular,' " 228. See my Introduction for Hall and for Richard Dyer's formulation of the "star image."

4. Dyer, *Stars,* 72.

5. I owe the latter term to Constance Penley.

6. Dyer, *Stars,* 71–72. Few if any studies by Woolf scholars are included in part 2, grounded as they are in an extensive knowledge of Woolf's writings and their critical history not ordinarily part of the popular debates.

7. Hall, "Notes on Deconstructing 'The Popular,' " 235.

8. Charles Gandee, "People Are Talking About," Mira Stout, "Raising Orlando," with photographs by Karl Lagerfeld, and Alexis Jetter, "Goodbye to the Last Taboo," *Vogue,* July 1993, 39, 138–43, 87.

9. Dyer, *Stars,* 38.

10. Rodden, *The Politics of Literary Reputation,* 55, 5, 91; in the first quotation, Rodden is quoting C. Day Lewis.

11. Mitchell, *Iconology,* 1.

12. Ibid., 43, 151.

13. Žižek, *Enjoy Your Symptom!* 140; Hanif Kureishi, *Sammy and Rosie Get Laid: The Script and the Diary* (London: Faber, 1988), 12–13.

TAKE TWO

1. Elson, *Time Inc.,* 5–9.

2. Schickel, *Intimate Strangers,* 74–76.

3. Edmund Wilson, "The All-Star Literary Vaudeville," *New Republic,* 30 June 1926, 158.

4. On Sherman, see Rubin, *Making of Middlebrow Culture,* 42–81.

5. Dyer, *Stars,* 68, 69.

6. It was not until 1975 that the *Sunday Times,* in imitation of the *New York Times,* initiated its list of best-sellers. I am grateful to John Sutherland for the information on the history of the best-seller in Britain.

7. See Jennifer Wicke, *Advertising Fictions: Literature, Advertisement, and Social Reading* (New York: Columbia University Press, 1988), 55–72, 79–86. Boorstin cites Barnum as one of the progenitors of the shift from ideals to images: *The Image,* 207–10.

8. Wicke, *Advertising Fictions,* 5, 81.

9. Leo Braudy, *The Frenzy of Renown: Fame and Its History* (New York and Oxford: Oxford University Press, 1986), 9 n. 1, 4, 377, 9.

10. My use of *persona* here borrows from Barry King's definition in "Articulating Stardom," in *Stardom: Industry of Desire,* ed. Christine Gledhill (London and New York: Routledge, 1991), 167–82. See, for example, his statement that "the persona is in itself a character, but one that transcends placement or containment in a particular narrative. . . . Indeed, the persona, buttressed by the discursive practices of publicity, hagiography and by regimes of cosmetic alteration and treatment,

is relatively durable and if sedimented in public awareness will tend to survive discrepant casting and performances" (179).

11. See Richard deCordova, *Picture Personalities: The Emergence of the Star System in America* (Urbana and Chicago: University of Illinois Press, 1990), 18ff.

12. Schickel, *Intimate Strangers,* 76.

13. On American advertising and publicity during the 1920s and 1930s, see John Tebbel, *A History of Book Publishing in the United States,* vol. 3 (New York: Bowker, 1978), 315–29; the use of the author's photograph to advertise books, still "in its infancy" in the late 1920s (Elizabeth P. Richardson, *A Bloomsbury Iconography* [Winchester: St. Paul's Bibliographies, 1989], 295) became common in the 1930s. For a more recent example of the use of photographs to make authors stars, this time academic authors, see Robert S. Boynton, "The Routledge Revolution," *Lingua Franca,* March–April 1995, 24–32, esp. 26.

14. Leonard Woolf, "On Advertising Books," *Nation and Athenaeum,* 19 March 1927, 849; quoted in J. H. Willis, Jr., *Leonard and Virginia Woolf as Publishers: The Hogarth Press, 1917–41* (Charlottesville: University Press of Virginia, 1992), 374.

15. In May 1937, wondering if she could afford some clothing she wanted, Woolf noted: "tho' they say The Years is in its 4th printing in America: only an advt. though, & H.B. not so scrupulous as we are": *The Diary of Virginia Woolf,* ed. Anne Olivier Bell, vol. 5 (San Diego: Harcourt Brace Jovanovich, 1984), 85 (4 May 1937).

16. Curiously, the picture that accompanies the review is not the Man Ray photo, but a drawing, based on a 1929 Lenare photograph, that had previously appeared in *Books* in a front-page article praising Woolf on June 28, 1931.

17. During the week of May 23, *The Years* took second place to *Gone with the Wind.* The blurb from the *Book-of-the-Month Club News* may indicate *The Years* had been chosen as an alternative, or it may have been a recommendation for readers; it was not a primary selection.

18. Woolf knew the book was a best-seller in America by May 26, 1937 (*The Letters of Virginia Woolf,* ed. Nigel Nicolson and Joanne Trautmann, vol. 6 [New York: Harcourt Brace Jovanovich, 1980], 130 [3251]; subsequent citations are to this edition). On June 1, she recorded in her diary that "H. Brace wrote & said they were happy to find that The Years is the best selling novel in America"; next to this entry she tracked the book's progress from June 14 through October 22: *Diary,* vol. 5, 90–91.

19. Braudy argues that during at least the nineteenth century "the expansiveness and expressiveness of the American context always placed a potential premium on visual appearance and appeal to an immediate public, so long as one could appeal to posterity or some higher value at the same time. But in Europe, the artistic mode was marked by both a scorn for public acceptance and a self-announced eccentricity— with both aristocratic and plebeian roots—that opposed the 'artist' of all sorts to the society around him. . . . The audience [in Europe] is not the 'people,' but (in Stendhal's phrase) the 'happy few' ": *The Frenzy of Renown,* 476.

20. "Hall of Fame," *Vogue London,* Late May 1924, 40; Garrity, "Dodging 'Intellectual Harlotry.' " On Beck and Macgregor, see Cecil Beaton, *British Photographers* (1944) (London: Bracken Books, 1987), 37–38.

21. "We Nominate for the Hall of Fame," *Vanity Fair,* September 1929, 93.

22. Cecil Beaton, *The Book of Beauty* (London: Duckworth, 1930), 37–38; *The Wandering Years; Diaries, 1922–1939* (London: Weidenfeld and Nicolson, 1961), 175.

23. For the history of their exchange, see Richardson, *Bloomsbury Iconography,* 296; Woolf's letters appeared in *Nation and Athenaeum,* 29 November and 20 December 1930.

24. A fictionalized portrait of Virginia Woolf as the novelist Jane Rose in Hugh Walpole's *Hans Frost* (1929) describes her as looking "like the wife of a Pre-Raphaelite painter"; see Hermione Lee, *Virginia Woolf* (London: Chatto & Windus, 1996), 567.

25. Beaton, *Book of Beauty,* 37; the rest of the entry uses descriptions of women from Woolf's novels to flesh out the portrait, including Clarissa Dalloway and Helen Ambrose.

26. See Wendy Lesser, *His Other Half: Men Looking at Women through Art* (Cambridge: Harvard University Press, 1991), 182–83.

27. This and subsequent quotes appear in "How Time Passes," 93–96.

28. Stuart Sherman had made a similar point in his 1925 *Tribune Books* profile of Woolf, noting that she "relishes *men's* authors and the qualities in them which appeal to robust and sinewy readers": "An Uncommon Essayist," 1.

29. Schickel, *Intimate Strangers,* 290; Joyce's *Time* appearance also signified to Schickel his "exemplary" success as a modernist avant-gardist in convincing people with money of the importance of not being understood, and hence of supporting his work. On the stereotypical representations of Joyce "essentialized in our popular culture," see Cheng, "The Joycean Unconscious," 180–81.

30. "Night Thoughts," *Time,* 8 May 1939, 78–84.

TAKE THREE

1. Hermione Lee speculates that the coroner's misquotation of Woolf's note to her husband at the time of her suicide and the subsequent news reports contributed to one aspect of the "posthumous myths": "that image of a sensitive, aesthetic, nervous creature, too fragile for her own good" (*Virginia Woolf,* 766). The misquotation implied Woolf killed herself because she couldn't "carry on" during the war, rather than because she feared another period of madness.

2. The process of marketing the writer had begun even before her death, when the Woolfs decided to publish a "Uniform Edition" of Virginia's works: "It was a decision which staked a claim for Virginia Woolf's commercial value and, at forty-seven, for the lasting value of her works. From then on, they also developed a practice of publishing some of her essays and short pieces as attractively designed pamphlets or short books: a way of 'maximising income from her minor works' ": Lee, *Virginia Woolf,* 558.

3. Gaines, *Contested Culture,* 228–29, 198, 198–99; see my Introduction.

4. W. H. Auden, "A Consciousness of Reality," *New Yorker,* 6 March 1954, 112; for an example of the dismissiveness, see Joseph Wood Krutch, "Bloomsbury's Mistress," *Saturday Review,* 13 March 1954, 17.

5. Mark Schorer, "A Writer's Mirror," *New Republic,* 1 March 1954, 18–19; Maxwell Geismar, "Art as Obsession," *Nation,* 27 February 1954, 175–76; and Krutch, "Bloomsbury's Mistress," 17.

6. Elizabeth Bowen, "The Principle of Her Art Was Joy," *New York Times Book Review,* 21 February 1954, 1, 26; Rumer Godden, "Virginia Woolf, Critical and Creative, Always the Dedicated Writer," *New York Herald Tribune Books,* 21 February 1954, 1; Auden, "A Consciousness of Reality," 111–16.

7. "Fragments of Time," *Times Literary Supplement,* 20 November 1953, 742.

8. Bowen, "The Principle of Her Art," 1; Auden, "A Consciousness of Reality," 112; Anne Fremantle, "The Diaries of Virginia Woolf," *Commonweal,* 19 March 1954, 603.

9. Schorer, "A Writer's Mirror," 19.

10. On the advent of the fan and its relationship to new forms of publicity in the eighteenth century, see Braudy, *The Frenzy of Renown,* 380ff.

11. DeCordova, *Picture Personalities,* 98.

12. Leonard Woolf, "Preface," in Virginia Woolf, *A Writer's Diary,* ed. Leonard Woolf (London: Hogarth, 1953), ix, vii.

13. Benedict Nicolson, "Books in General," *New Statesman and Nation,* 7 November 1953, 567–68; Nigel Nicolson, *Portrait of a Marriage* (London: Atheneum, 1973). Ben denies the value of the "juicy scandal" almost certainly in the diary, but not before alerting his readers to it.

14. This was also true of the publication of Leonard Woolf's autobiography, which began appearing in 1960.

TAKE FOUR

1. Martha Duffy, "V," *Time,* 20 November 1972, 93; Gordon S. Haight, "Virginia Woolf," *Yale Review* 62 (spring 1973): 426.

2. Posting on the e-mail Virginia Woolf list.

3. Dyer, *Heavenly Bodies,* 3; *Stars,* 3.

4. Lewis Funke, "News of the Rialto," *New York Times,* 21 October 1962, sec. 2, p. 1.

5. Virginia Woolf, "Jane Austen at Sixty," *Nation and Athenaeum,* 15 December 1923, 433.

6. Philip T. Hartung, review of *Who's Afraid of Virginia Woolf? Commonweal,* 22 July 1966, 474.

7. Malcolm Muggeridge, review of *Virginia Woolf: A Biography, Esquire,* March 1973, 38. Before the play opened, Albee sent the script to Leonard, who later saw the London production: Leonard Woolf, *Letters,* ed. Frederic Spotts (San Diego: Harcourt Brace Jovanovich, 1989), 522 and n., 536–37.

8. David Pryce-Jones, "The Rules of the Game," *Spectator,* 14 February 1964, 213.

9. As reported in the media, the costs of using the Disney tune forced Albee to substitute "Here We Go 'Round the Mulberry Bush" instead: "A Woolf in the Bush," *Theatre Arts,* December 1962, 8.

10. Lewis Funke, "News of the Rialto," *New York Times,* 18 November 1962, sec. 2, p. 1.

11. Janet Flanner (Gênet), "Letter from Paris," *New Yorker,* 26 December 1964, 68.

12. Diana Trilling, "Who's Afraid of the Culture Elite?" *Esquire,* December 1963, 69–92; "The Riddle of Albee's *Who's Afraid of Virginia Woolf?*" in *Claremont Essays,* 203–27. Unless otherwise noted, the citations in the text are to the Claremont version, identified where necessary as "Riddle"; the *Esquire* version is cited as "Culture Elite."

13. Trilling's strong anticommunism, with its roots in a reaction against mass culture as a form of Stalinism, lies behind this statement.

14. In the Claremont version, Trilling is more modest about which magazine is being raided, referring to "the literary quarterlies" (226) rather than the *Partisan Review,* where both she and her husband were regular contributors. Trilling repeats the *Partisan Review* version of this anecdote in her autobiography, where she also tells us she too wrote for the "popular" women's magazines: *The Beginning of the Journey: The Marriage of Diana and Lionel Trilling* (San Diego: Harcourt Brace, 1993), 346–47.

15. Diana Trilling, "Virginia Woolf's Special Realm," *New York Times Book Review,* 21 March 1948, sec. 7, pp. 1, 28–29; reprinted as "Virginia Woolf: A Special Instance," in *Claremont Essays,* 87–94.

16. See Huyssen, "Mass Culture as Woman," 188–207, and my discussion in part 1, section 3.

17. See Funke, "News of the Rialto," 18 November 1962.

18. Jo Coudert, "Letters to the Editor," *New York Times,* 2 December 1962, sec. 2, p. 5.

19. Howard Taubman, "Modern Primer: Helpful Hints to Tell Appearances vs. Truth," *New York Times,* 28 April 1963, X1. See also John M. Clum, *Acting Gay: Male Homosexuality in Modern Drama* (New York: Columbia University Press, 1992), 175–77.

20. Richard Schechner, "Who's Afraid of Edward Albee?" *Tulane Drama Review* 7/3 (spring 1963): 9–10.

21. "Who's Afraid . . . ," *Newsweek,* 4 July 1966, 84. The *Newsweek* review found its way into other reviews as well, as if to say, "see, it's not me but *Newsweek*"; see, e.g., H. H., "Who's Afraid of Virginia Woolf?" *Films in Review* 17 (1966): 448. British reviewers of the film, if they even mentioned this subtext, were more oblique; John Coleman notes only that "there's a sense that the line of attack relies too much on something stranger and more splenetic than the humdrum bitcheries of marriage. I think, as others have said, that some special bleeding is

before us": review of *Who's Afraid of Virginia Woolf? New Statesman*, 15 July 1966, 103.

22. For Albee's comment, see Kim Garfield, "Edward Albee's Delicate Balance," *Advocate*, 7 November 1989, 48; Vito Russo, *Celluloid Closet: Homosexuality in the Movies*, rev. ed. (New York: Harper & Row, 1987), 192.

23. Henry Hewes, "Who's Afraid of Big Bad Broadway?" *Saturday Review*, 27 October 1962, 29.

24. Susan Sontag, "Notes on 'Camp,' " *Partisan Review* 31 (fall 1964): 515–30. Writing in 1966 about "Homosexual Themes in the Cinema," Lee Atwell noted that "it is clear that many Hollywood directors find homosexuality a fashionable touch, although no more so than the Beatles or Camp": *Tangents* (April 1966): 9.

25. Edward Albee, *Who's Afraid of Virginia Woolf?* (New York: Pocket, 1963), 3; hereafter cited in text.

26. Majorie Garber, *Vested Interests: Cross-Dressing and Cultural Anxiety* (New York: Routledge, 1992), 91. For Albee's choice, see Garfield, "Edward Albee's Delicate Balance," 46; Sky Gilbert provides the commentary: "Closet Plays: An Exclusive Dramaturgy at Work," *Canadian Theatre Review* 59 (summer 1989): 58.

27. Philip Roth, "The Play That Dare Not Speak Its Name," *New York Review of Books*, 25 February 1965, 4.

28. Gilbert, "Closet Plays," 57–58.

29. Doty, *Making Things Perfectly Queer*, 84. Doty uses Albee's play as an example of gay men's presentation of "representations of 'straight women–as–gay men' " (131–32).

30. Fiedler, "The New Mutants," 394; see my discussion in part 1.

31. Cynthia Grenier, " 'Virginia Woolf' Claws Way to Compassion in Paris," *New York Herald Tribune* (Paris edition), 2 December 1964, n.p. The numerous comparisons of Albee's play to Strindberg's work in the reviews also suggest this reading.

32. David Halberstam, *The Fifties* (New York: Villard Books, 1993), 605–6; Steinem is quoted in Susan J. Douglas, *Where the Girls Are: Growing Up Female with the Mass Media* (New York: Times Books/Random House, 1994), 68–70; Fiedler, "The New Mutants," 391. Douglas also points to the publication of Helen Gurley Brown's *Sex and the Single Girl* in 1962 as exciting alarm.

33. Robert Brustein, "Albee and the Medusa-Head," *New Republic*, 3 November 1962, 29–30. See also Alfred Chester, "Edward Albee: Red Herrings and White Whales," *Commentary*, April 1963, 299, 297.

34. Boston Women's Health Book Collective, *Our Bodies, Ourselves* (New York: Simon & Schuster, 1973); quoted in *The Abortion Controversy: A Documentary History*, ed. Eva R. Rubin (Westport, Conn.: Greenwood Press, 1994), 66–67.

35. Brustein, "Albee and the Medusa-Head," 30. A letter "To the Editor of *Commentary*" in October 1963 makes a similar point: "Albee's theme . . . is the diminishing differences between the sexes today, or the increasing masculinity of the female, etc. The sterility of the characters . . . is essential to it."

36. Donald Kaplan, "Homosexuality and American Theatre: A Psychoanalytic

Comment," *Tulane Drama Review* 9/3 (spring 1965): 35, 36. Laurence A. Rickels makes a similar point to Marcuse's when he juxtaposes replication, in particular teenagers' "groupwide self-replication," to reproduction and reads it as a form of rebellion: "Psy Fi Explorations of Out Space: On Werther's Special Effects," in *Outing Goethe and His Age,* ed. Alice A. Kuzniar (Stanford: Stanford University Press, 1996), 148–49.

37. For readings of the fantasy child as "a latent homosexual fantasy" or as the "changeling boy," see, respectively, Axel Madsen, "Who's Afraid of Alfred Hitchcock?" *Sight and Sound* 37 (winter 1967–68): 27; and Garber, *Vested Interests,* 90–92.

38. Leonard Leff, "Play into Film: Warner Brothers' *Who's Afraid of Virginia Woolf?" Theatre Journal* 33 (December 1981): 454. The unnaturalness, the monstrosity, associated with both Virginia Woolf and Martha—as well as the link to Medusa—seems to have rubbed off on Elizabeth Taylor as well, at least for some writers on the actress; "Who's Afraid of Virginia Woolf?" Brenda Maddox states, "marked Elizabeth Taylor's debut as Medusa, the monster-woman with snaky hair and raging eyes that can transform mortals to stone": *Who's Afraid of Elizabeth Taylor?* (New York: M. Evans, 1977), 195.

39. Huyssen, "Mass Culture as Woman," 196, which includes the quotation from Le Bon.

40. The last line is Martha's reply: "I . . . am . . . George. . . . I . . . am . . ." (242).

41. See, for example, respectively, Neil Hertz, "Medusa's Head: Male Hysteria under Political Pressure," in *The End of the Line: Essays on Psychoanalysis and the Sublime* (New York: Columbia University Press, 1985), 161–215; Tobin Siebers, *The Mirror of Medusa* (Berkeley and Los Angeles: University of California Press, 1983); and Patricia Klindienst Joplin, "The Voice of the Shuttle Is Ours," in *Rape and Representation,* ed. Lynn A. Higgins and Brenda R. Silver (New York: Columbia University Press, 1991), 35–66.

42. Joplin, "The Voice of the Shuttle," 52; de Lauretis, *Alice Doesn't,* 109.

43. Ernest Callenbach, "Who's Afraid of Virginia Woolf?" *Film Quarterly* 20 (fall 1966): 48.

44. De Lauretis, *Alice Doesn't,* 109.

TAKE FIVE

1. Frances Spalding, "Leader of the Woolfpack," *Times Educational Supplement,* 13 September 1996, 6.

2. Lee, *Virginia Woolf,* 767.

3. For the latter figure as well as a list of other feminist landmarks during the period, see Ferguson et al., "Feminism and Antifeminism," 35–47.

4. The twenty-fifth anniversary of many of these events in 1997 brought them back to public attention, accompanied by retrospective assessments. See, e.g., Alix Kates Shulman's introduction to the anniversary issue of *Memoirs of an Ex-Prom*

Queen (New York: Penguin, 1997), ix; and Mary Thom, *Inside Ms.: 25 Years of the Magazine and the Feminist Movement* (New York: Holt, 1997). Reviewing Thom's book, Francine Prose notes that "great delicacy, skill and sympathetic imagination are required to help the reader fathom or recall how the most obvious facts (When you turn the faucet, water runs out! America has a power structure headed by rich white men!) could have seemed like epistemological breakthroughs, hot news so amazing as to provoke spells of revved up, reactive behavior": "How to Examine Your Cervix: More *Ms.*-story Than You Wanted," *New York Observer,* 14 July 1997, 30.

5. See Valerie Carnes, "Icons of Popular Fashion," in *Icons of America,* 236.

6. Simpson, *The Academic Postmodern,* 23. The groundwork for this transformation in the United States was laid in Richard Macksey and Eugenio Donato, eds., *The Structuralist Controversy: The Languages of Criticism and the Sciences of Man* (Baltimore: Johns Hopkins University Press, 1970); James Olney's influential retheorization of autobiography appeared in 1972: *Metaphors of Self: The Making of Autobiography* (Princeton: Princeton University Press, 1972).

7. Robert Gish, "Books and Authors," *North American Review,* summer 1973, 77.

8. See, e.g., William Maxwell, who states, "It isn't at all difficult to distinguish her successes from her failures, nor do her novels require elucidation": "Virginia Stephen/Virginia Woolf," *New Yorker,* 3 February 1973, 88; and Pearl K. Bell, "The Fin on the Sea," *New Leader,* 8 January 1973, 16.

9. Reviewers more sympathetic to the novels argued that Bell's decision allowed readers to form their own opinions.

10. Quentin Bell, *Virginia Woolf: A Biography* (New York: Harcourt Brace Jovanovich, 1972), vol. 1, xiii; my emphasis.

11. Maxwell, "Virginia Stephen/Virginia Woolf," 88; Gish, "Books and Authors," 77.

12. One notable example is the construction of Virginia Woolf as incest victim/survivor, a role that at times has seemed to obscure all other facets of her meaning.

13. William Pritchard, "Understanding Virginia," *Hudson Review,* summer 1973, 370, 368.

14. Leonard Woolf, *Downhill All the Way: An Autobiography of the Years 1919–1939* (London: Hogarth Press, 1967), 27.

15. Cynthia Ozick, "Mrs. Virginia Woolf," *Commentary,* August 1973, 42–43.

16. Barbara Hardy, "Granite and Rainbow," *Spectator* (London), 4 November 1972, 715.

17. See part 1, section 2, for another discussion of this subject.

18. "The Fears of Virginia Woolf," *Times Literary Supplement,* 27 October 1972, 1278; Muggeridge, review of *Virginia Woolf,* 38.

19. On the problematic "genius" attributed to Virginia Woolf, see Pritchard, who argues that "she was not a great novelist but a very fine and rewarding and

admirable writer. Of genius, if one can bear the term": "Understanding Virginia," 370.

20. Jill Johnston, "The virgins of the stacks," *Village Voice,* 16 November 1972, 28.

21. Ellen Hawkes Rogat, "The Virgin in the Bell Biography," *Twentieth Century Literature* 20 (April 1974): 96.

22. For Olivier Bell's critique, see Janet Malcolm, "A House of One's Own," *New Yorker,* 5 June 1995, 78. For the other quotations, see Stephen Spender, "Virginia Woolf: A Biography," *Washington Post Book World,* 19 November 1972, 1; Stanley Weintraub, "Those Horrible Voices," *New Republic,* 25 November 1973, 34; and Noel Annan, "Virginia Woolf in Close-Up," *Listener,* 26 October 1972, 544. In addition to being a hero or heroic, Leonard is often described as "saintly."

23. Ozick, "Mrs. Virginia Woolf," 34.

24. Ibid. Writing in *Commentary,* published by the American Jewish Committee, Ozick argues that the family, particularly Vanessa, needed a caretaker for Virginia, and that Leonard, in his desire for assimilation, needed Virginia Stephen and everything she stood for.

25. Malcolm, "A House of One's Own," 64, 78; the fact that Quentin twice reviewed his half-sister's memoir *Deceived with Kindness* (1984) even while questioning whether he should do so helped secure his authority. For another recent journalistic rendering of Virginia Woolf from the family's perspective, see Regina Marler, *Bloomsbury Pie: The Making of the Bloomsbury Boom* (New York: Henry Holt, 1997).

26. Robert Manson Myers, *From Beowulf to Virginia Woolf,* rev. ed., with cover by Edward Gorey (Urbana: University of Illinois Press, 1984); Alistair Cooke, Introduction to *A Room of One's Own,* directed by Patrick Garland, Masterpiece Theatre, PBS (WGBH-Boston), January 1991; John Simon, "Two from the Heart, Two from Hunger," *New York,* 18 March 1991, 76.

27. Nell Irvin Painter, *Sojourner Truth: A Life, a Symbol* (New York: Norton, 1996), 287.

28. Lee has been careful to acknowledge Bell's work and to eschew presenting hers as an antidote, even as she explicitly sets out to undo the family portraits (548); the facets she confronts and challenges include the influence of Vanessa's "caricature" of her sister (119, 169); "the legend" of her frigidity (244) and the Woolfs' sexless marriage (331–32); Quentin's, his siblings', and the grownups' "family image" (547–48); the view of her as apolitical (681–82): *Virginia Woolf.*

29. John Bayley, "Woolf in Child's Clothing," *Evening Standard,* 23 September 1996, 27.

TAKE SIX

1. Jackie Wullschlager, "A Woolf in the Family Fold," *Financial Times,* 14 September 1996, sec. 3, p. 15.

2. For the different approaches to identification in star theory, see Christine Gledhill, "Introduction," in *Stardom: Industry of Desire,* xv–xvi.

3. Rosemary J. Coombe, "The Celebrity Image and Cultural Identity: Publicity Rights and the Subaltern Politics of Gender," *Discourse* 14/3 (summer 1992): 59.

4. For the phrase, used in conjunction with (some) feminist critics, see Alex Zwerdling, *Virginia Woolf and the Real World* (Berkeley: University of California Press, 1986), 33.

5. Dyer, *Stars,* 37; see also Curry's *Too Much of a Good Thing.*

6. See Richardson, *Bloomsbury Iconography,* 284, for the date; Richardson is the source for all the dates in this section. She also describes each image in detail and records where it has been published. Here I am treating the Beresford profile, which exists in at least two almost identical versions, as one.

7. Lee, *Virginia Woolf,* 246.

8. Richardson distinguishes one of the Beresford profiles (A32) by noting "neck like Julia Stephen's": *Bloomsbury Iconography,* 285.

9. Virginia Woolf, "Julia Margaret Cameron," in *Victorian Photographs of Famous Men and Fair Women by Julia Margaret Cameron* (1926), rev. ed. (Boston: Godine, 1973), 13–20. Roger Fry provided an introduction to the photographs.

10. On Woolf's relationship to photography, see Diane F. Gillespie, " 'Her Kodak Pointed at His Head': Virginia Woolf and Photography," in *The Multiple Muses of Virginia Woolf,* ed. Gillespie (Columbia: University of Missouri Press, 1993), 113–47; and Helen Wussow, "Virginia Woolf and the Problematic Nature of the Photographic Image," *Twentieth Century Literature* 40/1 (spring 1994): 1–14, and "Travesties of Excellence: Julia Margaret Cameron, Lytton Strachey, Virginia Woolf, and the Photographic Image," in *Virginia Woolf and the Arts,* ed. Diane F. Gillespie and Leslie K. Hankins (New York: Pace University Press, 1997), 48–56.

11. My focus on the studio and professional portraits, often taken in conjunction with the publication of Woolf's books or the appearance of her essays in journals, underlines my emphasis on her public image. Although each sitting probably produced a dozen or so shots, the convention was to choose the one or two believed to be most characteristic of the sitter; see David Ellis, "Images of D. H. Lawrence: On the Use of Photographs in Biography," in *The Portrait in Photography,* ed. Graham Clarke (London: Reaktion Books, 1992), 166.

12. Beaton, *British Photographers,* 37–38; Beaton considered their portraits of Virginia Woolf, T. S. Eliot, and Lytton Strachey "particularly successful" (38). On Woolf's connection with *Vogue,* which under Dorothy Todd's editorship integrated "highbrow" writers and artists into the magazine, see Elgin W. Mellown, "An Annotated Checklist of Contributions by Bloomsbury . . . in *Vogue* Magazine during the Editorship of Dorothy Todd, 1923–27," *Bulletin of Bibliography* 53/3 (September 1996): 227–34; Nicola Luckhurst, *Bloomsbury in Vogue* (London: Cecil Woolf, 1998); and Garrity, "Dodging 'Intellectual Harlotry.' "

13. Quoted in Anthony Haden-Guest, "The Society Photograph," in *Lenare: The Art of Society Photography, 1924–1977,* ed. Nicholas deVille (London: Allen Lane, 1981), 11.

14. In a letter to *Time* after Woolf's cover appearance in 1937, the editor of *Harper's,* Carmel Snow, wrote that she was "horrified to see that the photograph . . . credited the photographer, Man Ray, but did not credit *Harper's Bazaar,* who

arranged to have Mrs. Woolf's picture taken and paid Man Ray a large sum for the exclusive rights to this beautiful picture": quoted in Richardson, *Bloomsbury Iconography*, 299, who also notes that no publication of the photo in *Harper's* has been traced.

15. For all five photographs, see Man Ray, *Photographs*, with an introduction by Jean-Hubert Martin (New York: Thames & Hudson, 1982), 218–19.

16. Man Ray, *Self-Portrait* (Boston: Little, Brown, 1963), 189; quoted in Richardson, *Bloomsbury Iconography*, 300.

17. Quoted in Arturo Schwarz, *Man Ray: The Rigour of Imagination* (New York: Rizzoli, 1977), 283. In general, writers received the lowest marks; T. S. Eliot also scored a 3, James Joyce a 6, Ernest Hemingway, Aldous Huxley, and Gertrude Stein a 10, and Henry Miller a 12. See also Richardson, *Bloomsbury Iconography*, 300.

18. See Gisèle Freund, *The World in My Camera*, trans. June Guicharnaud (New York: Dial, 1974), 129–37.

19. Ibid., 131, 134. For Woolf's letter to Ocampo (26 June 1939), see *The Letters of Virginia Woolf*, vol. 6, 342–43 [3528]. The apology, dated "20 May 1940," which does not appear in the *Letters*, was published in Spanish in the Argentinian journal *Sur* in 1980; in 1997 an English (re)translation by Paul Standish was posted on the Virginia Woolf e-mail list. In her apology, Woolf explains that "my displeasure at allowing myself to be photographed in colour is due to an old complex; I hate the imposition of the presence, of the personality of the writer before his work."

20. For the quotation, see Allan Sekula, "The Traffic in Photographs," *Photography against the Grain: Essays and Photoworks, 1973–1983* (Halifax: The Press of the Nova Scotia College of Art and Design, 1984), 85; see also Sekula, "The Body and the Archive," *October* 39 (winter 1986): 33–64. On the subject of physiognomy and portraiture, see Richard Brilliant, *Portraiture* (Cambridge: Harvard University Press, 1991), 38; and Mary Cowling, *The Artist as Anthropologist: The Representation of Type and Character in Victorian Art* (Cambridge: Cambridge University Press, 1989).

21. Graham Clarke, "Introduction," in *The Portrait in Photography*, 1, 41–43; Edward Weston, *Edward Weston on Photography*, ed. Peter C. Bunnell (Salt Lake City: Gibbs M. Smith, Inc., 1983), 135.

22. Brilliant, *Portraiture*, 11; Clarke, "Introduction," 3; Brilliant, 115, 141.

23. Roland Barthes, *Camera Lucida: Reflections on Photography*, trans. Richard Howard (New York: Hill & Wang, 1981), 26–27, 43. Virginia Woolf makes an unexplained appearance in Barthes's meditations on the *punctum*, providing a caption under a photograph of Queen Victoria and her groom that is the only caption not taken from Barthes's text itself: " 'Queen Victoria, entirely unaesthetic' " (56). For Barthes, the *punctum* in this photograph resided in the groom.

24. See Dawn Ades, "Duchamp's Masquerades," in *The Portrait in Photography*, 110; Nell Irvin Painter, "Representing Truth: Sojourner Truth's Knowing and Becoming Known," *Journal of American History* 81/2 (September 1994): 485.

25. Beaton, *Book of Beauty*, 4–5, 36.

26. Quoted in Georgina Howell, *In Vogue: Six Decades of Fashion* (London: Penguin, 1977), 61.

27. L. Fritz Gruber, *Beauty: Variations on the Theme WOMAN by Masters of the Camera—Past and Present* (London and New York: Focal Press, 1965), 133.

28. Trilling, "Virginia Woolf's Special Realm," 1.

29. Barthes, *Camera Lucida,* 34, 36.

30. Trilling's ambivalence continued throughout her life. In an interview published in 1989, she responds to the question, "What about literary heroines? George Eliot or Virginia Woolf?" by stating that her "admiration for Virginia Woolf is qualified, both as a person and as a writer." The qualifications include the limited scope of her "[novels] of sensibility" and the fact that "privately she really wasn't a very nice person"; the latter leads her to compare Virginia Woolf to Lillian Hellman, Trilling's legendary antagonist: Stephen Koch, "Journey's Beginning: A Talk with Diana Trilling," *New York Times Book Review,* 19 February 1989, sec. 7, p. 27.

31. Cowling, *The Artist as Anthropologist,* 145, 148.

32. For Strachey, see Cowling, *The Artist as Anthropologist,* 149; *The Letters of Virginia Woolf,* vol. 5 (1979), 273 [2850]. Elsewhere, commenting on a reproduction of one of the 1929 Lenare photographs of her, Woolf writes that "her nose looks sharp eno' to cut hay with": *Letters,* vol. 6, 235 [3395]. For a contrasting example, see the references to D. H. Lawrence's large but not aquiline nose in Ellis, "Images of D. H. Lawrence," 164.

33. Lee, *Virginia Woolf,* 57; Alan Bennett, *Forty Years On* (London: Faber & Faber, 1969), 74.

34. Rebecca West described both Vanessa and Virginia as untidy: "They always looked as if they had been drawn through a hedge backwards before they went out": in *Recollections of Virginia Woolf,* ed. Joan Russell Noble (New York: William Morrow, 1972), 90; Gordon Haight, reviewing *Recollections,* comments, "Though not poor, these precursors of the sloppy-jeans generation affected careless and ill-fitting clothes": "Virginia Woolf," 431.

35. See Diana Trilling, "Lionel Trilling: A Jew at Columbia," excerpted in *The Beginning of the Journey,* 319; and "A Visit to Camelot," *New Yorker,* 2 June 1997, 54–65.

36. Brilliant, *Portraiture,* 47–48, 68.

37. The Staff, *Everywoman's Center: Evolution of an Alternative* (Amherst, Mass.: Everywoman's Center, 1975), 36–37, 72.

38. On the function of the full-face portrait in establishing an " 'I-You' " relationship, see Louis Marin, "Toward a Theory of Reading in the Visual Arts: Poussin's *The Arcadian Shepherds,*" in *The Reader in the Text: Essays on Audience and Interpretation,* ed. Susan R. Suleiman and Inge Crosman (Princeton: Princeton University Press, 1980), 306.

39. Colin Symes, "Keeping Abreast with the Times: Towards an Iconography of T-Shirts," *Studies in Popular Culture* 12/1 (1989): 87; Roy Rivenburg, "When the Shirt Hits the Fan," *Los Angeles Times,* 29 May 1997, E5.

40. Richard Martin, curator of the Metropolitan Museum of Art's Costume Institute, quoted in Rivenburg, "When the Shirt Hits the Fan," 5. On the "gender-

bending effect" of the T-shirt, traced back to Jean Seberg in *Breathless* (1959), see J. D. Reed, "Hail to the T, the Shirt that Speaks Volumes," *Smithsonian,* April 1992, 98–99.

41. Reed, "Hail to the T," 99. On the process, see Rivenburg, "When the Shirt Hits the Fan," 5, and Reed, 100.

42. Amy Spindler, quoted in Ann Douglas, "High Is Low," *New York Times Magazine,* 29 September 1996, 187.

43. Edith Mayo, "Ladies and Liberation: Icon and Iconoclast in the Women's Movement," in *Icons of America,* 216ff., 222. For another first-wave feminist icon whose symbolic social meanings have a strong visual component, see Painter, *Sojourner Truth,* 173, and "Representing Truth," 482–88.

44. Alix Kates Shulman, "Dances with Feminists," *Women's Review of Books,* December 1991, 13.

45. One 1972 reviewer of the Bell biography noted that "the women's liberation Virginia Woolf primarily was the author of a most remarkable little book, *A Room of One's Own,*" as well as the lesser-known *Three Guineas:* Michele Murray, "Who's Afraid of Virginia? These Days, Not Many," *National Observer,* 25 November 1972, 25; Reed, "Hail to the T," 100.

46. Rickels, "Psy Fi Explorations of Out Space," 149.

47. Mitchell, *Iconology,* 143–44, 151.

48. Russo, *The Female Grotesque,* 75.

49. Hélène Cixous, "The Laugh of the Medusa," in *New French Feminisms: An Anthology,* ed. Elaine Marks and Isabelle de Courtivron (Amherst: University of Massachusetts Press, 1980), 245, 246, 255.

50. Tania Modleski, "Some Functions of Feminist Criticism; or, The Scandal of the Mute Body," in *Feminism without Women,* 46–47. Modleski is quoting J. L. Austin, who, she argues, provides the model for speech acts as initiating procedures: *How to Do Things with Words* (Cambridge: Harvard University Press, 1962), 26.

51. E. E. Evans-Pritchard, "Introduction," in Marcel Mauss, *The Gift: Forms and Functions of Exchange in Archaic Societies,* trans. Ian Cunnison (New York and London: Norton, 1967), ix. I speak here from personal experience; most of my Virginia Woolf objects, including my first T-shirt and the UMass poster, were gifts from colleagues, students, or friends.

52. Mitchell, *Iconology,* 151.

53. These included at least seven academic conferences and colloquia, as well as exhibitions at libraries and articles in *Modern Maturity;* for some examples, see *Virginia Woolf Miscellany* 19 (fall 1982). Europe also celebrated, as Quentin Bell noted approvingly, even while shaking his head at the American carnival; he tells us this in an introduction to the proceedings of the one British conference on Virginia Woolf, held at Cambridge University, seemingly at the suggestion of the organizer's wife: "Foreword," in *Virginia Woolf: A Centenary Perspective,* ed. Eric Warner (New York: St. Martin's Press, 1984), xiii; for the origins of the conference, see xiv.

54. Dudar, "The Virginia Woolf Cult," 32.

55. Heilbrun, "The Politics of Mind," 223. For a reading of (some of) Jane Austen's male admirers' self-presentation as a cult and "masculine" responses to them, see Claudia L. Johnson, "The Divine Miss Jane: Jane Austen, Janeites, and the Discipline of Novel Studies," *Boundary 2* 23/3 (fall 1996): 144–63.

56. Peter Watson, "Virginia Woolf Follows in Monroe's Footsteps," *Times* (London), 22 February 1982, 22.

57. Quoted in Reed, "Hail to the T," 100.

58. Malcolm, "A House of One's Own," 68. For two takes on the marketing of Bloomsbury, see Jo Griffiths, "Who Can Pay for Virginia Woolf?—Commodifying Bloomsbury," in *Virginia Woolf and Her Influences,* ed. Laura Davis and Jeanette McVicker (New York: Pace University Press, 1998), 215–20; and Jennifer Wicke, "*Mrs. Dalloway* Goes to Market: Woolf, Keynes, and Modern Markets," *Novel* 28/1 (fall 1994): 5–23, which reads Bloomsbury, past and present, as "an experiment in coterie consumption" (6).

59. *J'Accuse: Virginia Woolf,* written by Tom Paulin, directed and produced by Jeff Morgan, Fulmar Productions for Channel Four, London, 29 January 1991.

60. Paulin identifies the moment as the fiftieth anniversary of her suicide, but he doesn't mention that because of this anniversary, her works had (temporarily) gone out of copyright in Great Britain and at least four new editions had appeared, including two in paper; Woolf's works were being bought in bookstores ranging from the university to the railway station.

TAKE SEVEN

1. Michael Ratcliffe, "Me, I'm Afraid of Virginia Woolf," *Times* (London), 30 November 1978, 9; Chris Dunkley, "Saturday, Sunday, Monday," *Financial Times,* 6 December 1978, 19.

2. R. W. Burchfield, ed., *The New Fowler's Modern English Usage,* 3d ed. (Oxford: Oxford University Press, 1996); my reading extends the linguistic distinction into the social and cultural.

3. Gaines, *Contested Cultures,* 202.

4. Alan Bennett, *Me, I'm Afraid of Virginia Woolf: The Writer in Disguise* (London: Faber, 1985), 50; hereafter cited in text. The film, directed by Stephen Frears, can be seen at the British Film Institute.

5. F. R. Leavis, *The Great Tradition: George Eliot, Henry James, Joseph Conrad* (New York: New York University Press, 1967).

6. Francis Mulhern, *The Moment of "Scrutiny"* (London: NLB, 1979), 319; hereafter cited in text.

7. David Simpson, "New Brooms at Fawlty Towers," in *Intellectuals,* ed. Robbins, 252–53; hereafter cited in text.

8. Noel Annan writes that Leavis's "denunciation of the metropolitan culture purveyed by Bloomsbury's disciples won an immediate response from the grammar school boy or girl coming from the provinces to the university, often from a home where books were a rarity," who felt reassured and empowered by Leavis's clear-cut guidelines on what it was necessary for them to learn: "Bloomsbury and the

Leavises," in *Virginia Woolf and Bloomsbury: A Centenary Celebration*, ed. Jane Marcus (Bloomington: Indiana University Press, 1987), 33.

9. Forty years later Bradbury was writing a screenplay of *Flush*, Virginia Woolf's best-selling biography of Elizabeth Barrett Browning's spaniel: Malcolm Bradbury, "The Eminent Post-Victorian," *Weekly Standard*, 19 May 1997, 33.

10. Annan, "Bloomsbury and the Leavises," 35.

11. My own experience bears this out; when I was a visitor at University College London in 1975–76, the Moderns course, run by a woman trained at Cambridge, treated Woolf, briefly, as a formal experimenter but not a major novelist. Mark Hussey remembers *To the Lighthouse*'s being in the curriculum at Leeds University, but nothing else; "my sense is that Woolf was not much of a feature in the late seventies" (e-mail note to author). At Aberystwyth not even offers from other faculty to teach Woolf could convince the Leavisite head of the Moderns course to include her.

12. Nigel Nicolson, "Bloomsbury: The Myth and the Reality," in *Virginia Woolf and Bloomsbury*, ed. Marcus, 9.

13. For Simpson, the Leavisite attitude to English literature is more easily defined by what it was not—not classics or a foreign language or philology or history or science or philosophy—than by what it offered: "the language of the 'vital,' the 'concrete,' of the 'embodiment' of 'feeling,' and of 'human nature' ": "New Brooms," 255.

14. For one report on the conflicts, see Frances Spalding, "The Virginia Woolf Centenary Conference in England," *Virginia Woolf Miscellany* 19 (fall 1982): 1; for a transcript of some of the debate, see Warner, ed., *Virginia Woolf*, 158–62.

15. Leavis, *The Great Tradition*, 8–9.

16. Mrs. Tucker might well be echoing Queenie Leavis's famous attack on Woolf in her review of *Three Guineas*, where she criticizes Woolf for her lack of "acquaintance with the realities," including her lack of children: Q. D. Leavis, "Caterpillars of the Commonwealth Unite!" in *The Importance of Scrutiny*, ed. Eric Bentley (New York: New York University Press, 1964), 388.

17. Alan Bennett, *Writing Home* (London and Boston: Faber & Faber, 1994), xi. Bennett has a long-standing love/hate relationship with Virginia Woolf; his first play, *Forty Years On* (1968), includes a parodic "memoir" of Bloomsbury that focuses on Virginia Woolf (73–75). Woolf and Bloomsbury also appear in Bennett's highly satiric 1976 review of *Lady Ottoline's Album: Snapshots of Her Famous Contemporaries*, "Say Cheese, Virginia," which parodies the Bloomsbury craze, particularly, it would seem, among the middle classes (*Writing Home*, 387–89), and certainly Hopkins's students seem to know all about her. In his journal about the production of *Forty Years On* Bennett indicates, in a more serious way, the extensive knowledge about Woolf and Bloomsbury among common readers when recording the comment by a television executive at Granada that the Bloomsbury parody wouldn't work, "because nobody will have heard of Virginia Woolf": "He . . . has the defect, peculiar to high television executives and editors of popular newspapers, of thinking the public stupider than it is" (*Writing Home*, 255).

18. Julian Barnes, "Look Up Life," *New Statesman*, 8 December 1978, 796–97. Barnes describes the graffiti on Forster's portrait as "the addition of a Clint Eastwood cigar," a mark of his lack of "machismo." While more-or-less present throughout, Forster does not pose the same threat as Virginia Woolf, belying one reviewer's comment that the play might equally have been called " 'It's All Organ, Organ with You, Morgan' ": Nancy Banks-Smith, *Guardian*, 4 December 1978, 10. The reference is to Organ Morgan, the organist, in Dylan Thomas's *Under Milk Wood*.

19. Harriet Martineau, *Eastern Life*, quoted in John Barrell, "Death on the Nile: Fantasy and the Literature of Tourism, 1840–1860," *Essays in Criticism* 41/2 (April 1991): 103; Barrell, 103. Although the Egyptian Sphinx, unlike the Greek, was male, Martineau's use of "it" and Barrell's reading, as well as common misperceptions, transform it into an androgynous if not a female figure.

20. Cora Kaplan, "Deformity/Race/Feminism," unpublished MS.

21. Alan Bennett, letter to the author, December 1991.

22. Lester Friedman and Scott Stewart, "Keeping His Own Voice: An Interview with Stephen Frears," in *Re-Viewing British Cinema, 1900–1992*, ed. Wheeler Winston Dixon (Albany: State University of New York Press, 1994), 222, 224.

23. One of the creators of Channel Four, Jeremy Isaacs, stated in 1979, "I hope in the eighties to see more black Britons on our screens in programmes of particular appeal to them and aimed at us; more programmes made by women for women which men will watch; more programmes for the young, for the age group that watches television least partly because so little television speaks to them." Quoted in David Docherty, David E. Morrison, and Michael Tracey, *4 Keeping Faith? Channel Four and Its Audience* (London: John Libbey, 1988), 5.

24. Gayatri Chakravorty Spivak, "Sammy and Rosie Get Laid," in *Outside in the Teaching Machine* (New York: Routledge, 1993), 244.

25. Quoted in Friedman and Stewart, "Keeping His Own Voice," 233, 224; for the economic conditions, see Quart, "The Politics of Irony: The Frears-Kureishi Films," in *Re-Viewing British Cinema*, 241, and "The Religion of the Market: Thatcherite Politics and the British Film of the 1980s," in *Fires Were Started: British Cinema and Thatcherism*, ed. Lester Friedman (Minneapolis: University of Minnesota Press, 1993), 15–34.

26. Quoted in Henry Sheehan, "All About the Making of *Sammy and Rosie Get Laid*," *Reader*, 20 November 1987, 8; Kureishi, *Sammy and Rosie*, 64.

27. Alexander Walker, "Lovers Overlaid," *London Evening Standard*, 21 January 1988, 32.

28. For the quotations, see, respectively, Peter Porter, "Polemical Pairings," *Times Literary Supplement*, 28 January 1988, 87; review in *California*, November 1987, 36; Terrence Rafferty, "Films," *Nation*, 21 November 1987, 608.

29. See, respectively, Pat Aufderheide, "Love in the Ruins: Laying Foundations," *In These Times*, 7–13 October 1987, 21; Samir Hachem, " 'Sammy & Rosie Get Laid,' " *Hollywood Reporter*, 27 October 1987; Quart, "The Politics of Irony," 242.

30. Brenda R. Silver, "Textual Criticism as Feminist Practice: Or, Who's Afraid of Virginia Woolf, Part II," in *Representing Modernist Texts: Editing as Interpretation,* ed. George Bornstein (Ann Arbor: University of Michigan Press, 1991), 193–94; for "matron saint," see Zwerdling, *Virginia Woolf and the Real World,* 33.

31. Kureishi, *Sammy and Rosie,* 12–13.

32. Margaret Walters, "Laid in Britain," *Listener,* 21 January 1988, 30; Pauline Kael, "The Current Cinema," *New Yorker,* 16 November 1987, 141. See also J. Hoberman's reference to the poster as part of a "p.c. paradise" (British reviewers do not use the phrase): *Village Voice,* 10 November 1987, 57.

33. See, respectively, Leonard Quart, review of *Sammy and Rosie Get Laid, Cineaste* 3 (1988): 41; Bert Cardullo, review of *Sammy and Rosie Get Laid, Hudson Review* 41 (summer 1988): 356; and Kael, "The Current Cinema," 141.

34. Spivak, "Sammy and Rosie," 246, 245.

35. Raymond Williams, "The Bloomsbury Fraction," in *Problems in Materialism and Culture* (London: Verso, 1980), 165, 167.

36. Spivak, "Sammy and Rosie," 245.

37. Ibid., 245.

38. Bell hooks, "Stylish Nihilism: Race, Sex, and Class at the Movies," in *Yearning: Race, Gender, and Cultural Politics* (Boston: South End Press, 1990), 161, 160, 163, 162. Although no mainstream reviewers noted the absence of black women in the heterosexual interracial relationships, some noted the missing point of view: "What the rioting blacks or homeless squatters may think, the film doesn't tell us": David Denby, "Riot Act," *New York,* 9 November 1987, 115.

39. Bell hooks's reading of the whiteness of the angels in *Wings of Desire* provides a model here: "Representing Whiteness: Seeing Wings of Desire," in *Yearning,* 165–71.

40. Walker, *In Search of Our Mothers' Gardens,* 231–43.

41. Stephen Frears, letter to author, July 1997; in the last paragraph of his letter, Frears (deliberately?) recasts *Virginia* as *Virgina.*

42. Nigel Andrews, "It's the Method That Damns, Not the Matter," *Financial Times,* 22 January 1988, 13. Rosie's smile, variously described as enigmatic or snide or "acid and dangerous," reappears so often in the reviews as to become emblematic of the figure herself; see, e.g., Hilary Mantel, "Preaching Hell-Fire," *Spectator,* 30 January 1988, 38.

43. Spivak, "Sammy and Rosie," 244, 243.

44. Richardson, *Bloomsbury Iconography,* 295; Kael, "The Current Cinema," 141.

45. Stephen Heath, "Difference," *Screen* 19/3 (autumn 1978): 92.

46. Jean-Pierre Vernant, *Mortals and Immortals: Collected Essays,* ed. Froma I. Zeitlin (Princeton: Princeton University Press, 1991), 150.

47. Ibid., 117, 144.

48. Mitchell, *Iconology,* 151.

49. Several reviewers refer to the poem as graffiti; see, e.g., review, *California,* November 1987, 36.

50. Colette Lindroth, "*The Waste Land* Revisited: 'Sammy and Rosie Get Laid,' " *Film/Literature Quarterly* 17/2 (1989): 95–98.

51. Peter Wollen, "The Last New Wave: Modernism in the British Films of the Thatcher Era," in *Fires Were Started,* 35–51; "Wild Hearts," *London Review of Books,* 6 April 1995, 28–31.

52. *The Proposition,* directed by Lesli Linka Glatter, 1997; Woolf's words are spoken by a young man propositioned to impregnate her. Kevin Bacon's *Losing Chase* (1996) invokes *To the Lighthouse*'s Ramsays in a film about a surrogate mother-daughter relationship, but does not quote the novel itself. For Eliot, see Francis Ford Coppola's *Apocalypse Now* or Woody Allen's *Love and Death* or Peter Ormrod's *Eat the Peach.* Similarly, James Joyce's appearances in the popular films and television shows discussed by Vincent Cheng all involve verbal rather than visual references: "The Joycean Unconscious," 180–92.

53. *Lumière,* directed by Jeanne Moreau, 1976. The passages, spoken in French, can be found in Virginia Woolf, *Between the Acts* (1941) (San Diego: Harcourt Brace Jovanovich, 1969), 90, 140.

54. *King Lear,* directed by Jean-Luc Godard, 1987.

55. Peter S. Donaldson, *Shakespearean Films/Shakespearean Directors* (Boston: Unwin Hyman, 1990), 213–17.

56. Ibid., 216. For a history of the French critical reception of Woolf, see Pierre-Eric Villeneuve, "Virginia Woolf and the French Reader: An Overview," *South Carolina Review* 29/1 (fall 1996): 109–21.

TAKE EIGHT

1. Stephen Frears, letter to author, July 1997.

2. Richard Bernstein, "When It Comes to Film Biography, Everyone's a Critic," *New York Times,* 20 November 1994, 22; Anthony Lane, "Etherized," *New Yorker,* 12 December 1994, 126, 127.

3. Jonathan Freedman, "Autocanonization: Tropes of Self-Legitimation in 'Popular Culture,' " *Yale Journal of Criticism* 1 (fall 1987): 211, 203, 207–8.

4. Guillory, *Cultural Capital,* 174.

5. Freedman, "Autocanonization," 211n, 213.

6. Tom is played by Willem Dafoe, Viv by Miranda Richardson, whose performance earned her Oscar and BAFTA (British Academy of Film and Television Arts) nominations for Best Actress.

7. Two versions of the film exist; the version distributed by Miramax in the United States is shorter than the European version and contains a voiceover narration absent in the original. I am grateful to Peter Samuelson, one of the producers, for showing me the European version and for sharing his archives with me; both he and Brian Gilbert responded to my questions with great generosity.

8. Michael Hastings, "Introduction," in *Tom & Viv* (Harmondsworth: Penguin, 1992), xxix.

9. See, respectively, *The Diary of Virginia Woolf*, ed. Anne Olivier Bell, vol. 3 (New York: Harcourt Brace Jovanovich, 1980), 331; *The Letters of Virginia Woolf*, vol. 3 (1977), 508 [1902]; and *Letters*, vol. 5, 207 [2767].

10. See, for example, *The Diary of Virginia Woolf*, ed. Anne Olivier Bell, vol. 2 (New York: Harcourt Brace Jovanovich, 1978), 304; *Letters*, vol. 5, 71 [2600].

11. See, for example, *Diary*, vol. 3, 14; *Diary*, vol. 4 (New York: Harcourt Brace Jovanovich, 1982), 178; and *Letters*, vol. 5, 266 [2841].

12. Gary Susman, "Wasteland," *Boston Phoenix*, 17 February 1995, sec. 3, p. 9.

13. Lyndall Gordon, who has written biographies of both Woolf and Eliot, provides one response: "I want to be sympathetic to a woman, but one has to tell the whole truth and the whole truth is complex. . . . Virginia Woolf, for instance, was sympathetic to women's issues, but she makes it clear in her diary that Vivienne wasn't nice to be near": quoted in Sue Summers, "The Secret Wife of T. S. Eliot," *Daily Telegraph* (London), 5 April 1994, 15.

14. For one example of her attempt to become more fashionable and her friends' ridicule of the results, see Mellown, "An Annotated Checklist of Contributions by Bloomsbury," 228.

15. In Woolf's version of the scene, "On a wild wet day she dresses in white satin, and exudes ether from a dirty pocket handkerchief": *Letters*, vol. 5, 100 [2629]. For the photograph, see Lyndall Gordon, *Eliot's New Life* (New York: Farrar, Straus & Giroux, 1988), opposite p. 52. The picture is often cropped to exclude Vivienne.

16. Michael Hastings and Adrian Hodges, *Tom and Viv*, typescript.

17. Angie Errigo, "Tom & Viv," *Empire* (U.K.), May 1994, 30.

18. John Calhoun, "Tom & Viv," *TCI* (*Theatre Crafts International*), March 1995, 38.

19. Conversation with Brian Gilbert; see Lady Ottoline Morrell, *Lady Ottoline's Album*, ed. Carolyn G. Heilbrun (New York: Knopf, 1976).

20. Calhoun, "Tom & Viv," 39; David Cecil, "Introduction," in *Lady Ottoline's Album*, 6.

21. I owe many of these insights to Margaret Spicer, my costume consultant.

22. Michael Musto, "La Dolce Musto," *Village Voice*, 20 December 1994, 11; "Real Life Goes on the Back Burner for Art's Sake," *Daily Telegraph* (London), 15 April 1994, 20. One English reviewer refers to those threatened in the knife scene as "the wholly deserving Virginia Woolf and Ottoline Morrell": review in *Sunday Telegraph* (London), 17 April 1994, 6; and one American writes, "She once threatened Virginia Woolf with a knife but, given what a sad sack old Ginny was, who wouldn't?": Chris Hewitt, "Tom & Viv," *St. Paul Pioneer Press*, 17 February 1995.

23. *Charlie Rose*, PBS-TV, 7 December 1994.

24. Richard Alleva, "Another Wasteland: 'Tom & Viv,'" *Commonweal*, 27 January 1995, 25.

25. David Richards, "Vanessa Redgrave and Eileen Atkins Bring 20 Years of

Letters to Life," *New York Times,* 22 November 1994, C15; Nancy Franklin, "Two Tall Women," *New Yorker,* 12 December 1994, 131.

26. Ellen Cohn, "Eileen Atkins," *Mirabella,* September 1991, 56.

27. Jane Gaines, "Costume and Narrative: How Dress Tells the Woman's Story," in *Fabrications: Costume and the Female Body,* ed. Gaines and Charlotte Herzog (New York: Routledge, 1990), 189–91.

28. Bernstein, "When It Comes to Film Biography," 13; see, e.g., Howie Mawshavitz, "Seeing 'Tom & Viv' Like Being Etherized on Table," *Denver Post,* 17 February 1995, F6. In Britain, reviewers compared the debunking depiction of the artist to that of C. S. Lewis in *Shadowlands;* in the States the comparison was to *Mrs. Parker and the Vicious Circle.*

29. Michael Hastings, "Portrait of a Fascist Marriage," *London Evening Standard,* 14 April 1994, 42.

30. Michael Wilmington, "Man versus Wife," *Chicago Tribune,* 17 February 1995, sec. 7A, C; Derek Elley, "Tom & Viv," *Variety,* 18 April 1994; see also Roger Ebert, "Poetry in Commotion: 'Tom & Viv' is for Eliot Scholars Only," *Chicago Sun-Times,* 17 February 1995, 38.

31. In this sense, the reception parallels the doubleness of Joyce's representations in popular culture: seemingly disrespectful but, upon closer inspection, revealing a culture in which "Joyce *is* getting some respect": Cheng, "The Joycean Unconscious," 192.

32. Sean Callahan, "Well-Done 'Tom & Viv' More Than Another Celebrity Biopic," *Daily Southtown* (Chicago), 17 February 1995. This view is particularly strong in the British reviews; see, e.g., Brian Appleyard, "Hijack of the Great Poet," *Independent* (London), 18 August 1993, 21.

33. Caryn James, "The Dark Side of Genius and Its Supporting Cast," *New York Times,* 2 December 1994, C3.

34. For the first, see Rod Lurie, review of *Tom & Viv, Los Angeles Magazine,* December 1994, 170–71; the second is quoted in Hastings, "Portrait of a Fascist Marriage," 42.

35. Claire Monk, "Tom & Viv," *Sight and Sound* 4 (May 1994): 57.

36. Duane Byrge, "Tom & Viv," *Hollywood Reporter,* 30 November 1994.

37. Philip Horne, "T. S. Eliot as Lover and Squeamish Villain," *Times Literary Supplement,* 22 April 1994, 20; several reviewers label it a soap opera.

38. Monk, " 'Tom & Viv,' " 57; Rhoda Koenig, "Tom & Viv & Mike," *New York,* 11 February 1985, 30.

39. *Carrington,* written and directed by Christopher Hampton, 1995.

40. Mary Ann Caws, *Women of Bloomsbury: Virginia, Vanessa, and Carrington* (New York and London: Routledge, 1990). For a critique of what gets lost, see Frances Spalding, "Painting Out Carrington," *New Yorker,* 18 December 1995, 70–76.

41. This statement would alter if we included films adapted from novels by women writers, but that is a different story. Whether the situation would change

more rapidly if there were more women directors and cultural commentators remains to be seen.

42. In 1997 Louis Menand repeated this male-only litany in a witty essay about stardom, where Madonna, Roseanne, Dr. Ruth, and Erica Jong represent the popular end and Eliot, Camus, Saul Bellow, and William Blake represent the high: "The Iron Law of Stardom," *New Yorker,* 24 March 1997, 36–39.

43. Freedman, "Autocanonization," 213–14; Guillory, *Cultural Capital,* 175. Guillory is quoting Cleanth Brooks about "the greater poems of our tradition."

TAKE NINE

1. Kimberly Forrest, "Bloomsbury Forever," *W* (July 1996): 62. Forrest underestimates the reappearances; "Virginia Woolf, Meet Anne Klein," the *New York Times* declared about the 1994 fall collection (8 April 1994, B8), and in 1998 it touted Karl Lagerfeld's "new longer lengths," "suffused" with "poetry" and "a touch of Bloomsbury" (*New York Times Magazine,* 12 July 1998, 42–43).

2. Virginia Woolf, *Orlando: A Biography* (1928) (San Diego: Harcourt Brace Jovanovich, 1956), 188–89.

3. "Style," *Vogue* (G.B.), December 1996, 115.

4. This panache permeates another appearance of Virginia Woolf as fashionable come-on during 1996: the spring catalog for the J. Peterman Company, which prides itself on creating narratives meant to entice through their snob appeal. The heading on the first page of merchandise reads, " 'Leonard is entirely remaking the garden.'—Virginia Woolf"; the narrative begins, "Imagine Leonard and Virginia entertaining Tom Eliot at Monk [*sic*] House." The object being sold? A teak wheelbarrow bench you can roll from place to place once you have purchased it for $1,395: *Peterman's Eye,* the J. Peterman Company, spring 1996, 2. Further on, the Beresford profile of Virginia Woolf, "beautiful and brilliant," who, "even if you've never read her . . . influenced everything you read," urges us to buy a photograph collection from the National Portrait Gallery (32).

5. Frances Spalding, *Vanessa Bell* (New Haven and New York: Ticknor & Fields, 1983), 142, 244. For an example of Virginia rather than Vanessa as fashion setter, see Cecil Beaton: "At its best the taste exhibited by Englishwomen has a certain 'literary' quality; almost, one might say, a Virginia Woolf appreciation for clothes that possess the association of ideas": *The Glass of Fashion* (Garden City, N.Y.: Doubleday, 1954), 288. More recently an article on clothing designer Charles James, who in 1939 was perceived as "Left Bank and Bloomsbury combined, with a dash of Rue de la paix," includes the comment, "Virginia Woolf described a James dress as 'diabolical, and geometrically perfect' ": Laura Jacobs, "Gowned for Glory," *Vanity Fair,* November 1998, 121, 128.

6. Elizabeth Wilson, *Adorned in Dreams: Fashion and Modernity* (Berkeley and Los Angeles: University of California Press, 1987), 185.

7. Michiko Kakutani, "The Trickle-Down Theory," *New York Times Magazine,* 22 September 1996, 28, 30; "Letters to the Editor," *New York Times Magazine,* 4 October 1996, 28, and 11 October 1996, 18, 20.

8. Forrest, "Bloomsbury Forever," 62.

9. Peter Lindbergh, "London Beat," *Harper's Bazaar,* September 1996, 384.

10. Susannah Frankel, "Bohemian Rhapsody," *Guardian Weekend Fashion Special,* 28 September 1996, 8, 10.

11. Katherine Betts, "Runway '96," *Vogue* (U.S.), July 1996, 40, 48–49.

12. "Flap Happy" and "This Side of Paradise," *Vogue* (U.S.), September 1996, 235 and 596–615.

13. "Fashion Literate," *Fashions of the Times, New York Times Magazine,* part 2, fall 1996, 128.

14. Iris Marion Young, "Women Recovering Our Clothes," in *On Fashion,* ed. Shari Benstock and Suzanne Ferriss (New Brunswick, N.J.: Rutgers University Press, 1994), 207; Young is paraphrasing Roland Barthes in *The Fashion System,* trans. Matthew Ward and Richard Howard (New York: Hill & Wang, 1983), 256–57.

15. Sheryl Garratt, "Dispatches from Planet Fashion," *New Statesman,* 11 October 1996, 30.

16. Ibid.

17. Quoted in Kaja Silverman, "Fragments of a Fashionable Discourse," in *On Fashion,* ed. Benstock and Ferriss, 194.

18. Katherine Betts, "Vogue's View," *Vogue* (U.S.), July 1996, 49.

19. Holly Brubach, "Whose Vision Is It Anyway?" *New York Times Magazine,* 17 July 1994, 46, 47–48.

20. Brubach, "Whose Vision," 49; Valerie Steele, "The F-Word," *Lingua Franca,* April 1991, 1, 17–18, 20.

21. Wilson, *Adorned in Dreams,* 65–66; Jane Gaines, "Introduction: Fabricating the Female Body," in *Fabrications,* 4; Wilson, 65–66.

22. Arlene Stein, "All Dressed Up, But No Place to Go? Style Wars and the New Lesbianism," in *Out in Culture,* ed. Creekmur and Doty, 477–78.

23. Shari Benstock and Suzanne Ferriss, "Introduction," in *On Fashion,* 4–6.

24. See Gaines, "Introduction: Fabricating the Female Body," 5, 7–11.

25. Ibid., 8, 9. Dick Hebdige's *Subculture: The Meaning of Style* (1979) (London: Routledge, 1988), based on working-class men, provided a model; McRobbie extended the work done by the Centre for Contemporary Cultural Studies to working-class women.

26. See, respectively, Gaines, "Introduction: Fabricating the Female Body," 3, 23–27; Diana Fuss, "Fashion and the Homospectatorial Look," in *On Fashion,* 211–32; Judith Butler, *Gender Trouble: Feminism and the Subversion of Identity* (New York: Routledge, 1990); and Benstock and Ferriss, "Introduction," in *On Fashion,* 1–2.

27. "Opposing Forces," *W,* June 1996, 148; "Trend Watch," *W,* August 1996, 180–91; James Fallon and William Middleton, "Boom Town," *W,* September 1996, 262–64, 266, 268; Bridget Foley, "The Thrill Is Back," *W,* October 1996, 158–64.

28. Holly Brubach, "The Religion of Woman," *New Yorker,* 6 July 1992, 63.

29. See, for example, Gaines, "Introduction: Fabricating the Female Body," 15; Hebdige, *Subculture;* Andrew Ross, "Tribalism in Effect," in *On Fashion,* 284–99;

and Alice Gambrell, "You're Beautiful When You're Angry: Fashion Magazines and Recent Feminisms," *Discourse* 17/2 (winter 1994–95): 139–58.

30. Wilson, *Adorned in Dreams,* 231, 234–35; illustrations occur throughout the work. See also Anne Hollander's often cited argument that the pictorial representation of clothing in any particular period governs the depiction of the nude body, making the conventional seem natural: *Seeing through Clothes* (New York: Viking, 1978), xiii and passim; and Jennifer Craik, *The Face of Fashion: Cultural Studies in Fashion* (London and New York: Routledge, 1994), 1.

31. Wilson, *Adorned in Dreams,* 173.

32. Susan Bordo, *Unbearable Weight: Feminism, Western Culture, and the Body* (Berkeley and Los Angeles: University of California Press, 1993), 283.

33. Julia Emberley, "The Fashion Apparatus and the Deconstruction of Postmodern Subjectivity," in *Body Invaders: Panic Sex in America,* ed. Arthur and Marilouise Kroker (New York: St. Martin's, 1990), 47–60.

34. Bordo, *Unbearable Weight,* 254, 259.

35. Stein, "All Dressed Up," 482; Danae Clark, "Commodity Lesbianism," in *Out in Culture,* ed. Creekmur and Doty, 493.

36. Lucinda Rosenfeld, "Feminism in a Micromini," *New York Times Magazine,* 25 May 1997, 64.

37. Gaines, "Introduction: Fabricating the Female Body," 5.

38. Wilson, *Adorned in Dreams,* 157.

39. *Style with Elsa Klensch,* CNN, 28 June 1997.

40. Brubach, "The Religion of Woman," 65; Woolf's statement occurs in *A Room of One's Own,* 74. For an influential reevaluation of women's genres that evokes the Woolf passage, see Tania Modleski, *Loving with a Vengeance: Mass-Produced Fantasies for Women* (New York and London: Methuen, 1982), 11.

41. Linda Grant, "Seriously Fashionable," *Vogue* (G.B.), November 1996, 109; *Vogue* (U.S.), July 1994, 176. On shopping and the novel, see also Reginald Abbott, "What Miss Kilman's Petticoat Means: Virginia Woolf, Shopping, and Spectacle," *Modern Fiction Studies* 38/1 (spring 1992): 193–216; and Jennifer Wicke, "*Mrs. Dalloway* Goes to Market."

42. Brubach, "The Religion of Woman," 62.

43. Ibid., 64, 65, 64.

44. For a study of the mixed messages conveyed by fashion magazines from the 1960s to the 1990s, see Leslie W. Rabine, "A Woman's Two Bodies: Fashion Magazines, Consumerism, and Feminism," in *On Fashion,* 59–75.

45. Gambrell, "You're Beautiful When You're Angry," 139, 152–53, 140.

46. Ibid., 152, 140. Brubach's 1994 presentation of Mugler and Nochlin indicates more currency.

47. Grant, "Seriously Fashionable," 107, 109.

48. Gambrell, "You're Beautiful When You're Angry," 151–52.

49. See, e.g., the headline "New York—Virginia Woolf Would Not Have Looked Amiss in Perry Ellis's Ample, Stretched-out Sweaters": "Ellis Advance: The Bloomsbury Sweater," *WWD* (*Women's Wear Daily*), 11 April 1984, 1; the long sweater

also appeared in Anna Sui's 1996 Bloomsbury collection. Explaining the appeal of Bloomsbury, Jennifer Wicke anachronistically translates the trademark cardigan into "Woolf's sweater sets": "*Mrs. Dalloway* Goes to Market," 22.

50. Grant, "Seriously Fashionable," 108.

51. Mary Jacobus, "Is There a Woman in This Text?" *Reading Woman: Essays in Feminist Criticism* (New York: Columbia University Press, 1986), 97; James D. Watson, *The Double Helix: A Personal Account of the Discovery of the Structure of DNA* (New York: Atheneum, 1968), 17–20, 68–71. For the contradiction, see Anne Sayre, *Rosalind Franklin and DNA* (New York: Norton, 1975), 21.

52. Anita Brookner, *Hotel du Lac* (London: Jonathan Cape, 1984), 8, 10; hereafter cited in text.

53. Dyer, *Stars*, 72–73.

Part Three

MOVE ONE

1. Stephen Orgel, "The Authentic Shakespeare," *Representations* 21 (winter 1988): 2, 24.

2. Dyer, *Stars*, 72.

3. Orgel, "The Authentic Shakespeare," 5.

4. On the crossovers between performance and performativity in theater/performance studies, philosophy, etc., see Andrew Parker and Eve Kosofsky Sedgwick, "Introduction: Performativity and Performance," in *Performativity and Performance,* ed. Parker and Sedgwick (New York and London: Routledge, 1995), 1–18.

5. On textual clusters, see Leah Marcus, "The Shakespearean Editor as Shrew-Tamer," *English Literary Renaissance* 22/2 (spring 1992): 198; on the conjunction of text and performance, see Joseph Grigely, "The Textual Event," in *Devils and Angels: Textual Editing and Literary Theory,* ed. Philip Cohen (Charlottesville: University Press of Virginia, 1991), 170, 176–77.

6. Laurie Osborne, "The Texts of *Twelfth Night,*" *ELH* 57/1 (spring 1990): 40, 48.

7. Neil Sinyard, *Filming Literature: The Art of Screen Adaptation* (New York: St. Martin's Press, 1986), 117.

8. Peter L. Shillingsburg, "Text as Matter, Concept, and Action," *Studies in Bibliography* 44 (1991): 74.

9. Ibid., 71.

10. See *translate:* "To change in form, appearance, or substance; to transmute; to transform. . . . Of a tailor, to renovate, turn, or cut down (a garment)" (*OED*); the relevant example comes from Shakespeare's *A Midsummer Night's Dream* (III.i.122): "Blesse thee Bottome, blesse thee; thou art translated." I owe this reference to Ann Rosalind Jones and Peter Stallybrass, who explore the use of the term in different versions of the "Patient Griselda" story: "By translation, Petrarch had something quite radical in mind. 'Translatio' could refer not only to

a linguistic metamorphosis but also to a specific metamorphosis through clothing (thus Chaucer, translating Petrarch's version of the tale, describes Griselda as being '*translated*' by her new clothes)": "(In)Alienable Possessions: Griselda, Clothing and the Exchange of Women," in *Renaissance Habit: Clothing and the Materials of Memory* (Cambridge: Cambridge University Press, forthcoming).

11. See, respectively, Jerome McGann, *A Critique of Modern Textual Criticism* (Chicago: University of Chicago Press, 1983), 52; Grigely, "The Textual Event," 176–77; and Dyer, *Stars*, 72.

12. Orgel, "The Authentic Shakespeare," 5. For the crossover, see, e.g., Jonathan Goldberg on Shakespeare's texts: "We have no originals, only copies. The historicity of the text means that there is no text itself," or "If texts, even lexically identical texts, are never the same because of history, history, as the principle of difference, cannot be a principle of identity" ("Textual Properties," *Shakespeare Quarterly* 37/2 [summer 1986]: 214, 216); and Judith Butler on gender and identity: ". . . gender is not a performance that a prior subject elects to do, but gender is *performative* in the sense that it constitutes as an effect the very subject it appears to express," or "And if the 'I' is the effect of a certain repetition, one which produces the semblance of a continuity or coherence, then there is no 'I' that precedes the gender that it is said to perform; the repetition, and the failure to repeat, produce a string of performances that constitute and contest the coherence of that 'I,' " or "*gender is a kind of imitation for which there is no original;* in fact, it is a kind of imitation that produces the very notion of the original as an *effect* and consequence of the imitation itself" ("Imitation and Gender Insubordination," in *Inside/Out: Lesbian Theories, Gay Theories,* ed. Diana Fuss [New York and London: Routledge, 1991], 24, 18, 21).

13. See Butler, *Bodies That Matter,* 9–10; emphasis in original.

14. Orgel, "The Authentic Shakespeare," 14.

15. Woolf, *A Room of One's Own,* 46, 48; hereafter cited in text.

16. Jeffrey Hart, "Wimmin against Literature," *National Review,* 30 September 1988, 61; Hart was ostensibly talking about *The Norton Anthology of Literature by Women: The Tradition in English* (1985), edited by Sandra Gilbert and Susan Gubar. Hart's term on the board of the National Endowment for the Humanities under Ronald Reagan and his use of the politically volatile Carol Iannone, whose nomination to the NEH was defeated in 1991, as his expert witness make his views more than just academic.

17. On the various prepublication versions, see Virginia Woolf, *Women & Fiction: The Manuscript Versions of A ROOM OF ONE'S OWN,* ed. S. P. Rosenbaum (Oxford: Blackwell, 1992).

18. Patrick Garland, director, *A Room of One's Own,* with Eileen Atkins, Lamb's Theatre, New York, March 1991; the play also includes some voiceovers from Woolf's diaries. I am concerned only with the stage version in this essay.

19. Grigely, "The Textual Event," 172, 174; Harry Berger, Jr., "Text against Performance in Shakespeare: The Example of *Macbeth,*" in *The Power of Forms in the English Renaissance,* ed. Stephen Greenblatt (Norman, Okla.: Pilgrim, 1982), 51.

20. Mikhail Bakhtin, *Speech Genres and Other Late Essays* (1986); quoted in Grigely, "The Textual Event," 181.

21. This is confirmed by the care taken by Eileen Atkins—and noted in almost all the reviews—to project Woolf's gestures, clothing, and facial expressions; photographs of Woolf adorned her backstage dressing room in New York.

22. Osborne, "The Texts of *Twelfth Night*," 55.

23. Sylvie Drake, "A Visit to the Mind, Spirit of Woolf," *Los Angeles Times*, 17 October 1991, F9; Sid Smith, " 'Room' Adds Some Feeling to One Woman's Fight for Literary Freedom," *Chicago Tribune*, 9 October 1991, 22.

24. Rosemary Dinnage, "Creative Collaboration," *Times Literary Supplement*, 16 June 1989, 666. For many readers the "digressions" constitute the point of Woolf's text; see, e.g., Peggy Kamuf, "Penelope at Work: Interruptions in *A Room of One's Own*," *Novel* 16 (fall 1982): 5–18.

25. Stefan Kanfer, "A Trio of Solos," *New Leader*, 11–25 March 1991, 22–23; Howard Kissel, "A 'Room' of Great Dimensions," *Daily News*, 5 March 1991.

26. Simon, "Two from the Heart, Two from Hunger," 76.

27. When the play opened in New York, the *New Yorker* reported that American sales of *Room* had "reached seventy thousand" in the previous year: "Goings On about Town," 4 March 1991, 6.

28. See, e.g., Mary Cantwell, "A Stage of Her Own," *New York Times*, 8 May 1991, A22.

29. *Orlando*, directed by Sally Potter, with Tilda Swinton as Orlando, 1992; for the script, see Sally Potter, *Orlando* (London and Boston: Faber & Faber, 1994).

30. *Freak Orlando*, directed by Ulrike Ottinger, 1981; for the description see Therese Grisham, "An Interview with Ulrike Ottinger," *Wide Angle* 14/2 (April 1992): 31. The German avant-garde filmmaker also drew upon the novel in *Madame X—An Absolute Ruler* (1977), an exploration of sexuality and power, fantasy and reality, which features both a character and a ship named Orlando.

31. For the text, see "Virginia Woolf's Orlando," extracted and arranged by Darryl Pinckney and Robert Wilson, *TheatreForum* 6 (winter–spring 1995): 77–87. The German version was performed by Jutta Lampe at the Schaubühne Theater in Berlin, fall 1989; the French version, performed by Isabelle Huppert, opened in Lausanne in 1993.

32. Angela Carter, *The Curious Room: Collected Dramatic Works* (London: Chatto & Windus, 1996), 155–82.

33. Nicolson, *Portrait of a Marriage*, 218.

34. Cherry Smyth, *Lesbians Talk Queer Notions* (London: Scarlet Press, 1992), 5.

35. Peter L. Shillingsburg, *Resisting Texts: Authority and Submission in Constructions of Meaning* (Ann Arbor: University of Michigan Press, 1997), 112.

36. See, e.g., Tina Gaudoin, "Prisoner of Gender: Is Androgyny the New Sexual Ideal?" *Harper's Bazaar*, June 1993, 114–17, 158. One exception was *Vogue*, which featured an interview with Sally Potter by Mira Stout accompanied by photographs of Tilda Swinton in costume taken by Karl Lagerfeld in his eighteenth-

century Parisian apartment: "Raising Orlando," July 1993, 26, 138–43. An article devoted to Sandy Powell, who also designed the costumes for *The Crying Game,* notes Lagerfeld's praise for the costumes and states they are "getting equal time with Donna Karan and Giorgio Armani in American fashion magazines": Betty Goodwin, "Renaissance Woman," *Los Angeles Times,* 2 July 1993, E3.

37. Quentin Crisp, "Playing the Virgin Queen," *Marie Claire,* December 1992, 32, 34. For Potter's comment about Crisp, see, e.g., B. Ruby Rich, "Sexual Personae," *Mirabella,* May 1993, 40–45. The Avedon photographs appeared in the *New Yorker,* 8 March 1993, 72–75; Terence Rafferty's review appeared 14 June 1993, 96–97.

38. On Sony Pictures Classics' targeting of "women and homosexuals" in the States, see Lauren David Peden, "Big Little Movies Stand Up to Summer's Blockbusters," *New York Times,* 22 August 1993, sec. 2, p. 10. For reviews, see David Ehrenstein, "Who's Afraid of Virginia Woolf?" *Advocate,* 1 June 1993, 71–72, and the series of articles in the *Washington Blade,* 25 June 1993. The critiques of the film's failures of nerve in terms of lesbianism occur either in private conversations or in more mainstream journals, including *Ms.* and the *Women's Review of Books;* see also Alexis Jetter writing about the new lesbian visibility in the same *Vogue* that featured *Orlando:* "While [*Orlando*] the book was an homage to Woolf's married lesbian lover, Vita Sackville-West, you wouldn't know that from watching the movie": "Goodbye to the Last Taboo," *Vogue* (U.S.), July 1993, 87. For a reaction to the reviews, see June Cummins, "What Are They Really Afraid Of? Repression, Anxiety and Lesbian Subtext in the Cultural Reception of Sally Potter's *Orlando,*" in *Virginia Woolf and Her Influences,* ed. Davis and McVicker, 20–25.

39. Eve Kosofsky Sedgwick, *Tendencies* (Durham and London: Duke University Press, 1993), xii. See also Alexander Doty's exploration of the multiple "positions within culture that are 'queer' or non-, anti-, or contra-straight" and that operate in the reception of mass culture: *Making Things Perfectly Queer,* 3.

40. For interviews with Potter, see Walter Donohue, "Immortal Longing," *Sight and Sound* 3/3 (March 1993): 10–12; Pat Dowell, "Demystifying Traditional Notions of Gender," *Cineaste* 20/1 (1993): 16–17; David Ehrenstein, "Out of the Wilderness," *Film Quarterly* 47/1 (fall 1993): 2–7; and Gary Indiana, "Spirits Either Sex Assume," *Artforum* 31/10 (summer 1993): 88–91. For "refashioning," see Sheila Johnston, "Woolf in Chic Clothing," *Independent* (London), 12 March 1993, Arts 22.

41. For the "essential human being" and "suspension of disbelief," see Donohue, Dowell, and Ehrenstein. On the reasons for the sex change, see Indiana for the quotations (90); Stephen Holden, "Films from New Directors Taking Literary License," *New York Times,* 19 March 1993, C24; and Manohla Dargis, "Sally Potter: A Director Not Afraid of Virginia Woolf," *Interview,* 23 June 1993, 42. On her rejection of the term *feminist,* see Dargis, Dowell, Ehrenstein, and Bernard Weinraub, "How Orlando Finds Her True Self: Filming a Woolfian Episode," *New*

York Times, 15 February 1993, C11. Potter's response to "lesbian chic" appears in Ehrenstein, 6.

42. Rich, "Sexual Personae," 42.

43. See, respectively, Jane Marcus, "A Tale of Two Cultures," *Women's Review of Books,* January 1994, 11; John Simon, "A Rheum in Bloomsbury," *National Review,* 5 July 1993, 53–54; Robin Morgan, "Who's Afraid of Sally Potter?" *Ms.,* July–August 1993, 78–79; and Stanley Kauffman, "Unafraid of Virginia Woolf," *New Republic,* 28 June 1993, 26.

44. Simon, "A Rheum in Bloomsbury," 53, 54; Morgan, "Who's Afraid of Sally Potter?" 79.

45. Dargis, "Sally Potter," 42.

46. Reactions to the casting of Quentin Crisp, ranging from "inspired" to "creepy," also come into play here. Many American reviewers attribute the cross-casting, if not the entire film, to what they see as the disturbing British tradition of male transvestism in cabarets, on television, etc.

47. On the complexity of the moment, seen through the complexity of the label *queer,* including its questioning of "gay and lesbian orthodoxies," see Creekmur and Doty's "Introduction," in *Out in Culture,* 6.

48. Sedgwick, *Tendencies,* xii.

49. Jeffrey Rosen, "The Book of Ruth," *New Republic,* 2 August 1993, 20; the clipping was an advertisement for the film. For Katha Pollitt's essay, "Marooned on Gilligan's Island: Are Women Morally Superior to Men?" see *Reasonable Creatures,* 42–62.

50. For the the Wilson quotation and the commentary, see Maria Nadotti, "Exits and Entrances," trans. Marguerite Shore, *Artforum,* February 1990, 28, 27; Nadotti is writing about the German production.

51. Charles Spencer, "Virginia Woolf's Tedious Adventures in Wonderland," *Daily Telegraph,* 15 August 1996, 17; Benedict Nightingale, "Bland Backcloth for a Gender Bender," *Times,* 15 August 1996, Arts 33; Michael Billington, "Supplely Shifting through the Ages," *Guardian,* 15 August 1996, 2; Michael Coveney, "Chic in Woolf's Clothing," *Observer Review,* 18 August 1996, 12.

52. See, e.g., Will Eaves, "The Time of Her Life," *Times Literary Supplement,* 2 October 1992, 18; Michael Billington, *Guardian,* 19 August 1992, 31.

53. Russo, *The Female Grotesque,* 96–97.

54. Ibid., 100, 96; Susan Stewart, *On Longing: Narratives of the Miniature, the Gigantic, the Souvenir, the Collection* (Baltimore: Johns Hopkins University Press, 1984), 109–10. Film critic Manohla Dargis, who has written about both films, provides one of the most critical readings of Potter's reiteration of heterosexual norms: "Sally Potter," 42.

55. See, respectively, Grisham, "An Interview with Ulrike Ottinger," 31; Roswitha Mueller, "Interview with Ulrike Ottinger," *Discourse* 4 (winter 1981–82): 115; and Laurence Rickels, "Real Time Travel," *Artforum,* February 1993, 83.

56. Russo, *The Female Grotesque,* 104.

57. Ella Taylor, "Crying Woolf: Sally Potter Unsexes *Orlando,*" *L.A. Weekly,*

25 June–1 July 1993, 21, 22; David Elliott, "Life Is Just One Damned Era after Another . . . ," *San Diego Union-Tribune,* 24 June 1993, 20.

58. Indiana, "Spirits Either Sex Assume," 89.

59. Rickels, "Real Time Travel," 83.

60. Russo, *The Female Grotesque,* 12.

61. Scott MacDonald, "Interview with Sally Potter," *Camera Obscura* 35 (May 1995): 219.

62. Clark, "Commodity Lesbianism," 489; the article originally appeared in 1991. On "lesbian chic," see Jetter, "Goodbye to the Last Taboo."

63. Clark, " 'Commodity Lesbianism," 493, 497. For one visually subversive reappropriation of the film, see Leslie Hankins, "Two Orlandos: Controversies in Film and Fiction," in *Re:Reading, Re:Writing, Re:Teaching Virginia Woolf,* ed. Eileen Barrett and Patricia Cramer (New York: Pace University Press, 1995), 168–83.

64. Butler, *Bodies That Matter,* 233ff.; see also Parker and Sedgwick's introduction to *Performativity and Performance,* 13.

65. Butler, *Bodies That Matter,* 241.

MOVE TWO

1. Conversations with the owners of the Hardback Café and with Leslie Hankins, who knows the image and the history first-hand.

2. Žižek, *Enjoy Your Symptom!* 139–40.

3. Butler, *Bodies That Matter,* 10, 8, 10.

4. Brilliant, *Portraiture,* 119.

5. On Rosalind Franklin, see Sayre, *Rosalind Franklin and DNA,* 19; for a reading of disembodiment in Athena/Minerva and Medusa, see Jay Clayton, "Concealed Circuits: Frankenstein's Monster, the Medusa, and the Cyborg," *Raritan* 15/4 (spring 1996): 53–69; on Marilyn Monroe as "Woman," see Dyer, *Heavenly Bodies,* 21, 23.

6. Gloria Steinem, *Marilyn/Norma Jeane* (New York: Signet, 1986), 17, 19.

7. Dudar, "The Virginia Woolf Cult," 32.

8. Watson, "Virginia Woolf Follows in Monroe's Footsteps," 22.

9. *J'Accuse: Virginia Woolf;* see Take 6.

10. Caughie, *Virginia Woolf and Postmodernism,* xv.

11. Graham McCann, *Marilyn Monroe* (New Brunswick: Rutgers University Press, 1988), 7; the quotation is from *Orlando.*

12. Ibid., 44–45. Monroe is reading Molly Bloom's soliloquy; for histories of the photograph, see Richard Brown, "Marilyn Monroe Reading *Ulysses:* Goddess or Post-Cultural Cyborg?" in *Joyce and Popular Culture,* 170–79.

13. McCann, *Marilyn Monroe,* 147, 151.

14. Norman Mailer, *Marilyn: A Biography* (New York: Grosset & Dunlap, 1973), 17–18; Schorer, "A Writer's Mirror," 19 (see Take 3).

15. Mailer, *Marilyn,* 17.

16. In both cases commentators disagree about why they did not have children; my statement reflects the popularly accepted view.

17. McCann, *Marilyn Monroe,* 181, 145.

18. Vernant, *Mortals and Immortals,* 150.

19. Beaton, *Book of Beauty,* 37.

20. See Book IV of Ovid's *Metamorphoses* and Judith D. Suther, "The Gorgon Medusa," in *Mythical and Fabulous Creatures: A Source Book and Research Guide,* ed. Malcolm South (New York: Greenwood Press, 1987), 165. On Medusa's beauty, see also Vernant, *Mortals and Immortals,* 149; and Siebers, *The Mirror of Medusa,* 14. Drawing upon Pindar and Apollodorus, Siebers notes another tradition in which "Medusa dares to compare her beauty to Athena's, which angers the goddess of reason to such an extent that she crowns the Gorgon's head with a wreath of hissing serpents."

21. For the first, see Vernant, *Mortals and Immortals,* 112–13; for the next two, see Suther, "The Gorgon Medusa," 163.

22. Clayton, "Concealed Circuits," 61; Vernant, *Mortals and Immortals,* 144. Siebers traces the "recent and unfounded" version of the story in which Medusa dies upon seeing her image in the mirror of Perseus's shield: *The Mirror of Medusa,* 9–11.

23. Froma Zeitlin, in an editorial note in Vernant, *Mortals and Immortals,* 138 n. 48; women can, however, like Niobe, be "turned into stone through excessive grief."

24. Cohen, "Monster Culture (Seven Theses)," 12.

25. Susan Sontag, *On Photography* (New York: Doubleday, 1989), 15; Barthes, *Camera Lucida,* 89, 9, 97, 111.

26. Barthes, *Camera Lucida,* 21.

27. Victor Burgin, "Photography, Phantasy, Function," in *Thinking Photography,* ed. Burgin (London: Macmillan, 1982), 190, 189, 191; Burgin's essay provides an overview of the intersections of psychoanalytic discourse and photography.

28. Vernant, *Mortals and Immortals,* 137.

29. Burgin, "Photography, Phantasy, Function," 188.

30. Christian Metz, "Photography and Fetish," *October* 34 (fall 1985): 80, 87–88.

31. Mary Ann Doane, *Femmes Fatales: Feminism, Film Theory, Psychoanalysis* (New York and London: Routledge, 1991), 46–47, 67. For other readings of the associations among fetishism, the close-up, and the woman's face, see Laura Mulvey, "Visual Pleasure and Narrative Cinema," in *Feminism and Film Theory,* ed. Constance Penley (New York: Routledge, 1988), 62–63; and Griselda Pollock, *Vision and Difference: Femininity, Feminism and Histories of Art* (New York and London: Routledge, 1988), 120–54, esp. 121–23, 138–40.

32. W. J. T. Mitchell, "Ekphrasis and the Other," *South Atlantic Quarterly* 9/3 (summer 1992): 709–10, 710; defining *ekphrasis* as "a verbal representation of visual representation," Mitchell associates it with both a utopian desire by the (male) poet for an image represented as the female Other and a resistance, a fear. Mary Ann Doane notes that the result of Woman's position at the limits of what

is theorizable denies her not only knowledge or self-knowledge but speech: "The woman cannot say what she knows; that knowledge may exist but it always resides elsewhere": *Femmes Fatales,* 68.

33. Eleanor Wilner, "The Medusa Connection," *Triquarterly* 88 (fall 1993): 104–9. On Pegasus, see also David Adams Leeming, "The Chimera," in *Mythical and Fabulous Creatures,* 107–8.

34. Mitchell, "Ekphrasis and the Other," 711–12.

35. Cixous, "The Laugh of the Medusa," 255, 258.

36. For the monster and the abject, see Cohen, who reads it through the writings of Julia Kristeva and Judith Butler: "Monster Culture (Seven Theses)," 19; see also Butler, *Bodies That Matter,* 3, 243 n. 2.

37. On citation, see Butler, *Bodies That Matter,* 12–15; for Craig Owens, see "The Medusa Effect, or, The Specular Ruse," in *Beyond Recognition: Representation, Power, and Culture* (Berkeley and Los Angeles: University of California Press, 1992), 194, 195.

38. Wilner, "The Medusa Connection," 108.

39. See, respectively, Henrietta McCall, "Sphinxes," in *Mythical Beasts,* ed. John Cherry (San Francisco: Pomegranate Artbooks and British Museum Press, 1995), 137; Frank A. Scafella, "The Sphinx," in *Mythical and Fabulous Creatures,* 183; and Charles Lemmi, *The Classic Deities in Bacon: A Study in Mythological Symbolism* (1933), quoted in Scafella, 183.

40. Ironically, so might her incarnation as fashion icon: writers on fashion often refer to it as posing the Sphinx's question, Who are you?

41. Žižek, *Enjoy Your Symptom!* 113–14, 139–40.

42. Mario Praz, *The Romantic Agony,* trans. Angus Davison, 2d ed. (London: Oxford University Press, 1951), 31.

43. For the quotation and a survey of Aristotle's views, see Helene Foley, "Women in Greece," in *Civilizations of the Ancient Mediterranean: Greece and Rome,* ed. Michael Grant and Rachel Kitzinger (New York: Scribner's, 1988), 1306; on the conjunction of female bodies and monsters see Rosi Braidotti, *Nomadic Subjects: Embodiment and Sexual Difference in Contemporary Feminist Theory* (New York: Columbia University Press, 1994), 75–94. For readings of women as monsters, not victims, in horror films, many of them linked to (psychoanalytic) theories about women's bodies, see Linda Williams, "When the Woman Looks," in *Re-vision: Essays in Feminist Film Criticism,* ed. Mary Ann Doane, Patricia Mellencamp, and Linda Williams (Los Angeles: American Film Institute, 1984), 83–99; Barbara Creed, *The Monstrous Feminine: Film, Feminism, Psychoanalysis* (New York: Routledge, 1993); and Halberstam, *Skin Shows.*

There have been, and continue to be, numerous readings of the female body, many of them questioning its psychoanalytic and/or monstrous representations or rereading them through a feminist, lesbian, and/or queer perspective. For some examples of the wide range of approaches, see Susan Rubin Suleiman, ed., *The Female Body in Western Culture: Contemporary Perspectives* (Cambridge: Harvard University Press, 1986); Emily Martin, *The Woman in the Body: A Cultural Analysis of Reproduction* (Boston: Beacon Press, 1987); Teresa de Lauretis, *The*

Practice of Love: Lesbian Sexuality and Perverse Desire (Bloomington: Indiana University Press, 1994); Elizabeth Grosz, *Volatile Bodies: Toward a Corporeal Feminism* (Bloomington: Indiana University Press, 1994); Elizabeth Grosz and Elspeth Probyn, eds., *Sexy Bodies: The Strange Carnalities of Feminism* (London and New York: Routledge, 1995); Judith Halberstam and Ira Livingston, *Posthuman Bodies* (Bloomington: Indiana University Press, 1995); Amelia Jones, *Body Arts: Performing the Subject* (Minneapolis: University of Minnesota Press, 1998); and, of course, Butler, *Bodies That Matter.*

44. Simone de Beauvoir, *The Second Sex,* trans. H. M. Parshley (New York: Vintage, 1974), 189; Cohen, "Monster Culture (Seven Theses)," 4.

45. Braidotti, *Nomadic Subjects,* 81.

46. For an analysis of images of this vulnerability in her films and public statements, see Dyer, *Heavenly Bodies,* 46–50.

47. Diana Trilling, "The Death of Marilyn Monroe," *Claremont Essays,* 237, 239.

48. Steinem, *Marilyn/Norma Jeane,* 24. Other women have echoed Steinem: " 'I think that Marilyn alarmed me as I was growing up because she was so vulnerable and had that sort of liquid-eyed defenselessness. . . . I think that it was less that I repudiated it intellectually than that it scared me, alarmed me' ": Emma, in Joel Oppenheimer, *Marilyn Lives!* (New York: Delilah, 1981), 54. More recently, Susan Bordo has found, Marilyn Monroe's body frightens her students by its perceived excess in a culture that valorizes thinness and hardness; she reads this response as a fear of "maternal power, newly threatening in an age when women are making their way into arenas traditionally reserved for men": *Unbearable Weight,* 141, 208.

49. Gay men have not exhibited this fear; for some responses by gay men, see Oppenheimer, *Marilyn Lives!* 33, 46–50.

50. Mailer, *Marilyn,* 15, 23; Lesser, *His Other Half,* 200.

51. Norman Rosten, *Marilyn: A Very Personal Story* (London: Millington, 1980), 24. An oddly similar episode, which also occurs on a beach, appears in Wayne Koestenbaum's interpretation of Jackie as icon; on this occasion, as *Photoplay* magazine told it, " 'The photographers clicked away as she backed out into the ocean. . . . She could have been doomed, yet she courageously refused to come in out of the water. She just kept on pleading and crying for help' ": cited in Koestenbaum, *Jackie under My Skin,* 167–68.

52. Arthur Miller, *After the Fall* (New York: Penguin, 1980), 104. Paige Baty identifies Marilyn and the suicide not with Medusa, but with the Sphinx, "a monstrous female that keeps asking me and itself, 'How does it end? What does it mean?' ": *American Monroe,* 5 n. 6.

53. Lesser, *His Other Half,* 197; Beaton, *Book of Beauty,* 37.

54. Kathryn N. Benzel, "The Body as Art: Still Photographs of Marilyn Monroe," *Journal of Popular Culture* 25 (fall 1991): 24.

55. Baty, *American Monroe,* 146, 150.

56. Russo, *The Female Grotesque,* 39–40, 3.

57. Sayre, *Rosalind Franklin and DNA,* 19.

58. Watson, *The Double Helix,* 70. Mary Jacobus argues that even Watson's

representations of Franklin's scientific methodology adopt this trope, transforming her into a schoolmarm, "the sour spinster science by which theory knows itself young and virile": "Is There a Woman in This Text?" 98.

59. Moi, *Simone de Beauvoir*, 1, 78, 90–91.

60. Garber, *Vested Interests*, 372.

61. On Sontag, see Zoë Heller, "The Life of a Head Girl," *Independent on Sunday* (London), 20 September 1992, 10; on Thatcher, see "Britain: Maggie Improves on History," *Newsweek*, 5 June 1995, 36.

62. Fuss, "Fashion and the Homospectatorial Look," 211–32; see also Valerie Traub, "The Ambiguities of 'Lesbian' Viewing Pleasure: The (Dis)articulations of *Black Widow*," in *Body Guards: The Cultural Politics of Gender Ambiguity*, ed. Julia Epstein and Kristina Straub (New York: Routledge, 1991), 305–28.

63. Kurt Andersen, "Real People," *New Yorker*, 10 November 1997, 44. For a study of lesbian and queer theater performances that draw upon Medusa, see Lizbeth Goodman, "Who's Looking at Who(m)? Re-viewing Medusa," *Modern Drama* 39 (spring 1996): 190–210.

64. Quoted in Alan Levy, " 'A Good Long Look at Myself,' " in *Marilyn Monroe: A Composite View*, ed. Edward Wagenknecht (Philadelphia: Chilton, 1969), 18.

65. Alexander Walker, "Body and Soul: Harlow and Monroe," in *Marilyn Monroe: A Composite View*, 157, 160.

66. Moi, *Simone de Beauvoir*, 82.

67. Mailer, *Marilyn*, 171, 173, 184.

68. Steinem, *Marilyn/Norma Jeane*, 30.

69. Bourdieu, *Distinction*, 34–35; Bourdieu uses a passage from Woolf's essay "Mr. Bennett and Mrs. Brown" to illustrate his point.

70. Schickel, *Intimate Strangers*, 149, 124; John Ralston Saul, *Voltaire's Bastards: The Dictatorship of Reason in the West* (New York: Vintage, 1993). The image may be playing on the "double herm" "popular in cultivated Roman circles" that combined the faces of Greek and Roman intellectuals and artists to increase the Romans' stature: Brilliant, *Portraiture*, 120–21.

71. Dean MacCannell, "Marilyn Monroe Was Not a Man," *Diacritics* (summer 1987): 115–16; Trilling, *The Beginning of the Journey*, 347. A 1999 review of two new books on Monroe reiterates the wide range of her appeal, but in true self-styled "intellectual" fashion sardonically attributes at least a part of it to her attraction to "brainy men," the books she read, and her "quick wit, which always endears populist icons to the intelligentsia": Daphne Merkin, "Platinum Pain," *New Yorker*, 8 February 1999, 72.

72. Freedman, "Autocanonization," 211–12; Daniel Harris, "Make My Rainy Day," *Nation*, 8 June 1992, 791.

73. Harris, "Make My Rainy Day," 790.

74. I stress this point, because several people have suggested to me that unless the body was the famous photo of Monroe in her white dress standing over the subway grate, no one would know it was hers.

75. E-mail exchanges with the owner brought the information that the head was

an unspecified Gisèle Freund photograph; the body is still available as a cardboard cutout with head attached.

76. Rosemary Mahoney, "A Brilliant Woman," *Elle,* August 1994, 48.

77. Pat Oliphant, Cartoon, *New York Times,* 21 March 1993, sec. 4, p. 6.

78. Katha Pollitt, "First-Lady Bashing: The Male Media's Hillary Problem," *Nation,* 17 May 1993, 657.

79. In March 1993 *Mirabella* ran an article called "Of Women's Bondage," which fantasizes Murphy Brown as a dominatrix; "the point seems to be," Shari Benstock and Suzanne Ferriss write, "that to appear truly powerful women must still be seen as threatening, intimidating": Benstock and Ferriss, "Introduction," in *On Fashion,* 16 n. 9.

80. Pierre Saint-Amand, "Terrorizing Marie Antoinette," trans. Jennifer Curtiss Gage, *Critical Inquiry* 20 (spring 1994): 379, 393. Two years later Jane Kramer noted the continuing representation of feminists and/or "wildly successful women" as "gargoyles": "The Invisible Woman," *New Yorker* (Special Women's Issue), 26 February–4 March 1996, 146–47.

81. Conversation with Griselda Pollock.

82. Stewart, *On Longing,* 125.

83. Žižek, *Enjoy Your Symptom!* 139; Butler, *Bodies That Matter,* 10.

84. Doane, *Femmes Fatales,* 75.

85. Vernant, *Mortals and Immortals,* 113. Doane outlines Baubo's appearances in psychoanalytic literature as a figure who "resides outside the regime of phallocentrism": *Femmes Fatales,* 65–66.

86. Maurice Olender, "Aspects of Baubo: Ancient Texts and Contexts," in *Before Sexuality: The Construction of Erotic Experience in the Ancient Greek World,* ed. David M. Halperin, John J. Winkler, and Froma I. Zeitlin (Princeton: Princeton University Press, 1990), 104–6.

87. Russo, *The Female Grotesque,* 11, 12.

88. Donna Haraway, "A Cyborg Manifesto: Science, Technology, and Socialist-Feminism in the Late Twentieth Century," in *Simians, Cyborgs, and Women* (New York: Routledge, 1991), 180, 150, 150, 162, 177. For the Sphinx, see "A Manifesto for Cyborgs: Science, Technology, and Socialist Feminism in the 1980s," *Socialist Review* 80 (March–April 1985): 64. Haraway's vision does not prevent her from recognizing that the new reproductive technologies pose their own problems for women and their bodies, creating "boundaries newly permeable to both 'visualization' and 'intervention'" and making the question of "who controls the interpretation of bodily boundaries in medical hermeneutics . . . a major feminist issue" (169).

89. Jody Scott, *I, Vampire* (New York: Ace Science Fiction Books, Berkeley Publishing Group, 1984), 38, 50, 52. The dolphin image may allude to Woolf's well-known description of Vita Sackville-West and hence to *Orlando.*

90. Russo, *The Female Grotesque,* 58; Butler, *Bodies That Matter,* 241. For an argument that we have already achieved this state of indeterminacy, of multiple bodies, see Halberstam and Livingston, "Introduction," in *Posthuman Bodies,* 1–19.

91. Elizabeth Bronfen, *Over Her Dead Body: Death, Femininity and the Aesthetic* (New York: Routledge, 1992), 399; Butler, *Bodies That Matter,* 22, xi.

Afterword

1. Hilary Spurling, "There Is Plenty to Be Afraid of in a Female Chauvinist," *Daily Telegraph,* 14 September 1996, A7.

2. Daphne Merkin, " 'This Loose, Drifting Material of Life,' " *New York Times Book Review,* 8 June 1997, 13–14. See also James Wood, "Beneath the Waves," *New Republic,* 29 September 1997, 33–38, who complains as well about the stereotyping of male readers by women reviewers, an allusion to Merkin.

3. Lee, *Virginia Woolf,* 769.

4. Bowlby, *Virginia Woolf;* Caughie, *Virginia Woolf and Postmodernism.* For the reviews, see, e.g., Candia McWilliam, "Woolf Who Led the Pack," *Independent on Sunday* (London), 8 September 1996, 29, and Maureen Howard, "Woolf's Worlds," *Boston Sunday Globe,* 18 May 1997, N18.

5. Lee, *Virginia Woolf,* 175, 199.

6. Lee made her comment about the face during a talk at Waterstone's Bookstore, Kensington High Street, London, 9 October 1996. Many people found the portrait on the British edition by Fletcher Sibthorpe too somber; the British paperback uses the Beck and Macgregor portrait of the younger Woolf in front of a Japanese screen.

7. Ozick, "Mrs. Virginia Woolf," 44.

8. Caricature by Steven Cragg, Largely Literary Designs, 1992; the T-shirt was produced by the same man who created the Chapel Hill hybrid and evoked a similarly horrified response.

9. Rose, "Smashing the Teapots," 7.

10. "Letters," *New York Times Magazine,* 15 December 1996, 14, 16, 18.

11. John Miller, ed., *Legends: Women Who Have Changed the World through the Eyes of Great Women Writers,* with an Introduction by Anjelica Huston (Novato, Calif.: New World Library, 1998), x; Barbara Cady, *Icons of the 20th Century: 200 Men and Women Who Have Made a Difference* (Woodstock and New York: Overlook Press, 1998). In *Legends,* Virginia Woolf is visually represented by the familiar Man Ray photograph (fig. 6) and verbally presented by Claudia Roth Pierpont (62–63); in *Icons,* conceived as a "photo gallery" of the "visionaries, cult figures, revolutionaries, tyrants, trend-setters, and opinion-makers who have shaped our group *Zeitgeist*" (ix), Beresford's Virginia Stephen represents the writer (392–93). A similar absence of the "hero" characterizes a November 1998 article in *Vanity Fair,* advertised on the cover as a special report on "America's Most Influential Women: 200 Legends, Leaders and Trailblazers," which "hails . . . academics, politicians, designers, artists, writers, athletes, and businesswomen": *Vanity Fair,* November 1998, cover, 24.

12. Marianne Brace, "Who Is the Greatest of Them All?" *Daily Telegraph,* 23 November 1996, 2.

13. Robert Carr-Archer, letter to the author, 14 March 1997.

14. Gaines, *Contested Cultures,* 231; Tony Bennett, "Popular Culture as 'Teaching Object,' " quoted in Gaines, 232.

15. *Beverly Hills 90210,* season 3, episode 23: "Duke's Bad Boys," 3 March 1993, Fox.

16. *Murphy Brown,* episode 184, "The Feminine Critique," 30 October 1995, CBS.

17. *Absolutely Fabulous,* "The Last Shout," directed by Bob Spiers, Saunders and French Productions/Artworks, 1996.

18. The poster was purchased in 1994. For the Italian version, see Virginia Woolf, *Tra un atto e L'altro* (Parma: Guanda, 1978), 70; for the English, *Between the Acts,* 103.

INDEX

Page numbers in boldface indicate illustrations.

Channel Four (G.B.), 162
Chapel Hill hybrid, 31, 86, 207–8, 236, 252,
    256–58, 262, 264–65, 270
Charleston (Bell family home), 67, 149
Charleston Trust, 149
Charlie Rose show (TV), 181
Chekhov, Anton, on writers and politics,
    121
Cheng, Vincent, 286n. 13, 317n. 52, 319n.
    31
childlessness, 99, 110, 111–13, 171, 260–61
Chronicle of Higher Education: on public
    intellectuals, 66
Churchill, Winston, 7
Cicero, 37
citation, 23, 82, 248–49
City University of New York. *See* CUNY
Cixous, Hélène, 248; on Medusa, 147, 268
Claremont Essays (Trilling), 65, 104
Clark, Danae, 199, 234
Clarke, Graham, on portrait photographs,
    136
class, 2, 3, 141, 161–62; conflict, 15, 83,
    157; cultural, 58, 72, 94, 104–7; cultural
    capital and, 46; cultural *vs.* gender, 12, 25,
    36–37, 52, 68, 72, 75, 82, 151, 176, 186,
    262–64; privilege, 141–42, 154; social,
    12, 52, 58, 94, 141
Classics of the Western World (Erskine),
    70. *See also Great Books of the Western
    World;* Literature Humanities (Lit. Hum.)
Clayton, Jay, 245
Clinton, Bill (President), 1, 2, 225, 255
Clinton, Hillary Rodham, 3, 265–66, 267
clothing, 144; Potter's use of in *Orlando,*
    189; in *A Room of One's Own* (Garland),
    182; in *Tom & Viv,* 179–80, 182–83;
    and translation, 213, 323n. 10; in *Vita &
    Virginia,* 182; VW on cultural significance
    of, 189, 224. *See also* fashion
Cohen, Jeffrey, on monsters, 11, 246, 252,
    265
Cold Comfort Farm (film), 188
Coleridge, Samuel Taylor, 217
Columbia University, 29, 35–37, 40–41;
    academic politics at, 43–46; Butler
    Library, 45; core curriculum, 41–45
Commentary, 36, 54, 121

commodification: of cultural icon, 7, 98,
    149, 240, 243; of culture, 68, 70, 79, 175
Common Reader, The, 60, 106
Commonweal, 182
Communist Party, Rome, Italy, 8, 283
Cooke, Alistair, 125
Coombe, Rosemary, on star image, 129
Cornillon, Susan Koppelman, 24
"Costume and Narrative: How Dress Tells
    the Woman's Story" (Gaines), 183
costume design, 179–83, 189; and
    metaphors, 183. *See also* fashion
Cottom, Daniel, 36; on anger, historical
    specificity of, 4, 37–38
Crawford, Michael, 192
Crisp, Quentin, 226, 231
Criterion: Vivienne Eliot published in, 178
Cross, Timothy, 44, 68
cross-dressing, 86, 95, 225, 234, 270. *See
    also* fashion
Crying Game, The (film), 228
cult, 22, 239, 313n. 55; used as put-down,
    24, 71, 148–49, 263–64
Cultural Capital (Guillory), 45–47, 70
CUNY Graduate Center, New York City, 40,
    41
Curry, Ramona, 6
cyborg, 269, 333n. 88. *See also* monster,
    monstrous

Dalloway, Mrs.. See *Mrs. Dalloway*
Dark Lady, the, 50, 121, 294n. 38; Mary
    McCarthy as, 50; Susan Sontag as, 50,
    258
Davis, Bette, 109
death, 86, 173, 246, 271; beauty and, 92–94,
    237, 243–45, 252, 253, 258; postmortem
    property rights, 98
deCordova, Richard, 100
Decter, Midge, 58
De Gaye, Phoebe, 180
de Lauretis, Teresa, 115
Demeter, 268
Denby, David, 50, 53, 62, 70; on cultural
    capital, 46; on female academicians, 52;
    Great Books, 30, 41–42, 47–48
Deneuve, Catherine, 8
Derrida, Jacques, 54, 216

the women's movement, 4–5, 24, 29, 59, 94, 118, 221

Woolf, Virginia (writer/woman), 3, 9, 10, 47, 59, 67, 74–75, 102, 119; adaptations of her works, 31, 125–26, 182, 207–8, 211–35, 273, 290n. 62; beauty of, 18, 91–92, 130–37; as best-seller, 74–75, 79–80; biographies of, 59–60, 67, 117–27, 274–76; canonization of, 9–10, 28–29, 42, 44, 46, 48, 51, 221; centenary, 10, 148, 156, 239, 312n. 53; childlessness of, 99, 113, 156, 243, 260–61, 314n. 16; and clothing, 141, 179–80, 189, 320n. 5; diary of, 97–101, 117, 142; and family, 58–59, 92, 94, 97–98, 123–25, 130, 141; "highbrow" status, 12, 70–72, 164; inclusion in *GBWW*, 68; on limitations of biography, 240; and makeup, 134, 138, 179, 204–5; nose of, 140–41; photography, attitudes toward, 92, 130, 132, 135; as public intellectual, 48, 80, 273; suicide of, 83, 94, 138, 164, 169, 239, 240, 243, 277, 283, 302n. 1;

and Vivienne Eliot, 177–78, 318n. 13. *Works:* 9, 16; *Between the Acts,* 172, 283; *Common Reader, The,* 60, 106; *Flush,* 75, 130; *Jacob's Room,* 92; *To the Lighthouse,* 43, 74, 130, 240, 317n. 52; *Mrs. Dalloway,* 60, 74, 201, 203; *Night and Day,* 92; *Orlando: A Biography,* 31, 130, 189, 208, 222–23, 229; *Pargiters, The,* 62; *Room of One's Own, A,* 9, 31, 41, 42–43, 46–48, 215–18, 240, 271, 280; *Three Guineas,* 29, 41, 44, 48, 52, 62, 100, 122, 130, 143; *Voyage Out, The,* 92; *Waves, The,* 173; *Writer's Diary, A,* 97–101, 117, 142; *Years, The,* 62, 74, 75, 79, 80, 91, 97

Writer's Diary, A, 97–101, 117, 142; Oratorio (Argento), 290n. 62

Writing Home (Bennett), 157

Years, The, 62, 75, 80, 91, 97; on best-sellers list, 74, 79

Žižek, Slavoj, 11, 86, 250, 251, 256, 266